CIMA
STUDY TEXT

Intermediate Paper 11

Organisational Management

BPP'S STUDY TEXTS FOR CIMA'S NEW SYLLABUS

- Targeted to the **syllabus** and **learning outcomes**

- **Quizzes** and **questions** to check your understanding

- Incorporates CIMA's new Official Terminology

- Clear layout and style designed to save you time

- Plenty of **exam-style questions**

- **Chapter Roundups** and summaries to help revision

- **Mind Maps** to integrate the key points

BPP Publishing
July 2001

First edition July 2000

Second edition July 2001

ISBN 0 7517 3167 6 (Previous edition 7517 3142 0)

British Library Cataloguing-in-Publication Data
*A catalogue record for this book
is available from the British Library*

Published by

*BPP Publishing Ltd
Aldine House, Aldine Place
London W12 8AW*

www.bpp.com

*Printed in Great Britain by W M Print
Frederick Street
Walsall
West Midlands, WS2 9NE*

We are grateful to the Chartered Institute of Management Accountants for permission to reproduce past examination questions and questions from the pilot paper. The suggested solutions to the illustrative questions have been prepared by BPP Publishing Limited.

Contents

THE BPP STUDY TEXT

Aims of this Study Text

To provide you with the knowledge and understanding, skills and application techniques that you need if you are to be successful in your exams

This Study Text has been written around the **Organisational Management** syllabus.

- It is **comprehensive**. It covers the syllabus content. No more, no less.

- It is written at the **right level**. Each chapter is written with CIMA's precise learning outcomes in mind.

- It is targeted to the **exam**. We have taken account of the pilot paper, questions put to the examiners at the recent CIMA conference and the assessment methodology.

To allow you to study in the way that best suits your learning style and the time you have available, by following your personal Study Plan (see page (ix))

You may be studying at home on your own until the date of the exam, or you may be attending a full-time course. You may like to (and have time to) read every word, or you may prefer to (or only have time to) skim-read and devote the remainder of your time to question practice. Wherever you fall in the spectrum, you will find the BPP Study Text meets your needs in designing and following your personal Study Plan.

To tie in with the other components of the BPP Effective Study Package to ensure you have the best possible chance of passing the exam (see page (vi))

BPP PUBLISHING

Recommended period of use	Elements of the BPP Effective Study Package
Three to twelve months before the exam	**Study Text** Use the Study Text to acquire knowledge, understanding, skills and the ability to use application techniques. You might also use BPP's **i-Learn** product to reinforce your learning.
One to six months before the exam	**Practice & Revision Kit** Try the numerous examination-format questions, for which there are realistic suggested solutions prepared by BPP's own authors. Then attempt the two mock exams.
From three months before the exam until the last minute	**Passcards** Work through these short, memorable notes which are focused on what is most likely to come up in the exam you will be sitting.
One to six months before the exam	**Success Tapes** These audio tapes cover the vital elements of your syllabus in less than 90 minutes per subject. Each tape also contains exam hints to help you fine tune your strategy.
Three to twelve months before the exam	**Breakthrough Videos** Use a Breakthrough Video to supplement your Study Text. They give you clear tuition on key exam subjects and allow you the luxury of being able to pause or repeat sections until you have fully grasped the topic.

HELP YOURSELF STUDY FOR YOUR CIMA EXAMS

Exams for professional bodies such as CIMA are very different from those you have taken at college or university. You will be under **greater time pressure before** the exam - as you may be combining your study with work. There are many different ways of learning and so the BPP Study Text offers you a number of different tools to help you through. Here are some hints and tips: they are not plucked out of the air, but **based on research and experience**. (You don't need to know that long-term memory is in the same part of the brain as emotions and feelings - but it's a fact anyway.)

The right approach

1   The right attitude

Believe in yourself	Yes, there is a lot to learn. Yes, it is a challenge. But thousands have succeeded before and you can too.
Remember why you're doing it	Studying might seem a grind at times, but you are doing it for a reason: to advance your career.

2   The right focus

Read through the Syllabus and learning outcomes	These tell you what you are expected to know and are supplemented by Exam Focus Points in the text.
Study the Exam Paper section	Take note of the form of assessment that will be used in the exam *you* will be facing.

3   The right method

The big picture	You need to grasp the detail - but keeping in mind how everything fits into the big picture will help you understand better. • The **Introduction** of each chapter puts the material in context. • The **Syllabus content, learning outcomes** and **Exam focus points** show you what you need to **grasp**. • **Mind Maps** show the links and key issues in key topics.
In your own words	To absorb the information (and to practise your written communication skills), it helps to **put it into your own words.** • **Take notes.** • Answer the **questions** in each chapter. As well as helping you absorb the information, you will practise the assessment formats used in the exam and your written communication skills, which become increasingly important as you progress through your CIMA exams. • Draw **mind maps**. We have some examples. • Try 'teaching' a subject to a colleague or friend.

Give yourself cues to jog your memory	The BPP Study Text uses **bold** to **highlight key points** and **icons** to identify key features, such as **Exam focus points** and **Key terms.** • Try **colour coding** with a highlighter pen. • Write **key points** on cards.

4   The right review

Review, review, review	It is a **fact** that regularly reviewing a topic in summary form can **fix it in your memory**. Because **review** is so important, the BPP Study Text helps you to do so in many ways. • **Chapter roundups** summarise the key points in each chapter. Use them to recap each study session. • The **Quick quiz** is another review technique to ensure that you have grasped the essentials. • Use the **Key terms** as a quiz. • Go through the **Examples** in each chapter a second or third time.

Suggested study sequence

Tackle the chapters in the order you find them in the Study Text. Taking into account your individual learning style, you could follow this sequence.

Key study steps	Activity
Step 1 **Topic list**	Each numbered topic is a numbered section in the chapter.
Step 2 **Introduction**	This gives you the **big picture** in terms of the **context** of the chapter, the **content** you will cover, and the **learning outcomes** the chapter assesses - in other words, it sets your **objectives for study.**
Step 3 **Knowledge brought forward boxes**	In these we highlight information and techniques that it is assumed you have 'brought forward' with you from your earlier studies. If there are topics which have changed recently due to legislation for example, these topics are explained in more detail.
Step 4 **Explanations**	Proceed methodically through the chapter, reading each section thoroughly and making sure you understand.
Step 5 **Key terms and Exam focus points**	• **Key terms** can often earn you *easy marks* if you state them clearly and correctly in an appropriate exam answer (and they are highlighted in the index at the back of the text). • **Exam focus points** give you a good idea of how we think the examiner intends to examine certain topics.
Step 6 **Note taking**	Take brief notes if you wish, avoiding the temptation to copy out too much.

Key study steps	Activity
Step 7 **Examples**	Follow each through to its solution very carefully.
Step 8 **Case examples**	Study each one, and try to add flesh to them from your own experience – they are designed to show how the topics you are studying come alive (and often come unstuck) in the real world.
Step 9 **Questions**	Make a very good attempt at each one.
Step 10 **Answers**	Check yours against ours, and make sure you understand any discrepancies.
Step 11 **Chapter roundup**	Work through it very carefully, to make sure you have grasped the major points it is highlighting.
Step 12 **Quick quiz**	When you are happy that you have covered the chapter, use the **Quick quiz** to check how much you have remembered of the topics covered and to practise questions in a variety of formats.
Step 13 **Question in the Exam Question bank**	Either at this point, or later when you are thinking about revising, make a full attempt at the **Question** suggested at the very end of the chapter. You can find these at the end of the Study Text, along with the **Answers** so you can see how you did. We highlight those that are introductory, and those which are of the standard you would expect to find in an exam. Whether you are sitting the exam in November 2001 or May 2002, attempt **all the question formats provided**.

BPP
PUBLISHING

Developing your personal Study Plan

Preparing a Study Plan (and sticking closely to it) is one of the key elements in learning success.

Step 1. How do you learn?

First you need to be aware of your style of learning. There are four typical learning styles. Consider yourself in the light of the following descriptions and work out which you fit most closely. You can then plan to follow the key study steps in the sequence suggested.

Learning styles	**Characteristics**	**Sequence of key study steps in the BPP Study Text**
Theorist	Seeks to understand principles before applying them in practice	1, 2, 3, 4, 7, 8, 5, 9/10, 11, 12, 13 (6 continuous)
Reflector	Seeks to observe phenomena, thinks about them and then chooses to act	
Activist	Prefers to deal with practical, active problems; does not have much patience with theory	1, 2, 9/10 (read through), 7, 8, 5, 11, 3, 4, 9/10 (full attempt), 12, 13 (6 continuous)
Pragmatist	Prefers to study only if a direct link to practical problems can be seen; not interested in theory for its own sake	9/10 (read through), 2, 5, 7, 8, 11, 1, 3, 4, 9/10 (full attempt), 12, 13 (6 continuous)

Step 2. How much time do you have?

Work out the time you have available per week, given the following.

- The standard you have set yourself
- The time you need to set aside later for work on the Practice & Revision Kit and Passcards
- The other exam(s) you are sitting
- Very importantly, practical matters such as work, travel, exercise, sleep and social life

Note your time available in box A.

A [   ] Hours

Step 3. Allocate your time

- Take the time you have available per week for this Study Text shown in box A, multiply it by the number of weeks available and insert the result in box B.

B [   ]

- Divide the figure in Box B by the number of chapters in this text and insert the result in box C.

C [   ]

Step 4. Implement

Set about studying each chapter in the time shown in box C, following the key study steps in the order suggested by your particular learning style.

This is your personal **Study Plan**.

Short of time: Skim study technique?

You may find you simply do not have the time available to follow all the key study steps for each chapter, however you adapt them for your particular learning style. If this is the case, follow the **skim study** technique below (the icons in the Study Text will help you to do this).

- Study the chapters in the order you find them in the Study Text.

- For each chapter, follow the key study steps 1-3, and then skim-read through step 4. Jump to step 11, and then go back to step 5. Follow through steps 7 and 8, and prepare outline answers to questions (steps 9/10). Try the Quick quiz (step 12), following up any items you can't answer, then do a plan for the Question (step 13), comparing it against our answers. You should probably still follow step 6 (note-taking), although you may decide simply to rely on the BPP Passcards for this.

Moving on...

However you study, when you are ready to embark on the practice and revision phase of the BPP Effective Study Package, you should still refer back to this Study Text, both as a source of **reference** (you should find the index particularly helpful for this) and as a **refresher** (the Chapter roundups and Quick quizzes help you here).

And remember to keep careful hold of this Study Text – you will find it invaluable in your work.

SYLLABUS AND LEARNING OUTCOMES

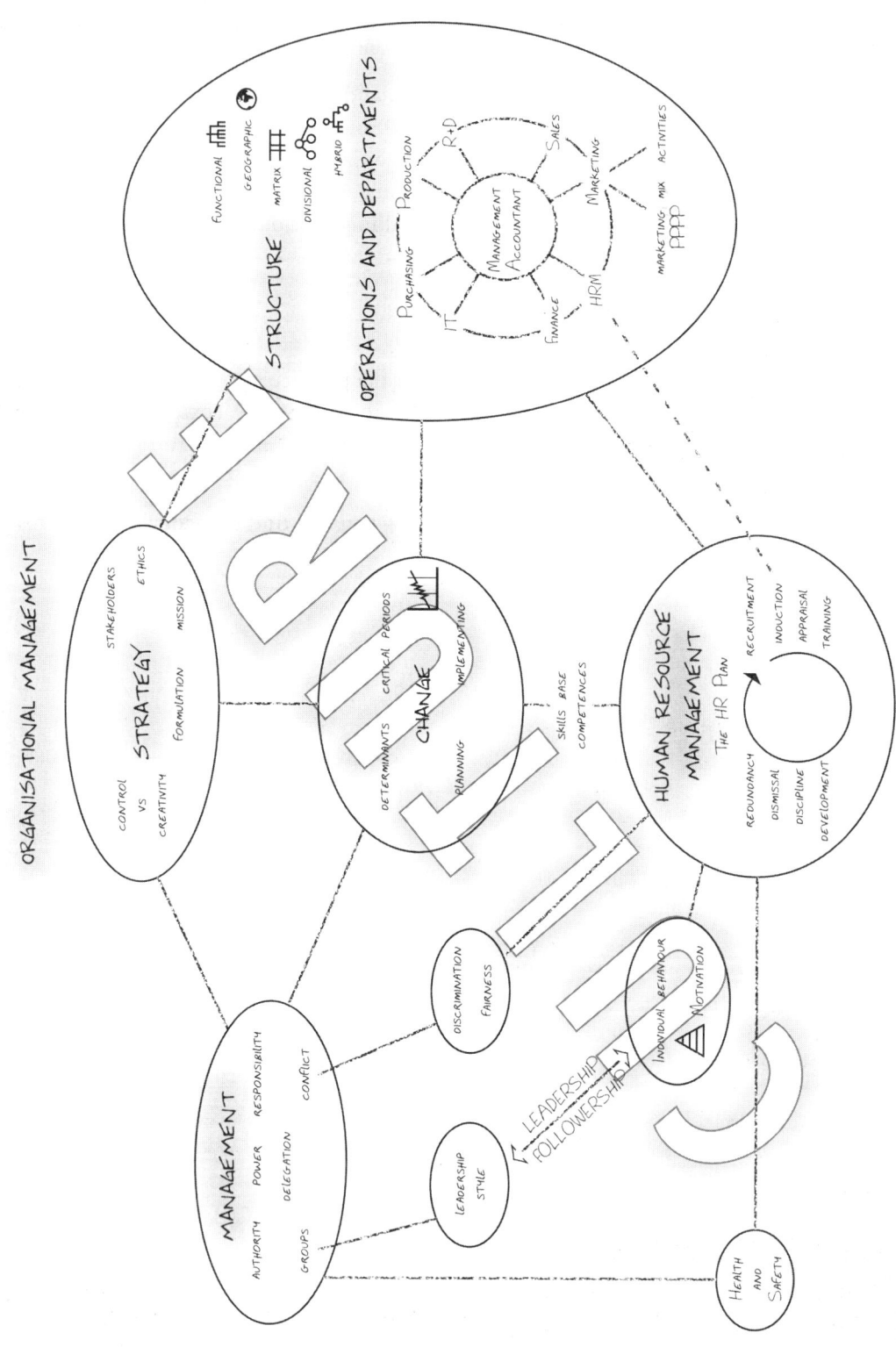

SYLLABUS AND LEARNING OUTCOMES

Syllabus overview

This syllabus introduces students to the concepts, tools and issues of management in organisations of all types. The emphasis is on the role of the Management Accountant as supervisor and manager of staff in an open social system and the relationships necessary with other specialists within the organisation. As well as their specialist role, Management Accountants are participants in the management process at the supervisory and managerial levels. This syllabus aims to provide candidates with an awareness of the skills required to operate effectively as a manager in the finance department of an organisation.

Aims

This syllabus aims to test the student's ability to:

- Evaluate and recommend improvements to the management of organisations in an international context

- Evaluate and recommend alternative structures for organisations

- Apply Human Resource Management techniques in the management of a finance department

- Advise on the management of working relationships

- Advise on the management of change

Assessment

There will be a written paper of 3 hours. The paper will compromise two sections. Section A will contain a series of compulsory questions each with its own scenario. Section B will offer a choice of questions, with or without short scenarios.

All learning outcomes and knowledge domains apply to both sections of the paper, but the optional questions are more likely to cover topical issues or specific areas.

Questions will not be phrased in such a way that they require knowledge of the work of specific writers. Examples of suitable alternatives are given for guidance, and candidates should use the theories or approaches with which they feel most comfortable, or which appear most appropriate to the circumstances described in the question. This is essentially a practical examination, and the theoretical models mentioned in the syllabus provide a framework for analysis and problem solving.

Learning outcomes and syllabus content

11(i) Organisational management - 25%

Learning outcomes

On completion of their studies students should be able to:

- Explain the concept of strategy and its possible effect on the structure and management of business organisation

- Identify the stakeholders of an organisation and explain their influence on its management and structure

- Recommend appropriate organisational goals

- Analyse and categorise the culture of an organisation, and recommend changes to improve organisational effectiveness

- Explain the importance of organisational and professional ethics

- Recommend ways in which ethical behaviour can be encouraged in organisations

- Discuss ways in which the conflict between centralised control and individual creativity can be managed

- Explain the usefulness of both classical and contemporary theories of management in practical situations

- Explain trends in the general management and structure of organisations

- Evaluate the management of an organisation and recommend improvements

Syllabus content

		Covered in chapter
•	The determinants and components of strategy	1
•	Organisational objectives (ie stakeholder analysis and organisational mission, goals and targets)	2
•	The reasons for conflict between the objectives of an organisation, or between the objectives of the organisation and its stakeholders, and the ways in which this conflict might be managed (eg compromise or identification of a dominant coalition)	2
•	The process of strategy formulation (ie the steps required and the order in which those steps might be undertaken)	1
•	The various approaches that might be adopted to determining an appropriate strategy for the organisation (ie rational, adaptive and interpretative approaches)	1
•	The determinants of culture, the different models available for categorising cultures (eg Deal and Kennedy, Harrison, McKinsey 7-S, Peters and Waterman, Peters)	4
•	The importance of culture in organisations (eg the 'organisational iceberg')	4
•	The expectations of stakeholders with regard to ethical behaviour, and the role of government (eg Cadbury report, ombudsman appointment) and professional bodies (eg CIMA) in determining ethical standards	5
•	The different models of organisational management available to achieve goal congruence while maintaining individual motivation (eg the creation of Strategic Business Units and the encouragement of entrepreneurial behaviour)	3

- The views expressed by both classical and contemporary writers on business management and the practical value and limitations of the approaches they propose (eg scientific management, administrative, human relations, systems and contingency approaches when compared with contemporary writers such as Peters or Handy)   3

- Trends in business management and structure as evidenced in the business press and other mass media   (eg demerger, strategic alliances, virtual organisations, service centres)

11(ii) The functional areas of organisations - 15%

Learning outcomes

On completion of their studies students should be able to:

- Explain the relative merits of a range of different organisation structures

- Explain the relationships necessary between the functional areas in order for an organisation to achieve its objectives

- Analyse a range of organisations, identifying their component parts, the relationships between those parts and any problems with those relationships

- Recommend and evaluate changes to the structure of organisations

- Explain the general characteristics and operation of the main functional areas of an organisation

- Explain the relationship between the work of the Management Accountant and the functional areas of an organisation

- Explain the workings of the marketing function of an organisation and the major tools and techniques used by marketing specialists

- Analyse the information needs of managers in each of the main functional areas of an organisation

Syllabus content

Covered in chapter

- The different structures which might be adopted by a business organisation and how the various components of those structures inter-relate (ie entrepreneurial, functional, divisional, matrix, network, complex)   6, 7

- The general operation of the main functional areas of business (ie operations, marketing, human resource management, finance, research and development, information systems management)   8

- The organisation and activities of the marketing function (ie marketing research, market segmentation, marketing strategy formulation)   8

- The concept of the marketing mix and the major tools therein (ie branding, product mix, pricing, advertising, sales promotion, public relations, packaging, distribution)   8

- The information required by managers in the various functional areas of a business organisation and the role of the Management Accountant in identifying and satisfying those information needs   9

BPP PUBLISHING

11(iii) Human Resource Management - 30%

Learning outcomes

On completion of their studies students should be able to:

- Explain the process of human resource planning and its relationship to other types of business plan

- Produce and explain a human resource plan for an organisation

- Produce a plan for the recruitment, selection and induction of finance department staff

- Produce a plan for the induction of new staff into the finance department of an organisation

- Explain the importance of human resource development planning

- Evaluate the tools which can be used to influence the behaviour of staff within a business, particularly within the finance department

- Explain the process of succession and career planning

- Produce a training and development plan for the staff of a finance department and analyse the major problems associated with the design and implementation of such a plan

- Produce and explain the planning and delivery of a training course on a finance related topic

- Evaluate a typical appraisal process

- Analyse the issues involved in managing the dismissal, retirement and redundancy of individual staff

Syllabus content

	Covered in chapter
• The relationship of the human resource plan to other types of business plan	10
• The determinants and content of a human resource plan (ie organisational growth rate, skills, training, development, strategy, technologies, natural wastage)	10
• The problems which may be encountered in the implementation of a human resource plan and the ways in which such problems can be avoided or solved	10
• The human issues relating to recruitment, dismissal and redundancy, and how to manage them	10
• The process of recruitment and selection of staff using different recruitment channels (ie advertisement, agencies, consultants, executive search)	10
• The content and format of job descriptions, candidate specifications and job advertisements	10
• The techniques that can be used in the selection of the most suitable applicant for a job (ie interviews, assessment centres, intelligence tests, aptitude tests, psychometric tests)	10
• The importance of negotiation during the offer and acceptance of a job	10

- The process of induction and the importance thereof   10

- The design of reward system   11

- A range of models of human behaviour and motivation and their application in a business context (eg Taylor, Schein, McGregor, Maslow, Herzberg, Handy, Lawrence and Lorsch)   11

- The distinction between development and training and the tools available to develop and train staff (ie education, training methods, management development programmes, promotion, succession and career planning, job redesign)   12

- The stages in the planning and conduct of a training course, the features and benefits of the various tools and visual aids used and the importance of feedback during and after a training course   12

- The importance of appraisals, their conduct and the problems often associated with them   13

- The relationship between performance appraisal and the reward system   13

11(iv) Management of relationships - 15%

Learning outcomes

On completion of their studies students should be able to:

- Explain the concepts of authority, power, responsibility and delegation

- Analyse the relationships between managers and subordinates

- Analyse situations where problems have been caused by the adoption of an ineffective or inappropriate management style and recommend remedial action

- Explain the formation of groups and the way in which groups and their members behave

- Identify the different roles adopted by members of a group, and explain the relevance of this to the management of the group

- Explain the problems of maintaining discipline and evaluate the tools available to help a manager achieve this

- Explain how the legal environment influences the relationship between the organisation and its employees, and between the employees of an organisation

- Explain the responsibilities of the organisation, its managers and staff in relation to health and safety and advise how a manager can ensure the health and safety of subordinates

- Explain the various ways in which fair treatment of employees can be achieved, and the role of government in ensuring this

- Analyse the causes of inter-group and interpersonal conflict in an organisation and recommend ways in which such conflict might be managed

Syllabus content

	Covered in chapter
• The concepts of power, authority, responsibility and delegation and their application to organisational relationships	14
• The characteristics of leaders and managers	14
• Management style theories (eg Likert, Tannenbaum and Schmidt, Blake and Mouton)	14
• The advantages and disadvantages of different styles of management	14
• Contingency approaches to management style (eg Adair, Fiedler)	14
• Theories of group development, behaviour and roles (eg Tuckman, Belbin)	14
• Disciplinary procedures and their operation, including the form and process of formal disciplinary action and dismissal	14
• The nature and effect of legal issues affecting work and employment, including the application of appropriate employment law (ie law relating to health, safety, discrimination, fair treatment, childcare, contracts of employment, working time)	14
• The sources of conflict in organisations and the ways in which conflict can be managed to ensure working relationships are productive and effective	15

Note:

Only the application of general legal principles will be required in this examination, and the English legal system will be used in suggested answers purely as an example. Candidates will be free to use relevant Law from their own country.

11(v) Management of change - 15%

Learning outcomes

On completion of their studies students should be able to:

• Evaluate the determinants of change in organisations and the different levels at which change must be managed

• Explain the process of organisational development and the problems associated with it

• Recommend ways in which planned change can be implemented at the organisational and departmental levels

• Evaluate how the organisation and its managers might deal with major critical periods in the development of the organisation

• Identify opportunities to improve the management of change and communicate recommendations to appropriate managers

Syllabus content

	Covered in chapter

- The impact on the organisation of external and internal change triggers (eg environmental factors, mergers and acquisitions, re-organisation and rationalisation) — 16

- The stages in the change process — 17

- Approaches to the management of organisational development and major cultural and structural change (eg Kanter, Lewin, Peters) — 16/17

- The importance of managing critical periods of change (start-up, rapid expansion, re-organisation, merger, redundancy programmes, close-down) and the ways in which these periods can be managed effectively — 16

BPP PUBLISHING

THE EXAM PAPER

Format of the paper

		Number of marks
Section A:	three compulsory 20 mark questions each with its own scenario	60
Section B:	choice of two 20 mark questions from four	40
		100

Time allowed: 3 hours

The examiner

The examiner for Organisational Management used to examine Organisational Management and Development, the equivalent paper under the old syllabus. We have prepared this Study Text in the light of the examiner's known practices.

Analysis of papers

May 2001

Section A

1   Stakeholders' interest and influence

2   Share incentive schemes and motivation

3   Adapting an authoritarian management style

Section B

4   Market segmentation – advantages and bases

5   Management accounting developments; finance department training

6   Organisational development – its nature; practitioner skills

7   Objectives and effectiveness of performance appraisal schemes

Pilot paper

Section A

1   Human resource planning: logic and process

2   Organisational culture and the market place

3   Conflict: causes and resolution

Section B

4   Management accounting: role and relationships

5   Divisional structure: for and against

6   Motivation: incentives and non-monetary methods

7   Implementing organisational change

WHAT THE EXAMINER MEANS

The table below has been prepared by CIMA to help you interpret exam questions.

Learning objective	Verbs used	Definition
1 Knowledge What you are expected to know	• List • State • Define	• Make a list of • Express, fully or clearly, the details of/facts of • Give the exact meaning of
2 Comprehension What you are expected to understand	• Describe • Distinguish • Explain • Identify • Illustrate	• Communicate the key features of • Highlight the differences between • Make clear or intelligible/state the meaning of • Recognise, establish or select after consideration • Use an example to describe or explain something
3 Application Can you apply your knowledge?	• Apply • Calculate/ compute • Demonstrate • Prepare • Reconcile • Solve • Tabulate	• To put to practical use • To ascertain or reckon mathematically • To prove with certainty or to exhibit by practical means • To make or get ready for use • To make or prove consistent/compatible • Find an answer to • Arrange in a table
4 Analysis Can you analyse the detail of what you have learned?	• Analyse • Categorise • Compare and contrast • Construct • Discuss • Interpret • Produce	• Examine in detail the structure of • Place into a defined class or division • Show the similarities and/or differences between • To build up or compile • To examine in detail by argument • To translate into intelligible or familiar terms • To create or bring into existence
5 Evaluation Can you use your learning to evaluate, make decisions or recommendations?	• Advise • Evaluate • Recommend	• To counsel, inform or notify • To appraise or assess the value of • To advise on a course of action

BPP PUBLISHING

Part A
Organisational management

Chapter 1

STRATEGY

Topic List		Syllabus reference	Ability required
1	What is strategy?	(i)	Comprehension
2	Planned strategies: an outline of the rational model	(i)	Comprehension
3	Crafting emergent strategies	(i)	Comprehension
4	'Muddling through' and logical incrementalism	(i)	Comprehension
5	Strategy and structure	(i)	Comprehension

Introduction

Strategy deals with how an organisation achieves its objectives. We look at contrasting ways in which different researchers consider that strategy *should be* made and how strategy *is* made. The **rational model** is outlined here.

- In the **rational model** (Section 2), decisions are made by logical analysis of the environment and the organisation. This is followed by the generation of alternative strategies, which are then evaluated objectively on their merits. The aim might be to secure a 'fit' with the environment.

- The **muddling through** approach suggests that strategies in many organisations are small-scale adjustments, which react to events.

- The **bounded rationality** and logical incrementalist models seek a middle ground between these two extremes.

- The **emergent strategies** model (Section 3) differs from the others above, in that it says that strategy can be generated from the 'bottom up' as well as from the 'top down'. Strategic management can mean 'crafting strategies as they emerge'.

Finally, we consider the influence of strategy on **structure**.

Learning outcome covered in this chapter

- Explain the concept of strategy and its possible effect on the structure and management of business organisations

Syllabus content covered in this chapter

- The determinants and components of strategy

- The process of strategy formulation (ie the steps required and the order in which those steps might be taken)

- The various approaches that might be adopted to determining an appropriate strategy for the organisation (ie rational, adaptive and interpretative approaches)

1 WHAT IS STRATEGY?

> **KEY TERM**
>
> **Strategy**: A course of action, including the specification of resources required, to achieve a special objective.

1.1 Strategy is about the higher direction of an enterprises. In organisations it is the concern of top management. In less exalted contexts it might be a simple technique.

> **Exam focus point**
>
> The November 1998 Examiner's report on the old syllabus equivalent of this paper noted a startling lack of knowledge of strategy models, including the rational model.

1.2 An organisation's objective is the desired outcome of the organisation's activities. The strategy specifies in broad terms how this should be achieved. (**Tactics** are the 'most efficient deployment of resources in an agreed strategy'.) This can be summarised in a diagram.

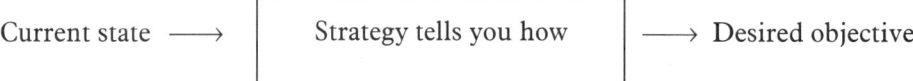

Current state ⟶ | Strategy tells you how | ⟶ Desired objective

1.3 An overall **objective** of a government's road safety policy might be to reduce deaths and injuries. There might be several **strategies** to achieve this objective.

- More stringent law enforcement
- Advertising
- Speed limits

1.4 CIMA's *Official Terminology* suggests the following example for a company. If the primary objective is 25% return on capital, and the secondary objective is to increase market share a **strategy** would be to 'sell on the basis that a 20% increase in sales and production capacity will reduce unit costs by 25%. Use £10m capital'.

1.5 What distinguishes strategy from other types of organisation decision? *Johnson and Scholes* have summarised the characteristics of **strategic decisions** for an organisation in their book *Exploring Corporate Strategy*.

(a) **Scope.** Strategic decisions will be concerned with the **overall, long-term direction** of activities.

(b) **Environment.** Strategy involves the matching of an organisation's **activities** to the **environment** in which it operates.

(c) Strategy also involves the matching of an organisation's activities to its **resource capability**. Strategic decisions include the allocation or re-allocation of resources.

(d) Strategic decisions will **affect operational decisions**, because they will set off a chain of lesser decisions and operational activities, involving the use of resources.

(e) Strategic decisions will be affected by the **values and expectations of the people in power** within the organisation.

(f) Strategic decisions have implications for **change** throughout the organisation, and so are likely to be **complex** in nature.

Case example

Hongkong Telecom

Hongkong Telecom is a subsidiary of Cable & Wireless. The Chinese telecoms market is conservatively estimated to be worth more than £368 billion: only one in six Chinese households currently possesses a land-based phone line. The company has seen double-digit growth over the past three years in a highly competitive market, and is, according to chief executive Linus Chiang, "poised on the cusp of a reincarnation".

Competition

The company lost its domestic monopoly in 1995. 'We were printing money,' Cheung says. 'Suddenly we were faced with competition and huge technological advances. We were good technically and technologically, but not in terms of service and efficiency. But we are taking a long-term view and using competition as a driving force, an agent for change.'

Culture and human resources

The key to success, he asserts, is 'attitude, a performance culture and a service culture'. Hongkong Telecom employees are judged against three key criteria: 'One, are you bold and decisive? Two, are you results-rather than activity-oriented? Three, are you effective – in other words, do you make things simple for internal and external audiences?'.

Cheung introduced Operation Excel, a programme that focuses on revenue enhancement and cost control, and rewards initiative, performance, teamwork and results, as an antidote to the complacency bred by monopoly. The programme has helped effect transition to a dynamic performance culture.

Product/service innovation

Most significantly, the company has switched its focus from international direct dialling to other areas, including fixed line, mobile, and interactive services. They won the licence for video-on-demand and home shopping in November, and it is a world first, using complex technology to deliver laser disk quality movies, karaoke, gambling, computer games, TV shopping, etc. Another innovation is Netvigator, an Internet access service launched into a marketplace of 80 competitors. To differentiate their offering, they focused on the customer interface, delivering useful, immediate information.

Competitive strategy

Hongkong Telecom's competitive differentiator is to respond to customer needs. Finance director David Prince explains: We are trying to bring more creativity in marketing and customer service to telecoms. We differentiate ourselves from the competition on quality rather than price, by providing a total package to suit individuals' lifestyles.

Summary

Hongkong Telecom's long-term *objective* appears to be survival and growth in the face of competition.

This is achieved by strategies for *products and markets* which involve offering new products/services and, in future, exploiting the Chinese market. These products and services enable it to *differentiate* its offering.

---

2 PLANNED STRATEGIES: AN OUTLINE OF THE RATIONAL MODEL

KEY TERM

Rational model. Rational models can be set up for most human behaviour. In the context of management, 'rational model' usually means a comprehensive and systematic system of strategic planning.

2.1 A **plan is a consciously intended course of action**. Many early books on business strategy supposed that strategy making was **necessarily a planning process**. Often, this involved delegating the task of strategic planning to a separate department.

2.2 *Drucker* defines strategic planning as having three aspects.

(a) 'The continuous process of **making present risk-taking decisions** systematically and with greatest knowledge of their futurity' (ie their future effect)

(b) '**Organising systematically** the efforts needed to carry out these decisions'

(c) '**Measuring the results** of these decisions ... through organised, systematic feedback'

The need for planning

2.3 **Advantages of having a plan**

- It helps organisations cope with the future, which is uncertain.
- It guides the allocation of resources.
- It directs the activities of various parts of the organisation.
- It sets a standard by which the actual performance of the organisation is measured.

The rational model

2.4 The rational model of strategic planning is a logical and comprehensive approach. It attempts to consider all relevant information and options. It is iterative; there is a planning cycle (usually annual) in which the results of one cycle become an input into the next.

2.5 **Characteristics of strategic plans**

- They are written down.
- They are circulated to interested parties in the organisation.
- They specify the outcomes (eg where the business wishes to be in five years' time).
- They specify how these are going to be achieved.
- They trigger the production of operational plans lower down the hierarchy.

The rational model

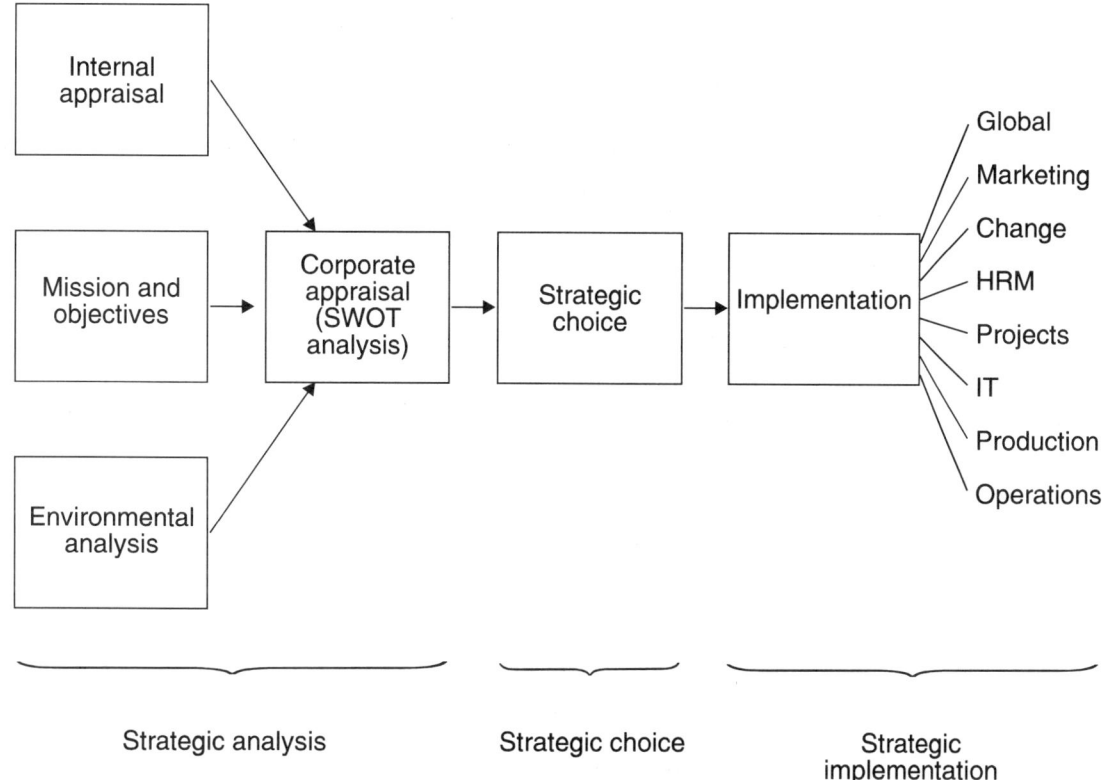

Strategic analysis   Strategic choice   Strategic implementation

Strategic analysis

2.6 **Strategic analysis** is concerned with understanding the strategic position of the organisation in the widest terms.

(a) The organisation operates within its **environment**. This has political/legal, economic, social and technological (PEST) aspects. The environment contains both **threats** and **opportunities.**

(b) The **resources** of the organisation (its **strengths** and **weaknesses**), how it adds value and its **distinctive competences** (what it does best or uniquely) must be matched to opportunities.

(c) **Mission and objectives.** The firm sets goals. The expectations of **stakeholder groups** must be considered. For example, if the organisation is financed by venture capitalists, a strategy might require sufficient growth generation to allow them to recover their investment.

Strategic choice

2.7 **Strategy development** has three phases.

(a) **Strategic options generation.** A variety of options can be set up for consideration. The aim is to build on the firm's capabilities exploit market opportunities.

(b) **Strategic options evaluation.** Each option is then examined on its merits.

- Is it **feasible?**
- Is it **suitable,** considering the firm's existing position?
- Is it **acceptable** to stakeholders?

A variety of techniques is used to assess and value strategies. Some will be assessed on financial criteria such as net present value. Where this is not possible, or where the uncertainty in the environment is great, other models are used. For instance, scenario building postulates a number of possible futures based on different assumptions about such things as world-wide economic growth, interest rates and competitors.

(c) **Strategy selection.** A strategy is chosen, according to the evaluation above. This process is strongly influenced by the **values** of the managers concerned.

Implementation

2.8 The chosen strategy is embodied in a corporate plan. From this, plans for operations are developed. The diagram below relates the corporate strategy to the activities of the sales force.

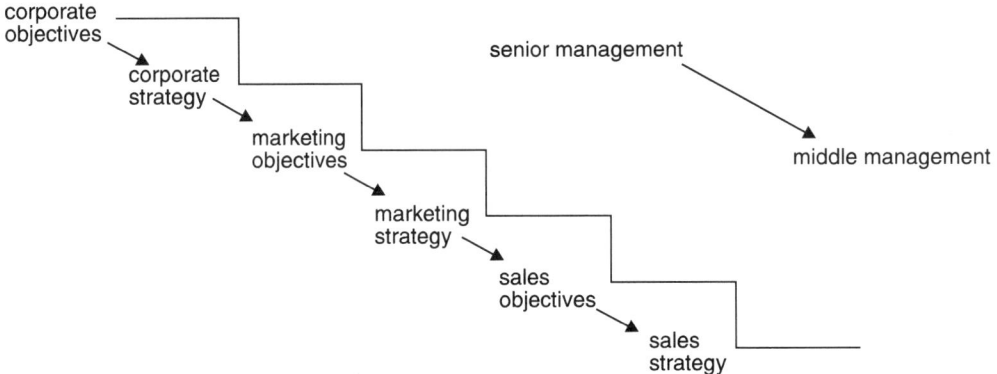

In this case what is defined as 'strategic' is in part determined by where you are, and your own relation to the plan. Similar cascades will relate corporate strategy to the plans of other departments such as production and HRM.

Levels of strategy

2.9 Some writers have developed this idea further. *Hofer and Schendel* make the following distinction.

(a) **Corporate strategy** is the most general level of strategy in an organisation. (In the words of *Johnson and Scholes*, corporate strategy 'is concerned with what types of business the company as a whole should be in and is therefore concerned with decisions of **scope**'). An example would be choosing between diversifying and limiting the activities of the business.

(b) **Business strategy** defines how an organisation approaches a particular **market**, or the activity of a particular **business unit**. For example, this can involve decisions as to whether, in principle, a company should segment the market and specialise in particularly profitable areas or compete by offering a wider range of products.

(c) **Operational and functional strategies** involve decisions of strategic importance, but which are made or determined at operational levels. These decisions include product pricing, investment in plant, personnel policy and so forth. The contributions of these different functions determine the success of the strategy as, effectively, a strategy is only implemented at this level.

Question 1

Ganymede Ltd is a company selling widgets. The finance director says: 'We plan to issue more shares to raise money for new plant capacity - we don't want loan finance - which will enable us to compete better in the vital and growing widget markets of Latin America. After all, we've promised the shareholders 5% profit growth this year, and trading is tough.'

Identify the corporate, business and functional strategies in the above quotation.

Answer

The corporate objective is profit growth. The corporate strategy is the decision that this will be achieved by entering new markets, rather than producing new products. The business strategy suggests that those markets include Latin America. The operational or functional strategy involves the decision to invest in new plant (the production function) which is to be financed by shares rather than loans (the finance function).

Case example

Goold and Quinn (in *Strategic Control*) cite Ciba-Geigy, a Swiss-based global firm with chemicals and pharmaceuticals businesses as an example of formal strategic control and planning processes.

(a)   Strategic planning starts with the identification of strategic business sectors, that is identifiable markets where profit, management and resources are largely independent of the other sectors.

(b)   Strategic plans containing long term objectives, key strategies and funds requirements are drawn up, based on a 'comprehensive analysis of market attractiveness', competitors and so on.

(c)   At corporate level, these plans are reviewed. Head office takes all the different plans, and, with a 7-10 year planning horizon, the total risk, profitability, cash flow and resource requirements are assessed. Business sectors are allocated specific targets and funds.

Problems with planning

2.10   The very concept of formal processes for strategy generation (and the limited success of strategic planning in practice) has led to **criticisms of the rational model**.

(a)   It is inappropriate to adhere to a block diagram or flowchart. Strategy formation cannot be broken down into a series of steps, since it depends on **flair, judgement, inspiration** and **experience**.

(b)   The assumption of **detachment** (that strategy can be easily divorced from operations) is dangerous. Planners rarely have to **implement** the strategies they devise and feedback occurs too late or is badly filtered. Similarly, many developments of strategic significance, or information about them, occur at **operational** level.

(c)   An organisation cannot know what its strengths and weaknesses are until they have been tested and implemented. Strategy making is a **learning process** more than a **planning process**.

(d)   Planning assumes the future can be **forecast** and **controlled**. Only in conditions of stability can extrapolation be used as a forecasting technique.

The criticisms are directed less at planning in principle, than at the assumption that **planning can create strategies** as opposed to publicising strategic decisions, co-ordinating them and mobilising resources.

3   CRAFTING EMERGENT STRATEGIES

3.1   The case example below shows how a spectacularly successful strategy developed, *against* managers' conscious intentions.

BPP PUBLISHING

Case example

Honda

Honda is credited with identifying and targeting an untapped market for small 50cc bikes in the US, which enabled it to expand, trounce European competition and severely damage indigenous US bike manufacturers. By 1965 Honda had 63% of the US market.

In practice, there was no clearly thought out-strategy at all. Honda had wanted to compete with the larger European and US bikes of 250ccs and over. These bikes had a defined market, and sold through dedicated motor bike dealerships. Disaster struck when Honda's larger machines developed faults - they had not been designed for the hard wear and tear imposed by US motorcyclists. Honda was unable to sell the larger machines.

Honda had made little effort to sell the small 50cc motorbikes - its staff rode them on errands around Los Angeles. Sports good shops, ordinary bicycle and department stores had expressed an interest, but Honda did not want to confuse its image in the target market of men who bought the larger bike.

The faults in Honda's larger machines meant that reluctantly Honda *had* to sell the small 50cc bike. It proved very popular with people who would *never* have bought motor-bikes before. *Eventually* the company adopted this new market with enthusiasm with the slogan: 'You meet the nicest people on a Honda'. Effectively, the strategy had emerged, against the conscious 'planned' intentions of management. However, Honda exploited the new market and *crafted* a strategy to deal with it.

KEY TERM

Emergent strategies arise from ad hoc or even uncontrolled responses to circumstances. If they work and have potential, the quick solutions may be developed into strategies.

3.2

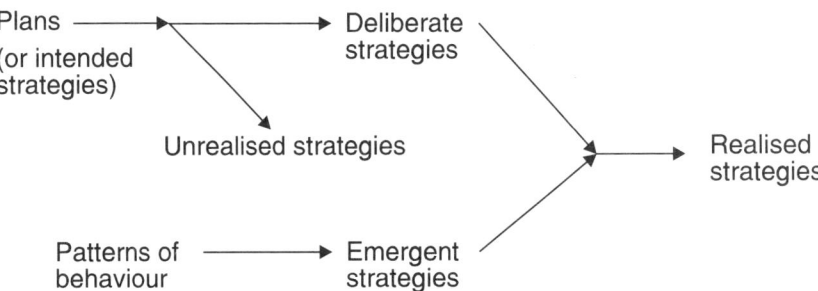

(a) **Intended strategies** are plans. Those plans or aspects of plans which are actually realised are called **deliberate strategies**.

(b) **Emergent strategies** are those which develop out of patterns of behaviour. 'Because big strategies can grow from little ideas ... almost anyone in an organisation can prove to be a strategist.' A sales person may sell to some new customers, with the upshot that the company enters a whole new market.

Question 2

Aldebaran Ltd is a pubic relations agency founded by an entrepreneur, Estella Grande, who has employed various talented individuals from other agencies to set up in business. Estella Grande wants Aldebaran Ltd to become the largest public relations agency in North London. Management consultants, in a planning document, have suggested 'growth by acquisition.' In other words, Alderbaran should buy up the other public relations agencies in the area. These would be retained as semi-independent business units, as the Alderbaran Ltd group could benefit from the goodwill of the newly acquired agencies. When Estella presents these ideas to the Board there is a general consensus that this is a good idea, with one significant exception. Livia Strange, the marketing director, is horrified. 'How am I going to sell this to my staff? Ever since we've been in business, we've won

business by undercutting and slagging off the competition. My team have a whole culture based on it. I give them champagne if they pinch a high value client. Why acquire these new businesses - why not stick to pinching their clients instead?'

Comment on the models of strategy formation in conflict here.

Answer

Livia Strange's department has generated its own pattern of competitive behaviour. It is an emergent strategy. It conflicts directly with the planned strategy proposed by the consultants. This little case history also makes the additional point that strategies are not only about numbers, targets and grand plans, but about the organisational cultures influencing a person's behaviour.

3.3 The task of strategic management is to control these emergent strategies in the light of a broader insight into the business's capabilities.

3.4 Emergent strategies can be driven by new business.

Case example

BPP began life as a training company. Lecturers had to prepare course material. This was offered for sale in a bookshop in the BPP building. Owing to the demand, BPP began offering its material to other colleges, in the UK and world-wide. BPP Publishing, which began as a small offshoot of BPP's training activities, is now a leading publisher in the market for targeted study material for the examinations of several professional bodies. It is unlikely that this development was anticipated when the course material was first prepared.

Crafting strategy

3.5 There will come a point when even an emergent strategy will need some conscious direction, perhaps to change its course. Alternatively, senior managers, when faced with an emergent strategy, might favour some aspects of it over others. For example a company might pride itself on the high quality of its products, even though this involves expensive labour costs. If the quality strategy is favoured, management might try to develop practices which reduce the cost of this given quality.

3.6 *Mintzberg* uses the phrase **crafting strategy** to help understand this idea. The planning approach encountered already implies rational control and systematic analysis of competitors and markets, and of company strengths and weaknesses. However, the idea of strategy as a **craft** evokes an idea of 'skill, dedication, perfection, through mastery of detail.' More importantly, forming a strategy and implementing it are 'fluid processes of learning through which creative strategies evolve'.

3.7 Mintzberg uses the image of a potter's wheel. The clay is thrown, and through shaping the clay on the wheel, the potter gives shape to the clay lump through a gradual process. Mintzberg believes this is a good analogy of how strategies are actually developed and managed.

(a) The potter can introduce innovations during the process of shaping. The potter is both the producer and consumer of the vase. The gap between thinking and doing is short.

(b) A sales representative who discovers a new way of providing customer satisfactions may have to convince large numbers of people within the organisation of the idea's merits. The gap between insight and execution is a long one.

3.8   The trouble with the long feedback loop is that there is a separation between 'thinking' and 'doing' when it comes to strategy. This has the following results.

(a)   A **purely deliberate strategy prevents learning** (once the formulators have stopped formulating). For example, it is hard with deliberate strategies to learn from mistakes, or stumble by accident into strategic growth.

(b)   A **purely emergent strategy defies control**. It may in fact be a bad strategy, dysfunctional for the organisation's future health.

3.9   **Deliberate strategies** can introduce strategic change as a sort of quantum leap in some organisations. In this case, a firm has only a few strategic changes in a short period but these are very dramatic.

Case examples

(a)   *Mercedes-Benz*, having concentrated on large expensive cars, has recently changed its strategy. Its boss recently stated that the company's strategy of expecting customers to pay premium prices for 'over-engineered' cars is no longer tenable. The company intends to produce a much wider range of cars, including small cars, than hitherto. This is a major, planned change of direction.

(b)   In other organisations, however, strategic change can be *haphazard*. Mintzberg mentions the example of the *Canadian National Film Board*. This used to make short documentaries but ended up by chance with a feature film. This forced it to learn the marketing of such films, and so it eventually became much more involved in feature length productions than before - 'strategy by accident'.

How to craft strategy

3.10   Mintzberg mentions the following essential activities in strategic management.

- Managing stability
- Detecting discontinuity
- Knowing the business
- Managing patterns
- Reconciling change and continuity

3.11   **Managing stability**

(a)   Most of the time, managers should be effectively implementing the strategies, not planning them.

(b)   Obsessions with change are dysfunctional. **Knowing when to change** is more important. You cannot **assume** perpetual environmental turbulence (chaos or whatever).

(c)   Formal planning is the detailed working out of the agreed strategy.

3.12   **Detecting discontinuity**

(a)   Environments do not change regularly, nor are they always turbulent.

(b)   Strategists should realise that some small environmental changes are much more significant than others, though guessing which these are is a problem.

(c)   Technological developments are hard to assess. Drucker quotes the example of Hoffmann-LaRoche a Swiss based pharmaceutical company, which began as a small firm making dyes. It acquired the patents to vitamins when no one else wanted them, and invested and borrowed all it could into producing and selling them. It is now an

industry leader. Other technologies, combined with cheap production processes, can revolutionise certain industries (eg the motor car revolutionised transportation).

(d) International developments are frequent causes of uncertainty. Spotting international trends which are important to the organisation (which markets are likely to grow and so forth) must be supplemented by assessments of commercial and political risks.

3.13 **Knowing the business.** Strategic management involves an intimate feel for the business. This has to include an **awareness and understanding of operations**.

3.14 **Managing patterns.** 'A key to managing strategy is the ability to detect emerging patterns and to help them take shape'. Some emergent strategies must be uprooted, others nurtured.

3.15 **Reconciling change and continuity.** 'Crafting strategy ...... requires a natural synthesis of the future, present and past'. Obsessions with change and or continuity can both be counterproductive.

Question 3

Britannia Hospital has just appointed a new director, Florian Vole, imported from the private sector, where he had run 'Hanky House' a niche retail operation specialising in handkerchiefs and fashion accessories. The recession put the business into receivership, but Mr Vole was sought out to inject his private sector expertise in running a public sector institution. He calls a meeting of the hospital's senior managerial, medical and nursing staffs. 'What the public sector has been missing too long is vision, and when you're eyeball-to-eyeball with change, it's vision you need, not planning documents and statistics. We need to be nimble and quick to adapt to our customer's ever changing needs. That is our strategy!'

What do think of Florian Vole's approach?

Answer

Mr Vole hasn't quite made the transition from the fashion industry, where desire for silk handkerchiefs is relatively fickle, to an institution like Britannia Hospital. Here planning *is* necessary. Resources must be obtained to cope with future needs. 'Customer needs' are likely to be fairly basic (ie security, comfort, medical attention, stimulation). However, in the actual delivery of care and services, Florian Vole has a point: experimentation with new care techniques might improve the hospital's service to its patients. In this case, pursuing his 'vision' rather than simply following old procedures might be a good approach.

4 'MUDDLING THROUGH' AND LOGICAL INCREMENTALISM

Bounded rationality

4.1 **Rationalism** and **incrementalism** are the two models which are generally represented as occupying opposite ends of the spectrum of approaches to strategy-making.

4.2 *Lindblom* argued that comprehensive rational planning was impossible, and likely to result in disaster if actively pursued. Strategy making involving **small scale extensions of past practices** was more likely to be successful: it would avoid major errors, and was more likely to be acceptable, because consultation, compromise and accommodation were built into the process.

4.3 **Critics argued that such muddling through was not a good prescriptive model -** strategists should aspire to do better.

(a) **Muddling through does not work where radical new approaches are needed**, and it has a **built-in conservative bias.** Lindblom denied the accusation of conservative bias, and suggested that it was possible to achieve a radical shift in policy over a period as a result of a series of incremental shifts. But he partially conceded the case for some forward planning in later versions of his model.

(b) Even as a descriptive model of the public sector, it does not always fit. Some changes do not seem incremental, but involve dramatic shifts. Examples include the reorganisation of the UK National Health Service.

(c) The approach does not seem to highlight **the role of corporate culture** in decision making, it filters out unacceptable choices.

A middle way? Logical incrementalism

4.4 **Logical incrementalism** was identified by *James Brian Quinn*. Logical incrementalism is **not just muddling through**: 'it is a purposeful, effective, proactive management technique for integrating **both** the **analytical** and **behavioural** aspects of strategy formation.'

(a) **Strategy is best described as a learning process**, by which managers have to deal with major internal or external events. One of the problems is that it is impossible to predict the long term consequences of decisions made in those situations of crisis or change. for example, the ramifications of a radical new technology may not be foreseen.

(b) **Managers have some notion as to where the organisation should be.** They 'may be able to predict the broad direction but not the precise nature of the strategy that will result'.

(c) **Managers deliberately keep their decisions small scale**, so that they can be *tested* in small steps, as there is so much uncertainty. However, unlike muddling through which appears simply reactive, the logical incremental model suggests a *conscious* process of decision making.

4.5 The implications of the rational model and incrementalism can be expressed in diagrammatic form.

(a) **Rational planning model**

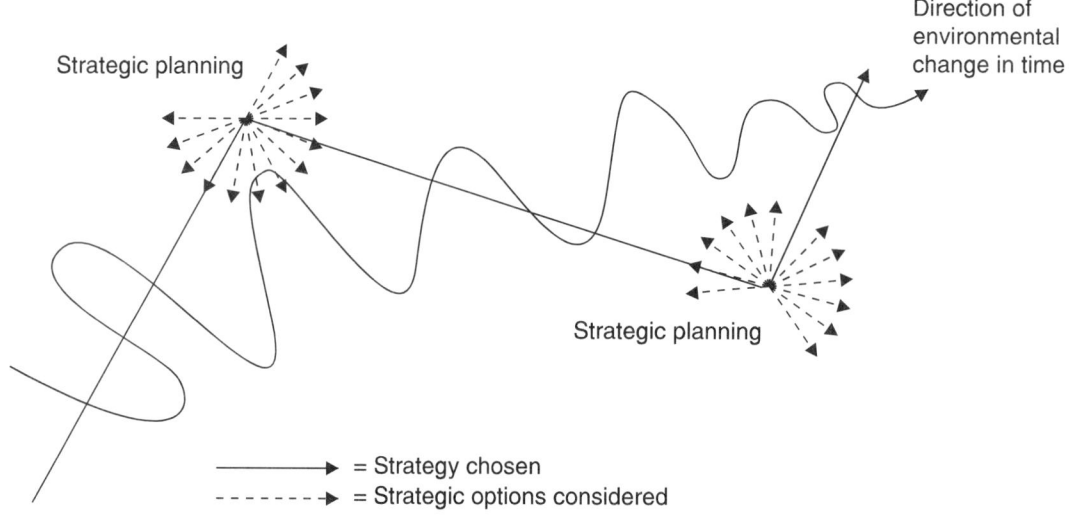

The dangers of the rational model are that the environment may change too quickly for the planning processes to react. All directions are considered, however.

(b) **Incremental model**

As we can see, the advantage of incrementalism is that it can map the environment closely. However, incremental change may not be enough as the number of strategic options considered may be insufficiently radical in terms of their ability to cope with environmental shift.

Direction of environmental
change in time

⟶ = Strategy chosen
- - - - → = Strategic options considered

4.6   **The two models are not mutually exclusive.**

(a) The rational model may be appropriate where the change in the environment is significant or where incrementalism is not enough.

(b) Incrementalism may be appropriate where there is significant uncertainty, so that the organisation follows, rather than pre-empts, changes in the environment.

4.7   Both the rational model and logical incrementalism contrast with the idea of emergent strategies, in that they hold that strategy is made by managers, whereas in the emergent strategy model it can grow from the lower levels of the organisation.

5   STRATEGY AND STRUCTURE

5.1   To what extent does an organisation's **structure** follow its strategy? *Alfred Chandler* conducted a detailed historical study of the development of four major US corporations: *Du Pont, General Motors, Standard Oil of New Jersey* and *Sears Roebuck*. He found that all four had evolved a decentralised structure based on operating divisions, though by different routes.

5.2   Chandler suggested that during the period 1850 to 1920 (which he describes as the formative years of modern capitalism), the development of high volume production to serve mass markets forced the replacement of entrepreneurial, owner management by innovative professional managers. These managers created the modern, multi-unit corporation as the best response to the administrative problems associated with growth. The divisionalised organisation is thus a response to strategy in its broadest sense.

5.3   Chandler discerned two main types of strategy, positive and negative. Positive strategy is aggressive, seeks new markets and leads to **growth by product diversification**. Negative strategy seeks to defend a current position and leads to **growth by vertical integration** based on mergers and acquisitions. In both cases, the initial structural response is likely to be centralised control based on functional departments. Both Du Pont and Sears Roebuck went through this stage.

5.4 Unfortunately, this approach has important disadvantages, especially where there is geographic dispersion. These disadvantages are discussed in Chapter 7. Du Pont therefore created an innovative decentralised structure of largely autonomous product-based business units co-ordinated rather than controlled by the corporate headquarters. General Motors copied the idea to overcome a lack of overall control in its loose federation of operating units. Standard Oil of New Jersey followed suit after a series of *ad hoc* responses to crises of control; its particular problem was the need to allocate and co-ordinate resources. Sears Roebuck went through essentially the same process as Du Pont.

5.5 The creation of the multi-unit structures thus a logical managerial response to the problems associated with strategies that create very large organisations.

5.6 Chandler described four levels of management activity typical of this structure.

(a) The **general office** is the headquarters, responsible for overall performance. It allocates resources to the divisions and controls their performance by setting targets. Divisions are responsible for a product line or sales region.

(b) The **divisional central office** is responsible to the general office. Divisions are organised internally on a functional basis.

(c) Each function, such as production or sales has a **departmental headquarters, which** manages **field units** such as manufacturing plants or a sales team. Only at field unit · level do managers carry out day-to-day operational work.

5.7 It has been argued that an established and well-functioning structure can influence strategy, as, for instance, when two retail organisations merge because the geographical pattern of their branches is complementary. However, this is really an aspect of organisational strengths and weaknesses analysis. Structure should, if necessary, be adjusted to suit the chosen strategy.

Chapter roundup

- One definition of strategy is that it is 'a course of action, including the specification of resources required to achieve a specific objective'.

- Strategic decisions affect the scope of an organisation's activities, the environment, resource capability and allocation, and the organisation's long-term direction.

- Strategic plans are formal statements of direction. The planning process suggests a sequence of strategic analysis (of the environment and the organisation), strategy generation and evaluation (several options are weighed up and compared) and strategic choice of the best alternative. Such, strategy making is the job of a strategic planning department.

- Emergent strategies are those which develop out of pattern of behaviour, which is not consciously thought out, but which eventually has a long-term, 'strategic' effect. Emergent strategies need to be crafted by mangers and shaped to the organisation's advantage.

- Logical incrementalism is an approach which holds that strategy is a series of incremental changes rather than big leaps. It suggests practical limits to the rational model. People make strategic decisions on the basis of precedent, accepting satisfactory rather than ideal solutions.

- An important aspect of strategy is the relation an organisation has with its environment. Strategy is sometimes seen as a means of ensuring a continual matching between the organisation's capability and environmental demands.

- Structure generally follows strategy.

Quick quiz

1 Define strategy.

2 List the characteristics of strategic decisions.

3 Why is planning useful?

4 Describe the rational model of the strategic planning process.

5 Distinguish between corporate strategy, business strategy and operational strategy.

6 What is an emergent strategy?

7 What is a deliberate strategy?

8 What is involved in crafting strategy?

9 What is meant by bounded rationality?

10 What are the drawbacks to incrementalism?

Answers to Quick Quiz

1 A course of action, including the specification of resources required to achieve a specific objective.

2 Wide and long term scope; securing fit with the environment and resources; defining effect on operational decisions; reflects expectations of power-holders; complexity.

3 It helps in coping with an uncertain future; guides the allocation of resources; provides overall direction of activities; and sets standards of performance.

4 The rational model has three main parts.

   • Strategic analysis considers aims, capabilities and external influences.

   • Strategic choice generates options, considers them and chooses an overall plan.

   • Strategic implementation lays down the framework of the corporate plan from which detailed operational plans can be developed.

5 Corporate strategy is the highest level of strategy and is concerned with decisions of scope, such as entering and leaving industries. Business strategy defines how a company approaches a particular market. Operational strategies are concerned with the implementation of the higher levels of planning.

6, 7 One which comes about by the exploitation of circumstances rather than through a conscious planning process; the latter is a deliberate strategy.

8 By crafting strategy, Mintzberg means the refinement of an emergent strategy through 'fluid processes of learning'.

9 Lindblom argued that there are limits to the usefulness of a totally reasoned approach to strategy-making, because of the immense complexity of the business environment.

10 Development in slow, incremental steps does not allow for the revolutionary developments that destroy old markets and create new ones.

Now try the question below from the Exam Question Bank

Number	Level	Marks	Time
Q1	Exam	20	36 mins

Chapter 2

MISSION AND GOALS

Topic List	Syllabus Reference	Ability required
1 Mission	(i)	Evaluation
2 Subverting mission	(i)	Evaluation
3 Goals and objectives	(i)	Evaluation
4 Stakeholders	(i)	Comprehension

Introduction

In this chapter, we cover the two of the elements of the strategic analysis process: an organisation's objectives and its mission.

- Mission (Section 1) describes an organisation's basic function in society. It has implications for a firm's business strategies, and for the values espoused by employees. It can be expressed in a statement. For business, profitability is a key element of mission.

- Goals and objectives (Section 3) will be set to implement the mission, for the organisation as a whole and for the units within it. Goals often conflict, and the trade-offs made between them can be a political process as much as a rational one. Not all goals and objectives can be quantified.

- In practice managers can direct the organisation so as to subvert its mission (Section 2).

- Stakeholders have important influences on the organisation's mission and goals.

Learning outcomes covered in this chapter

- Identify the stakeholders of an organisation and explain their influence on its management and structure.

- Recommend appropriate organisational goals.

Syllabus content covered in this chapter

- Organisational objectives (ie stakeholder analysis and organisational mission, goals and targets)

- The reasons for conflict between the objectives of an organisation, or between the objectives of the organisation and its stakeholders, and the ways in which this conflict might be managed (e.g. compromise or identification of a dominant coalition)

1 MISSION

1.1 **Mission** 'describes the organisation's basic function in society, in terms of the products and services it produces for its clients' (*Mintzberg*).

Case example

In its *Vision for the new Millennium*, CIMA defines its mission like this:

To be the acknowledged world leader in:

* The qualification and support of Chartered Management Accountants
* The science of Management Accountancy

1.2   It is possible, however, to give a broader definition of mission to include four elements.

(a) **Purpose**. Why does the company exist, or why do its managers and employees feel it exists? Who does the organisation exist for? (eg shareholders, and possibly other stakeholders such as employees, customers). Here are some possibilities.

(i)   To create wealth for shareholders, who take priority over all other stakeholders.

(ii)   To satisfy the needs of all stakeholders (including employees, society at large, for example).

(iii)   To reach some higher goal ('the advancement of society'). This element appears to include both operational and non-operational goals.

(b) **Strategy**. This provides the commercial logic for the company, and so defines the nature of the firm's business, the markets it competes in and the competences and competitive advantages by which it hopes to prosper.

(c) **Policies and standards of behaviour**. Strategy needs to be converted into everyday performance. For example, a service industry that wishes to be the best in its market must aim for standards of service, in all its operations, which are at least as good as those found in its competitors. In service businesses, this includes simple matters such as politeness to customers and the speed with which phone calls are answered.

(d) **Values**. These relate to the organisation's culture, and are the basic, perhaps unstated, beliefs of the people who work in the organisation. For example, a firm's moral principles might mean refusing an assignment if it believes the client will not benefit, even though this refusal means lost revenue. Mintzberg sometimes defines values as ideology, in other words, a means of control through shared beliefs. A sense of mission, or emotional bond, is where employees' personal values coincide with organisational values.

For there to be a strong sense of mission, the elements above must be mutually re-inforcing.

Case example

CIMA's *vision for the new millennium* went on to state its **vision** and **strategy**. We might feel that these are parts of its **mission statement** (see below).

The Vision

* An Institute renowned and respected for the quality of its members, staff, qualification, technical products and services

* An Institute which stands out by reason of its effectiveness, its ability to anticipate and its agility in delivery

* An Institute which thrives on partnerships, worldwide

* An Institute which is inventive and innovative, and which maximises the potential of technology.

The Strategy

* To make the CIMA qualification relevant and accessible in key markets

BPP PUBLISHING

- To establish a network of alliances and partnerships to enable the Institute to increase its influence and/or penetration in those key markets

- To develop, maintain and exploit a range of management accountancy products which anticipate and meet the needs of members and business

- To anticipate and respond speedily to customer demand and market opportunities by structuring the institute accordingly

- To attract, develop and retain talented staff who are empowered to reach stretch goals, and who are directly responsible and accountable for their performance

1.3 You may feel that philosophical discourse about values and principles is not relevant to organisational performance, and is so much hot air. None of it can be quantified, and so, from an accountant's point of view, this must reduce its value. There are several reasons, however, why this scepticism as to the value of mission, because of its emotional content, is misplaced.

(a) **Values and feelings are integral elements of consumers' buying decisions**, as evidenced by advertising, branding and market research. Therefore they should be considered during a company's decision-making processes.

(b) **Accountants are a small segment of the population as a whole**, and a respect for numbers that add up and quantifiable information is part of their professional culture and training. This is not necessarily shared by other people, who hold the issues of value and emotional content, when dealing with customers and doing their job, to be important.

(c) **Employees are motivated by more than money**. A sense of mission and values can help to motivate employees. In some jobs such as nursing, a sense of vocation and professionalism is bound up with the organisation's mission.

(d) Many organisations do in practice take the cultural aspect of mission seriously.

Mission statements

KEY TERM

A **mission statement** is a formal declaration of underlying purpose. It says what an organisation exists to do.

1.4 **Mission statements** might be reproduced in a number of places, such as at the front of an organisation's annual report, on publicity material, in the chairman's office and in communal work areas. There is no standard format, but they should have certain qualities.

- **Brevity** will make them easier to understand and remember.
- **Flexibility** will enable them to accommodate change.
- They should be **distinctive**, to make the firm stand out.

Scott Adams, creator of *Dilbert*, defines a mission statement as 'a long awkward sentence that demonstrates management's inability to think clearly'. This illustrates the main problem with mission statements, which is getting people to take them seriously.

Case examples

The following statements were taken from annual reports of the organisations concerned. Are they 'mission statements'? If so, are they any good?

(a) **Glaxo** 'is an integrated research-based group of companies whose corporate purpose is to create, discover, develop, manufacture and market throughout the world, safe, effective medicines of the highest quality which will bring benefit to patients through improved longevity and quality of life, and to society through economic value.'

(b) **IBM (UK)**: 'We shall increase the pace of change. Market-driven quality is our aim. It means listening and responding more sensitively to our customers. It means eliminating defects and errors, speeding up all our processes, measuring everything we do against a common standard, and it means involving employees totally in our aims'.

(c) **Matsushita**: 'the duty of the manufacturer is to serve the foundation of man's happiness by making man's life affluent with an inexpensive and inexhaustible supply of life's necessities.'

(d) **Guinness Group**: Guinness plc is one of the world's leading drinks companies, producing and marketing an unrivalled portfolio of international best-selling brands, such as Johnnie Walker, Bell's and Dewar's Scotch whiskies, Gordon's and Tanqueray gins, and Guinness stout itself - the world's most distinctive beer. The strategy is to focus resources on the development of the Group's alcoholic drinks businesses. The objectives are to provide superior long-term financial returns for shareholders, to create a working environment in which people can perform to their fullest potential and to be recognised as one of the world's leading consumer brand development companies.

(e) **British Film Institute**. 'The BFI is the UK national agency with responsibility for encouraging and conserving the arts of film and television. Our aim is to ensure that the many audiences in the UK are offered access to the widest possible choice of cinema and television, so that their enjoyment is enhanced through a deeper understanding of the history and potential of these vital and popular art forms.'

Mission and planning

1.5 Although the mission statement might be seen as a set of abstract principles, **it can play an important role in the planning process**.

(a) **Plans should outline the fulfilment of the organisation's mission**. To take the example of a religious organisation (the best example of a **missionary organisation**), the mission of spreading the gospel might be embodied in plans to send individuals as missionaries to various parts of the world, plans for fund-raising activities or even targets for the numbers of new converts.

(b) **Evaluation and screening**. Mission acts as a yardstick by which plans are judged. Take the example of a financial services organisation which runs a number of ethical investment funds which exclude from their portfolios shares in firms involved in alcohol, tobacco and armaments. If a new fund manager proposed to invest in shares of a diversified company, would be examined to see if its activities included those which the investment fund considered unethical. The investment strategy would be assessed with reference to the investment fund's mission. Mission helps to ensure **consistency in decisions**.

(c) **Implementation**. Mission also affects the implementation of a planned strategy and can be embodied in the **policies and behaviour standards of** the firm.

2 SUBVERTING MISSION

2.1 Mintzberg provides a useful analysis of the sorts of goals that organisations, and people in them, actually pursue.

(a) **Ideological goals** usually focus on the organisation's mission. They are shared sets of beliefs and values.

(b) **Formal goals** are imposed by a dominant individual or group. People work to attain these goals, as a means to their personal goals. (For example, you do what your boss tells you to in order to earn a wage to support your family.)

(c) **Shared personal goals**. Individuals reach a consensus about what they want out of an organisation. A group of academics might decide they want to pursue research in a particular field.

(d) **System goals** derive from the organisation's existence as an organisation, independent of mission. See below.

(e) The inherent danger of mission is that it will not be implemented. Mintzberg writes 'organisations, too, can have trouble operationalising their lofty goals, with the result that their *official* goals - what they claim to be their goals - often do not correspond with the end they *actually* seem to pursue. Sometimes, of course, the official goals are merely for public consumption, not for internal decision making'.

(f) *Warringer* said that the official statements of organisational purpose must be considered as 'fictions produced by an organisation to account for, explain, or rationalise its existence to particular audiences': PR in other words.

2.2 Mintzberg argues that **system goals** are those which organisations as systems pursue. **These goals have a habit of subverting mission**, by making mission subordinate to them. Here are some system goals.

System goal	Comment
Survival	Individuals benefit from the organisation's existence (as their employer, for their social life), irrespective of what the organisation actually does. People invest time and effort in an organisation: consequently its demise is more than simply *economic* failure for the people that work for it. Organisations are also places where people build careers. There is a strong incentive for an organisation to survive simply because it keeps its managers in work. Hence the purchase, say, by a tobacco company of an insurance company to safeguard the 'future of the organisation'. Shareholders could simply have switched investments.
Efficiency	This is the greatest benefit for a given cost. However, an organisation can be efficient (doing things well) as opposed to being effective (doing the right things). Efficiency takes precedence over effectiveness according to Mintzberg because it is easier to measure costs than benefits, and because it is harder to measure social costs and benefits than economic costs and benefits.
Control	Organisations may attempt 'to exercise some control over their own environments'. Examples of control are vertical integration (eg to control supply) and diversification (to reduce uncertainty).
Growth	Managers benefit directly from growth, in terms of salaries and status. 'Growth is the natural goal of the manager' as it reduces vulnerability to the environment and other organisations.

2.3 Technical experts such as work study analysts are less concerned with mission than exercising their specialisation for whoever is interested. They have less interest in the survival of the organisation than do line managers.

Question 1

The Octagon company is a firm which employs about 150 managers and staff. It has recently obtained a stock market listing. Its business is the supply of unusual high quality fabrics in small quantities to fashion designers in London. There is no likely competition. The Managing Director feels that he needs a Director of Information Systems; one is appointed to the Board. About six months into his appointment, the new director of information systems produces a plan to the board, which he has largely dreamed up from scratch. 'If we are to grow,' he says, 'we'll need new systems.'

'Grow where? Why?' says the MD.

Why do you think the MD is querying the new plan outlined by the Director of Information Systems?

Answer

Growth would expand the Information Director's power and influence, and also the power and influence of other senior managers. The MD is quite happy with the market as it is. Growth is a system goal, in this case.

3 GOALS AND OBJECTIVES

3.1 Goals are '**the intentions behind decisions or actions**, the states of mind that drive individuals or collectives of individuals called organisations to do what they do.' (Mintzberg: *Power In and Around Organisations*)

(a) **Operational goals** can be expressed as **objectives**. Mintzberg says that **an objective is a goal expressed in a form by which its attainment can be measured.** Here is an example.

- **Mission**: deliver a quality service
- **Goal**: enhance manufacturing quality
- **Objectives**: over the next twelve months, reduce the number of defects to 1 part per million

(b) **Non-operational goals or aims** on the other hand cannot be expressed as objectives. Mintzberg quotes the example of a university, whose goal might be to 'seek truth'. This cannot really be expressed as a quantified objective. To 'increase truth by 5% this year' does not make a great deal of sense.

3.2 Objectives should meet the SMART criteria.

- Specific
- Measurable
- Attainable
- Results-orientated
- Time-bounded

3.3 However, not all goals, as we have seen, can be measured, or can ever be attained completely. **Customer satisfaction** is a goal, but satisfying customers and ensuring that they remain satisfied is a **continuous process** that does not stop when one target has been reached.

BPP PUBLISHING

3.4 **Features of goals and objectives in organisations**

(a) **Goal congruence.** Goals should be consistent with each other.

    (i) **Across all departments.** There should be **horizontal** consistency. In other words, the goals set for different parts of the organisation should be consistent with each other.

    (ii) **At all levels.** Objectives should be consistent **vertically,** in other words at all levels in the organisation.

    (iii) **Over time.** Objectives should be consistent with each other over the **same time span.**

(b) An objective should **identify the beneficiaries** as well as the nature and size of the benefit.

> **Exam focus point**
>
> You should be able to define mission and to be able to elaborate on the functions of mission statements.
>
> As a rule of thumb, if you have any difficulty, ask yourself 'What and who is this organisation for?' and possibly 'What does this organisation do?'

Corporate and unit goals and objectives

3.5 **Corporate objectives** are concerned with the firm as a whole or the strategic business units in the firm. A strategic business unit (SBU) which is a part of the company that for 'all intents and purposes has its own distinct products, markets and assets'. Objectives should be explicit, quantifiable and capable of being achieved. The corporate objectives outline the expectations of the firm and the strategic planning process is concerned with the means of achieving the objectives. Objectives should relate to the **critical success factors** for business success, which are typically the following.

- Profitability (return on investment)
- Market share
- Growth
- Cash flow

- Customer satisfaction
- The quality of the firm's products
- Industrial relations
- Added value

3.6 **Unit objectives are specific to individual units of an organisation.** Here are some examples.

(a) **For businesses**

    (i) Increasing the number of customers by x% (an objective of a sales department).

    (ii) Reducing the number of rejects by 50% (an objective of a production department).

    (iii) Producing monthly reports more quickly, within 5 working days of the end of each month (an objective of the management accounting department).

(b) **For the public sector**

    (i) To introduce x% more places at nursery schools (an objective of a borough education department).

    (ii) Responding more quickly to calls (an objective of a local police station, fire department or hospital ambulance service).

Primary and secondary objectives

3.7 Some objectives are more important than others. In the hierarchy of objectives, there is a **primary corporate objective** (restricted by certain constraints on corporate activity) and other **secondary objectives** which are strategic objectives which should combine to ensure the achievement of the overall corporate objective.

(a) For example, if a company sets itself a primary objective of growth in profits, it will then have to develop strategies by which this primary objective can be achieved.

(b) Secondary objectives might then be concerned with matters such as sales growth, continual technological innovation, customer service, product quality, efficient resource management (eg labour productivity) and reducing the company's reliance on debt capital. Secondary objectives have to be ranked in order of priority.

3.8 *Kaplan and Norton* suggested a **balanced scorecard** approach which looks at the business in four perspectives; performance in all must be satisfactory if the business is to prosper.

- The **financial perspective**, or 'how do we look to shareholders?'

- The **customer perspective**, or 'how do customers see us?'

- The **internal business perspective**, or 'what must we excel at?'

- The **innovation and learning perspective**, or 'can we continue to improve and create value?'

It is necessary for each business to set **goals** and establish **performance measures** for each perspective. Some will be fairly simple and traditional. For instance, shareholders will want to see their company survive and grow; suitable measures here would be cash generation and profits respectively. The internal perspective will vary widely between companies but will concentrate on efficiency goals and measures. Measuring customer satisfaction can be done in a variety of ways such as counting complaints or starting a programme of interviews. The innovation and learning perspective will, perhaps, be the most difficult to handle. Kaplan and Norton give the example of an electronics company with several goals in this perspective; one is technology leadership and the chosen measure is how long it takes to develop a new generation of product.

Trade-off between objectives

3.9 When there are several key objectives, some might be achieved only at the expense of others. For example, attempts to achieve a good cash flow or good product quality, or to improve market share, might call for some sacrifice of profits.

3.10 There will be a trade-off between objectives when strategies are formulated, and a choice will have to be made. For example, there might be a choice between the following two options.

Option A 15% sales growth, 10% profit growth, a £2 million negative cash flow and reduced product quality and customer satisfaction.

Option B 8% sales growth, 5% profit growth, a £500,000 surplus cash flow, and maintenance of high product quality/customer satisfaction.

If the firm chose option B in preference to option A, it would be trading off sales growth and profit growth for better cash flow, product quality and customer satisfaction. Note that the long-term effect of reduced quality has not been considered.

Long-term and short-term objectives

3.11 Objectives may be long-term and short-term.

   (a) company that is suffering from a recession in its core industries and making losses in the short term might continue to have a primary objective in the long term of achieving a steady growth in earnings or profits, but in the short term, its primary objective might switch to survival.

   (b) Secondary objectives will range from the short term to the long term. Planners will formulate secondary objectives within the guidelines set by the primary objective, after selecting strategies for achieving the primary objective.

3.12 For example, a company's primary objective might be to increase its earnings per share from 30p to 50p in the next five years. Strategies for achieving the objective might include those below.

   • Increasing profitability in the next twelve months by cutting expenditure
   • Increasing export sales over the next three years
   • Developing a successful new product for the domestic market within five years.

3.13 Secondary objectives might then be re-assessed.

   (a) Improving manpower productivity by 10% within twelve months

   (b) Improving customer service in export markets with the objective of doubling the number of overseas sales outlets in selected countries within the next three years

   (c) Investing more in product-market research and development, with the objective of bringing at least three new products to the market within five years

Conflict: how trade-offs are made

3.14 There are conflicts between different types of goals (eg long-term vs short-term). *Daft* indicates, in addition to rational analysis, four ways of dealing with **goal conflict**.

   (a) **Bargaining**. Managers with different goals will compete with each other, and will form alliances with other managers to achieve them.

   (b) **Satisficing**. Organisations do not aim to maximise performance in one area if this leads to poor performance elsewhere. Rather they will accept satisfactory, if not excellent, performance in a number of areas.

   (c) **Sequential attention**. Goals are dealt with one by one, as it were, in a sequence.

   (d) **Priority setting**. Certain goals get priority over others. This is determined by senior managers, but there are quite complicated systems to rank goals and strategies according to certain criteria.

Question 2

What type of trade-off mechanisms are being used in the following cases?

(a) 'Next year, we'll flood the market with the stuff. But we've got to get the quality right first.'
(b) 'Don't bother about the third coat of varnish, as long as we get the job done by Saturday.'

Answer

(a) Sequential attention
(b) Satisficing

Stakeholders

3.15 Managers are not completely free to set objectives; they have different groups of stakeholders to consider.

3.16 For a business, return or profit is the yardstick, but elsewhere managers might have to bow to other key external stakeholders, when setting objectives.

4   STAKEHOLDERS   5/01

> **KEY TERM**
>
> **Stakeholders**: groups or individuals having a legitimate interest in the activities of an organisation

4.1   There are three broad types of stakeholder in an organisation.

- **Internal** stakeholders such as employees and management
- **Connected** stakeholders such as shareholders customers, suppliers and financiers
- **External** stakeholders such as the community, government and pressure groups

Internal stakeholders

4.2   Because employees and management are so intimately connected with the company, **their objectives are likely to have a strong and immediate influence on how it is run**. They are interested in the **organisation's continuation and growth**. The organisation is a place where management and employees spend a great deal of their time and energy. It pays them. Management and employees have a special interest in the organisation's continued existence. This interest may not be held by shareholders. For example, if the organisation has surplus funds, the management might try and invest them in new projects whereas shareholders might prefer these funds to be returned to them, so that they can make up their own minds.

4.3   Managers and employees also have **individual interests and goals**.

- Security of income
- Increases in income
- A safe and comfortable working environment
- A sense of community
- Interesting work
- Skills and career development
- A sense of doing something worthwhile

Connected stakeholders

4.4   There are several groups of connected stakeholders.

(a)   **Shareholders**. Their prime interest is a return on their investment, whether in the short or long term. As shareholders own the business, this is a commercial organisation's prime objective. Some shareholders are concerned with a corporation's ethical performance, hence the growth of investment funds designed to avoid certain companies. Shareholders are now being asked to take a more involved interest in a company's affairs.

(b) **Bankers** are also interested in a firm's overall condition, but from the point of view of the security of any loans they make. A bank is keen to minimise the risk of interest not being paid, or of its security being eroded.

(c) **Customers** want products and services. Large customers have significant power over prices and procedures.

(d) **Suppliers** will expect to be paid and will be interested in future business.

External stakeholders

4.5 External stakeholder groups - the government, local authorities, pressure groups, the community at large, professional bodies - are likely to have quite diverse objectives and have a varying ability to ensure that the company meets them.

(a) **Central government** is interested in tax revenues, compliance with legislation (eg on health and safety), statistics and so on.

(b) **Local authorities** are interested, since companies can bring local employment. Also they can affect the local environment for instance by increasing road traffic.

(c) **Professional bodies** are interested to ensure that members who work for companies comply with professional ethics and standards.

(d) **Pressure groups** will have an interest in particular issues.

Case example

Saatchi and Saatchi

An example of the role and power of different stakeholders is provided by the changes in the Saatchi and Saatchi advertising agency in 1995.

Upset about the share price, a number of shareholders (key stakeholders) wanted changes to the agency's management, in particular a reduction in the roles of the Saatchi brothers, who had founded the agency. The Saatchi brothers eventually left the agency they founded, which was renamed Cordiant. Round 1 to the shareholders.

For an industrial company, such boardroom manoeuvrings are not uncommon. However, advertising is very much a 'people' business; and shareholders perhaps worried about the change when shortly after the Saatchis departed key personnel followed them and many key customers ceased their relationship with Cordiant, in favour of the Saatchi brothers' new agency.

Since that time, Cordiant has decided to demerge.

Stakeholder power

4.6 How stakeholders relate to the management of the company depends very much on what type of stakeholder they are - internal, connected or external - and on the level in the management hierarchy at which they are able to apply pressure. Clearly a company's management will respond differently to the demands of, say, its shareholders and the community at large. The way in which the relationship between company and stakeholders is conducted again is a function of the character of the relationship, the parties' relative bargaining strength and the philosophy underlying each party's objectives. This can be shown as a spectrum.

Spectrum of relationship between organisation and stakeholders

		Weak				Stakeholders' bargaining strength				Strong	

Company's conduct of relation- ship	{	Command/ dictated by company	Consultation and consideration of stakeholders' views	Negotiation	Participation and acceptance of stakeholders' views	Democratic voting by stakeholders	Command/ dictated by stakeholders

Conflict with stakeholders

4.7 *Mendelow* classifies stakeholders on a matrix whose axes are power held and likelihood of showing an interest in the organisation's activities. These factors will help define the type of relationship the organisation should seek with its stakeholders.

Level of interest

	Low	High
Low	A	B
Power		
High	C	D

(a) **Key players** are found in segment D: strategy must be *acceptable* to them, at least. An example would be a major customer.

(b) Stakeholders in segment C must be treated with care. While often passive, they are capable of moving to segment D. They should, therefore be **kept satisfied.** Large institutional shareholders might fall into segment C.

(c) Stakeholders in segment B do not have great ability to influence strategy, but their views can be important in influencing more powerful stakeholders, perhaps by lobbying. They should therefore be **kept informed.** Community representatives and charities might fall into segment B.

(d) Minimal effort is expended on segment A.

4.8 Stakeholder mapping is used to assess the significance of stakeholders. This in turn has implications for the organisation.

(a) The framework of **corporate governance** should recognise stakeholders' levels of interest and power.

(b) It may be appropriate to seek to **reposition** certain stakeholders and discourage others from repositioning themselves, depending on their attitudes.

(c) Key **blockers** and **facilitators** of change must be identified.

4.9 A relationship in which **conflict** between stakeholders is vividly characterised is that between **managers and shareholders**. The relationship can run into trouble when the managers' decisions focus on maintaining the corporation as a **vehicle for their managerial skills** while the shareholders wish to see radical changes so as to enhance their **dividend stream and increase the value of their shares**. The shareholders may feel that the business is a **managerial corporation** run for the benefit of managers and employees without regard for the objectives of the owners. The conflict in this case can be seriously detrimental to the company's stability.

(a) Shareholders may force resignations and divestments of businesses, while managers may seek to preserve their empire and provide growth at the same time by undertaking risky policies.

(b) In most cases, however, managers cannot but acknowledge that the shareholders have the major stake as owners of the company and its assets. Most companies therefore focus on making profits and increasing the market value of the company's shares, sometimes at the expense of the long term benefit of the company. Hence long term strategic plans may be 'hijacked' by the need to make a sizeable profit in one particular year; planning horizons are reduced and investment in long term business prospects may be shelved.

Clearly, each stakeholder group considers itself in some way **a client of the organisation**, thus broadening the debate about organisation effectiveness.

Exam focus point

The May 2001 exam included a question on stakeholders and their influence. The organisation in question was a very large and successful football club. Note the following points.

- The organisation is **not** an ordinary commercial concern. The examiner is always likely to choose slightly unusual settings. Do not be put off!

- It is always worth remembering that in the UK, and in many other countries, the behaviour of any large organisation is likely to be of interest of **government**. Government was not mentioned in the setting, but you may assume that it will always be tempted to interfere in any setting that involved large scale adverse publicity, as this one did.

Chapter roundup

- Mission includes both the organisation's value system and an answer to the question 'What business are we in?'

- A mission (sometimes referred to as 'official goals') is often embodied in a mission statement.

- Goals or objectives are the intentions or decisions behind actions. Some goals are quantified. Quantified objectives (or operational goals) normally describe what an organisation hopes to achieve over a specific period and can be measured. They include indicators such as profitability and market share.

- Objectives are sometimes in conflict. In such a case, managers can adopt four ways of reconciling them.

  Internal bargaining
  Satisficing
  Sequential attention
  Priority setting

- People in organisations pursue a variety of goals, not necessarily related to the product-market circumstances of the business. *Systems goals* (Mintzberg) derive from an organisation's existence as an organisation. They include survival of the organisation, whereas shareholders can switch investments, growth etc.

- There are internal, connected and external stakeholders. All stakeholders aim to influence the behaviour of the organisation. Sometimes, the stakeholder groups are in conflict with one another.

Quick quiz

1 Define mission.

2 Why is mission, as a set of values, relevant to an organisation?

3 What four sorts of goals does Mintzberg suggest that organisations (or the people within them) pursue?

4 List some corporate objectives.

5 What is meant by 'satisficing'?

6 List three types of stakeholder.

7 What interests do shareholders have?

Answers to quick quiz

1   Mintzberg defines an organisation's mission as its 'basic function in society, in terms of the products and services it produces for its clients'.

2   When the members of an organisation subscribe to common values, those values create a framework of control over what the organisation does and how it does it.

3   Ideological goals, formal goals, shared personal goals and system goals

4   Increase sales by 5%. Cut headcount by 2%. Increase return on investment to 17%. Reduce debtor days to 55.

5   The acceptance of satisfactory rather than exemplary performance.

6   Internal, connected, external.

7   Return on investment, dividends, capital growth, corporate survival, ethical behaviour.

Now try the question below from the Exam Question Bank

Number	Level	Marks	Time
Q2	Exam	20	36 mins

Chapter 3

MANAGEMENT

Topic List		Syllabus reference	Ability required
1	The functions of management	(i)	Comprehension
2	Innovation	(i)	Analysis
3	Centralisation and decentralisation	(i)	Analysis

Introduction

Management is responsible for **directing** the activities of the organisation, so that it fulfils its **mission**. They have to work through the organisation structure and mobilise the organisation's resources. How the management task should be achieved has been the subject of much debate. Early writers produced lists of **functions** which the manager should fulfil. Management was often seen as a single discipline which was applicable to organisations of all types. Beginning with *Drucker*, we illustrate the more modern view that management of commercial organisations is firmly differentiated by the economic role of the profit making business.

An important tension at the heart of business is the need both to retain control and to encourage entrepreneurial activity and innovation. Top management must establish systems and practices which encourage the congruence of subordinate managers' goals with those of the company as a whole, while rewarding the development of new ideas.

Learning outcomes covered in this chapter

- Discuss ways in which the conflict between centralised control and individual creativity can be managed.

- Explain the usefulness of both classical and contemporary theories of management in practical situations.

- Explain trends in the general management and structure of organisations.

- Evaluate the management of an organisation and recommend improvements.

Syllabus content covered in this chapter

- The different models of organisational management available to achieve goal congruence while maintaining individual motivation (eg the creation of Strategic Business Units and the encouragement of entrepreneurial behaviour).

- The views expressed by both classical and contemporary writers on business management and the practical value and limitations of the approaches they propose (eg scientific management, administrative, human relations, systems and contingency approaches when compared with contemporary writers such as Peters or Handy).

BPP PUBLISHING

1 THE FUNCTIONS OF MANAGEMENT

The purpose of management

1.1 Management is needed for a variety of reasons.

- **Objectives have to be set** for the organisation.

- These **objectives have to be met,** and somebody has to ensure that this happens.

- **Corporate values** must be sustained.

- **Mission** must be followed.

- The organisation's **key stakeholders must be satisfied**.

Question 1

John, Paul, George and Ringo set up in business together as repairers of musical instruments. Each has contributed £5,000 as capital for the business. They are a bit uncertain as to how they should go about achieving success, and, when they discuss this in the pub, they decide that attention needs to be paid to planning what they do, reviewing what they do and controlling what they do.

Suggest two ways in which John, Paul, George and Ringo can manage the business, assuming no other personnel are recruited.

Answer

The purpose of this exercise has been to get you to separate the issues of management functions from organisational structure and hierarchy. Here are some extreme examples.

(a) All the management activities could be the job of one person. Paul, for example, could plan direct and control the work and the other three would do the work.

(b) Division of management tasks between individuals (eg: repairing drums **and** ensuring plans are adhered to would be Ringo's job, and so on).

(c) Management by committee. All of them could sit down and work out the plan together.

> **KEY TERM**
>
> **Management** is a diffuse activity and there is no one definition that is universally valid. So try Rosemary Stewart's: 'Deciding *what* should be done and then getting other people to do it'. (In other words, 'getting things done through other people'.)

1.2 In large organisations, if everybody participated in management nothing would get done, so management tasks are done by a separate group of people. Over the years, there have been many changes in what managers are supposed to do.

General management functions: early theories

The classical school

1.3 *Fayol* listed the **functions** of management.

Function	Comment
Planning	Selecting objectives and the strategies, policies, programmes and procedures for achieving them.
Organising	Establishing a **structure of tasks** to be performed to achieve the goals, **grouping these tasks into jobs** for individuals, creating **groups of jobs** within departments, **delegating authority** to carry out the jobs, providing **systems of information,** and co-ordinating activities.
Commanding	Giving instructions to subordinates to carry out tasks over which the manager has authority for decisions and responsibility for performance.
Co-ordinating	**Harmonising** the activities of individuals and groups within the organisation.
Controlling	**Measuring** the activities of individuals and groups, to ensure that their performance is in accordance with plans. Deviations from plan are identified and corrected.

Question 2

Group the activities of a manager in your organisation into Fayol's five functions. What do you think is left out from Fayol's list? What do you think is wrong with it? or inadequate about it?

Answer

You might regard **commanding** as a bit old-fashioned. After all, it is widely realised that managers have to **motivate** as well as command. Moreover, if a manager and a subordinate work with each other over a long period, the manager's approach will have a significant effect on the subordinate's development. Drucker, for example, mentions 'developing people' as a key function.

Scientific management: planning work

1.4   *Frederick W Taylor* pioneered the **scientific management** movement. He argued that management should be based on 'well-recognised, clearly defined and fixed principles, instead of depending on more or less hazy ideas.' Taylor was an engineer and mostly concerned with **engineering** management. His aim was increased **efficiency** in production, that is, increased productivity. His methods were later applied to many other types of work.

1.5   **Principles of scientific management**

(a) **The development of a true science of work.** 'All knowledge which had hitherto been kept in the heads of workmen should be gathered and recorded by **management**. Every single subject, large and small, becomes the question for scientific investigation, for reduction to law.'

(b) **The scientific selection and progressive development of workers:** workers should be carefully trained and given jobs to which they are best suited.

(c) **The bringing together of the science and the scientifically selected and trained men.** The application of techniques to decide what should be done and how, using workers who are both properly trained and willing to maximise output, should result in maximum productivity.

(d) **The constant and intimate co-operation between management and workers:** 'the relations between employers and men form without question the most important part of this art.' There is much that is relevant today in this approach and the pursuit of productivity is still a major preoccupation for management at all levels. 'Business Process Re-engineering' is lineally descended from Scientific Management.

1.6 Scientific management in practice

(a) **Work study techniques** established the 'one best way' to do any job. No discretion was allowed to the worker. Subsequently, *Henry Ford's* approach to mass production broke each job down into its smallest and simplest component parts: these single elements became the newly-designed job. Such work is dehumanising and boring but very productive.

(b) **Planning the work and doing the work were separated.** Workers lost any control over what they did, and all knowledge was assumed to reside in the heads of work study analysts. This is probably the greatest contrast between Scientific Management and today's approach. Remember, many work people are much better educated than their predecessors were 100 years ago. It is almost always a good idea to make the best use of the abilities people being to their work by encouraging their input. This is the basis of much modern management thought, including such ideas as *empowerment* and the *learning organisation*.

(c) **Workers were paid incentives** on the basis of acceptance of the new methods and output norms as the new methods greatly increased productivity and profits.

(d) All aspects of the work environment were tightly controlled in order to attain maximum productivity.

Case example

It is useful to consider an application of Taylor's principles. In testimony to the House of Representatives Committee in 1912, Taylor used as an example the application of scientific management methods to shovelling work at the Bethlehem Steel Works.

(a) Facts were first gathered by management as to the number of shovel loads handled by each man each day, with particular attention paid to the relationship between weight of the average shovel load and the total load shifted per day. From these facts, management was able to decide on the ideal shovel size for each type of material handled in order to optimise the speed of shovelling work done. Thus, scientific technique was applied to deciding how work should be organised.

(b) By organising work a day in advance, it was possible to minimise the idle time and the moving of men from one place in the shovelling yard to another. Once again, scientific method replaces 'seat-of-the-pants' decisions by supervisors.

(c) Workers were paid for accepting the new methods and 'norms' and received 60% higher wages than those given to similar workers in other companies in the area.

(d) Workers were carefully selected and trained in the art of shovelling properly; anyone consistently falling below the required norms was given special teaching to improve his performance.

(e) 'The new way is to teach and help your men as you would a brother; to try to teach him the best way and to show him the easiest way to do his work. This is the new mental attitude of the management towards the men....'

(f) At the Bethlehem Steel Works, Taylor said, the costs of implementing this method were more than repaid by the benefits. The labour force required fell from 400 - 600 men to 140 men for the same work.

Reactions to classical theories and scientific management

Human relations: promotion of job satisfaction

1.7 In the 1930s, a critical perception of scientific management emerged. *Elton Mayo* was pioneered a new approach called **human relations**. This concentrated mainly on the concept of 'Social Man' *(Schein)*: **people are motivated by 'social' or 'belonging' needs**, which are satisfied by the social relationships they form at work.

1.8 Attention shifted towards people's higher psychological needs for growth, challenge, responsibility and self-fulfilment. *Herzberg* suggested that only these things could positively motivate employees to improved performance.

1.9 The human relations approaches contributed an important awareness of the influence of the human factor at work on organisational performance.

(a) Most theorists offered guidelines to enable practising managers to satisfy and motivate employees and so (theoretically) to obtain improved productivity.

(b) However, as far as the practising manager is concerned there is still **no simple link between job satisfaction and productivity** or the achievement of organisational goals.

Drucker: the management process

1.10 *Peter Drucker* was a business adviser to a number of US corporations and a prolific writer on management. He grouped the operations of management into five categories.

(a) **Setting objectives for the organisation**. Managers decide what the objectives of the organisation should be and quantify the targets of achievement for each objective. They must then communicate these targets to other people in the organisation.

(b) **Organising the work**. The work to be done must be divided into manageable activities and manageable jobs. The jobs must be integrated into a formal organisation structure, and people must be selected to do the jobs.

(c) **Motivation**. Managers must motivate employees and communicate information to them to enable them to do their work.

(d) **The job of measurement**. Management must establish yardsticks of performance, measure actual performance, appraise it against the yardsticks, and communicate the findings both to subordinate employees and to superiors.

(e) **Developing people**. The manager 'brings out what is in them or he stifles them. He strengthens their integrity or he corrupts them'.

1.11 It is clear from this analysis that Drucker was much more concerned than Fayol with the human resource aspects of management. He also differed from Fayol in suggesting that management of commercial enterprises was fundamentally different from managing other types of organisation. He argued that the manager of a business has a fundamental responsibility - **economic performance**. Management can only justify its existence and authority by the economic results it produces. He suggested there were three aspects.

(a) **Managing a business**. This revolves around marketing and innovation.

(b) **Managing managers**. Drucker was the first to use the phrase 'management by objectives'.

(c) **Managing worker and work**.

Handy

1.12 *Charles Handy* suggested that a definition of a manager or a manager's role is likely to be so broad as to be fairly meaningless. His own analysis of being a manager was divided into three aspects.

1.13 **The manager as a general practitioner.** Managers are the first recipients of the organisation's problems. They must identify the symptoms (such as falling sales); diagnose the cause of the trouble (such as increased competition); decide how it might be dealt with (for instance by increasing promotional spending); and start the treatment. Handy suggested that typical strategies for health would involve changing **people**, either literally or figuratively, restructuring **work** or making changes to **systems and procedures**.

1.14 **The managerial dilemmas.** Managers are regularly faced with dilemmas which have to be resolved.

   (a) **The dilemma of the cultures.** Management must guide the development of an appropriate culture. As managers rise in seniority, they will find it necessary to behave in a **culturally diverse** manner to satisfy the requirements of both work and the expectations of employees.

   (b) **The dilemma of time horizons.** The manager must reconcile the frequent conflict between short and long term priorities.

   (c) **The trust-control dilemma.** Management must delegate, but this inevitably reduces immediacy of control.

   (d) **The commando leader's dilemma.** Junior managers often prefer working in project teams, to working within the bureaucratic structure of a large organisation. Unfortunately, having too many ad hoc groups leads to confusion.

1.15 **The manager as a person.** Management is increasingly seen as a profession and managers accorded appropriate status. However, at the same time the manager is coming under more pressure from customers to deliver and from employees and society to exercise social responsibility.

1.16 Handy's analysis contrasts with both Fayol's and Drucker's in its lack of prescription. Instead of specifying a list of functions, Handy discusses some of the types of problems the manager may have to solve.

Mintzberg

1.17 Handy's rather vague approach is much improved upon by Henry Mintzberg's empirical research into how managers in fact do their work. He contends 'The classical view says that the manager organises, co-ordinates, plans and controls; the facts suggest otherwise.' Mintzberg instead identifies three types of role which a manager must play.

1.18 **Interpersonal roles.** Senior manager spend much of their time in figurehead or ceremonial roles. The leader role involves hiring, firing and training staff, motivating employees and reconciling individual needs with the requirements of the organisation. The liaison role is performed when managers make contacts outside the vertical chain of command.

1.19 **Informational roles.** As a leader, a manager has access to every member of staff, and is likely to have more external contacts than any of them. Managers are a channels of information from inside the department to outside and vice versa. The manager **monitors**

the environment, and receives information from subordinates or peers, much of it informally. The manager **disseminates** information both formally and informally to subordinates. As a **spokesman** the manager provides information to interested parties.

1.20 **Decisional roles**. The manager takes decisions of several types relating to the work of the department.

(a) A manager acts as a sort of **entrepreneur** by initiating projects to improve the department or to help it react to a changed environment.

(b) A manager responds to pressures and is therefore a **disturbance handler** taking decisions in unusual situations which are impossible to predict.

(c) A manager takes decisions relating to **the allocation of scarce resources**.

(d) **Negotiation** inside and outside the is a vital component of managerial work.

1.21 Mintzberg drew a number of conclusions about managerial work which contrast strongly with Fayol's prescriptions and even Drucker's more pragmatic approach.

(a) Managerial work is disjointed and planning is conducted on a day to day basis, in between more urgent tasks.

(b) Managers perform a number of routine duties, particularly of a ceremonial nature, such as receiving important guests.

(c) Managers prefer *verbal* communication. Information conveyed in an informal way is likely to be more current and concrete than that produced by a formal management information system.

(d) General management is, in practice, a matter of judgement and intuition, gained from experience in particular situations rather than from abstract principles. 'The manager is . . . forced to do many tasks superficially. Brevity, fragmentation and verbal communication characterise his work.'

Excellence

1.22 *Peters and Waterman* designated certain companies as **excellent** because over a 20 year period they had given an above average return on investment and they had a reputation for innovation.

1.23 Peters and Waterman identified eight attributes of excellence.

- **A bias for action** rather than analysis
- **Closeness to customers**
- **Autonomy and entrepreneurship**
- **Productivity through people**
- **Hands-on, value driven**. There is a commitment to shared corporate value
- **Stick to the knitting**: avoid conglomerate diversification
- **Simplicity.** Excellent companies are not over-complicated
- **Simultaneous loose-tight properties**: few rules and procedures but strong values

1.24 Peters and Waterman found that the '**dominance and coherence of culture**' **was an essential feature of the 'excellent'** companies they observed. A 'handful of guiding values' was more powerful than manuals, rule books, norms and controls formally imposed (and resisted).

BPP PUBLISHING

1.25 **Excellence theories have been criticised**. Key problems are:

- Many 'excellent' companies, such as IBM, have stumbled.
- It concentrates on operational issues rather than long term strategy.
- Strong cultures can impede necessary change.
- It proposes that there is 'one best way' to succeed.

1.26 Excellence does not appear to involve any long-term strategic thinking, other than as a by-product of 'sticking to the knitting' and keeping 'close to customers' and sharing 'core values'. IBM was close to its customers because customers had no alternative: IBM had control of a proprietary and expensive technology.

2 INNOVATION

2.1 **Innovation** is a major responsibility of modern management, particularly in commercial organisations. This is because both technology and society are developing extremely rapidly; new products must be matched with new market opportunities if businesses are to survive and prosper.

2.2 One of the sources of innovation is increased **delegation**. In itself delegation has great value - morale and performance are improved, top management is freed for strategic planning and decisions are made by those 'on the ground' and therefore more 'in the know'. Most importantly the organisation benefits from the imagination and thinking of its high flyers.

2.3 Warning bells ring, however, when delegation is confused with **lack of control**.

> 'The line between efficient corporate performance through delegation and anarchy resulting from a loss of total control is a very fine one.'   Alec Reed MD, Reed Accounting

2.4 **The dilemma then is between the need to be innovative so as to deal with a chaotic environment and the need to retain control so as to prevent anarchy**. This can be done simply by giving employees and managers parameters within which discretion can be exercised, and by ensuring that they know they are accountable for their actions.

2.5 To encourage innovation the objective for management should be to create a more outward-looking organisation. People should be encouraged to use their initiative to look for new products, markets, processes, designs and ways to improve productivity.

2.6 *Thomas Attwood* suggests the following steps to encourage innovation.

- Ensure management and staff know what innovation is and how it happens.
- Ensure that senior managers welcome, and are seen to welcome, changes for the better.
- Stimulate and motivate management and staff to think and act innovatively.
- Understand people in the organisation and their needs.
- Recognise and encourage potential 'entrepreneurs'.

Company size

2.7 **Small companies** appear to produce a disproportionate number of innovations because the sheer number of attempts by small-scale entrepreneurs means that some ventures will survive. The 90 to 99 per cent that fail are distributed widely throughout society and receive little attention.

2.8 On the other hand, **large companies** must absorb all potential failure costs; even if an innovation is successful, the organisation may face costs that newcomers do not have to bear, like converting current operations and customer-profiles to the new solution.

Small organisations and innovation

2.9 The research suggests that the following factors are crucial to the success of innovative small organisations.

(a) **Need orientation.** Lacking resources, successful small entrepreneurs soon find that it pays to approach potential customers early, test their solutions in the user's hands, learn from their reactions and adapt their designs rapidly.

(b) **Experts and fanatics.** Commitment allows the entrepreneur to persevere despite the frustrations, ambiguities and setbacks that always accompany major innovations.

(c) **Long time horizons.** Time horizons for radical innovations make them essentially 'irrational' from a present-value viewpoint - delays between invention and commercial production/success can range from three to 25 years.

(d) **Low early costs.** Innovators incur as few overheads as possible, their limited resources going directly into their projects. They borrow whatever they can and invent cheap equipment or processes, often improving on what is available in the marketplace.

(e) **Multiple approaches.** Committed entrepreneurs will tolerate the chaos of random advances in technology, adopting solutions where they can be found, unencumbered by formal plans that would limit the range of their imaginations.

(f) **Flexibility and quickness.** Undeterred by committees, the need for board approvals and other bureaucratic delays, the inventor/entrepreneur can experiment, recycle and try again, with little time lost. They quickly adjust their entry strategies to market feedback.

(g) **Incentives.** Tangible personal rewards are foreseen if success is achieved and the prospect of these rewards (which may not be principally of a monetary nature) is a powerful driver.

Large organisations and innovation

2.10 Within large organisations, by contrast, the following **barriers to innovation and creativity** may typically be encountered.

(a) **Top management isolation.** Financially-focused top managers are likely to perceive technological innovation as more problematic than, say, acquisitions or organic growth: although these options are just as risky, they may appear more familiar.

(b) **Intolerance of fanatics.** Big companies often view entrepreneurial fanatics as embarrassments or trouble-makers.

(c) **Short time horizons.** The perceived corporate need to report a continuous stream of upward-moving, quarterly profits conflicts with the long time-spans that major innovations normally require.

(d) **Accounting practices.** A project in a big company can quickly become an exposed political target, its potential net present value may sink unacceptably, and an entry into small markets may not justify its sunk costs (ie its already-incurred expenses).

(e) **Excessive rationalism.** Managers in large organisations often seek orderly advance through early market research studies or systematic project planning.

(f) **Excessive bureaucracy.** Bureaucratic structures require many approvals that cause delays; the interactive feedback that fosters innovation is lost, important time windows can be missed and real costs and risks rise for the corporation.

(g) **Inappropriate incentives.** When control systems neither penalise opportunities missed nor reward risks taken, the results are predictable.

2.11 Successful large organisations, have developed techniques that emulate or improve on the approaches used in small, fleet-of-foot companies.

(a) **Atmosphere and vision.** Continuous innovation occurs largely because top managers appreciate innovation and atmosphere in order to support it. They project clear long-term vision for the organisation that go beyond simple economic measures.

(b) **Orientation to the market.** Within innovative organisations, managers focus primarily on seeking to anticipate and solve customers' emerging problems.

(c) **Small, flat hierarchies.** Development teams in large organisations normally include only six to seven key people; operating divisions and total technical units are kept below 400 people.

(d) **Multiple approaches.** Where possible, several prototype programmes are encouraged to proceed in parallel. Such redundancy helps the organisation to cope with uncertainties in development, motivates people through competition and improves the amount and quality of information available for making final choices on scale-ups or new-product/service introductions.

(e) **Development shoot-outs.** The most difficult problem in the management of competing projects lies in re-integrating the members of the losing team. For the innovative system to work continuously, managers must create a climate that honours high-quality performance whether a project wins or loses, reinvolves people quickly in their technical specialities or in other projects and accepts rotation among tasks and groups.

(f) **Skunkworks.** This is the name given the system in which small teams of engineers, technicians, designers and model makers are placed together with no intervening organisational or physical barriers, to develop a new product from idea to commercial prototype stage. This approach eliminates bureaucratic controls; allows fast, unfettered communications; permits rapid turnround times for experiments; and instils a high level of group identity and commitment.

(g) **Interactive learning.** Recognising that the random, chaotic nature of technological change cuts across organisational and even institutional lines, the big company innovators tap into multiple sources of technology from outside as well as to their customers' capabilities.

2.12 Many large companies seek to retain some of the innovation and flexibility supposedly characteristic of small firms. They are converging on a balance between bureaucracy (the old order) and entrepreneurship/innovation (the new order) based on **synergies** and **alliances**.

(a) A **synergy** is a combination of businesses, internal services and organisation structures which means that the whole is worth more in value than the sum of the parts. People at all levels focus on doing what they do best.

(b) Organisations are also seeking to extend their reach without increasing their size by forming **strategic alliances** (closer working relationships) with other organisations. This involves partnerships and joint ventures as well as contracting out services to outside suppliers. It results in improved access to information and technology, and quicker responses. However, alliances are vulnerable to management failures and so must be carefully selected; in addition they involve genuine moves away from bureaucracy and hierarchy.

2.13 **An innovation strategy calls for a management policy of giving encouragement to innovative ideas.** This will require positive action.

(a) **Financial backing to innovation,** by spending on R & D and market research and risking capital on new ideas.

(b) **Giving employees the opportunity to work in an environment where the exchange of ideas for innovation can take place**. Management style and organisation structure can help here. Management can actively encourage employees and customers to put forward new ideas. Participation by subordinates in development decisions might encourage employees to become more involved with development projects and committed to their success. Development teams can be set up and an organisation built up on project team-work.

(c) Where appropriate, **recruitment policy should be directed towards appointing employees with the necessary skills for doing innovative work**. Employees should be trained and kept up to date.

(d) Certain managers should be made responsible for obtaining **information from outside the organisation about innovative ideas**, and for communicating this information throughout the organisation.

(e) Strategic planning should result in **targets being set for innovation**, and successful achievements by employees should if possible be rewarded.

3 CENTRALISATION AND DECENTRALISATION

> **KEY TERMS**
>
> **Centralisation** means a greater degree of central control.
>
> **Decentralisation** means a greater degree of delegated authority to regions or sub-units.

3.1 The degree of centralisation in an organisation has a significant effect on the way its managers do their jobs.

> 'From decentralisation we get initiative, responsibility, development of personnel, decisions close to the facts, flexibility - in short, all the qualities necessary for an organisation to adapt to new conditions. From co-ordination we get efficiencies and economies. It must be apparent that co-ordinated decentralisation is not an easy concept to apply'. (*A Sloan*)

3.2 **Advantages of centralisation**

Advantage	Comment
Control	Senior management can exercise greater control over the activities of the organisation and co-ordinate their subordinates or sub-units more easily.
Standardisation	Procedures can be standardised throughout the organisation.
Corporate view	Senior managers can make decisions from the point of view of the organisation as a whole, whereas subordinates would tend to make decisions from the point of view of their own department or section.
Balance of power	Centralised control enables an organisation to maintain a balance between different functions or departments.
Lower overheads	When authority is delegated, there is often a duplication of management effort (and a corresponding increase in staff numbers) at lower levels of hierarchy.
Leadership	In times of **crisis**, the organisation may need strong leadership by a central group of senior managers.

3.3 **Advantages of decentralisation**

Advantage	Comment
Innovation	Delegation of responsibility encourages different approaches and solutions.
Workload	It reduces the stress and burdens of senior management.
Job	It provides subordinates with greater job satisfaction by giving them more say in making decisions which affect their work.
Local knowledge	Subordinates may have a better knowledge than senior management of 'local' conditions affecting their area of work.
Flexibility and speed	Delegation should allow greater flexibility and a quicker response to changing conditions. If problems do not have to be referred up a scalar chain of command to senior managers for a decision, decision-making will be quicker.
Training	Management at middle and junior levels are 'groomed' for eventual senior management positions.

3.4 **Contingency approach.** Centralisation suits some functions more than others.

(a) The **research and development function** might be centralised into a single unit, as a resource for each division.

(b) Sales departments might be decentralised on a terroritial basis.

Factors influencing the degree of decentralisation

3.5 **Geography** is a major influence on the degree of decentralisation in an organisation. Remoteness from the centre encourages a degree of autonomy, though **information technology** can draw scattered elements together by setting up an **intranet** using **internet** technology to share information. Multi-national organisations will need extensive decentralisation to deal effectively with local legal, cultural and market requirements.

3.6 **Heterogeneity of activity or product range** will promote decentralisation as varying specialist skill and knowledge will be required to manage the different parts of the organisation.

3.7 Rapid **environmental change** will lead to decentralisation to speed up response to developments in technology and markets.

3.8 **Management style and organisational culture** will affect the degree of decentralisation. An autocratic culture and style is not compatible with delegation and decentralisation. Such a style may indicate a lack of trust in subordinates; this may or may not be justified.

3.9 Whatever system is set up, it is of paramount importance that all managers at all levels should clearly know where they fit into the organisation. They should know the nature and extent of their authority and responsibility and that of fellow managers at all levels. Managers can then exercise as much authority and carry as much responsibility as possible within the constraints of the policies set by the organisation and the commitments they have made to their own superior executive.

Decentralisation in very large companies

3.10 There are more and more very large businesses, most of them operating in more than one country and many of them in more than one economic sector. These companies are too large to be managed by a single board of directors. This topic is discussed in more detail later. Here, we may simply remark that such organisations are likely to be decentralised in an emphatic way. **Strategic business units** may be established, each of which is run as an **autonomous business** by its own board and chief executive, pursuing its own goals and exploiting its own markets.

Centralisation and strategic planning

3.11 *Goold and Campbell* categorised three types of strategic planning organisation, according to whether:

- Decisions are made at the centre or by subsidiaries
- How the centre measures and controls the performance of subsidiaries.

3.12 They identified **three strategic management styles**.

(a) **Strategic planners** (such as *Cadbury-Schweppes*) have a small number of core businesses. Head office plays a big part in making the strategic planning decisions for all its businesses, and subsidiaries are required to implement these global plans.

(b) **Strategic controllers** tend to be diversified. Headquarters are remote. Strategic planning involves general guidelines issued from head office, on going objectives and background assumptions.

(c) **Financial controllers** (such as *GEC* and *Tarmac*) are groups where most strategic decisions are made by the subsidiaries without head office interference. Head office exercises control over subsidiaries according to results - ie financial performance and success or failure in achieving financial targets.

Question 3

XYZ has over 500 profit centres (ranging from baggage handling equipment to stockings) and revenues of £7bn. Head office staff amount to 47. Each profit centre must provide the following.

(a) The *annual profit plan*. This is agreed in detail every year, after close negotiation. It is regarded as a commitment to a preordained level of performance.

(b) A *monthly management report*, which is extremely detailed (17 pages). Working capital is outlined in detail. Provisions (the easiest way to manipulate accounts) are highlighted.

Is XYZ a strategic planner, a strategic controller or a financial controller?

Answer

Financial controller.

Chapter roundup

- It is difficult to define management without discussing its nature at some length.

- Fayol proposed a list of functions which he thought were applicable to all management work. FW Taylor was specifically concerned with delivering productivity in engineering work, though his ideas were applied in many other areas. He popularised the idea of management as a rational discipline. The importance of the human factor began to be recognised after the work of Elton Mayo and continues as an important branch of management study.

- Drucker was the first to speak of managing by objectives and emphasised business management's responsibility for achieving economic success. Handy and Mintzberg concerned themselves with the problems managers face and exactly how they spend their time. Mintzberg found that managerial work was disjointed and depended heavily on judgement and intuition.

- Small companies seem disproportionately innovative, partly because larger companies seem to erect barriers to innovation. It is possible to take steps to encourage innovation.

- The degree of centralised control in an organisation has important effects on its success. There is no single policy which suits all organisations and a number of factors have effect.

Quick quiz

1. What did Fayol say were the functions of management?

2. What did Fayol mean by 'organising'?

3. What did FW Taylor see as the principles of scientific management?

4. Drucker introduced a new idea to the discussion of the manager's job. What was it?

5. How did Mintzberg classify the roles played by a manager?

6. How may innovation be encouraged generally?

7. What do large organisations do to overcome their barriers to creativity?

8. State 3 advantages of decentralised control and 3 disadvantages.

9. What factors influence the degree of decentralisation?

10. How do very large companies achieve decentralisation?

Answers to quick quiz

1   Planning, organising, commanding, co-ordinating, controlling.

2   Establishing a structure of tasks, grouping the tasks into jobs and the jobs into departments, delegating authority and providing information systems.

3   The development of a true science of work; the scientific selection and progressive development of workers; bringing the science and the worker together; constant and intimate co-operation between management and worker.

4   The fundamental responsibility of a manager of a commercial organisation is economic performance.

5   Interpersonal, informational and decisional roles.

6   Delegation

7   Atmosphere and vision; market orientation; flat hierarchies; multiple approaches; skunkworks and interactive learning.

8   Advantages: innovation, reduced stress on senior managers, increased job satisfaction for junior managers, better local knowledge, increased flexibility and speed of response, management development.

    Disadvantages: reduced control, lack of standardisation, parochial decision making, unbalanced corporate development, duplication of effort and costs, fragmented response to crisis.

9   Geography, heterogeneity of activity or product range, environmental change, management style, organisational culture.

10   Strategic business units are established, each run as an autonomous business by its own board and chief executive.

Now try the question below from the Exam Question Bank

Number	Level	Marks	Time
Q3	Exam	20	36 mins

BPP
PUBLISHING

Chapter 4

ORGANISATIONAL CULTURE

Topic List	Syllabus Reference	Ability required
1 What is culture?	(i)	Analysis
2 Culture and structure	(i)	Analysis
3 Culture, the environment and strategy	(i)	Analysis

Introduction

This chapter looks at organisation culture, in other words the culture that exists within the organisation's boundaries.

After completing this chapter, you should have learned the following points.

- An organisation's culture is a set of beliefs and assumptions which people have within the organisation, which influences their behaviour and their approaches to the environment (Section 1).

- Culture is found in visible artefacts and underlying values.

- In some cases, culture, can have an intimate relationship with an organisation's structure (Section 2). It may be that people are individually disposed to work better in some cultures than in others.

- Culture can also relate to an organisation's vulnerability to the environment, and the rate of change. In particular you should understand the cultures of consistency, mission, involvement and adaptability (Section 3).

- A powerful culture can be a source of strength for an organisation. However, strong cultures resist change.

Learning outcome covered in this chapter

- Analyse and categorise the culture of an organisation, and recommend changes to improve organisational effectiveness.

Syllabus content covered

- The determinants of culture, the different models available for categorising cultures (eg Deal and Kennedy, Harrison, McKinsey 7-S, Peters and Waterman, Peters).

- The importance of culture in organisations (eg the 'organisational iceberg').

1   WHAT IS CULTURE?

1.1   Through contact with a particular culture, individuals learn a language, acquire values and learn habits of behaviour and thought.

(a)   **Beliefs and values.** Beliefs are what we feel to be the case on the basis of objective and subjective information (eg people can believe the world is round or flat). Values are

beliefs which are relatively enduring, relatively general and fairly widely accepted as a guide to culturally appropriate behaviour.

(b) **Customs.** Customs are modes of behaviour which represent culturally accepted ways of behaving in response to given situations.

(c) **Artefacts.** Artefacts are all the physical tools designed by human beings for their physical and psychological well-being, including works of art, technology, products.

(d) **Rituals.** A ritual is a type of activity which takes on symbolic meaning; it consists of a fixed sequence of behaviour repeated over time.

The learning and sharing of culture is made possible by **language** (both written and spoken, verbal and non-verbal).

Case example

Islamic banking

Islamic banking is a powerful example of the importance of culture in an economy. The Koran abjures the charging of interest, which is usury. However whilst interest is banned, profits are allowed. A problem is that there is no standard interpretation of the sharia law regarding this. Products promoted by Islamic banks include:

(a) Leasing (the Islamic Bank TII arranged leases for seven Kuwait Airways aircraft)
(b) Trade finance
(c) Commodities trading

The earlier Islamic banks offered current accounts only, but depositors now ask for shares in the bank profits. To tap this market, Citibank, the US bank, opened an Islamic banking subsidiary in Bahrain.

1.2 Knowledge of the culture of a society is clearly of value to businesses in a number of ways.

(a) **Marketers** can adapt their products accordingly, and be fairly sure of a sizeable market. This is particularly important in export markets.

(b) **Human resource managers** may need to tackle cultural differences in recruitment. For example, some ethnic minorities have a different body language from the majority, which may be hard for some interviewers to interpret.

1.3 Culture in a society can be divided into **subcultures** reflecting social differences. Most people participate in several of them.

Subculture	Comment
Class	People from different social classes might have different values reflecting their position of society.
Ethnic background	Some ethnic groups can still be considered a distinct cultural group.
Religion	Religion and ethnicity are related.
Geography or region	Distinct regional differences might be brought about by the *past* effects of physical geography (socio-economic differences etc). Speech accents most noticeably differ.
Age	Age subcultures vary according to the period in which individuals were socialised to an extent, because of the great shifts in social values and customs in this century. ('Youth culture'; the 'generation gap' etc).

Sex	Some products are targeted directly to women or to men.
Work	Different organisations have different corporate cultures, in that the shared values of one workplace may be different from another.

Case example

Consider the case of a young French employee of *Eurodisney*.

(a) The employee speaks the French language - part of the national culture - and has participated in the French education system etc.

(b) As a youth, the employee might, in his or her spare time, participate in various 'youth culture' activities. Music and fashion are emblematic of youth culture.

(c) As an employee of Eurodisney, the employee will have to participate in the corporate culture, which is based on American standards of service with a high priority put on friendliness to customers.

1.4 Cultural change might have to be planned for. There has been a revolution in attitudes to female employment, despite the well-publicised problems of discrimination that still remain.

Organisational culture

KEY TERM

Culture in an organisation is the sum total of the beliefs, knowledge, attitudes of mind and customs to which people are exposed during their interaction with the organisation.

1.5 Culture is both internal to an organisation and external to it. The culture of an organisation is embedded in the culture of the wider society.

1.6 There are certain patterns of behaviour, assumptions and beliefs which members of the organisation share because of their common background and experience.

- The country where they live
- Their status or class position within that society
- Their profession (eg as accountants, marketers)
- Their membership of the organisation

1.7 *Peters and Waterman*, in their book *In Search of Excellence*, found that the 'dominance and coherence of culture' was an essential feature of the 'excellent' companies they observed. A 'handful of guiding values' was more powerful than manuals, rule books, norms and controls formally imposed (and resisted). They commented: 'If companies do not have strong notions of themselves, as reflected in their values, stories, myths and legends, people's only security comes from where they live on the organisation chart.'

1.8 All organisations will generate their own cultures, whether spontaneously or under the guidance of positive managerial strategy. The culture will exist in three main areas.

(a) **Basic, underlying assumptions** which guide the behaviour of the individuals and groups in the organisation. These may include customer orientation, or belief in

quality, trust in the organisation to provide rewards, freedom to make decisions, freedom to make mistakes and the value of innovation and initiative at all levels.

(b) **Overt beliefs** expressed by the organisation and its members, which can be used to condition the assumptions mentioned above. These beliefs and values may emerge as sayings, slogans and mottoes, such as IBM's motto, 'think'. They may emerge in a rich mythology of jokes and stories about past successes and heroic failures.

(c) **Visible artefacts** - the style of the offices or other premises, dress rules, display of trophies, the degree of informality between superiors and subordinates and so on.

Management can encourage this by selling a sense of the corporate mission, or by promoting the corporate image. It can reward the right attitudes and punish (or simply not employ) those who are not prepared to commit themselves to the culture.

1.9 *Charles Hampden-Turner* listed a number of characteristics of an organisation culture in *Corporate Culture*.

(a) **Culture lies in the organisation's individual members.** They use it to reinforce ideas, feelings and information consistent with their beliefs and to discourage or repress information and sentiments inconsistent with their beliefs. A culture then, is partly *exclusive*. It gives a bias to information.

(b) **Cultures embody the needs and aspirations** of a group's members, thus setting the criteria by which people are judged, and defining prestige for particular achievements.

(c) Culture is strong where people need **reassurance and certainty**.

(d) Cultures have **consequences** (sometimes in the manner of self-fulfilling prophecies).

(e) **A corporate culture is coherent**, and its actions follow on from the beliefs and assumptions underlying it.

(f) Cultures provide their members with some sense of **continuity and identity**, especially as things change over time.

(g) A culture is in a **state of balance between different values**. It is not a division of labour, but a re-integration of labour into a coherent whole.

(h) **A culture is partly self-correcting**. Feedback from customers, for example, might help reinforce an organisation's attempts to conform to its culture. (Is it living up to its standards?)

(i) **Cultures are patterns**. Hampden-Turner argues that the way a member of staff treats a customer will be similar to the way in which the member of staff is treated by his or her supervisor.

(j) **Cultures communicate support**, in that they facilitate the sharing of information and experiences. They make members supportive of each other (to the point of reinforcing wishful thinking).

(k) **Cultures deal with synergies**, which in this case means that the values of management and staff must work together harmoniously.

(l) **Cultures and organisations can learn**. The concept of the **learning organisation** implies that knowledge and innovation are not simply the result of a creative individual, but resides in cultures and relationships. (Hampden-Turner argues that the stereotype of the 'creative individual' gains its force from the fact that so many UK corporate cultures are resistant to innovation.)

(m) Cultures mediate **dilemmas** (eg minimise cost vs maximise quality) and provide ways of solving them.

1.10 A culture can be defined as follows. 'Culture comes from within people and it is put together by them to reward the capacities they have in common. Culture gives continuity and identity to the group. It balances contrasting contributions and operates as a self-steering system which learns from feedback. It works as a pattern of information and can greatly facilitate the exchange of understanding. The values within a culture are more or less harmonious.'

Case example

To get an idea of how a culture operates, we can consider a company's dress code: this is the type of clothes deemed appropriate for office or business use.

BT's elaborate dress code, and the problems it caused, were described by John Kay (*Financial Times*, 12 January 1996).

(a) After privatisation, senior employees were told to adopt 'suitable business dress'. People complained that they did not know what this meant, so the firm promulgated a dress code. Senior male employees were to wear smart suits, collared shirts and ties.

(b) Somebody came in wearing a red suit: 'undeniably smart, but it was the smartness of a night club rather than a boardroom'. The dress code was amended to specify colour (not red) and brightness (dark blues: OK; bright blues: not OK).

(c) Ties were a more intractable problem, given the enormous variety: 'A clearance procedure seemed the best answer. Anyone who bought a new tie could submit it to the dress code department, which had 42 days to rule on whether or not it was suitable business dress' ... but of course this depended on the 'suit and the shirt that went with it'.

(d) This raised the issue of an appeal mechanism, but letting the dress code department be 'judge and jury in implementing regulations it had devised ... violated natural justice'.

(e) Therefore a small group of senior directors and an independent fashion adviser 'would hear complaints from employees who felt their ties had been unreasonably rejected'.

(f) Moreover, to cope with the problem of changing fashion, 'a well-known fashion designer agreed to chair a standing working party to advise the company on fashion trends.'

(g) 'By this time, the dress code extended to 50 pages, largely impenetrable ... Knowledge of its contents was confined to the dress department which by this time consisted of 20 people, mostly lawyers, the union representative who negotiated over it, and a few cranks...'

New management felt they had two options: supply a uniform or reissue the instruction to wear business dress. They did the latter. If anybody was in doubt, they would ask the dress regulator, a wise and experienced individual.

1.11 An organisation's culture is influenced by many factors.

(a) **The organisation's founder.** A strong set of values and assumptions is set up by the organisation's founder, and even after he or she has retired, these values have their own momentum. Or, to put it another way, an organisation might find it hard to shake off its original culture. Peters and Waterman believed that 'excellent' companies began with strong leaders.

(b) **The organisation's history.** *Johnson and Scholes* state that the way an organisation works reflects the era when it was founded. Farming, for example, sometimes has a craft element to it. The effect of history can be determined by stories, rituals and

symbolic behaviour. They legitimise behaviour and promote priorities. (In some organisations certain positions are regarded as intrinsically more 'heroic' than others.)

(c) **Leadership and management style**. An organisation with a strong culture recruits managers who naturally conform to it.

(d) **Structure and systems** affect culture as well as strategy. Handy's description of an Apollonian role culture (bureaucracy) is an example (among others) where **organisational form** has **cultural consequences**.

Exam focus point

A question in the old exam was divided into three parts. Part (a), worth 6 marks asked simply for the meaning of corporate culture. Parts (b) and (c), worth 6 and 8 marks respectively, required the application of the idea of culture to the scenario in detail. This will be typical of Paper 11 questions; they require theoretical knowledge but offer the bulk of the marks for application.

1.12 The McKinsey 7-S model was designed to show how the various aspects of a business relate to one another. It is a useful illustration of the way culture fits into an organisation. In particular, it shows the links between the organisation's behaviour and the behaviour of individuals within it.

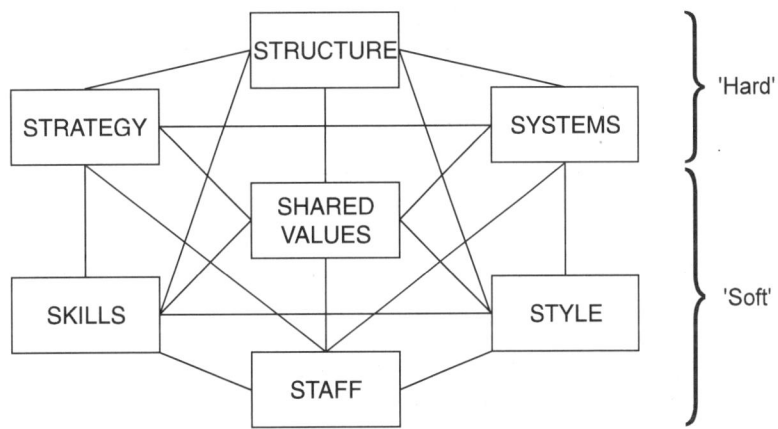

1.13 Three of the elements are considered 'hard'.

(a) **Structure**. The organisation structure determines division of tasks in the organisation and the hierarchy of authority from the most senior to junior.

(b) **Strategy**. Strategy is way in which the organisation plans to outperform its competitors, if it is a business, or how it intends to achieve its objectives.

(c) **Systems**. Systems include the technical systems of accounting, personnel, management information and so forth.

These 'hard' elements are easily quantified or defined, and deal with **facts and rules**.

1.14 However, the McKinsey model suggests that certain 'soft' elements are equally important.

(a) **Shared values** are the guiding beliefs of people in the organisation as to why it exists. (For example, people in a hospital seek to save lives.) It forms part of the corporate culture.

(b) **Staff** are the people in the organisation. They have their own complex concerns and priorities.

(c) **Style** is another aspect of the **corporate culture,** which includes the shared assumptions, ways of working and attitudes of management.

(d) **Skills** are those things that the organisation does well. For example, BT is good at providing a telephone service, but even if the phone network is eventually used as a transmission medium for television/film programmes, BT is unlikely to make those programmes itself.

The importance of the 'soft' elements for success was emphasised by *Peters and Waterman* in their study of 'excellent' companies.

1.15 **The organisational iceberg**

French and Bell described the' organisational iceberg' in which formal aspects are **overt** and informal aspects are **covert** or hidden, rather as the bulk of an iceberg is underwater. The formal aspects are similar to the McKinsey 'hard' elements while the informal aspects correspond to the 'soft' elements in the 7-S model.

1.16 **Formal aspects**

- Goals
- Terminology
- Structure
- Policies and procedures
- Products
- Financial resources

1.17 **Informal aspects**
- Beliefs and assumptions
- Perceptions
- Attitudes
- Feelings 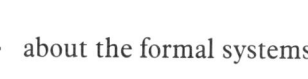 about the formal systems
- Values
- Informal interactions
- Group norms

1.18 Some of these issues we will explore in later chapters. **All elements must pull in the same direction for the organisation to be effective**.

2 CULTURE AND STRUCTURE

2.1 Writing in 1972, *Roger Harrison* suggested that organisations could be classified into four types. His work was later popularised by *Charles Handy* in his book 'Gods of Management'. The four types are differentiated by their structures, processes and management methods. The differences are so significant as to create distinctive cultures, to each of which Handy gives the name of a Greek god.

2.2 **Zeus** is the god representing the **power culture** or **club culture**. Zeus is a dynamic entrepreneur who rules with snap decisions. Power and influence stem from a central source, perhaps the owner-directors or the founder of the business. The degree of formalisation is limited, and there are few rules and procedures. Such a firm is likely to be organised on a functional basis. Important decisions are made rapidly by key people. In Mintzberg's terms it is perhaps a **simple structure**, but with some co-ordination by mutual adjustment.

(a) The organisation, since it is not rigidly structured, is capable of adapting quickly to meet change. However, success in adapting will depend on the luck or judgement of the key individuals who make the rapid decision.

(b) Personal influence decreases as the size of an organisation gets bigger. **The power culture is therefore best suited to smaller entrepreneurial organisations, where the leaders have direct communication with all employees**.

(c) Personnel have to get on well with each other for this culture to work. Staff have to empathise with each other. These organisations are clubs of 'like-minded people introduced by the like-minded people, working on empathetic initiative with personal contact rather than formal liaison.'

2.3 **Apollo** is the god of the **role culture** or **bureaucracy. Everything and everybody are in their proper place. There is a presumption of logic and rationality**.

(a) These organisations have a formal structure, and operate by well-established rules and procedures. Job descriptions establish definite tasks for each person's job and procedures are established for many work routines, communication between individuals and departments, and the settlement of disputes and appeals. Individuals are required to perform their job to the full, but not to overstep the boundaries of their authority. Individuals who work for such organisations tend to learn an expertise without experiencing risk; many do their job adequately, but are not over-ambitious. Psychological sensitivity is a feature of this culture.

(b) **The bureaucratic style can be very efficient** in a stable environment, when the organisation is large and when the work is predictable.

(c) The Civil Service, insurance companies and many large well established companies with relatively unchanging products have been associated with bureaucratic organisations and the role culture. Unfortunately, bureaucracies are very slow to adapt to change and when severe change occurs (eg an economic depression) many run into financial difficulties or even bankruptcy (eg British Leyland and the British Steel Corporation in the late 70s). Otherwise they respond to change by doing more of the same (eg by generating cross functional liaison teams and a bureaucracy to support them).

2.4 **Athena** is the goddess of the **task culture. Management is seen as completing a succession of projects or solving problems**.

(a) The task culture is reflected in a **matrix organisation** or else in project teams and task forces. In such organisations, **there is no dominant or clear leader. The principal concern in a task culture is to get the job done**. Therefore the individuals who are important are the **experts** with the ability to accomplish a particular aspect of the task. Each individual in the team considers he or she has more influence than he or she would have if the work were organised on a formal 'role culture' basis. Expertise and talent are more important than length of service.

(b) Performance is judged by results. Such organisations are flexible and constantly changing; for example, project teams are disbanded as soon as their task has been completed.

(c) Task cultures are expensive, as experts demand a market price.

(d) Task cultures also depend on variety, and to tap creativity requires a tolerance of perhaps costly mistakes. They are ideal when funds are available, in expanding industries or new situations. Where cost is a worry, controls are necessary.

(e) Since job satisfaction tends to be high owing to the degree of individual participation and group identity, 'behavioural' management theorists might recommend this type of organisation structure as being the most efficient available.

2.5 **Dionysus** is the god of the **existential culture**. In the three other cultures, the individual is subordinate to the organisation or task. **An existential culture is found in an organisation whose purpose is to serve the interests of the individuals within it**. These organisations are rare, although an example might be a partnership of a few individuals who do all the work of the organisation themselves (with perhaps a little secretarial or clerical assistance).

(a) Doctors come together to form a practice.

(b) Barristers (in the UK) work through chambers. The clerk co-ordinates their work and hands out briefs, but does not control them.

(c) Management in these organisations are often lower in status than the professionals and are labelled secretaries, administrators, bursars, registrars and chief clerk.

(d) The organisation depends on the **talent of the individuals;** management is derived from the consent of the managed, rather than the delegated authority of the owners.

2.6 The descriptions above interrelate four different strands.

- The individual
- The type of the work the organisation does
- The culture of the organisation
- The environment

Organisational effectiveness perhaps depends on an appropriate fit of all of them.

Case example

Handy cites a pharmaceutical company which at one time had all its manufacturing subcontracted, until turnover and cost considerations justified a factory of its own. The company hired nine talented individuals to design and run the factory. Result:

(a) The *design team* ran on a task culture, with a democratic/consultative leadership style, using project teams for certain problems. This was successful while the factory was being built.

(b) After its opening, the factory, staffed by 400, was run on similar lines. There were numerous problems. Every problem was treated as a project, and the workforce resented being asked to help sort out 'management' problems. In the end, the factory was run in a slightly more autocratic way. Handy states that this is a classic case of an *Athenian* culture to create a factory being superseded by an *Apollonian* culture to run it. Different cultures suit different businesses.

Question 1

Which of Handy's cultures would you say is prevalent in your office?

Question 2

Review the following statements. Ascribe each of them to one of the four approaches.

People are controlled and influenced by:

- the personal exercise of rewards, punishments or charisma;
- the impersonal exercise of economic and political power to enforce procedures and standards of performance;

- communication and discussion of task requirements leading to appropriate action, motivated by personal commitment, to achieve the goal;
- intrinsic interest and enjoyment in the activities to be done, and/or concern and caring for the needs of the other people involved.

Answer

- Power
- Role
- Task
- Existential

3 CULTURE, THE ENVIRONMENT AND STRATEGY

3.1 Culture is an important filter of information and an interpreter of it, as suggested in the diagrams below.

Ignoring culture

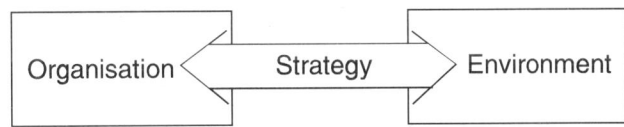

Including culture

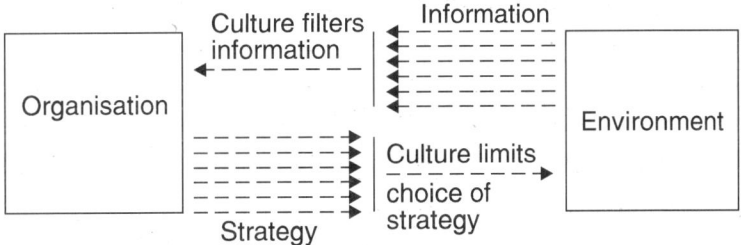

Culture filters and reconfigures environmental information. (A tragic example is the events in Waco, where members of the Branch Davidian cult interpreted environmental information as presaging the end of the world.) At the same time culture filters out a number of strategic choices. For example, a firm might have a cultural predisposition against embarking on risky ventures. Another culture might have an ingrained 'Buy British' approach. Finally, **if culture is embodied in *behaviour*, it may make an incompatible strategy impossible to implement**.

3.2 A model of culture which focuses specifically on a firm's approach to strategy was suggested by *Miles and Snow*, who outlined three strategic cultures, and a fourth 'non-strategic' culture.

(a) **Defenders like low risks, secure niche markets, and tried and trusted solutions.** These companies have cultures whose stories and rituals reflect historical continuity and consensus. Decision-taking is relatively formalised. (There is a stress on 'doing things right' ie efficiency.) Personnel are drawn from within the industry.

(b) **Prospectors are organisations where the dominant beliefs are more to do with results** (doing the right things ie effectiveness). They seek to expand and increase market presence, and move into new areas.

(c) **Analysers try to balance risk and profits**. They use a core of stable products and markets as a source of earnings, like defenders, but move into areas that prospectors have already opened up. Analysers follow change, but do not initiate it.

(d) **Reactors**, unlike the three above, **do not have viable strategies**, other than living from hand to mouth.

Case example

Miles and Snow's analysis was applied to the responses by the regional electricity companies (RECs) to takeover bids in the Autumn of 1995. (The RECs are responsible for supplying and distributing electricity.) As at October 1995, seven of the 12 RECs in England and Wales had received takeover bids. (*Financial Times,* 4 October 1995).

At privatisation they 'shared a common heritage and hence ... greater similarities than would be found in more well-established private sector market places'.

• The largest REC, Eastern Group, 'embraced' the possibility of an alliance with Hanson. Eastern exhibits the characteristics of a 'prospector'. Its chief executive is 'non-REC' 'with a North American corporate pedigree and a greater interest in activities outside the traditional REC field'.

• Norweb and Midlands were 'cautious prospectors' which allow significant degrees of decentralisation, and a 'willingness to bring in executives with experience external to the industry'. They countenance 'strategic alliances'.

• Many of the RECs 'have demonstrated classical defender strategies'. They have specific features.

  ○ Hierarchical company structures

  ○ Board membership drawn from within the industry

  ○ Incremental growth, rather than more rapid growth by entering new business areas; little enthusiasm for diversification

---

3.3 *Denison's* model uses a grid to assess the relationship of culture with the environment. There are two dimensions.

(a) How orientated is the firm to the environment rather than to its internal workings? (An internal orientation is not always a bad thing, eg maintaining the safety of a nuclear installation.)

(b) To what extent does the environment offer stability or change?

Organisation's strategic orientation

		Internal	External
Environmental responses Required	Stability	Consistency	Mission
	Change/flexibility	Involvement	Adaptability

3.4 In Denison's analysis there are thus four possible cultures.

(a) **Consistency culture**. This exists in a stable environment, and its structure is well integrated. Management are preoccupied with efficiency. Such cultures are characterised by formal ways of behaviour. Predictability and reliability are valued. This has some features in common with the Apollonian culture.

(b) **Mission culture**. The environment is relatively stable, and the organisation is orientated towards it (eg 'customers'). A mission culture, whereby members' work activities are given meaning and value, is appropriate. For example, hospitals are preoccupied with the sick: inevitably their values are 'customer' orientated. A church is concerned with saving souls.

(c) **Involvement culture**. This is similar to clan control identified in an earlier chapter. The basic premise behind it is that the satisfaction of employees' needs is necessary for them to provide optimum performance. An example might be an orchestra, whose performance depends on each individual. Involvement and participation, as discussed in an earlier chapter, are supposed to create a greater sense of commitment and hence performance. For example, if you train people well enough, it is assumed that they will perform well. An involvement culture might take a 'human relations' approach to management.

(d) **Adaptability culture**. The company's strategic focus is on the external environment, which is in a state of change. Corporate values encourage inquisitiveness and interest in the external environment. Fashion companies are an example: ideas come from a variety of sources. Customer needs are fickle and change rapidly.

Question 1

(a) What do you think is the most significant contrast between Denison's model and Harrison's model?

(b) Which is better?

Answer

(a) Harrison's model places much more emphasis on organisation structure and systems, which both determine and are determined by culture. Harrison's model describes actual cultures. Denison's model describes *ideal* cultures, and is more concerned with the environment and a firm's external orientation than its structure. Denison suggests that if the environment is stable *and* the business is most effective with an internal orientation, *then* a consistency culture will be *best* etc.

(b) It depends on what you wish to use each model for.

3.5 *Deal and Kennedy* (*Corporate Cultures*) consider cultures to be a function of the willingness of employees to take **risks**, and how quickly they get **feedback** on whether they got it right or wrong.

High risk

BET YOUR COMPANY CULTURE ('Slow and steady wins the race') Long decision-cycles: stamina and nerve required eg oil companies, aircraft companies, architects	**HARD 'MACHO' CULTURE** ('Find a mountain and climb it') eg entertainment, management consultancy, advertising
PROCESS CULTURE ('It's not what you do, it's the way that you do it') Values centred on attention to excellence of technical detail, risk management, procedures, status symbols eg banks, financial services, government	**WORK HARD/PLAY HARD CULTURE** ('Find a need and fill it') All action - and fun: team spirit eg sales and retail, computer companies.

Slow feedback (left) — *Fast feedback* (right)

Low risk

Excellence, culture and motivation

3.6 Peters and Waterman also discuss the central importance of *positive reinforcement* in any method of motivation as critical. 'Researchers studying motivation find that the prime

factor is simply the self-perception among motivated subjects that they are in fact doing well ... Mere association with past personal success apparently leads to more persistence, higher motivation, or something that makes us do better.'

3.7 Positive reinforcement - whether in the form of bonuses, prizes, 'reaffirming the heroic dimension' of the job itself, identifying workers with the company's success, or enhancing self-image in the workforce - is the method Peters and Waterman observed *succeeding*, although other research has shown that 'tough' managers, applying sanctions on undesirable behaviour, can also get improved performance out of their subordinates.

3.8 Peters and Waterman argue that employees can be 'switched on' to extraordinary loyalty and effort in the following cases.

(a) **The cause is perceived to be in some sense great.** Commitment comes from believing that a task is inherently worthwhile. Devotion to the *customer*, and the customer's needs and wants, is an important motivator in this way.

(b) **They are treated as winners.** 'Label a man a loser and he'll start acting like one.' Repressive control systems and negative reinforcement break down the employee's self-image.

(c) **They can satisfy their dual needs, both to** be a conforming, secure part of a successful team to be stars in their own right.

3.9 This means applying control (through firm central direction, and shared values and beliefs) but also allowing maximum individual autonomy (at least, the illusion of control) and even competition between individual or groups within the organisation. Peters and Waterman call this *loose-tight* **management.** Culture, peer pressure, a focus on action, customer-orientation and so on are 'non-aversive' ways of exercising control over employees. In other words, the control system used is **cultural control.**

3.10 The implication of this for work behaviour affects the way in which individuals can be motivated and managed. As Peters and Waterman argue, a strong 'central faith' (ie a mission), which binds the organisation together as a whole, should be combined with a strong emphasis on individual self-expression, contribution and success: individuals should be given at least the 'illusion of control' over their destinies, while still being given a sense of belonging and a secure, perceived meaningful framework in which to act.

Management cultures

3.11 A factor which has an impact on the culture of transnational organisations, or organisations competing in global markets, is **management culture.** This is the views about managing held by managers, their shared educational experiences, and the 'way business is done'. Obviously, this reflects wider cultural differences between countries, but national cultures can sometimes be subordinated to the corporate culture of the organisation (eg the efforts to ensure that staff of EuroDisney are as enthusiastic as their American counterparts).

3.12 The way in which business practice can be affected by management culture can be indicated by an example.

(a) The Harvard Business Review reported (July-August 1991) that 'the successful development of executives depends on creating a distinctive shared identity, a sense of belonging to the French managerial class'. Further quotations are illuminating:

'French managers see their work as an intellectual challenge, requiring the remorseless application of individual brainpower. They do not share the Anglo-Saxon view of management as an interpersonally demanding exercise, where plans have to be constantly "sold" upward and downward using personal skills. The bias is for intellect rather than for action. People who run big enterprises must above all else be clever - that is, they must be able to grasp complex issues, analyse problems, manipulate ideas and evaluate solutions. A revealing witticism contains this rejoinder, supposedly from one senior French civil servant to another: "That's fine in practice, but it will never work in theory'.

(b) The 'world leadership survey' conducted by the *Harvard Business Review* asked a variety of questions to managers in different countries. Although the response to the survey (which appeared in business magazines) was self-selected, it could be concluded that managers in different countries do not have the same priorities when it came to business issues. When asked what they thought of as the three most important factors in organisation success, these were listed as follows, in order of priority.

> **Japan**: product development, management, product quality
> **Germany**: workforce skills, problem solving, management
> **USA**: customer service, product quality, technology

3.13 The existence of these different systems of priorities and ways of doing business affects the competitive environment, international marketing and the success of joint ventures. UK managers, who were described by the survey as among the least cosmopolitan, may have some adapting to do.

The Hofstede model

3.14 The **Hofstede model** was developed in 1980 by Professor *Geert Hofstede* in order to explain national differences by identifying **key dimensions** in the value systems of all countries. Each country is represented on a scale for each dimension so as to explain and understand values, attitudes and behaviour. Global businesses have to be sensitive to these issues.

3.15 In particular, Hofstede pointed out that countries differ on the following dimensions.

(a) **Power distance**. This dimension measures how far superiors are expected to exercise power. In a high power-distance culture, the boss decides and people do not question.

(b) **Uncertainty avoidance**. Some cultures prefer clarity and order, whereas others are prepared to accept novelty. This affects the willingness of people to *change* rules, rather than simply obey them.

(c) **Individualism-collectivism**. In some countries individual achievement is what matters. In a collectivist culture people are supported and controlled by their in-group and put the interests of the group first.

(d) '**Masculinity**'. In 'masculine' cultures assertiveness and acquisitiveness are valued. 'Masculine' cultures place greater emphasis on possessions, status, and display as opposed to quality of life and caring for others.

Hofstede grouped countries into eight clusters using these dimensions. Here are some examples.

3.16 Countries in the **Anglo** group (the UK, the USA)

- Low to medium power-distance
- Low to medium uncertainty avoidance
- High individualism

- High 'masculinity'

3.17 Countries in the **nordic** group (Scandinavia and also The Netherlands)

- Low power distance
- Low to medium uncertainty avoidance
- Medium individualism
- Low 'masculinity'

3.18 Countries in the **more developed Asian** group (ie Japan)

- Medium power distance
- High uncertainty avoidance
- Medium individualism
- High 'masculinity'

Chapter roundup

Culture is important both in organisations and in the wider world. It is the knowledge, beliefs, customs and attitudes which people adhere to. In wider society it is affected by factors such as age, class, race and religion, while in organisations it is defined by assumptions, beliefs and artefacts. These, in turn, are influenced by history, management, structure and systems. The McKinsey 7-S model shows how culture relates to other aspects of the organisation.

Harrison's four-fold classification of organisations is a useful analysis of some common aspects of culture.

- The **power** culture depends on the holder of centralised power.

- The **role** culture is associated with bureaucracy and emphasises rules and procedures.

- The **task** culture is focused on delivering the current goal.

- The **existential** culture supports individual independence and aspiration.

Culture colours the organisation's view of its environment and hence influences its strategy. **Defenders** like low risk solutions and niche markets. **Prospectors** are more adventurous and concerned with results. **Analysers** try to balance risk and profits. **Reactors** do not have viable strategies. Deal and Kennedy analyse culture in terms of inherent risk in the industry and the speed with which feedback is available on strategic decisions.

Holstede discerns cultural differences between businesses in different areas of the world, analysing them in terms of power distance, uncertainty avoidance, individualism–collectivism and masculinity – femininity.

Quick quiz

1   What constitutes culture in a general sense?

2   What are the main aspects of organisational culture?

3   What influences organisational culture?

4   Draw the McKinsey 7-S model.

5   Describe Harrison's analysis of organisations.

6   How did Miles and Snow analyse strategic culture?

7   Describe Deal and Kennedy's analysis of culture.

8   What are the cultural characteristics of the 'Anglo' group of countries in Hofstede's terms?

Answers to quick quiz

1   Beliefs, values, customs, artefacts, rituals

2   Underlying assumptions, overt beliefs and visible artefacts.

3   Many factors, including the founder, history, management style, structure, systems

4

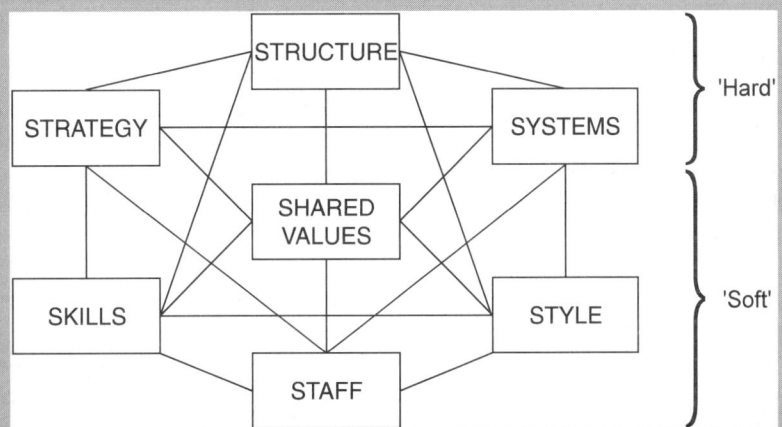

5   Harrison analysed organisations into four types based on their structure and culture.

- Organisations structured around a dynamic leader display a power culture.

- The role culture is typical of bureaucracy.

- Organisations that are run by project teams or have a matrix structure tend to display the task culture.

- The existential culture pervades the loose organisation which exists to serve the interests of its principal members.

6   Defenders like low risks and secure markets. Prospectors constantly seek improved results. Analysers try to balance risk and profit. Reactors live from hand to mouth.

7   Deal and Kennedy suggest that culture is determined by two things: the degree of risk inherent in the business and how quickly the results of risk-taking become apparent. High risk and slow feedback lead to cautious and deliberate cultures. High risk and rapid feedback produce a culture of boldness. Low risk and fast feedback produce action and good humour. Low risk and slow feedback lead to emphasis on technical excellence, procedure and status.

8   Low to medium power-distance and uncertainty-avoidance; high individualism and high 'masculinity'.

Now try the question below from the Exam Question Bank

Number	Level	Marks	Time
Q4	Exam	20	36 Mins

BPP
PUBLISHING

Chapter 5

ETHICS AND SOCIAL RESPONSIBILITY

Topic List	Syllabus Reference	Ability required
1 Boundary management	(i)	Comprehension
2 The social and ethical environment	(i)	Comprehension
3 The social responsibility of organisations and managers	(i)	Comprehension
4 Ethics in organisations	(i)	Evaluation

Introduction

Social responsibility and ethical issues relate to many aspects of the firm: its environment; its culture; and management practice. It is one of the firm's objectives or goals. This subject is also examinable in later papers, so a good grasp now will stand you in good stead. However, it is the nature of ethics to deny easy answers; furthermore, in the context of business, ethical prescriptions have to be practical to be of any use.

After completing this chapter, you should:

(a)   appreciate the importance and complexity of the issues surrounding ethics and social responsibility, so far as organisations and their various stakeholders are concerned

(b)   accept that organisations should be consciously concerned with their public posture so far as ethics and social responsibility are concerned

(c)   be able to discriminate between ethical and non-ethical actions undertaken by employees acting individually or employees as representatives of their organisations

(d)   cope with the difficulties of translating broad concepts of ethics and social responsibilities into the everyday operational actions of employees within organisations.

Learning outcomes covered in this chapter

- Explain the importance of organisational and professional ethics.

- Recommend ways in which ethical behaviour can be encouraged in organisations.

Syllabus content covered in this chapter

- The expectations of stakeholders with regard to ethical behaviour, and the role of government (eg Cadbury report, ombudsman appointment) and professional bodies (eg CIMA) in determining ethical standards.

1   BOUNDARY MANAGEMENT

1.1   A business supplies goods and services to customers, and employs people; **it is an integral part of society and is subject to the pressures of that society.** Many companies share similar aspirations.

(a) To seek a good public image

(b) To protect the environment from pollution, and the waste of non-renewable resources

(c) To be good employers

(d) To provide facilities or welfare to the local community or the country as a whole (eg the sponsorship of sports, which is not always associated with a blaze of advertising and publicity, donations to charity)

1.2 There are differing views about the extent to which external pressures modify business objectives and form boundaries to the exercise of management discretion.

(a) **The stakeholder view of company objectives** is that many groups of people have a stake in what the company does. Shareholders own the business, but there are also suppliers, managers, workers and customers. A business depends on appropriate relationships with these groups, otherwise it will find it hard to function. Each of these groups has its own objectives, so that a compromise or balance is required. **Management must balance the profit objective with the pressures from the non-shareholder groups in deciding the strategic targets of the business.**

(b) **The consensus theory of company objectives** was developed by *Cyert and March*. They argued that managers run a business but do not own it and that 'organisations do not have objectives, only people have objectives'. Managers do not necessarily set objectives for the company, but rather they look for objectives which suit their own inclinations. However, objectives emerge as a consensus of the differing views of shareholders, managers, employees, suppliers, customers and society at large, but (in contrast to the stakeholder view) **they are not all selected or controlled by management.**

1.3 *Ansoff* suggested that a company has a number of **different levels of objectives**.

(a) A **primary economic objective**, aimed at optimising the efficiency and effectiveness of the firm's 'total resource-conversion process'.

(b) **Non-economic, social objectives**, which are secondary and modify management behaviour. These social objectives are the result of inter-action among the individual objectives of the differing groups of stakeholders.

(c) **Responsibilities** are obligations which a company undertakes, but which do not form a part of its 'internal guidance or control mechanism'. Responsibilities would include charitable donations, contributions to the life of local communities.

(d) **Boundaries** are rules that restrict management's freedom of action, and include government legislation (on, for instance, pollution levels, health and safety at work, employment protection, redundancy and monopolies) and agreements with trade unions.

2 THE SOCIAL AND ETHICAL ENVIRONMENT

> **KEY TERM**
>
> **Ethics**: a set of moral principles to guide behaviour

2.1 Whereas the political environment in which an organisation operates consists of laws, regulations and government agencies, the social environment consists of the customs,

attitudes, beliefs and education of society as a whole, or of different groups in society; and the ethical environment consists of a set (or sets) of well-established rules of personal and organisational behaviour.

2.2 Social attitudes, such as a belief in the merits of education, progress through science and technology, and fair competition, are significant for the management of a business organisation. Other beliefs have either gained strength or been eroded in recent years:

(a) There is a growing belief in preserving and improving the quality of life by reducing working hours, reversing the spread of pollution, developing leisure activities and so on. Pressures on organisations to consider the environment are particularly strong because most environmental damage is irreversible and some is fatal to humans and wildlife.

(b) Many pressure groups have been organised in recent years to protect social minorities and under-privileged groups. Legislation has been passed in an attempt to prevent racial discrimination and discrimination against women and disabled people.

(c) Issues relating to the environmental consequences of corporate activities are currently debated, and respect for the environment has come to be regarded as an unquestionable good.

2.3 The ethical environment refers to justice, respect for the law and a moral code. The conduct of an organisation, its management and employees will be measured against ethical standards by the customers, suppliers and other members of the public with whom they deal.

Ethical problems facing managers

2.4 Managers have a duty (in most enterprises) to aim for profit. At the same time, modern ethical standards impose a duty to guard, preserve and enhance the value of the enterprise for the good of all touched by it, including the general public. Large organisations tend to be more often held to account over this than small ones.

2.5 In the area of **products and production**, managers have responsibility to ensure that the public and their own employees are protected from danger. Attempts to increase profitability by cutting costs may lead to dangerous working conditions or to inadequate safety standards in products. In the United States, product liability litigation is so common that this legal threat may be a more effective deterrent than general ethical standards. The Consumer Protection Act 1987 and EU legislation generally is beginning to ensure that ethical standards are similarly enforced in the UK.

2.6 Another ethical problem concerns **payments by companies to government or municipal officials** who have power to help or hinder the payers' operations. In *The Ethics of Corporate Conduct*, *Clarence Walton* refers to the fine distinctions which exist in this area.

(a) **Extortion.** Foreign officials have been known to threaten companies with the complete closure of their local operations unless suitable payments are made.

(b) **Bribery.** This refers to payments for services to which a company is not legally entitled. There are some fine distinctions to be drawn; for example, some managers regard political contributions as bribery.

(c) **Grease money.** Multinational companies are sometimes unable to obtain services to which they are legally entitled because of deliberate stalling by local officials. Cash payments to the right people may then be enough to oil the machinery of bureaucracy.

(d) **Gifts**. In some cultures (such as Japan) gifts are regarded as an essential part of civilised negotiation, even in circumstances where to Western eyes they might appear ethically dubious. Managers operating in such a culture may feel at liberty to adopt the local customs.

2.7 Business ethics are also relevant to competitive behaviour. This is because a market can only be free if competition is, in some basic respects, fair. There is a distinction between competing aggressively and competing unethically. The dispute between British Airways and Virgin centred around issues of business ethics.

Examples of social and ethical objectives

2.8 Companies are not passive in the social and ethical environment. Many organisations pursue a variety of social and ethical objectives.

2.9 **Employees**

- A minimum wage, perhaps with adequate differentials for skilled labour
- Job security (over and above the protection afforded by legislation)
- Good conditions of work (above the legal minima)
- Job satisfaction

2.10 **Customers** may be regarded as entitled to receive a produce of good quality at a reasonable price.

2.11 **Suppliers** may be offered regular orders and timely payment in return for reliable delivery and good service.

2.12 **Society as a whole**

- Control of pollution
- Provision of financial assistance to charities, sports and community activities
- Co-operation with government authorities in identifying and preventing health hazards in the products sold

2.13 As far as it is possible, social and ethical objectives should be expressed quantitatively, so that actual results can be monitored to ensure that the targets are achieved. This is often easier said than done - more often, they are expressed in the organisation's mission statement which can rarely be reduced to a quantified amount.

2.14 Many of the above objectives are commercial ones - for example satisfying customers is necessary to stay in business. The question as to whether it is the business of businesses to be concerned about wider issues of social responsibility *at all* is discussed shortly.

3 THE SOCIAL RESPONSIBILITY OF ORGANISATIONS AND MANAGERS

3.1 Not only does the environment have a significant influence on the structure and behaviour of organisations, but also organisations have some influence on their environment.

3.2 Since organisations have an effect on their environment, it is arguable that they should act in a way which shows **social awareness and responsibility**.

> 'A society, awakened and vocal with respect to the urgency of social problems, is asking the managers of all kinds of organisations, particularly those at the top, what they are doing to discharge their social responsibilities and why they are not doing more.'
>
> Koontz, O'Donnell and Weihrich

BPP PUBLISHING

3.3 Social responsibility is expected from all types of organisation.

(a) **Local government** is expected to provide services to the local community, and to preserve or improve the character of that community, but at an acceptable cost to the ratepayers.

(b) **Businesses** are expected to provide goods and services, which reflect the needs of users and society as a whole. These needs may not be in harmony - arguably, the development of the Concorde aeroplane and supersonic passenger travel did not contribute to the public interest, and caused considerable inconvenience to residents near airports who suffer from excessive aircraft noise. A business should also be expected to anticipate the future needs of society; examples of socially useful products might be energy-saving devices and alternative sources of power.

(c) **Pollution control** is a particularly important example of social responsibility by industrial organisations, and some progress has been made in the development of commercial processes for re-cycling waste material. British Coal attempts to restore the environment by planting on old slag heaps.

(d) **Universities and schools** are expected to produce students whose abilities and qualifications will prove beneficial to society. A currently popular view of education is that greater emphasis should be placed on vocational training for students.

(e) In some cases, **legislation** may be required to enforce social need, for example to regulate the materials used to make crash helmets for motor cyclists, or to regulate safety standards in motor cars and furniture. Ideally, however, organisations should avoid the need for legislation by taking **earlier self-regulating action**.

Social responsibility and businesses

3.4 Arguably, institutions like hospitals, schools and so forth exist because health care and education are seen to be desirable social objectives by government at large, if they can be afforded.

3.5 However, where does this leave businesses? How far is it reasonable, or even appropriate, for businesses to exercise 'social responsibility' by giving to charities, voluntarily imposing strict environmental objectives on themselves and so forth?

3.6 One school of thought would argue that **the management of a business has only one social responsibility, which is to maximise wealth for its shareholders**. There are two reasons to support this argument.

(a) The business is owned by the shareholders and the assets of the company are, ultimately, the shareholders' property. Management has no moral right to dispose of business assets (like cash) on non-business objectives, as this has the effect of reducing the return available to shareholders. The shareholders might, for example, disagree with management's choice of beneficiary. Anyhow, it is for the shareholders to determine how their money should be spent.

(b) A second justification for this view is that management's job is to **maximise wealth, as this is the best way that society can benefit from a business's activities**.

(i) Maximising wealth has the effect of increasing the tax revenues available to the state to disburse on socially desirable objectives.

(ii) Maximising wealth for the few is sometimes held to have a 'trickle down' effect on the disadvantaged members of society.

(iii) Many company shares are owned by pension funds, whose ultimate beneficiaries may not be the wealthy anyway.

3.7 This argument rests on one fact and two assumptions.

(a) It is a fact that the *rights* of legal ownership take precedence over all other *interests* in a business: while other stakeholders may have an interest, they have few legal rights over the wealth created.

(b) The first assumption is that a business's *only* relationship with the wider social environment is an economic one. After all, that is what businesses exist for, and any other activities are the role of the state.

(c) The second assumption is that the defining purpose of business organisations is the maximisation of the wealth of their owners.

3.8 *Henry Mintzberg* (in *Power In and Around Organisations*) suggests that simply viewing organisations as vehicles for shareholder investment is inadequate.

(a) In practice, he says, organisations are rarely controlled effectively by shareholders. Most shareholders are passive investors.

(b) Moreover, businesses do receive a lot of government support. The public pays for roads, infrastructure, education and health, all of which benefits businesses.

(c) Large corporations can manipulate markets. Social responsibility, forced or voluntary, is a way of recognising this.

(d) Strategic decisions by businesses always have wider social consequences. In other words, says Mintzberg, the firm produces two outputs: **goods and services** and the **social consequences of its activities** (eg pollution).

It is possible to refute the first two of Mintzberg's arguments. The second two points are more significant.

Externalities

3.9 If it is accepted that businesses do not bear the total social cost of their activities, then the exercise of social responsibility is a way of compensating for this. An example is given by the environment. Industrial pollution is injurious to health: if someone is made ill by industrial pollution, then arguably the polluter should pay the sick person, as damages or in compensation, in the same way as if the business's builders had accidentally bulldozed somebody's house.

3.10 In practice, of course, while it is relatively easy to identify statistical relationships between pollution levels and certain illnesses, mapping out the chain of cause and effect from an individual's wheezing cough to the dust particles emitted by Factory X, as opposed to Factory Y, is quite a different matter.

3.11 Of course, it could be argued that these external costs are met out of general taxation: but this has the effect of spreading the cost amongst other individuals and businesses. Moreover, the tax revenue may be spent on curing the disease, rather than stopping it at its source. Pollution control equipment may be the fairest way of dealing with this problem. Thus advocates of social responsibility in business would argue that business's responsibilities then do not rest with paying taxes.

3.12 However, is there any justification for social responsibility outside remedying the effects of a business's direct activities. For example, should businesses give to charity or sponsor the arts? There are several reasons why they should.

(a) If the **stakeholder concept** of a business is held, then the public is a stakeholder in the business. A business only succeeds because it is part of a wider society. Giving to charity is one way of encouraging a relationship.

(b) Charitable donations and artistic sponsorship are a useful medium of **public relations** and can reflect well on the business. It can be regarded, then, as another form of promotion, which like advertising, serves to enhance consumer awareness of the business, while not encouraging the sale of a particular brand.

3.13 The arguments for and against social responsibility of business are complex ones. However, ultimately they can be traced to different assumptions about society and the relationships between the individuals and organisations within it.

Question 1

The Heritage Carpet Company is a London-based retailer which imports carpets from Turkey, Iran and India. The company was founded by two Europeans who travelled independently through these countries in the 1970s. The company is the sole customer for carpets made in a number of villages in each of the source countries. The carpets are hand woven. Indeed, they are so finely woven that the process requires that children be used to do the weaving, thanks to their small fingers. The company believes that it is preserving a 'craft', and the directors believe that this is a justifiable social objective. Recently a UK television company has reported unfavourably on child exploitation in the carpet weaving industry. There were reports of children working twelve hour shifts in poorly lit sheds and cramped conditions, with consequent deterioration in eyesight, muscular disorders and a complete absence of education. The examples cited bear no relation to the Heritage Carpet Company's suppliers although children are used in the labour force, but there has been a spate of media attention. The regions in which the Heritage Carpet Company's supplier villages are found are soon expected to enjoy rapid economic growth.

What boundary management issues are raised for the Heritage Carpet Company?

Answer

Many. This is a case partly about boundary management and partly about enlightened self-interest and business ethics. The adverse publicity, although not about the Heritage Carpet Company's own suppliers, could rebound badly. Potential customers might be put off. Economic growth in the area may also mean that parents will prefer to send their children to school. The Heritage Carpet Company as well as promoting itself as preserving a craft could reinvest some of its profits in the villages (eg by funding a school), or by enforcing limits on the hours children worked. It could also pay a decent wage. It could advertise this in a "code of ethics" so that customers are reassured that the children are not simply being exploited. Alternatively, it could not import child-made carpets at all. (This policy, however, would be unlikely to help communities in which child labour is an economic necessity. Children already living on the margins of subsistence might end up even more exploited, in begging or prostitution.)

4 ETHICS IN ORGANISATIONS

4.1 Ethics is a code of moral principles that people follow with respect to what is right or wrong. Ethical principles are not necessarily enforced by law, although the law incorporates moral judgements (murder is wrong ethically, and is also punishable legally).

4.2 Companies have to follow legal standards, or else they will be subject to fines and their officers might face similar charges. Ethics in organisations relates to **social responsibility** and **business practice**.

4.3 People that work for organisations bring their own values into work with them. Organisations contain a variety of ethical systems.

(a) **Personal ethics** (eg deriving from a person's upbringing, religious or non-religious beliefs, political opinions, personality). People have different ethical viewpoints at different stages in their lives. Some will judge situations on 'gut feel'. Some will consciously or unconsciously adopt a general approach to ethical dilemmas, such as 'the end justifies the means'.

(b) **Professional ethics** (eg CIMA's code of ethics, medical ethics).

(c) **Organisation cultures** (eg 'customer first'). We discussed culture in an earlier chapter; culture, in denoting what is normal behaviour, also denotes what is the right behaviour in many cases.

(d) **Organisation systems**. Ethics might be contained in a formal code, reinforced by the overall statement of values. A problem might be that ethics does not always save money, and there is a real cost to ethical decisions. Besides, the organisation has different ethical duties to different stakeholders. Who sets priorities?

Case example

Organisation systems and targets do have ethical implications. The Harvard Business Review reported that the US retailer, Sears, Roebuck was deluged with complaints that customers of its car service centre were being charged for unnecessary work: apparently this was because mechanics had been given targets of the number of car spare parts they should sell.

Leadership practices and ethics

4.4 The role of culture in determining the ethical climate of an organisation can be further explored by a brief reflection on the role of leaders in setting the ethical standard. A culture is partly a collection of symbols and attitudes, embodying certain truths about the organisation. Senior managers are also symbolic managers; inevitably they decide priorities; they set an example, whether they like it or not. Remember, too, that one of the roles of managers, according to Mintzberg is the **ceremonial one**.

4.5 **There are four types of cultural leadership in organisations.** (Note that these should *not* be confused with leadership styles.)

(a) **Creative**. The culture of an organisation often reflects its founder, and it is therefore reasonable to expect that the founding visionary should set the ethical tone. Such leaders create the ethical style.

(b) **Protective**. Such leaders sustain, or exemplify, the organisation's culture: for example a company which values customer service may have leaders who are 'heroic' in their efforts to achieve it.

(c) **Integrative**. Other leaders aim to create consensus through people, and perhaps flourish in an involvement culture. The danger is that this can turn to political manipulation; the 'consensus' created should work towards some valued cultural goal.

(d) **Adaptive**. These leaders change an existing culture or set of ethics. (When appointed to run *British Airways, Colin Marshall* changed the sign on his door from Chief Executive to his own name.) However, a leader has to send out the right signals, to ensure that competitive behaviour remains ethical, to avoid bad publicity if nothing else.

Two approaches to managing ethics

4.6   *Lynne Paine (Harvard Business Review*, March-April 1994) suggests that ethical decisions are becoming more important as penalties, in the US at least, for companies which break the law become tougher. (This might be contrasted with UK, where a fraudster whose deception ran into millions received a sentence of community service.) Paine suggests that there are two approaches to the management of ethics in organisations.

- **Compliance**-based
- **Integrity**-based

Compliance-based approach

4.7   A compliance-based approach is primarily designed to ensure that the company **acts within the letter of the law**, and that violations are prevented, detected and punished. Some organisations, faced with the legal consequences of unethical behaviour take legal precautions such as those below.

- Compliance procedures to detect misconduct
- Audits of contracts
- Systems for employees to report criminal misconduct without fear of retribution
- Disciplinary procedures to deal with transgressions

4.8   Corporate compliance is limited in that it relates only to the law, but legal compliance is 'not an adequate means for addressing the full range of ethical issues that arise every day'. This is especially the case in the UK, where **voluntary** codes of conduct and self-regulation are perhaps more prevalent than in the US.

4.9   An example of the difference between the **legality** and **ethicality** of a practice is the sale in some countries of defective products without appropriate warnings. 'Companies engaged in international business often discover that conduct that infringes on recognised standards of human rights and decency is legally permissible in some jurisdictions.'

4.10   The compliance approach also overemphasises the threat of detection and punishment in order to channel appropriate behaviour. Arguably, some employers view compliance programmes as an insurance policy for senior management, who can cover the tracks of their arbitrary management practices. After all, some performance targets are impossible to achieve without cutting corners: managers can escape responsibility by blaming the employee for not following the compliance programme, when to do so would have meant a failure to reach target.

4.11   Furthermore, mere compliance with the law is no guide to **exemplary** behaviour.

Integrity-based programmes

4.12   'An integrity-based approach combines a concern for the law with an **emphasis on managerial responsibility** for ethical behaviour. Integrity strategies strive to define companies' guiding values, aspirations and patterns of thought and conduct. When integrated into the day-to-day operations of an organisation, such strategies can help prevent damaging ethical lapses, while tapping into powerful human impulses for moral thought and action.

4.13   It should be clear to you from this quotation that an integrity-based approach to ethics treats ethics as an issue of organisation culture.

4.14 Ethics management has several tasks.

- To define and give life to an organisation's defining values.
- To create an environment that supports ethically sound behaviour
- To instil a sense of shared accountability amongst employees.

4.15 The table below indicates some of the differences between the two main approaches.

	Compliance	Integrity
Ethos	Knuckle under to external standards	Choose ethical standards
Objective	Keep to the law	Enable legal and responsible conduct
Originators	Lawyers	Management, with lawyers, HR specialists etc
Methods (both includes education, and audits, controls, penalties)	Reduced employee discretion	Leadership, organisation systems
Behavioural assumptions	People are solitary self-interested beings	People are social beings with values
Standards	The law	Company values, aspirations (including law)
Staffing	Lawyers	Managers and lawyers
Education	The law, compliance system	Values, the law, compliance systems
Activities	Develop standards, train and communicate, handle reports of misconduct, investigate, enforce, oversee compliance	Integrate values *into* company systems, provide guidance and consultation, identify and resolve problems, oversee compliance

4.16 In other words, an integrity-based approach **incorporates** ethics into corporate culture and systems.

Case example

Charles Hampden-Turner (in his book *Corporate Culture*) notes that attitudes to safety can be part of a corporate *culture*. He quotes the example of a firm called (for reasons of confidentiality) *Western Oil*.

Western Oil had a bad safety record. 'Initially, safety was totally at odds with the main cultural values of productivity (management's interests) and maintenance of a macho image (the worker's culture) ... Western Oil had a culture which put safety in conflict with other corporate values.' In particular, the problem was with its long-distance truck drivers (which in the US have a culture of solitary independence and self reliance) who drove sometimes recklessly with loads large enough to inundate a small town. The company instituted *Operation Integrity* to improve safety, in a lasting way, changing the policies and drawing on the existing features of the culture but using them in a different way.

The culture had five dilemmas.

(a) *Safety-first vs macho-individualism.* Truckers see themselves as 'fearless pioneers of the unconventional lifestyle ... "Be careful boys!" is hardly a plea likely to go down well with this particular group'. Instead of trying to control the drivers, the firm recommended that they become *road safety consultants* (or design consultants). Their advice was sought on improving the system. This had the advantage that 'by making drivers critics of the system their roles as outsiders were preserved and promoted'. It tried to tap their heroism as promoters of public safety.

(b) *Safety everywhere vs safety specialists.* Western Oil could have hired more specialist staff. However, instead, the company promoted cross functional safety teams from existing parts of the business, for example, to help in designing depots and thinking of ways to reduce hazards.

(c) *Safety as cost vs productivity as benefit.* 'If the drivers raced from station to station to win their bonus, accidents were bound to occur ... . The safety engineers rarely spoke to the line manager in charge of the delivery schedules. The unreconciled dilemma between safety and productivity had been evaded at management level and passed down the hierarchy until drivers were subjected to two incompatible injunctions, work fast and work safely'. To deal with this problem, safety would be built into the reward system.

(d) *Long-term safety vs short-term steering.* The device of recording 'unsafe' acts in operations enabled them to be monitored by cross-functional teams, so that the causes of accidents could be identified and be reduced.

(e) *Personal responsibility vs collective protection.* It was felt that if 'safety' was seen as a form of management policing it would never be accepted. The habit of management 'blaming the victim' had to stop. Instead, if an employee reported another to the safety teams, the person who was reported would be free of *official* sanction. Peer presence was seen to be a better enforcer of safety than the management hierarchy.

4.17 It has also been suggested that the following institutions can be established.

(a) An **ethics committee** is a group of executives (perhaps including non-executive directors) appointed to oversee company ethics. It rules on misconduct. It may seek advice from specialists in business ethics.

(b) An **ethics ombudsperson** is a manager who acts as the corporate conscience.

4.18 Accountants can also appeal to their professional body for ethical guidance.

4.19 **Whistle-blowing** is the disclosure by an employee of illegal, immoral or illegitimate practices on the part of the organisation. In theory, the public ought to welcome the public trust: however, confidentiality is very important in the accountants' code of ethics. Whistle-blowing frequently involves **financial loss** for the whistleblower.

(a) Whistle-blowers may lose their jobs.

(b) A whistle-blower who is a member of a professional body cannot, sadly, rely on that body to take a significant interest, or even offer a sympathetic ear. Some professional bodies have narrow interpretations of what is meant by ethical conduct. For many the duties of **commercial confidentiality** are felt to be more important.

Exam focus point

The ethics codes described above can be related to mission, culture and control strategies. A compliance-based approach suggest that bureaucratic control is necessary; an integrity based approach relies on cultural control.

Chapter roundup

- The stakeholder view holds that there are many groups in society with an interest in the organisation's activities. Some firms have objectives for these issues. Some argue, however, that a business's only objective should be to make money: the state, representing the public interest, can levy taxes to spend on socially desirable projects or can regulate organisational activities.

- Firms have to ensure they obey the law: but they also face ethical concerns, because their reputations depend on a good image.

- Inside the organisation, a compliance based approach highlights conformity with the law. An integrity based approach suggests a wider remit, incorporating ethics in the organisation's values and culture.

- Organisations sometimes issue codes of conduct to employees. Many employees are bound by professional codes of conduct.

Quick quiz

1 Distinguish between responsibilities and boundaries.

2 What ethical problems face management?

3 What objectives might a company have in relation to wider society?

4 To whom might management have responsibilities, and what are some of these responsibilities?

5 Why does Mintzberg say that the profit motive is not enough?

6 Describe two approaches to the management of ethics in an organisation.

7 What systems of ethics might you find in an organisation?

8 What is whistle blowing?

Answers to quick quiz

1 In Ansoff's analysis, boundaries are imposed rules; they restrict management's freedom of action. Responsibilities are voluntarily undertaken obligations such as charitable donations.

2 There is a constant tension between the need to achieve current profitability, the need to safeguard the stakeholders' long term investment and the expectations of wider society.

3 Protection of the environment, support for good causes, a responsible attitude to product safety.

4 Managers of businesses are responsible to the owners for economic performance and to wider society for the externalities related to their business operations.

5 Large businesses are rarely controlled by their shareholders; they receive a lot of support from public funds; and their activities have wider consequences.

6 A compliance–based approach aims to remain within the letter of the law by establishing systems of audit and review so that transgressions may be detected and punished. An integrity-based approach tries to promote an ethical culture in which individuals will do the right thing.

7 Personal ethics, professional ethics, organisation culture, organisation systems.

8 Informing outside regulatory agencies about transgressions by one's organisation.

Now try the question below from the Exam Question Bank

Number	Level	Marks	Time
Q5	Exam	20	36 mins

Part B
The functional areas of organisations

Chapter 6

ORGANISATION STRUCTURE: GENERAL PRINCIPLES

Topic List		Syllabus Reference	Ability required
1	Components of the organisation	(ii)	Evaluation
2	Hierarchy and span of control	(ii)	Evaluation
3	Line, staff and functional authority	(ii)	Evaluation
4	The informal organisation	(ii)	Evaluation

Introduction

In this chapter we look at some basic ideas relating to organisational structure. We begin with *Mintzberg's* influential analysis of structure and how he uses it to classify organisations. This is a very important aspect of theory. Parts 2 and 3 deal with fundamental ideas about the way relationships in organisations can be set up, while section 4 deals with the informal, social structure which exists alongside the official hierarchy. The ideas in parts 2 and 3 give you a basic vocabulary and are unlikely to be examined in detail. However, the informal aspects of organisation underpin many exam questions.

Learning outcomes covered in this chapter

- Explain the relative merits of a range of different organisation structures.

- Explain the relationships necessary between the functional areas in order for an organisation to achieve its objectives.

- Analyse a range of organisations, identifying their component parts, the relationships between those parts and any problems with those relationships

- Recommend and evaluate changes to the structure of organisations.

Syllabus content covered in this chapter

- The different structures which might be adopted by a business organisation and how the various components of those structures inter-relate (ie entrepreneurial, functional, divisional, matrix, network, complex).

1   COMPONENTS OF THE ORGANISATION

1.1   *Mintzberg* suggests that the structure of any business depended on a number of **design parameters,** which can be embodied in an organisation in a variety of ways.

- **Job specialisation:** the number of tasks in a given job, the division of labour
- **Behaviour formalisation:** in other words, the standardisation of work processes
- **Training:** to achieve work standardisation
- **Indoctrination** of employees in the organisation's culture

- **Unit grouping:** organisation by function, geographical area, or product, for example
- **Unit size:** the number of people in the work group
- **Planning and control systems** for the standardisation of outputs
- **Liaison devices** to achieve mutual adjustment
- **Decentralisation:** the diffusion of decision making power

1.2   Mintzberg identifies five structural components to an organisation. These are shown in this diagram.

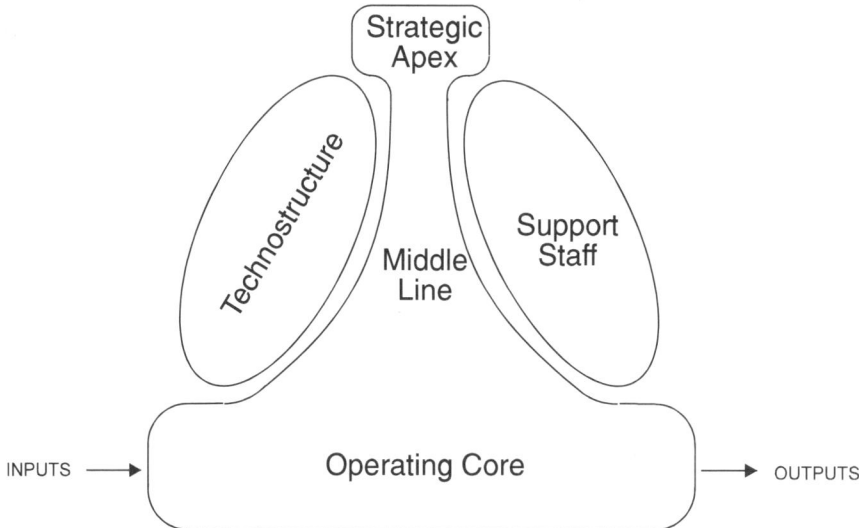

The organisation has a sixth essential component which Mintzberg calls 'ideology'. This is exactly equivalent to **culture.**

KEY TERMS

The **operating core** contains those people directly involved in production (ie in securing inputs and processing them into outputs and distributing those outputs). In other words, they might be directly responsible for the **primary activities of the value chain.** In small organisations, they are co-ordinated through mutual adjustment.

The **strategic apex** emerges with the need for supervision and control. It ensures that the organisation follows its mission and serves the needs of its owners. Its job is supervision, boundary management and strategy. The strategic apex might consist of the owner on the board of directors.

The **middle line** is the hierarchy of authority between the operating core and the strategic apex. People in this area administer the work done. The chain of middle managers with formal authority runs from senior managers to front line supervisors. It converts the wishes of the strategic apex into the work of the operating core.

The **technostructure** standardises the work. This is a further layer of administration and planning. Work-study analysts (eg engineers) standardise work processes by analysing and determining the most efficient method of doing a job. Planners (eg quality staff, accountants) standardise outputs. Personnel analysts standardise skills by arranging for training programmes.

Support staff provide ancillary services such as public relations, legal counsel, the cafeteria. Support staff are different from the technostructure, as they do not plan or standardise production. They function independently of the operating core.

The examiner has told BPP that Mintzberg's approach is 'a major theory of structure'.

> **Exam focus point**
>
> It is a good idea to learn the components of organisations described above, as you can apply them in real exam questions. Be careful, though, to read the question. The words 'configuration' and 'Mintzberg' should indicate that you use the approach in this section. The words 'organisation structure' or 'structural form' are more ambiguous – generally, you should use the type of approach described in later sections and the next chapter.

1.3 **These elements are linked in five ways**.

(a) There is an **organisation hierarchy** of formal authority. This is discussed in section 2 of this chapter.

(b) An organisation is a **flow of regulated activity**. Inputs are processed into outputs. The activities in the value chain are controlled and linked.

(c) There is a flow of **informal communications**. This denotes the real structure of communication, supplementing or bypassing the formal communication system.

(d) An organisation is **a system of work constellations**. Groups of people work on distinct tasks. For example, the members of the accounts department work together. These constellations might be temporary. For example, in producing a set of annual financial statements, people from the finance department (for the numbers), the sales department (for detailed statistics) and public relations (for presentation) need to be involved.

(e) An organisation is a system of **ad hoc decision processes**. A decision process involves recognising a problem, diagnosing its causes, finding a solution and implementing it. For any one decision, these activities occur in a number of different places in the organisation. For example, customer care personnel might first hear of a problem with faulty goods, but the decisions as to how to prevent the problem happening again will be taken in the production department.

2 HIERARCHY AND SPAN OF CONTROL

Authority, accountability and responsibility

2.1 It is easy to confuse authority, accountability and responsibility since they are all to do with the allocation of power within an organisation.

Authority

> **KEY TERM**
>
> **Organisational authority:** the scope and amount of discretion given to a person to make decisions, by virtue of the position he or she holds in the organisation.

2.2 The authority and power structure of an organisation defines two things.

- The part which each member of the organisation is expected to perform
- The relationship between the members

2.3 A person's (or office's) authority can come from a variety of sources, including from above (supervisors) or below (if the position is elected). Managerial authority thus has three aspects.

- Making decisions within the scope of one's own managerial authority
- Assigning tasks to subordinates
- Expecting and requiring satisfactory performance of these tasks by subordinates

Responsibility

2.4 **Responsibility** is the liability of a person to discharge duties. Responsibility is the obligation to do something; in an organisation, it is the duty of an official to carry out assigned tasks.

2.5 With responsibility, we must associate **accountability**. Managers are accountable *to* their superiors *for* their actions and are obliged to report to their superiors how well they have exercised the authority delegated to them.

Delegation

2.6 **Delegation of authority** occurs in an organisation where a superior gives to a subordinate the discretion to make decisions within a certain sphere of influence. This can only occur if the superior initially possesses the authority to delegate; a subordinate cannot be given organisational authority to make decisions unless it would otherwise be the superior's right to make those decisions. Delegation of authority is the process by which a superior gives a subordinate the authority to carry out an aspect of the superior's job. Without delegation, a formal organisation could not exist.

2.7 When a superior delegates authority to a subordinate, the subordinate is accountable to the superior. However, the superior **remains fully accountable** to **his** superiors; responsibility and accountability cannot be abdicated by delegation.

Authority and power

2.8 If an organisation is to function as a co-operative system of individuals, some people must have authority or power over others. Authority and power flow **downwards** through the formal organisation.

   (a) **Authority** is the right to do something; in an organisation it is the right of a manager to require a subordinate to do something in order to achieve the goals of the organisation.

   (b) **Power** is distinct from authority, but is often associated with it. **Whereas authority is the right to do something, power is the ability to do it**.

Power and influence

2.9 Influence is the process by which one person in an organisation, A modifies the behaviour or attitudes of another person, B. An individual may have the ability to make others act in a certain way, without having the organisational authority to do so: informal leaders are frequently in this position.

2.10 The following types of power from different sources have been identified (by Handy and others).

(a) **Physical power** is the power of superior force. Physical power is absent from most organisations (except the prison service and the armed forces), but it is sometimes evident in poor industrial relations (eg shop floor intimidation). Power based on fear of punishment is known as **coercive power**.

(b) **Resource power** is the control over resources which are valued by the individual or group to be influenced. Senior managers may have the resource power to grant promotion or pay increases to subordinates, in which case it is **reward power**. Trade unions possess the resource power to take their members out on strike. The amount of power a person has then depends on how far he controls the resource, how much the resource is valued by others, and how scarce it is.

(c) **Position power** or **legitimate power** is the power which is associated with a particular job in an organisation. **It is more or less the same as authority**. Handy noted that position power has certain 'hidden' benefits.

   (i) Access to information

   (ii) Access to people: for example, entitlement to membership of committees and contact with other powerful individuals in the organisation

   (iii) The right to organise conditions of working and methods of decision-making

(d) **Expert power** is the power which is based on **expertise**, although it only works if others **acknowledge** that expertise. Many staff jobs in an organisation (eg computer systems analysts and personnel department managers) rely on expert power to influence line management. If the expert is seen to be incompetent or if his area of expertise is not widely acknowledged (which is often the case with personnel department staff) he will have little or no expert power.

(e) **Personal power** lies in the personality of the individual. Personal power is capable of influencing the behaviour of others, and helps to explain the strength of informal organisations.

(f) **Negative power** is the use of disruptive attitudes and behaviour to stop things from happening. It is associated with low morale, latent conflict or frustration at work. Negative power is destructive and potentially very damaging to organisational efficiency.

2.11 Influence, the act of directing or modifying the behaviour of others, may be achieved in a variety of ways.

(a) The application of force, such as physical or economic power

(b) The establishment of rules and procedures that are enforced through position and/or resource power

(c) Bargaining and negotiation, which depend on the relative strengths of each party's position

(d) Persuasion

Power at different levels in organisation

2.12 The **degree** of power people exercise, and the **types** of power they are able to exploit, differ depending in part on their position in the organisation hierarchy. The effects of personal power vary: the chief executive's use of personal power will be more far-reaching in the organisation as a whole than that of a junior manager.

Senior management

2.13 Senior management enjoy position power. In theory, senior managers take the major decisions and set constraints over the decisions taken by other people. In practice, however, the senior manager's power is never absolute. Senior managers depend on decisions and information supplied by subordinates, and it is quite possible that the information is shaped at a lower level. Senior managers are likely to play a number of the managerial roles suggested in the previous chapter.

2.14 Senior managers have coercive and reward powers, and most importantly take decisions relating to personnel.

2.15 Finally, it helps managers to be on a 'network'. This means that if a manager's allies are placed in certain positions, their loyalty might be useful.

Middle managers

2.16 Middle managers have a number of power sources. They have some reward power over their own subordinates. They may have expert power and negative power to delay or subvert decisions taken by senior managers. They need legitimate power, hence the need for formal job descriptions, authorisation limits and so on.

2.17 People at lower levels of the organisation derive power from several sources.

- Expert power (about organisational activities, or specific processes)
- Resource power over information
- Access to other important people
- Negative power

Interest groups

2.18 There are also formal interest groups, that is, groups which are perceived to represent the interests of their members. Such groups tend to wield greater power in conflict situations than their members as individuals.

(a) **Trade unions** are organisations whose purpose it is to promote their members' interests. The power of trade unions has been much reduced.

(b) **Occupational and professional groups** represent the interests of their members and of their clients. Professional bodies and other occupational associations are concerned to preserve standards of skill and knowledge, to ensure appropriate financial rewards (theoretically commensurate with their skills and knowledge) and to create a measure of independence, for example, in the right to control their own affairs.

Departmental power

2.19 The power exercised by **individual departments** will vary.

Some departments in the technostructure exercise power by the use of **functional authority,** for instance, by specifying procedures. Other departments are important as they deal with **key strategic contingencies**. These are 'events and activities both inside and outside an organisation that are essential for attaining organisational goals'. They can arise in several ways.

(a) **Dependency**. A department which depends on anther department may not be in a position to exercise power over that department, without support at a higher level. A department may use its **resource power** to make other departments dependent on it.

(b) **Financial resources**. This is another sort of dependency, but a department with a larger budget can spend it with more discretion.

(c) **Centrality**. How critical is the department in the **primary** activities of the organisation?

(d) **Non-substitutability**. Some departments cannot easily be broken up and their activities carried out elsewhere. This used to be the case with information systems departments, before the advent of cheap personal computers and software.

(e) **Uncertainty**. A department which reduces the levels of uncertainty faced by other departments (in dealing with key environmental variables) has a sort of expert power.

Scalar chain

2.20 The formal arrangement of power, authority and delegation is known as the **organisation hierarchy**. The **scalar chain** connects the strategic apex to the operating core. Formal communication is up and down the **scalar chain**. If, however, interaction between different branches of the chain is necessary, horizontal communication saves time and is likely to be more accurate, as long as superiors know that such communication is taking place.

2.21 An organisation has many such chains of authority and command, but all of them originate at the topmost management authority which in a company is the board of directors. Managers at different levels in the hierarchy are all links in a chain of command.

2.22 There might be a tendency for chains of command within a single organisation to get longer as the organisation grows older. The length of the chain of command depends on a number of factors.

- The size of the organisation
- The type and complexity of the products it makes or services it provides
- The diversity of its products and services
- Its geographical spread
- The number and complexity of controls required
- The type of people it employs

2.23 No rules have been (or can be) laid down for how chains of command should be structured or how many links or levels there should be, but a general observation is that chains of command should be kept as short as possible.

(a) Management structure should be organised for business performance. The scalar chain should promote rather than inhibit effective management.

(b) A problem with long chains of command is that it can take time for the organisation to react, as decisions have to go up several levels and through several hands. This can be slow moving and cumbersome, especially if senior managers only delegate with reluctance.

(c) Short chains of command, with a reduction in the number of management layers, have become more common.

(d) Chains of command are also useful in developing tomorrow's managers: both short and long chains have advantages in this respect. Short chains of command help junior managers to develop as they get valuable insights into management problems and thinking 'at the top' which help their own development as manager. However, long chains of command do enable mangers to be given progressively greater authority. A danger is that some managers may be frustrated by the delay and might leave.

BPP
PUBLISHING

Span of control

2.24 The **span of control** or span of management is the number of subordinates working for a superior official. In other words, if a manager has five subordinates, the span of control is five. Clearly, the width of the average span of control in an organisation is directly linked to the length of the scalar chain: a generally narrow span of control implies many layers of management and vice versa.

2.25 **Advantages of a narrow span of control**

- Tight control and close supervision

- Time for the manager to think and plan

- Reduced delegation: managers can do more of their work themselves.

- Better communication with subordinates

2.26 **Advantages of a wide span of control**

- Greater decision-making authority for subordinates
- Fewer supervisory costs
- Less control, but perhaps greater motivation through job satisfaction

2.27 It is reasonable to accept the view that there is a limit to a supervisor's capabilities and that the span of control should be limited. However, the span of control is now thought to be dependent on several factors.

- The nature of the manager's work load.

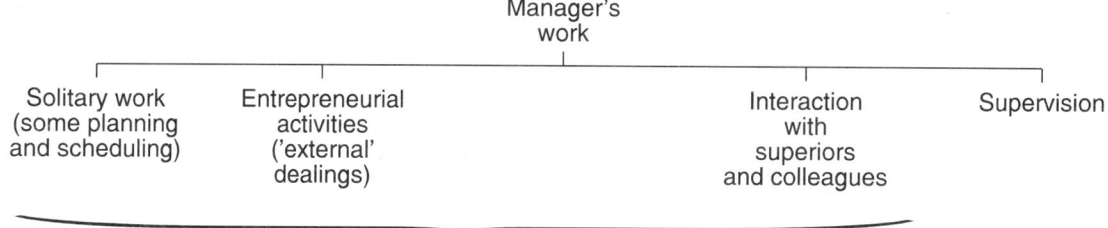

The greater the proportion of non-supervisory work in a manager's work load the narrower the span of control should be or the greater the delegation of authority to subordinates should be.

- Wide geographical dispersion probably makes a wide span of control impossible.

- If the subordinates' work is all of a similar nature a wide span is possible.

- The more complex the potential work problems, the narrower the span should be.

- With close interaction between subordinates, a wider span should be possible.

- The more competent management and subordinates are, the wider the span may be.

- Small groups may achieve better team work.

- Help from staff functions makes a wider span possible.

2.28 There is no universally correct size for the span of management, and no current writer on organisations would suggest that a correct span exists, without considering the particular circumstances of any particular individual organisation or department.

Question 1

Draw up an organisation chart for your department (or firm).

- How many layers are there in the scalar chain?
- What is your span of control?
- What is your supervisor's span of control?
- What is the average span of control?
- Can you improve this design?

Current issues in organisation hierarchy

Tall and flat organisations: delayering

2.29 The span of control concept has implications for the shape of an organisation.

    (a) A **tall organisation** is one which, in relation to its size, has a large number of management levels, and small spans of control.

    (b) A **flat organisation** is one which has a smaller number of hierarchical levels and hence wider spans of control. These are outlined in the diagram below.

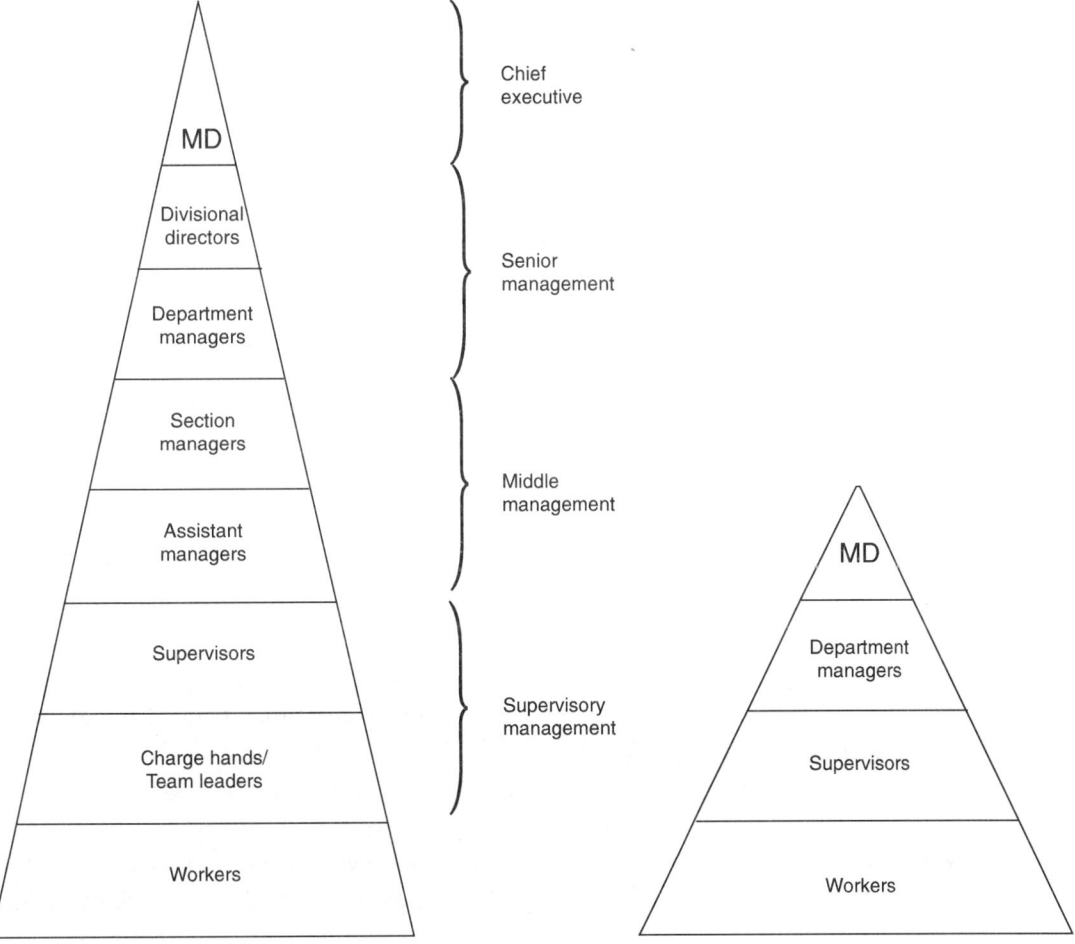

2.30 Currently, many believe a **tall organisation structure is inefficient**.

    (a) It increases overhead costs, especially middle management salaries.

    (b) It creates extra communication problems. Senior managers are more remote from the work done at the bottom end of the organisation. Information tends to get distorted or blocked on its way up or down through the organisation hierarchy.

(c) It slows down decision-making. It is easy for people to 'pass the buck'.

(d) Management responsibilities tend to overlap and become confused as the size of the management structure gets larger. Different sections or departments may seek authority over the same territory of operations, and superiors may find it difficult to delegate sufficient authority to satisfy subordinates.

(e) The same work passes through too many hands.

(f) Planning is more difficult because it must be organised at more levels in the organisation.

2.31 Nevertheless, not all researchers favour flat organisation structures.

(a) If work is organised on the basis of small groups or project teams and therefore narrow spans of control and a tall organisation structure), group members would be able to plan their work in an orderly manner, encourage participation by all group members in decision-making and monitor the consequences of their decisions better, so that their performance will be more **efficient** than the work of groups in a flat structure with a wide span of control.

(b) In the case of large organisations such a banks, 'it is virtually impossible for so complex an organisation as an international bank to work with less than five or six executive levels.' *D Vander Weyer* (*Management and People in Banking*).

(c) Flat organisations offer few avenues for **promotion**, and the organisation may find it hard to retain staff.

(d) Flat organisations depend on a workforce **empowered to take decisions**, and senior managers interested in operational issues. This does not always occur.

(e) Flat organisations may be inconsistent with some management controls.

(f) There might be wide discrepancies in decision-making.

2.32 There is a trade-off between the span of control and the tallness/flatness of an organisation. The span of control should not be too wide, but neither should an organisation be too tall.

Tall organisations	
Reasons in favour	*Reasons against*
1 Keeps span of control narrow.	1 A wide span of control means that more authority will be delegated to subordinates. Greater discretion leads to job enrichment and motivation.
2 A large number of career/promotion steps are provided in the hierarchical ladder. More frequent promotions possible.	2 With many rungs in the hierarchical ladder, the *real* increases in authority between one rung and another might not seem obvious to managers.
	3 Tall organisations are more expensive in management overheads costs.
	4 Tall organisations tend to suffer from worse communications.

2.33 Flat organisations are becoming more common with the current fashion for **delayering**, in other words, the abolition of the number of tiers between the highest to the lowest layers.

(a) This depends on the **empowerment** of employees so that they make more decisions and need less supervision.

(b) Much of the work of middle management consists of receiving, filtering, analysing and relaying **information**. Much of this information processing is now done by IT systems.

Downsizing

2.34 Delayering has gone hand in hand with a trend towards **downsizing** whereby large numbers of managers and staff have been made redundant.

(a) CIMA defines **downsizing** as:

'Organisational restructuring involving *outsourcing* activities, replacing permanent staff with contract employees and reducing the number of levels within the organisation hierarchy, with the intention of making the organisation more flexible, efficient and responsive to its environment.'

(b) In theory, this makes organisations **leaner and more flexible**. Often, however, it is a simple short-term cost cutting exercise with no fundamental change to the business. Cutting staff numbers and management levels reduces capacity, and where there is no fundamental examination of how the organisation works, this does not necessarily offer enhanced profits over the long term. Furthermore, such **corporate anorexia** can in fact reduce flexibility as there is no time for experimentation or creativity.

Case examples

The September 1992 edition of *Accountancy* reported a decimation of middle managers - not just 'pen pushers' but technicians also - at a number of large British companies.

(a) BP. In 1990, a new chairman announced 1,000 job losses of which 160 were head office managers - a 30% cut at head office.

(b) BT. Project Sovereign in 1990 involved a change in structure. Of a total cut in jobs of 19,000, 6,000 came from management ranks. Recently, BT has announced it also wanted to cut senior management jobs.

(c) Harley Davidson, in the US, cut the number of production controllers at one of its plants from 27 to 1.

Reasons for this trend are as follows.

(a) Information technology makes the information processing work of middle managers redundant.

(b) The trend towards team-working, whereby responsibility is devolved to groups of workers, renders redundant the directing and controlling role of middle managers.

Exam focus point

De-layering and downsizing were the subjects of a 20-mark theory question in May 1997. You had to describe what they were and why managers are adopting these approaches – the question hinted that cost cutting is one reason.

Homeworking and supervision

2.35 So far our discussion of span of control has implied that an individual is under the direct physical supervision of a manager or supervisor. Advances in communications technology have, for some tasks, reduced the need for the **actual presence of an individual in the office**. This is particularly true of tasks involving computers.

(a) The employee can, for example, do tasks involving data entry at home.

(b) The keyed-in data can be sent over a telecommunications link to head office.

(c) Some firms see benefits in employing the services of a pool of freelance workers, when there is a demand. This approach is being adopted in publishing and journalism.

2.36 This is sometimes known as homeworking (or, occasionally, telecommuting if it involves IT). The practice is not new in itself, but it is relatively new to the management of the office.

2.37 **Advantages to the organisation of homeworking**

(a) **Cost savings on space**. Office rental costs and other charges can be very expensive. If firms can move some of their employees on to a homeworking basis, money can be saved.

(b) **A larger pool of labour**. The possibility of working at home might attract more applicants for clerical positions, especially from people who have other demands on their time (eg ferrying children to and from school) which cannot be fitted around standard office hours.

(c) If the homeworkers are freelances, then the organisation **avoids the need to pay them** when there is insufficient work, when they are sick or on holiday.

2.38 **Advantages to the individual of homeworking**

(a) No time is wasted commuting to the office. Perhaps commuting time is more a problem of the congested metropolis of London than in some other areas, but commuting can often take up over two hours a day.

(b) The work can be organised flexibly around the individual's **domestic commitments** (eg school trips).

(c) Jobs which require **concentration** can sometimes be done better at home without the disruption of the office.

2.39 The problems for the organisation might superficially appear to be problems of control. Managers who practise close supervision will perhaps feel a worrying loss of control. Managers who take a pessimistic view of human nature might view homeworking as an opportunity for laziness and slack work.

2.40 However, these problems of control are partly illusory. Studies show that many people welcome homeworking. Instead, there may be other problems for the organisation.

(a) **Co-ordination** of the work of different homeworkers. The job design should ensure that homeworkers perform to the required standard.

(b) **Training**. If a homeworker needs a lot of help on a task, this implies that the task has not been properly explained.

(c) **Culture**. A homeworker is relatively isolated from the office and therefore, it might be assumed, from the firm. However, questions of loyalty and commitment do not apply for an organisation's sales force, whose members are rarely in the office. A freelance worker, however, cannot be expected to have the same loyalty as a permanent or part time employee who has at least some job security.

Outsourcing and management problems

2.41 Outsourcing has been adopted by many organisations, and it has implications for scalar chain and span of control. Let us take the example of office cleaning.

(a) In the past the office cleaners would have been recruited by the firm, and they would probably have reported to the person in charge of maintaining the physical structure of the building, who would have reported to an administration manager.

(b) With outsourcing arrangements, the chain of command is effectively broken. The firm has a contract with the external supplier, and therefore has no direct management control over the cleaning staff.

2.42 For functions such as cleaning (and catering), this causes few problems, although there are certain management issues.

(a) Someone has to manage and monitor the contract, to ensure that the firm supplying cleaning services keeps to the precise terms of the contract.

(b) Any breach requires compensation and disputes can easily end up in court. The firm cannot simply discipline the supplier's employee for poor performance. Managers save money but perhaps at the expense of operational flexibility.

2.43 For minor matters such as cleaning and catering the issues are very clear cut. However, government departments and local governments outsource a substantial proportion of their activities and so contract management becomes a major management task. The Inland Revenue, for example, has outsourced some of its IT operations.

3 LINE, STAFF AND FUNCTIONAL AUTHORITY

3.1 The technostructure, as we have seen, is involved in standardising work processes or outputs. But how is this authority exercised over the middle line and the operating core? When analysing the types of authority which a manager or a department may have, the terms **line**, **staff** and **functional** authority are often used.

KEY TERMS

Line authority is the authority a manager has over a subordinate.

Staff authority is the authority one manager or department may have in giving specialist advice to another manager or department, over which there is no line authority. Staff authority does not entail the right to make decisions in the advisee department or direct its activities.

Functional authority is a hybrid of line and staff authority, whereby a specialist staff manager or department has the authority, in certain circumstances, to direct activities or procedures. An example is where a finance manager has authority to require timely reports from, say, production managers. Functional authority is the way by which the technostructure **controls** operations, by enforcing standards.

3.2 This means that managers must know whether their authority is line, staff or functional to avoid confusion.

Question 2

What sort of authority is exercised:

(a) by the financial controller over the chief accountant?
(b) by the production manager over the production workforce?
(c) by the financial controller over the production manager?

Answer

(a) and (b) are both examples of line authority.
(c) is staff or perhaps functional authority.

3.3 In small organisations, most functions of the technostructure and support staff may be provided by external agencies: for example, a computer bureau may take on many data processing applications (eg payroll work). Owing to specialisation of work, there must be both middle line, a technostructure and support staff management within an organisation of any size, despite the trend to outsourcing.

3.4 **Too much authority to the technostructure** might have the following consequences.

(a) Technostructure managers sometimes have **divided loyalties** between their organisation and their speciality. Computer specialists, for example, might want to introduce the most up to date computer systems when these might not be the most appropriate for the organisation.

(b) Many expert managers have skills which can be marketed to other organisations, so that their career is not necessarily tied to one company. Middle line managers, on the other hand, might be trained exclusively for service in one company, or one type of company or organisation (eg a bank or the Civil Service). When specialist managers do not necessarily have a vested, long term interest in their organisation, it might be argued that their authority should be kept under restraint. However, keep in mind the concept of **systems goals**: a vested interest is not necessarily a good thing.

(c) Technostructure managers tend to introduce **rules and procedures** and these tend to increase the bureaucratic nature of the formal organisation. This might restrict a line manager's freedom of choice and flexibility.

(d) When an organisation has a **multi-divisional structure**, each subsidiary or division might have its own support functions. When there is a technostructure management at group level, divisional level and below divisional level, a further organisational problem is created because of overlapping interests, boundaries of authority and influence, and conflicting advice and opinions between the different levels of functional staff.

(e) When the technostructure builds up an **empire of influence and authority**, it may be difficult to measure the benefits to the organisation of various aspects of their work. The only way to restrict the growth of costly, unjustifiable staff work might be to appoint outside consultants from time to time to carry out a cost/benefit analysis of a staff department on behalf of senior management.

Implications of line and staff authority for organisational design

3.5 There are drawbacks to the power of the technostructure.

(a) There is a danger that experts in the technostructure may **undermine the authority** of line managers or even try to usurp it.

(b) **Friction** may occur when managers in the technostructure report to a higher authority in the scalar chain of command. For example, a management accountant may submit reports about the performance of a manager in the middle line to the production director or the managing director.

(c) Technostructure managers have little **responsibility** for what actually happens other than within their own area of expertise.

(d) The technostructure's ideas may be **unrealistic** and **impracticable**; line managers, having received poor advice from one staff expert, might tar all technostructure managers with the same brush and resist all future expert help.

3.6 The solutions to these problems are easily stated, but not easy to implement in practice.

(a) Authority must be clearly **defined**, and distinctions between line authority and staff advice clearly set out.

(b) Senior management must encourage managers in the middle line to make positive efforts to discuss work problems with the technostructure, and to be prepared to accept their advice.

(c) Managers in the technostructure must be fully informed about the **operational** aspects of the business. By providing them with detailed information they should be less likely to offer impractical advice.

(d) When expert advisers are used to plan and implement changes in the running of the business, they must be kept involved during the implementation, monitoring and review of the project. Specialists must be prepared to accept responsibility for their failures and this is only really possible if they advise during the implementation and monitoring stages.

Question 3

A large multinational firm of accountants provides audit, tax, and consultancy services. The firm has a strong Technical Department which designs standardised audit procedures. The firm has just employed a marketing manager who is held in high regard by the firm's senior partner. The marketing manager regards an audit as a 'product', part of the entire marketing mix including price (audit fees), place (usually on the client's premises) and promotion (advertising in professional journals). The marketing manager and the senior partner have unveiled a new strategic plan, drawn up in conditions of secrecy, which involves a tie-up with an advertising agency. The firm will be a 'one-stop shop' for business services and advice to management on any subject. Each client, or 'customer' will have a dedicated team of auditors, consultants and advertising executives. Obviously, a member of staff will be a member of a number of different teams.

In the light of what we have covered in this section, what do you think will be the organisational influences of the proposed strategy?

Answer

Accountants have divided loyalties - to their firm, and to their profession.

The Technical Department will almost certainly resist such a change, as the proposals devalue audit to being one of only many business services to management. An audit is undertaken for the benefit of shareholders, not the company management. The Technical Department (the firm's technostructure) is also powerful as enforcement of the standards it will suggest should reduce professional negligence costs. The technostructure will thus exert a powerful influence over strategy and business practices. External influences include professional associations which have a technostructural influence on the profession as a whole. (The marketing manager may also be misled as to the degree to which customers want a 'one-stop shop' for accounting and advertising services.)

4 THE INFORMAL ORGANISATION

4.1 An **informal organisation** exists side by side with the formal one in all organisations. When people work together, they establish **social relationships** and **customary ways of doing things**.

(a) They form social groups, or cliques (sometimes acting against one another).

(b) They develop **norms of behaviour** which are different in character from those imposed by the formal organisation.

4.2 Social groups, or cliques, may act collectively for or against the interests of their company; the like-mindedness which arises in all members of the group strengthens their collective attitudes or actions. Whether these groups work for or against the interests of the company depends to some extent on the **type of supervision** they get. If superiors involve them in decision-making, they are more likely to be management-minded.

4.3 The informal organisation of a company (given an acceptable social atmosphere) improves communications, facilitates co-ordination and establishes **unwritten methods for getting a job done**. These may bypass formal communication channels or lengthy procedures; they may be more flexible and adaptable to change than the formal ways of doing things.

4.4 Certain individuals can have an important informal influence in an organisation because of their **experience, skill or personal qualities**. These people can use their influence to support or undermine the efforts of the formal organisation.

4.5 The informal structure of a company may take over from the formal organisation when the formal structure is slow to adapt to change.

4.6 When employees are dissatisfied with aspects of formal organisation (if they dislike the work they do or the person they work for, say) they are likely to rely more and more heavily on an informal organisation at work to satisfy their **personal needs in their work situation**. When this happens the informal organisation will act against the efficiency of the formal organisation. If employees are properly motivated, the informal organisation should operate to the advantage of the formal organisation's efficiency and effectiveness.

4.7 A conclusion might therefore be that management should seek to **harness the informal organisation** to operate to the benefit of the formal organisation. In practice, however, this will be difficult because, unlike formal organisation, which does not change even when the individual employees move into and out of jobs (by promotion, transfer, appointment, resignation or retirement), most informal organisations depend on **individual personalities**. If one member leaves, the informal organisation is no longer the same, and new informal organisations will emerge to take its place.

Case example

The *Harvard Business Review* in July-August 1993 reported the significance of informal relationships.

- They are often reasons for high staff turnover.
- They indicate where people *actually* look for advice.
- They indicate who people trust.

A senior manager in a Californian-based computer company was having difficulty in getting staff to work together on a strategic plan. The co-ordinator on the task force could not get the others to work together because of his weak position on the 'trust network'. A replacement co-ordinator was then appointed who was more trusted by a wider group of people and who was able to get people to work together. Thus the senior manager exploited the informal organisation.

Informal communication channels

4.8 The formal pattern of communication in an organisation is always supplemented by an informal one, which is sometimes referred to as the grapevine. People like to gossip about rumours and events.

4.9 The danger with informal communication of this type is that it might be malicious, contain inaccurate rumour or half-truths, or simply be wild speculation. This type of gossip can be unsettling to people in an organisation, and make colleagues mistrust one another or act cautiously.

Chapter roundup

- Organisations exist to co-ordinate the activities of different individuals. Co-ordination can be achieved by mutual adjustment, direct supervision, standardisation of work processes, outputs, and skills and knowledge.

- An organisation can be analysed into five components: strategic apex, middle line, operating core, technostructure and support staff.

- These are linked by: formal hierarchies of authority, flows of regulated activity, informal communications, work groups, and decision processes.

- Formal organisation hierarchy is based on the principles of the scalar chain and span of control. There is a possible trend towards flatter organisations (fewer management levels and wider spans of control than hitherto).

- Line authority is the direct authority a superior has over a subordinate. Staff authority derives from the giving of specialist advice. Functional authority is the exercise of specialist advice. Functional authority is the exercise of staff authority through procedures, or the right by staff departments to require certain actions by line managers. The technostructure exercises staff and possibly functional authority over other parts of the organisation.

- The informal organisation is the system of personal and 'political' relationships in an organisation, outside the normal hierarchy.

Quick quiz

1 What principles does Mintzberg suggest underlie organisations?

2 Describe the five component parts of an organisation.

3 What is scalar chain?

4 What are the arguments in favour of and against tall organisations.

5 Give three factors which influence span of control

6 What is functional authority?

7 What are the drawbacks to the power of the technostructure?

8 What is the informal organisation?

Answers to quick quiz

1 Job specialisation, behaviour formalisation, training, indoctrination, unit grouping, unit size, planning and control systems, liaison devices, decentralisation.

2 The operating core converts inputs into outputs. The strategic apex provides strategic control and boundary management. The middle line is the hierarchy of authority between the strategic apex and the operating core. The technostructure standardises work of all types. The support staff provide ancillary services.

3 Scalar chain is the hierarchical structure which links the organisation from top to bottom.

4 A tall organisation implies small spans of control and therefore closer supervision; this allows for less skilled workers or enables more complex work to be done and can improve control. Many levels of management offer opportunities for career development. On the other hand, a flat organisation, with wide spans of control leads to greater delegation of authority, which increases job satisfaction and motivation and which may make the organisation more responsive to change. Tall organisations are more expensive in management costs and can suffer from poor communication.

5 The extent of the manager's other responsibilities; the degree of geographical dispersion, the nature and complexity of the subordinates' work; subordinates' abilities; the degree of group cohesion needed; the amount of input from staff functions.

6 The authority exercised by managers outside their own departments over matters for which they are responsible.

7 Divided loyalty between the organisation and the speciality; possible lack of long-term commitment; proliferation of rules and procedures; conflict in multi-divisional organisations between the divisional technostructures; empire-building.

8 The informal relationships, customs, communication links, groups and norms of behaviour which exist alongside the formal structure.

Chapter 7

ORGANISATION DESIGN

Topic List	Syllabus Reference	Ability required
1 Structural configurations: Mintzberg	(ii)	Evaluation
2 Design of the formal hierarchy: departmentation	(i)	Evaluation
3 Multifocused hierarchies: hybrid and matrix designs	(i), (ii)	Evaluation
4 Designs for global businesses	(i), (ii)	Evaluation
5 Mechanistic and organic structures	(ii)	Evaluation
6 Influences on organisation structure	(ii)	Evaluation

Introduction

Chapter 6 described general principles of organisation theory and design. This chapter goes on to discuss how some of these principles can be applied, in terms of the different approaches to organisation hierarchy, and the forces that the different organisational components exert over its structure, management and mechanisms of co-ordination.

By the end of this chapter you should understand the following.

(a) Each of the component parts of the organisation exerts a 'pull' to a particular organisational *configuration* (eg the technostructure exerts a pull to a machine bureaucracy).

(b) The departments in an organisation can be structured according to the work specialism, geography, product etc.

(c) The influence of the environment on the organisation, and the extent to which the organisation's components integrate with each other or become more differentiated from each other, are elements of the contingency approach.

(d) The differences between organic and mechanistic organisations: mechanistic organisations are characterised by hierarchy. Organic organisations are more flexible.

Learning outcomes covered in this chapter

- Analyse a range of organisations, identifying their component parts, the relationships between those parts and any problems with those relationships.

- Recommend and evaluate changes to the structure of organisations.

- Explain trends in the general management and structure of organisations.

Syllabus content covered in this chapter

- The different structures which might be adopted by a business organisation and how the various components of those structures inter-relate (i.e. entrepreneurial, functional, divisional, matrix, network, complex).

1   STRUCTURAL CONFIGURATIONS: MINTZBERG

1.1   *Henry Mintzberg's* theory of organisational configuration is a way of expressing the main features by which both formal structure and power relationships are expressed in organisations. These were identified in Chapter 6.

1.2   Mintzberg has written that there are five ideal types of organisation, each of which configures the five components above in a significantly different way. Why should this be so?

1.3   Mintzberg believes that each component of the organisation has its own **dynamic**, which **leads to a distinct type of organisation**.

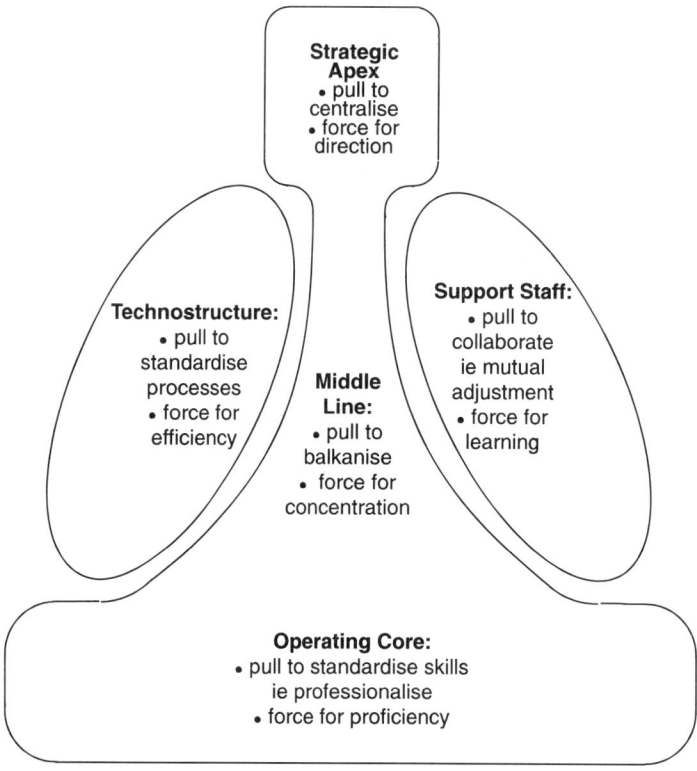

(a)   The **strategic apex** wishes to retain control over decision-making. An example is a manager's refusal to delegate. A more direct example is the decision-making structure in a dictatorship, where power is closely controlled at the centre. It achieves this when the co-ordinating mechanism is **direct supervision**. The force this most relates to is the **force for direction** (in other words for the need for people to be told what to do).

(b)   The **technostructure's** reason for existence is the design of **procedures** and **standards**. For example, the preparation of accounts is highly regulated. This acts as a **force for efficiency**.

(c)   The members of the **operating core** seek to minimise the control of administrators over what they do. They prefer to work autonomously, achieving what other co-ordination is necessary by **mutual adjustment**. As professionals, they rely on outside training (such as medical training) to standardise skills. This corresponds to the **force for proficiency**.

(d)   The managers of the **middle line** seek to increase their **autonomy** from the strategic apex, and to increase their control over the operating core, so that they can concentrate on their own segment of the market or with their own products. This corresponds to the **force for concentration** (on individual product areas).

(e) **Support staff** only gain influence when their expertise is vital. **Mutual adjustment** is the co-ordinating mechanism. This corresponds to the **force for learning**.

The **forces for co-operation and competition** largely determine how these elements relate to each other.

The simple structure (or entrepreneurial structure)

1.4 The **strategic apex** wishes to retain control over decision-making, and so exercises what Mintzberg describes as a **pull to centralise**. Mintzberg believes that this leads to a **simple structure**.

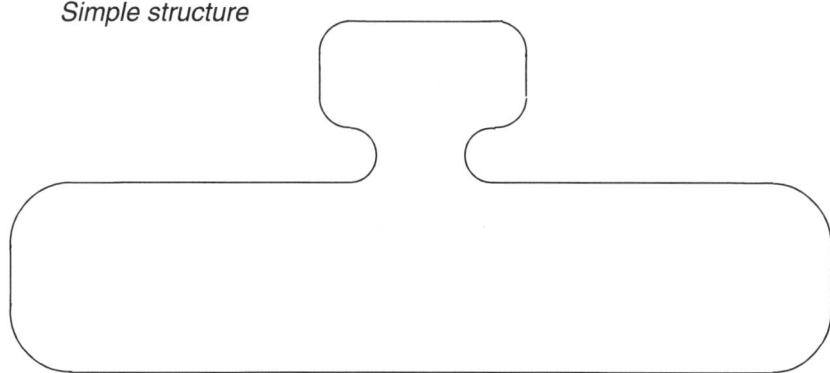

Simple structure

(a) **The simple structure is characteristic of small, young organisations**.

(b) In small firms, a single entrepreneur or management team will dominate (as in the power culture). If it grows, the organisation might need more managerial skills than the apex can provide. Strategies might be made on the basis of the manager's hunches.

(c) Centralisation is advantageous as it reflects management's full knowledge of the operating core and its processes. However, senior managers might intervene too much.

(d) It is risky as it depends on the expertise of one person. Such an organisation might be prone to **succession crises**. Who takes over if the boss dies? This problem is often encountered in family businesses.

(e) This structure can handle an environment that is relatively simple but fast moving, where standardisation cannot be used to co-ordinate activities.

(f) **Co-ordination is achieved by direct supervision,** with few formal devices. It is thus flexible.

(g) This structure has its own particular characteristics : wide span of control; no middle line and hence minimal hierarchy; and no technostructure, implying little formalisation or standardisation of behaviour.

The machine bureaucracy

1.5 The **technostructure** exerts a pull for standardisation of work processes. It creates a **machine bureaucracy**.

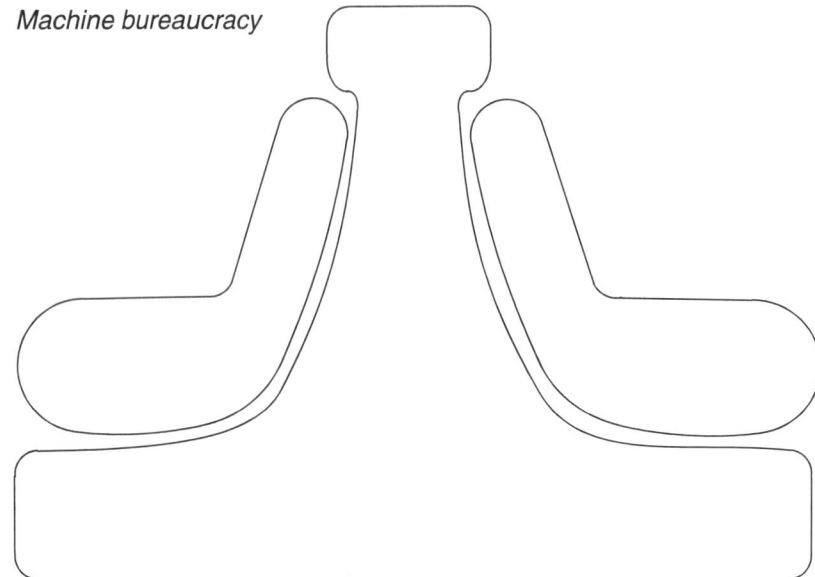

Machine bureaucracy

(a) This is the classic bureaucracy, working on a sophisticated and well-tuned set of **rules and procedures**. Machine bureaucracies are associated with routine technical systems and repetitive tasks. The bureaucracy can function if people leave, as jobs are designed precisely.

(b) **The technostructure is the key part**. Power rests with analysts who standardise other people's work. The key management philosophy is **scientific management**.

(c) The work of the operating core is highly standardised. Direct supervision by the strategic apex is limited as **standardisation of work processes ensures co-ordination**.

(d) There is a strong emphasis on the **division of labour**, and in particular **on control**. Uncertainty has to be eliminated. The elaborate middle line monitors and directs the operating core. Outsourcing would be embraced reluctantly so the firm employs its own legal and PR specialists. (For example, many big firms have a central legal department.)

(e) Formal communication is most important. Authority is hierarchical.

(f) Conflict is rife between different departments, between line and staff, and between operating core and management.

(g) The environment must be simple and stable.

(h) The machine bureaucracy is the most efficient structure for integrating sets of simple and repetitive tasks.

(i) Machine bureaucracies cannot adapt rapidly they are designed for specialised purposes. They are driven by performance, not problem solving.

The professional bureaucracy

1.6 The **operating core** has a pull for standardisation, not of work processes but of **individual skills**. A machine bureaucracy would lay down exactly how financial transactions should be posted, whether people understood them or not. A **professional bureaucracy** would employ accountants who should know what is involved. The operating core seeks to minimise the influence of administrators (mainly the middle line and technostructure) over work. Examples are hospitals and accountancy firms.

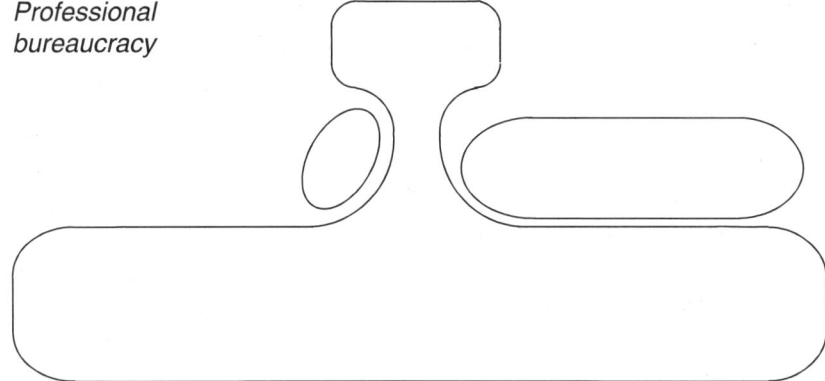

Professional bureaucracy

(a) It hires trained specialists who are all imbued with the skills and values of the profession. A school is an example. Teachers' work in the classroom is not directly supervised but all teachers are trained.

(b) **Co-ordination is achieved by standardisation of skills**, which originate outside its structure. (Teacher training occurs at independent colleges.)

(c) **Power is often based on expertise**, not formal position in the organisation hierarchy.

(d) Work processes are **too complex** to be standardised by a technostructure.

(e) The **operating core** is the key part. There is an elaborate support staff to service it. A technostructure might exist for budgeting, but not for designing work processes.

(f) Work is decentralised. **Professionals control their own work**, and seek collective control over the administrative decisions which affect them.

(g) There might be **two** organisation hierarchies: one, relatively informal, for the operating core doing the work; another, more formal for the support staff. An example is a barristers' chambers. Barristers are co-ordinated by the Clerk, but they retain collective authority over the clerk. The clerk, on the other hand, will exercise direct control over secretarial services.

(h) Professional administrators also manage much of the organisation's boundary.

(i) It can be democratic.

(j) The professional bureaucracy cannot always cope with any variations of standards, as control is exercised through training.

The divisional form (or diversified form)

1.7 The middle line seeks as much autonomy for itself as possible. It exerts a **pull to balkanise** (ie to split into small self-managed units). The result is the **divisional form**, by which autonomy is given to managers lower down the line. The prime co-ordinating mechanism is **standardisation of outputs**: these are usually performance measures such as profit, which are set by the strategic apex.

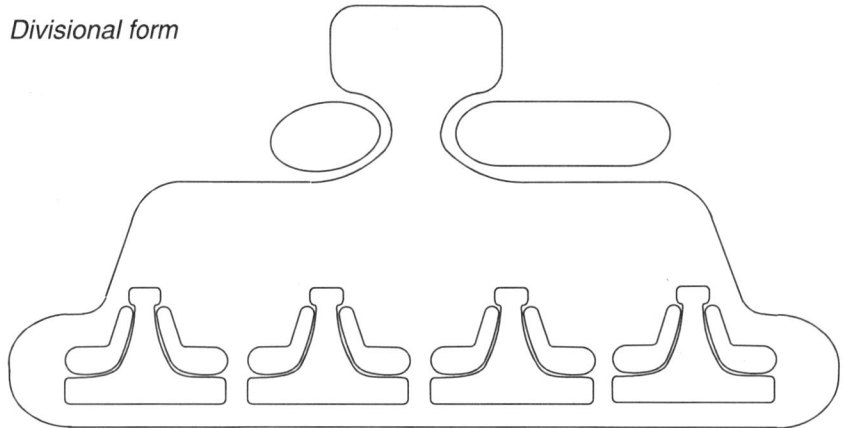

Divisional form

(a) Divisionalisation is the division of a business into **autonomous regions** or product businesses, each with its own revenues, expenditures and profits.

(b) Because each division is monitored by its objective performance towards a single integrated set of goals determined by the strategic apex, **each division is configured as a machine bureaucracy**.

(c) Communication between divisions and head office is restricted, formal and related to performance standards. Influence is maintained by headquarters' power to hire and fire the managers who are supposed to run each division.

(d) Divisionalisation is a function of organisation size, in numbers and in product-market activities.

1.8 Mintzberg believes there are **inherent problems in divisionalisation**.

(a) A division is partly **insulated** by the holding company from shareholders and capital markets, which ultimately reward performance.

(b) It 'piggybacks on the machine bureaucracy in a simple stable environment, and may feel drawn back to that form'.

(c) The economic advantages it offers over independent organisations 'reflect fundamental inefficiencies in capital markets'. (In other words, different product-market divisions might function better as independent companies.)

(d) The divisions are **more bureaucratic** than they would be as independent corporations, owing to the performance measures imposed by the strategic apex.

(e) Big companies bring a threat to competitive markets.

(f) Headquarters management have a tendency to **usurp divisional profits** by management charges, cross-subsidies, head office bureaucracies and unfair transfer pricing systems.

(g) In some businesses, it is impossible to identify completely independent products or markets for which divisions would be appropriate.

(h) Divisionalisation is only possible at a fairly senior management level, because there is a limit to how much independence in the division of work can be arranged.

(i) It is a halfway house, relying on personal control over performance by senior managers and enforcing cross-subsidisation.

(j) Divisional performance is not directly assessed by the market.

(k) Many of the problems of divisionalisation are those of **conglomerate diversification**. Each business might be better run independently than with the others. The different businesses might offer different returns for different risks which shareholders might prefer to judge independently.

1.9 The multi-divisional structure might be implemented in one of two forms.

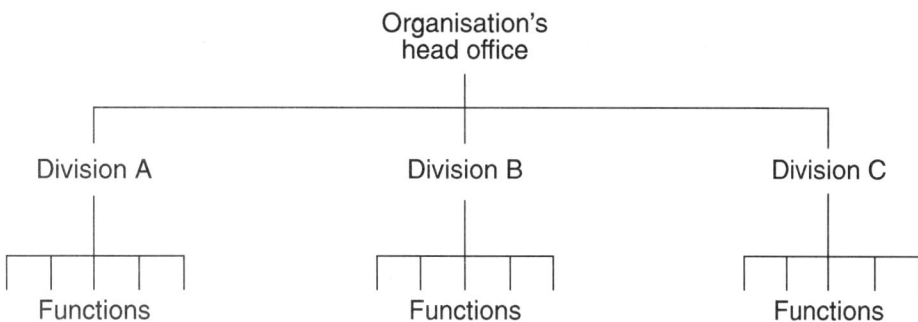

This enables concentration on particular product-market areas, overcoming problems of functional specialisation at a large scale. Problems arise with the power of the head office, and control of the resources. Responsibility is devolved, and some central functions might be duplicated.

1.10 The holding company (group) structure is a radical form of divisionalisation. **Subsidiaries are separate legal entities**. The holding company can be a firm with a permanent investment or one which buys and sells businesses.

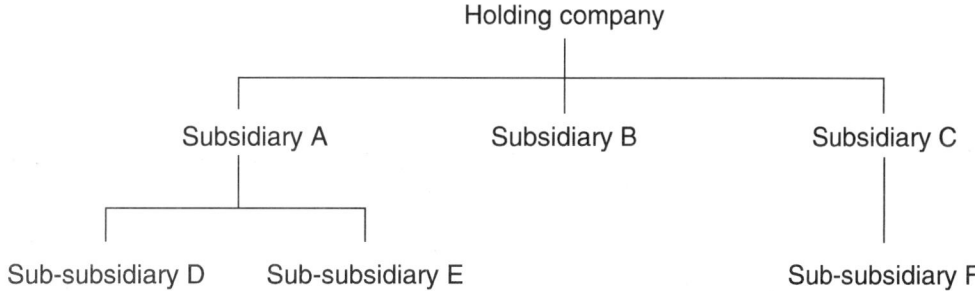

1.11 Divisionalisation has some advantages, despite the problems identified above.

(a) It focuses the attention of subordinate management on business performance and results.

(b) Management by objectives can be applied more easily. 'The manager of the unit knows better than anyone else how he is doing, and needs no one to tell him'.

(c) It gives more authority to junior managers, and therefore provides them with work which grooms them for more senior positions in the future.

(d) It tests junior managers in independent command early in their careers, and at a reasonably low level in the management hierarchy.

(e) It provides an organisation structure which reduces the number of levels of management. The top executives in each divisions should be able to report direct to the chief executive of the holding company.

BPP PUBLISHING

1.12 **Rules for successful divisionalisation.**

(a) Divisional management should be free to use their authority to do what they think is right for their part of the organisation, but they must be held properly accountable to head office (eg for profits earned).

(b) A division must be large enough to support the quantity and quality of management it needs. It must not rely on head office for excessive management support.

(c) Each division must have a potential for growth in its own area of operations.

(d) There should be scope and challenge in the job for the management of the division.

(e) Division should exist side by side with each other. If they deal with each other, it should be as an arm's length transaction. Where they touch, it should be in competition with each other. There should be no insistence on preferential treatment to be given to a 'fellow unit' by another unit of the overall organisation.

The adhocracy

1.13 The **support staff** exert a pull of their own, towards **collaboration**. The **adhocracy** does not rely on standardisation to co-ordinate its activities, yet it is much more complex than the simple structure which also does not use standardisation.

Adhocracy

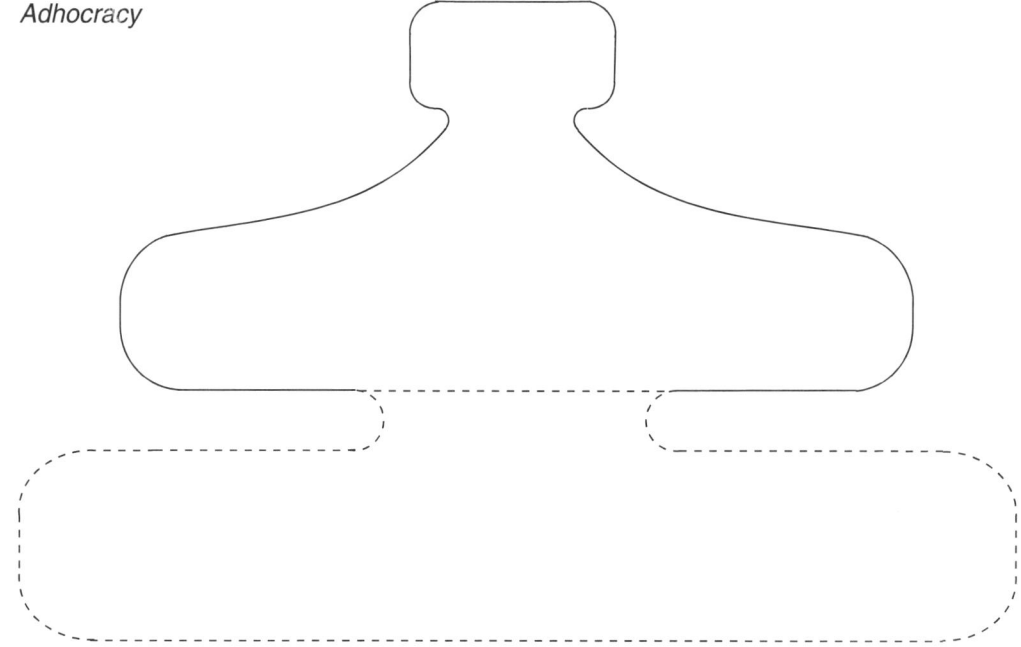

(a) The adhocracy is **complex and disorderly**. There is little formalisation of behaviour. Specialists are deployed in market-based project teams which group together and disperse as and when a project arises and ends. Co-ordination is informal, by mutual adjustment.

(b) The adhocracy relies on the expertise of its members, **but not through standardised skills**. Instead, the *mix* of skills is important. For example, a film is made by a director, actors, camera people, set designers and so on.

(c) A matrix structure might exist, but there are a large number of management roles such as project managers. Managers do not plan or supervise, but co-ordinate.

(d) Decision-making power depends on the type of decision and the situation in which it is made, rather than level in hierarchy. 'No-one ... monopolises the power to innovate'.

(e) Strategy is hard to determine in the adhocracy. It depends partly on the projects that come along (like a film studio). The strategic apex does not *formulate* strategies, but is engaged in battles over strategic *choices* (eg which films shall we make?) and liaisons with the outside parties.

(f) The adhocracy is positioned in a dynamic and complex environment.

(g) The adhocracy is driven to bureaucratise itself as it ages. The organisation will eventually **specialise in what it does best**, driving it to more stable environmental conditions and predictable work processes, leading perhaps to a professional bureaucracy.

1.14 The adhocracy is concerned with **innovation**.

(a) The **operating adhocracy** seeks to **innovate** to serve its clients, whereas the professional bureaucracy seeks perfection. (Mintzberg uses an analogy of a theatre company. An adhocratic theatre company produces new plays. A professional bureaucratic one would seek to produce ever more perfect renditions of Shakespeare.) The operating core is retained.

(b) The **administrative adhocracy** innovates to serve its **own convenience**. Note that the operating core is split off, frequently subcontracted or automated, or even forms a separate organisation. The support staff are important, a central pool of expert talent from which project teams are drawn.

1.15 Adhocracies sometimes exist because the complexity of their technical systems require a trained support staff to operate them.

(a) The adhocracy is an ambiguous environment for work. This elicits complex human responses, as many people dislike ambiguity.

(b) The adhocracy is not suitable for **standardised** work; it is better at dealing with unique projects.

(c) It has a high cost of communication, and workloads are unbalanced.

Concluding thoughts

1.16 The usefulness of Mintzberg's theory of structural configuration is that it covers many issues, over and above formal organisation structure.

- The type of work the organisation does (customised or standardised)
- The complexity it has to deal with (simple or complex)
- The environment (stable or dynamic)

We can summarise some of these in the table below.

BPP
PUBLISHING

Configuration	Co-ordination mechanism	Key part	Environment? (see Ch 6)	Possible characteristics
Simple	Direct supervision	Strategic apex	Simple/dynamic (even hostile)	Small, young, centralised, personality-driven. Crisis of leadership
Machine bureaucracy	Standardised work processes	Techno-structure	Simple/stable	Old, large, rule-bound, specialised
Professional bureaucracy	Standardised skills	Operating core	Complex/stable	Decentralised, emphasis on training
Divisional form	Standardised outputs	Middle line	Varies; each division is shielded to a degree	Old, large, divisions are quasi-autonomous, decentralised, bureaucratic
Adhocracy	Mutual adjustment	Support staff	Complex/ dynamic	Innovative, disorderly

1.17 Mintzberg mentions one other co-ordinating factor: **mission. A missionary organisation** is one welded together by ideology or culture. There is job rotation, standardisation of values (*norms*) and little external control (eg like a religious sect). This relates to ideology, the **force for co-operation**.

1.18 As a cautionary note, these 'ideal types do not exist as such; they are **simplified models of real organisations**: most contain elements of all types.'

Exam focus point

Be on the alert for ambiguities in the question. The word 'configuration' refers to Mintzberg's analysis above. The word 'form' might be interpreted as configuration or in terms of the departmentation approaches discussed in the next section. This confusion was evident in November 1995.

Question 1

Joan Porely has recently been appointed general manager of a prestigious eye hospital in the UK. Together with the most senior eye surgeon in the hospital, Dr Iris Glass, she is touring the world to find examples of best practice not only in surgical procedures and medical technology but also in the organisation of the hospital's work. In their travels, they visit the St Petersburg Research Institute of Eye Microsurgery. This is run by Doctor Fyodr Sviatorov, and has become a multi-million pound business. This hospital has pioneered the use of surgery to correct sight defects like short-sightedness. An operation is typically performed as follows.

1   The patient receives an anaesthetic outside the operating theatre, and lies down on a conveyor belt which takes the patient into the operating theatre.

2   A computer calculates the depth of the cuts to the cornea of the eye.

3   Surgeon A marks exactly the depth and lengths of the cuts.

4   Surgeon B makes between eight and sixteen cuts with a diamond scalpel

5   Surgeon C adjusts the cut to ensure maximum eyesight gain.

6   Surgeon D cleans and dresses all the wounds.

7   A doctor administers any necessary antibiotics.

About 200 patients per day can be processed on this conveyor belt system. Doctor Sviatorov says: 'The important thing is to make sure you know what you're doing in advance, and for the sort of standard operation that we do, that's quite easy. We employ senior surgeons, myself included, to design the operation process. They scour the medical press for any new techniques which our surgeons in the theatres can be trained to use: we try to minimise the discretion they can use so they can concentrate on accuracy. One day, I'd be happy to use robots to do all the dirty work. But still, I'm hoping to set up satellite hospitals in Minsk and Kiev. Even in the West one day!'

Doctor Glass is curious. She says: 'I think this system has some uses. But it stifles individual initiative and professional judgement, especially in more complex operations. You need professionally qualified surgeons who are able to oversee all aspects of an operation. And what if something goes wrong on this production line? And I do not doubt that we in London can be just as productive if we had proper administrative support and technical backup. I feel compelled to add that I have my doubts as to the long term safety and suitability of surgery on eyes to correct standard problems like short-sightedness. Glasses and contact lenses are cheaper and safer. I'm not sure how I could justify it in terms of medical ethics, either. After all, we want to help people, not make money out of them.'

Joan Porely is impressed with the work, especially as it makes a profit for the hospital: she has already been looking at ways to improve her hospital's financial position. Such a unit in London, she feels, could attract patients from all over Europe, the Middle East, and even North America, and this quick operation could even be sold, as Doctor Sviatorov has suggested, as part of a package holiday. ('It brings a whole new dimension to sightseeing,' he says.)

Required

Analyse the above case in the light of Mintzberg's theory of structural configurations and organisation goals.

Answer

Although the details of this case seem far-fetched, the description of the conveyor belt approach to simple eye surgery is based on fact. Such techniques are practised by the Moscow Research Institute of Microsurgery, run by Professor Sviatoslav Fiodorov. Buchanan and Huczynski *(Organisational Behaviour)* note that: 'Foreigners can buy an operation package holiday, operation included, for £2,000 for a two-week stay. Professor Fiodorov is planning to replace the surgeons on his assembly line with robots'.

Mintzberg's theory of structural configurations holds that an organisation can be analysed into five components.

(a) *An operating core* is where the work is carried out. In the case of the St Petersburg Research Institute the operating core consists of the following.

   (i)   The doctors who carry out the initial diagnosis, who conduct the eye tests to see the deficiency that needs to be corrected and to check for any other complaints that might make the treatment dangerous (this you could have inferred from the data).

   (ii)   The anaesthetist.

   (iii) Surgeons A, B, C and D who carry out the operation.

   (iv) The doctor who administers antibiotics at the end.

   (v)   Any ancillary nursing staff, hospital cleaners, cooks etc.

   (vi) The computer, which calculates the cut, is a vital component of the process. However, the operating core is by no means entirely automated so it is not an administrative adhocracy.

(b) The *strategic apex*. Doctor Sviatorov set up the hospital and has plans for its expansion. He is responsible for strategic decision making.

(c) The *middle line* is not described in the case: the work is heavily planned, but Doctor Sviatorov probably has deputies to deal with administrative matters (eg receiving bookings from the patients, purchasing supplies.)

(d) The *technostructure* does not manage the work of the operating core, but it designs the work process. The speed of the conveyor belt, the programming of the computer, the exact sequence of cuts to be made and so forth are all determined in advance, by technicians who have designed the safest and most economical sequence of movements.

(e) *Support staff* provide ancillary functions, such as legal advice, public relations and so forth. If Doctor Sviatorov wants to expand in the West, he will need a good support staff to win over the approval of people such as Doctor Glass, before such procedures are allowed to be imported by other countries.

With Mintzberg's categorisation, we can easily outline the differing approaches taken by Doctor Glass and Doctor Sviatorov.

(a) Most hospitals, according to Mintzberg, are professional bureaucracies. In other words, the doctors and surgeons generally speaking decide how the work is to be done. Their professional training gives them the necessary expertise. Their work is not managed like the work, say, of a factory. In the past, hospitals in the UK were often run by committees of the medical staff. Doctor Glass's hospital, or her ideal of it, sounds like a professional bureaucracy, even though the appointment of a general manager who is not a doctor means a change.

(b) Doctor Sviatorov's hospital appears more like a machine bureaucracy, in that for some of the work at least, the procedures are standardised to the extent that surgeons can be replaced by robots. The design of the work process is out of the hands of those who carry it out. However, professional specialists will be the designers, so they have a doctor's normal skill and training. This is quite an unusual configuration for a hospital. It could not be generally applied, as most hospital operations are more complex than the simple sequence of cuts that the eye operation needs.

---

2 DESIGN OF THE FORMAL HIERARCHY: DEPARTMENTATION

KEY TERM

Departmentation: the division of an organisation into departments.

2.1 As an organisation grows in size, it employs more people and is able to specialise.

(a) It is able to take advantage of economies of scale, which in turn may call for the establishment of departments of specialist or experts (eg research and development, management scientists).

(b) The number of levels in the organisation hierarchy increases, so that problems of delegation of authority and control arise.

(c) Specialist support teams (eg service and maintenance, quality control, corporate planning, organisation and methods, data processing) are created to ease the burdens and complexities of line management. Such support teams need to be slotted into the hierarchical structure.

(d) Separate groups and departments continue to be formed as specialisation extends; new problems of communication and co-ordination (or integration) now arise.

2.2 The creation of departments is known as **departmentation**. Different patterns of departmentation are possible, and the pattern selected will depend on the individual circumstances of the organisation. Various methods of departmentation are described below.

Geographic departmentation

2.3 Some authority is retained at Head Office (organised, perhaps, on a functional basis) but day-to-day service operations are handled on a territorial basis. Within many sales departments, the sales staff are organised territorially.

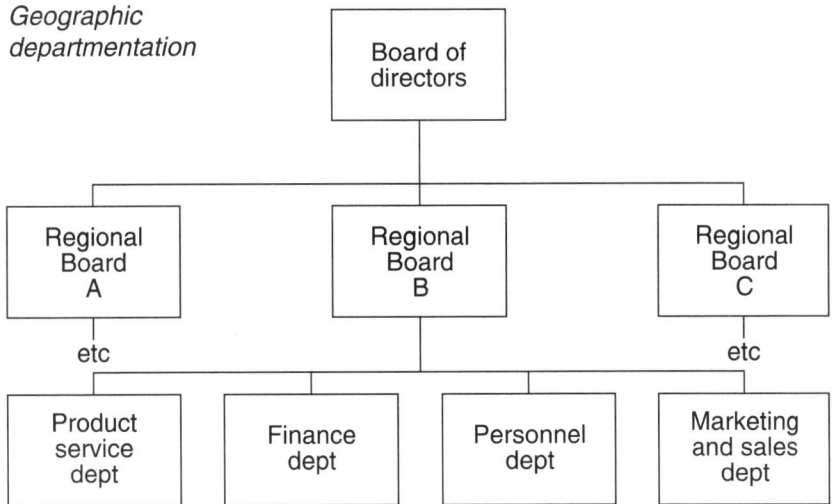

2.4 Advantages of geographic departmentation

(a) Better and quicker local decision making at the point of contact between the organisation (eg a salesman) and its customers.

(b) It may be less costly to establish area factories/offices than to run everything centrally (eg costs of transportation and travelling may be reduced).

(c) It might be essential for overseas operations.

2.5 The **disadvantage** of geographic departmentation is the duplication of management effort. For example, a national organisation divided into ten regions might have a customer liaison department in each regional office. If the organisation did all customer liaison work from head office it might need fewer managerial staff.

Functional departmentation

2.6 Functional organisation means that departments are defined by their **functions,** that is, the work that they do. It is a traditional, common sense approach and many organisations are structured like this. Primary functions in a manufacturing company might be production, sales, finance, and general administration. Sub-departments of marketing might be selling, advertising, distribution and warehousing.

2.7 Advantages of functional departmentation

- It is based on work specialism and is therefore logical.
- The firm can benefit from economies of scale.
- It offers a career structure.

2.8 Disadvantages

- It does not reflect the actual business processes by which **value is created**.
- It is hard to identify where profits and losses are made on individual products.
- People do not have an understanding of how the *whole* business works.
- There are problems of co-ordinating the work of different specialisms.

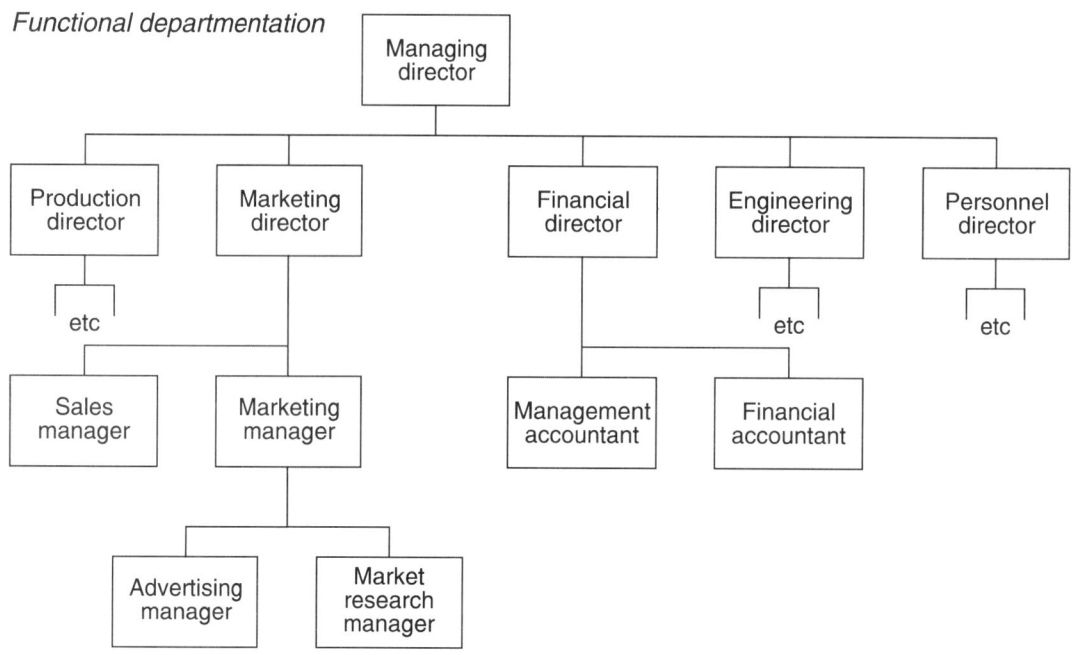

Functional departmentation

Product/brand departmentation

2.9 **Product.** Some organisations group activities on the basis of products or product lines. Some functional departmentation remains (eg manufacturing, distribution, marketing and sales) but a divisional manager is given responsibility for the product or product line, with authority over personnel of different functions.

2.10 **Advantages of product departmentation**

(a) Individual managers can be held accountable for the **profitability** of individual products.

(b) Specialisation can be developed. For example, some salesmen will be trained to sell a specific product in which they may develop technical expertise and thereby offer a better sales service to customers. Service engineers who specialise in a single product should also provide a better after sales service.

(c) The different functional activities and efforts required to make and sell each product can be co-ordinated and integrated by the divisional/product manager.

(d) It should be focused on how a business makes its profits.

2.11 The **disadvantage of product departmentation** is that it increases the overhead costs and managerial complexity of the organisation.

2.12 **Brand.** A brand is the name (eg 'Persil') or design which identifies the products or services of a manufacturer or provider and distinguishes them from those of competitors. Large organisations may produce a number of different brands of the same basic product, such as washing powder or toothpaste. This is viable because branding brings the product to the attention of buyers and creates brand loyalty - often the customers do not realise that two rival brands are in fact produced by the same manufacturer.

(a) Because branding is linked with unique marketing positions it becomes necessary to have brand departmentation. As with product departmentation, some functional departmentation remains (especially on the manufacturing side) but brand managers have responsibility for the brand's marketing and this can affect every function.

(b) Brand departmentation has similar advantages and disadvantages to product departmentation. In particular, overhead costs and complexity of the management structure are increased, the relationships of a number of different brand departments with the manufacturing department, if there is only one, being particularly difficult.

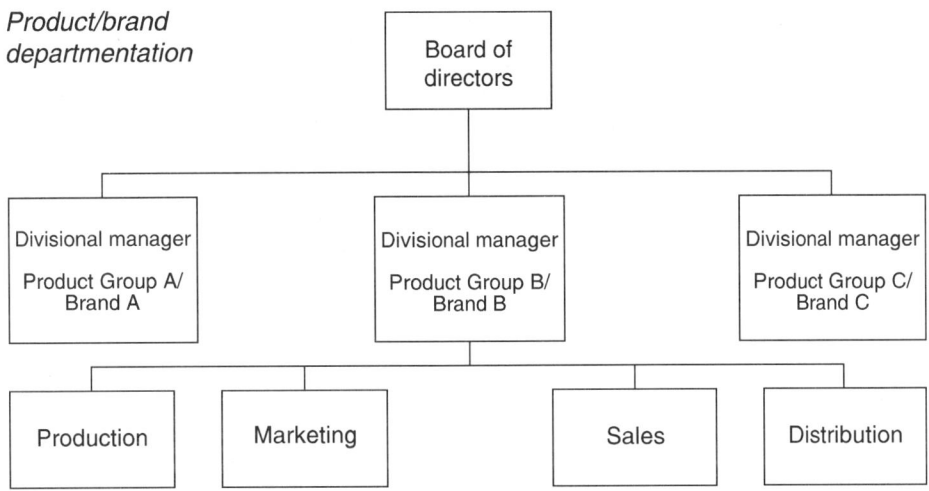

Customer or market segment departmentation

2.13 **Customer or market segment**

(a) A manufacturing organisation may sell goods through wholesalers, export agents and by direct mail. It may therefore organise its sales, marketing and distribution functions on the basis of types of customer, or market segment. Departmentation by customer is commonly associated with sales departments and selling effort, but it might also be used by a jobbing or contracting firm where a team of managers may be given the responsibility of liaising with major customers.

(b) Another example is where firms distinguish between domestic consumers and business customers, with a different marketing and supply efforts for each.

Divisionalisation

2.14 **Divisionalisation** is the division of a very large enterprise into **autonomous** segments, each with its own revenues, expenditures and capital asset purchase programmes, and therefore each with its own profit and loss responsibility. Divisions of the organisation might be subsidiary companies under the holding company or profit or investment centres within a single company. Divisionalisation was discussed in Section 1 of this chapter.

3   MULTIFOCUSED HIERARCHIES: HYBRID AND MATRIX DESIGNS

3.1 Many organisation hierarchies in practice combine elements of a number of these approaches. In the example below, research and development is centrally organised, but the operating activities of the firm are geographically arranged. This is an example of a **hybrid structure**.

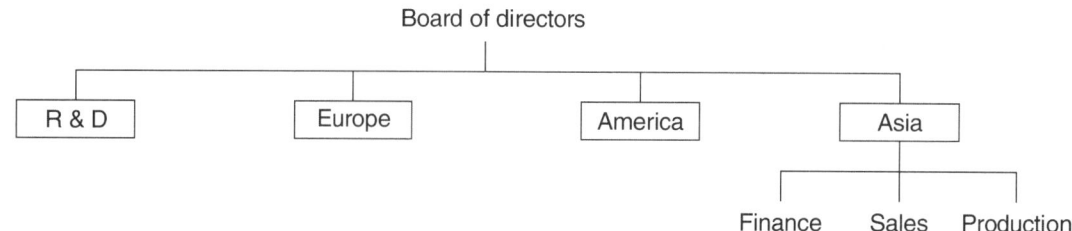

3.2 Another example is given below. R&D, human resources and finance are centralised functions: other activities are arranged on a product basis.

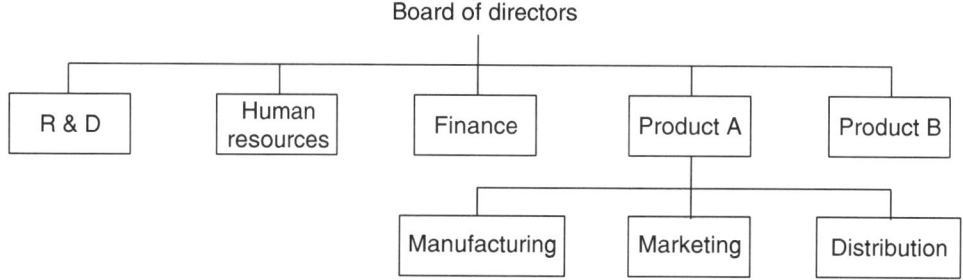

3.3 Most organisations contain features of the hybrid structure.

(a) Certain business activities are better arranged or centralised on a **functional basis** for reasons of **economies of scale,** and pooling of knowledge and efficiency (eg R&D).

(b) Other activities are best organised on a **product or territorial basis,** with the particular advantages of **specialisation, local knowledge,** and **flexibility** (eg marketing).

Question 2

The Erewhon Bank plc has branches in the UK, Eire, France, Germany and Denmark. It grew from the merger of a number of small local banks in these countries. These local banks were not large enough to compete single-handedly in their home markets. The Erewhon Bank hopes to attract both retail and corporate customers, through its use of home banking services and its heavily advertised Direct Bank service, which is a branchless bank to which customers telephone, fax or post their instructions. The bank also specialises in providing foreign currency accounts, and has set up a revolutionary service whereby participating customers can settle their own business transactions in Euros.

What sort of organisation structure do you think would be appropriate?

Answer

Although some of the technical details of the products described might have appeared daunting, you should have realised that the bank basically serves two markets, the personal sector and the corporate sector. However, you would perhaps be ill advised to organise the bank *solely* on that basis. Why?

(a) The banking needs of customers in the personal sector are likely to be quite distinct. This market is naturally segmented geographically. Users of the telephone banking service, for example, will want to speak in their own language. Also, despite the Single European Market, the competitive environment of financial services is likely to be different in each country (eg credit cards are widely used in France, but hardly used at all in Germany).

For the personal sector, a geographic organisation would be appropriate, although with the centralisation of common administrative and account processing functions and technological expertise, so that the bank gains from scale economies and avoids wasteful duplication.

(b) For the corporate sector, different considerations apply. If the bank is providing sophisticated foreign currency accounts, these will be of most benefit to multi-nationals or companies which regularly export from, or import to, their home markets. A geographical organisation structure may not be appropriate, and arguably the bank's organisation should be centralised on a Europe wide basis, with the country offices, of course, at a lower level.

Matrix and project organisation

3.4 Matrix organisation is a structure which provides for the formalisation of management control between different functions, whilst at the same time maintaining functional departmentation. It can be a mixture of a functional, product and territorial organisation.

3.5 A golden rule of classical management theory is **unity of command**: an individual should have one boss. (Thus, staff management can only act in an advisory capacity, leaving authority in the province of line management alone.) Matrix and project organisation may possibly be thought of as a reaction against the classical form of bureaucracy by establishing a structure of **dual command** either temporary (in the form of projects) or permanent (in the case of matrix structure).

Projects

3.6 A project normally has a defined task. Many projects are interdisciplinary, and might require, for instance the contributions of an engineer, a scientist, a statistician and a production expert, who would be appointed to the team while retaining membership and status within their own functional department.

(a) Members of the project team would provide formal lateral lines of communication and authority, superimposed on the functional departmental structure.

(b) Project teams are, essentially, temporary arrangements.

Matrix organisation

Case example

Matrix management first developed in the 1950s in the USA in the aerospace industry. Lockheed-California, the aircraft manufacturers, were organised in a functional hierarchy. Customers were unable to find a manager in Lockheed to whom they could take their problems and queries about their particular orders, and Lockheed found it necessary to employ 'project expediters' as customer liaison officials. From this developed *project co-ordinators*, responsible for co-ordinating line managers into solving a customer's problems. Up to this point, these new officials had no functional responsibilities.

Owing to increasingly heavy customer demands, Lockheed eventually created 'programme managers', with authority for project budgets and programme design and scheduling. These managers therefore had functional authority and responsibilities, thus a matrix management organisation was created.

3.7 The matrix organisation imposes the multi-disciplinary approach on a permanent basis. For example, it is possible to have a product management structure superimposed on top of a functional departmental structure in a matrix; product or brand managers may be responsible for the sales budget, production budget, pricing, marketing, distribution, quality and costs of their product or product line, but may have to co-ordinate with the

R&D, production, finance, distribution, and sales departments in order to bring the product on to the market and achieve sales targets.

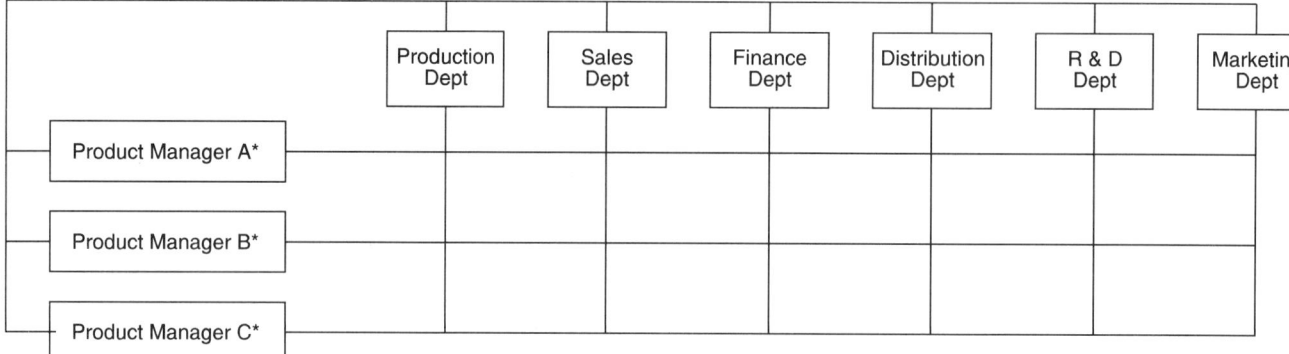

* The product managers may each have their own marketing team; in which case the marketing department itself would be small or non-existent.

3.8 The authority of product managers may vary from organisation to organisation.

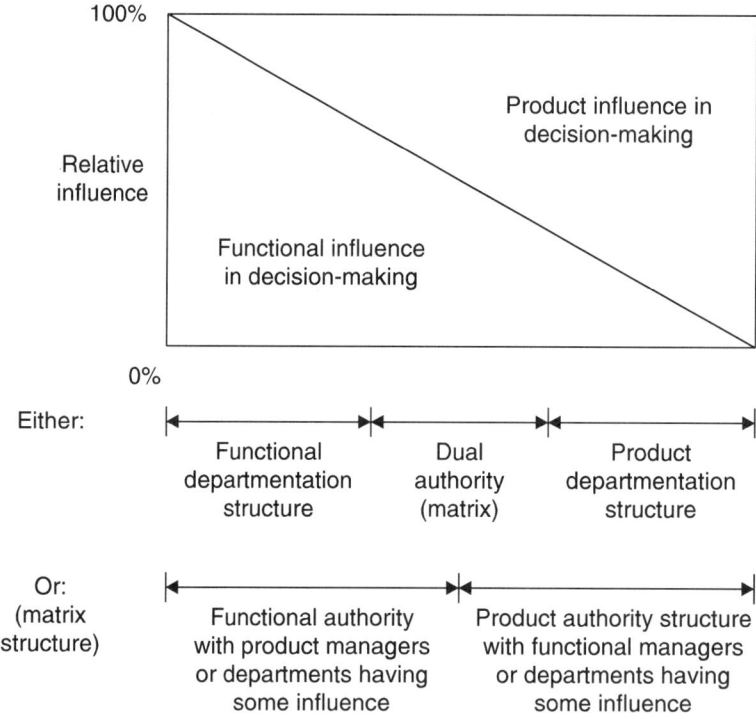

Once again, the division of authority between product managers and functional managers must be carefully defined.

3.9 Matrix management thus **challenges classical ideas** about organisation by rejecting the idea of one person, one boss.

3.10 A subordinate cannot easily take orders from two or more bosses, and so an arrangement has to be established, perhaps on the following lines.

(a) A subordinate takes orders from one boss (the functional manager) and the second boss (the project manager) has to ask the first boss to give certain instructions to the subordinate.

(b) A subordinate takes orders from one boss about some specified matters and orders from the other boss about different specified matters. The authority of each boss would have to be carefully defined. Even so, good co-operation between the bosses would still be necessary.

3.11 Advantages of a matrix structure

(a) It offers greater **flexibility**. This applies both to **people,** as employees adapt more quickly to a new challenge or new task, and develop an attitude which is geared to accepting change; and to **task and structure,** as the matrix may be short-term (as with project teams) or readily amended (eg a new product manager can be introduced by superimposing his tasks on those of the existing functional managers). Flexibility should facilitate efficient operations in the face of change.

(b) It should improve **communication** within the organisation.

(c) Dual authority gives the organisation **multiple orientation** so that functional specialists do not get wrapped up in their own concerns.

(d) It provides a **structure for allocating responsibility to managers for end-results**. A product manager is responsible for product profitability, and a project leader is responsible for ensuring that the task is completed.

(e) It provides for **inter-disciplinary co-operation** and a mixing of skills and expertise.

3.12 A matrix organisation is most suitable in the following situations.

(a) There is a fairly large number of different functions, each of great importance.

(b) There could be communications problems between functional management in different functions (eg marketing, production, R&D, personnel, finance).

(c) Work is supposed to flow smoothly between these functions, but the communications problems might stop or hinder the work flow.

(d) There is a need to carry out uncertain, interdependent tasks. Work can be structured so as to be **task centred**, with task managers appointed to look after each task, and provide the communications (and co-operation) between different functions.

(e) There is a need to achieve common functional tasks so as to achieve savings in the use of resources - ie product divisions would be too wasteful, because they would duplicate costly functional tasks.

(f) There are many geographic areas with distinct needs, but the firm wishes to exploit economies of scale.

3.13 Disadvantages of matrix organisation

(a) Dual authority threatens a **conflict** between managers. Where matrix structure exists it is important that the authority of superiors should not overlap and areas of authority must be clearly defined. A subordinate must know to which superior he is responsible for each aspect of his duties.

(b) One individual with two or more bosses is more likely to suffer **role stress** at work.

(c) It is sometimes more **costly** - eg product managers are additional jobs which would not be required in a simple structure of functional departmentation.

(d) It may be **difficult for the management to accept** a matrix structure. It is possible that a manager may feel threatened that another manager will usurp his authority.

(e) It required consensus and agreement which may slow down decision-making.

4   DESIGNS FOR GLOBAL BUSINESSES

4.1   In an earlier chapter, we identified four possible stages through which an organisation might pass in dealing with global markets. A key factor is the extent to which the different parts of the organisation are involved in international activity.

- A multi-domestic strategy treats each country as a **separate market**.
- A global strategy treats the world as a **single market**.

4.2   The following diagram describes the types of organisation structure which might arise from these problems.

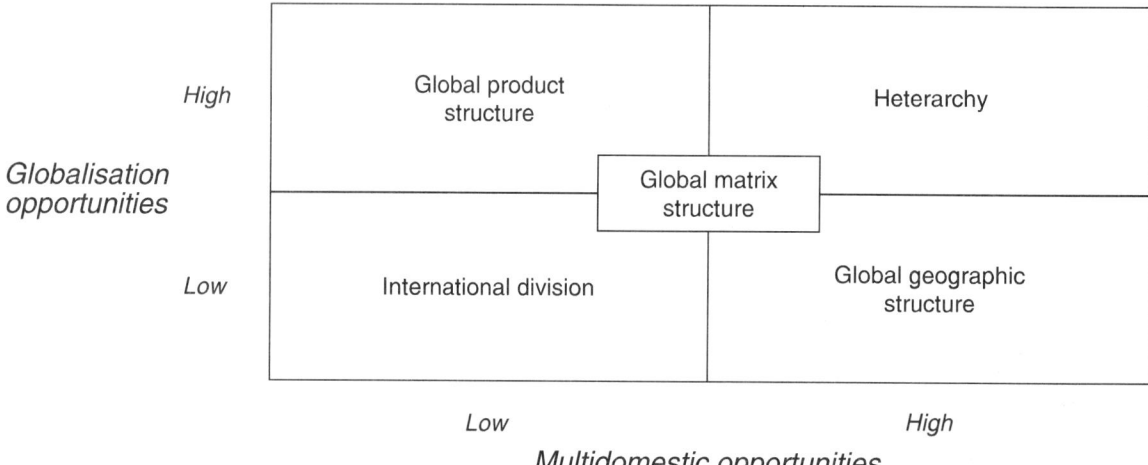

(a)   An **international division** might be set up to co-ordinate all of a firm's overseas activities. Such a division might have developed from an export department. The international division is a **separate department** in a functionally organised firm, or alongside product divisions in a product organised form, or even alongside the domestic market's area divisions in a geographic-orientated firm. The international division itself is probably organised on an area basis by country.

(b)   **Global product division structure**. This might exist in a firm where there are few opportunities to customise products for each separate market. Aircraft engines are an example. The firm is primarily organised by product.

(c)   **Global geographic division structure**. This is similar to organisation by geographic area, writ large on to a global basis. Each area can operate with effective autonomy. There is a small corporate staff. It implies that products can be adapted to each market.

(d)   **Global matrix structure**. This has effectively been described above, in Section 3, in that individual business units report both on an area basis and on a product divisional (or functional) basis.

(e)   **Global heterarchy**. The heterarchy is characteristic of large and very complex international firms: the matrix is simple in comparison.

4.3   **Features of the heterarchy.**

(a)   **Some headquarters functions are diffused geographically.** For example, R&D might be in the UK, marketing in the US. Or again certain products will be made in one country, and others elsewhere. (Motor manufacturers do not make every model of car at each factory.) Some central functions might be split up: many firms are experimenting with having several centres for R&D.

(b)   **Subsidiary managers have a strategic role for the corporation as a whole** (eg through bargaining and coalition forming).

(c) **Co-ordination is achieved through corporate culture and shared values** rather than a formal hierarchy. Employees with long experience might have worked in a number of different product divisions.

(d) **Alliances** can be formed with other company parts and other firms, perhaps in joint ventures or consortia.

Global or stateless corporations

4.4 However, it is a long way even from global heterarchy to a truly **global organisation**. The argument is that because companies now produce, invest and sell in a wide variety of countries, they make decisions primarily with regard to their global ambitions, and do not take their legal nationality into account. In short, there is supposed to be an increasing number of **stateless corporations**, whose activities transcend national boundaries, whose personnel can come from any country, and who have no particularly strong links with any country.

4.5 This theory has some attractive evidence, particularly in a relatively open economy like that of the UK, which is host to a number of multinational corporations and has attracted a fair degree of inward investment. *Robert B Reich* (in his book *The Work of Nations*), has argued that firms are places where 'enterprise webs' are spun, which **tie together capital, resources, skills and technology from all over the world**.

4.6 Do these global or stateless corporations really exist? Against Reich's view the following **factual objections** have been raised as a result of research.

(a) Most multinationals, other than those based in small nations, have fewer than half of their employees abroad.

(b) Ownership and control of multinationals remain restricted. This is partly because of the way in which capital markets are structured. Few so-called global companies are quoted on more than two stock markets. While capital may be mobile, different firms raise money from different sources, and investors might have different expectations of the returns they expect and the risk.

(c) Top management is rarely as multinational as the firm's activities. This is particularly true of Japanese companies. A foreigner is rarely seen on the Tokyo-based board of a Japanese multinational. In 1991, only 2% of board members of large American companies were foreigners.

(d) National residence and status is important for tax reasons. Boundary-less corporations are not recognised as such by lawyers or tax officials.

(e) The bulk of a multinational's research and development is generally done in the home country, where strategic decisions are made.

(f) Where capital is limited, global companies stick to the home market rather than developing overseas ones.

(g) Finally, profits from a global company must be remitted somewhere. Firms such as Reuters are quoted on a number of stock exchanges worldwide, but they are exceptional.

The best that can be said is that some firms are moving towards globalisation, even though few, if any firms, actually exemplify it.

4.7 It has generally been assumed that a multinational or global company must be **big**, no matter how decentralised. This view is increasingly being challenged.

(a) In the past, big companies were the only ones able to surmount formidable **trade barriers** and the **legal and tax complications** of operating in more than one country.

Open markets and common standards now make it easier for small firms to sell products worldwide, as these barriers are lower.

(b) **The use of technology**. When technology was expensive only big firms could afford it, so only they could benefit from the resulting scale economies. Cheap computers offer technological benefits to small firms and the scale at which economies are found is falling. The Internet, for example, is an inexpensive way of advertising.

(c) **Capital markets**. Previously, international capital markets could only be accessed by large companies. More efficient capital markets are now open to smaller companies.

Case examples

The two examples below suggest the varying pressures underlying the structure of a business on a worldwide scale.

Shell

In March 1995 (*Financial Times*, 30.3.95) Shell announced the end of its old matrix organisation. For historical reasons the firm had a complicated structure. Each country or region had its own operating companies.

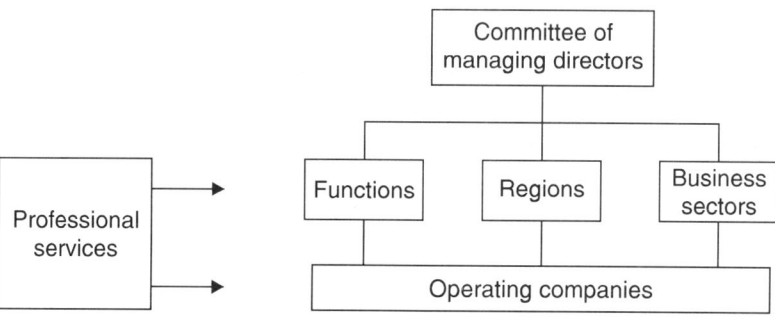

A given operating company could be defined by geography, or business sector for example. The structure was very elaborate and required the support of large groups of executives, representing 'national or regional units, business sections (or divisions) and functions such as finance. It is felt that the company can no longer afford the army of coordinators to "police" such a matrix'. This old structure is all to go. The change will 'cut the larger regional baronies'. It should speed decision making.

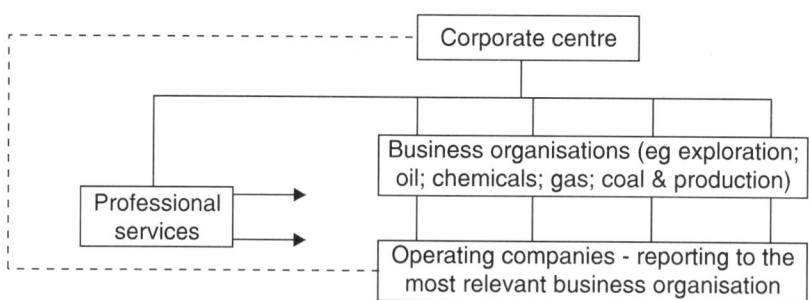

The operating companies are unchanged, so a local basis is maintained and the operating companies still have a link to the corporate centre.

Ford

However, whilst many firms are trying to reduce their head offices and have dismantled their matrices (eg BP) and others (IBM) are streamlining them, some companies have decided to *install* them. Ford has announced a matrix structure to avoid duplication.

Ford had suffered for a long time from duplication: for example the North American and European Escorts were quite separate cars. However, the Mondeo was launched as a world car, and the lessons learned from that exercise have been absorbed elsewhere. The following comes from the *Financial Times* 3 April 1995.

First of all, its previously independent automative operations have been integrated into one. This will reduce duplication.

To avoid costly duplication, there is one worldwide product development organisation with five 'vehicle centres' for different ranges of car.

A matrix management system will replace the old 'functional chimneys' of the old organisation.

'Most employees will report to two or more managers, for example, both within a vehicle centre team and in a functional discipline, such as manufacturing, finance, sales and marketing or purchasing.

'Under the new system career development is a responsibility of the functional head, while performance evaluation is the responsibility of the vehicle programme team leader.'

'The balance of power has been shifted to the vehicle programme teams and this has been reinforced by co-locating people.'

'The first loyalty will not be to function, say crash testing or NVH (noise, vibration and harshness), but to the car team.' says Parry-Jones. 'It is like a Formula One team. If a problem occurs, everyone works on it. You always race, and you always race to win. It's no use saying afterwards that the chassis worked perfectly, but it was a shame about the engine.'

'Ford believes it is guaranteeing empowerment by making it virtually impossible for managers to 'micro manage'. The entire Ford automotive operation has been flattened from as many as 14 levels of management in its largest organisations to only 7.'

---

5   MECHANISTIC AND ORGANIC STRUCTURES

Bureaucracy and mechanistic structures

5.1   Bureaucracy is perhaps the term most commonly used to describe a hierarchical rule-bound organisation. Many of the organisational structures described earlier could be classified as bureaucracies. When the term was first coined, bureaucracy was regarded as a social advance. There are still cases where a bureaucratic approach is best suited to an organisation's objectives.

5.2   *Weber* specified several general characteristics of bureaucracy, which he described as 'a continuous organisation of official functions bound by rules'.

5.3   Mintzberg, as we have seen, identifies two kinds of bureaucracy.

(a)   Machine bureaucracy, similar to Weber's description, based on standardisation of work processes, functional groupings, size.

(b)   Professional bureaucracy (eg hospitals) based on standardisation of skills.

Criticisms of bureaucracies

5.4   The very strength of some of the characteristics of bureaucracy may in some cases be turned into a cause of weakness. *Gouldner* argued that rules are **both functional** and **dysfunctional** in a bureaucracy.

(a)   **Rules are functional**: they take away from subordinates the feeling that their superiors, in issuing orders, hold power over them. This in turn reduces the interpersonal tensions which otherwise exist between superiors and subordinates.

(b)   **Rules are dysfunctional**: employees use rules to learn what is the **minimum** level of behaviour expected from them, and there is a tendency for employees to work at this minimum level of behaviour. This, in turn, suggested Gouldner, creates a requirement for close supervision. Greater pressure from supervisors will make subordinates more aware of the power the supervisor holds over them, thereby increasing tension within the work group.

5.5 Undesirable features of bureaucracy

(a) Committees and reports slow down the decision-making process.

(b) Conformity creates ritualism, formalism and 'organisation man'.

(c) Personal growth of individuals is inhibited - although bureaucracies tend to attract, select and retain individuals with a tolerance for such conditions.

(d) Innovation is discouraged.

(e) Control systems are frequently out of date. According to Michael Crozier, the control mechanism (whereby feedback on errors is used to initiate corrective action) is hampered by rigidity: bureaucracies cannot learn from their mistakes!

(f) Bureaucracies are slow to change. *Michael Crozier* stated that 'a system of organisation whose main characteristic is its rigidity will not adjust easily to change and will tend to resist change as much as possible'.

(g) Over prescriptive rules produce a simplistic approach to problems.

5.6 The financial and technical advantages of bureaucratic organisations **usually outweigh** the disadvantages, especially in circumstances of slow change and a large customer/client base, to which bureaucracy is well suited. The dysfunctions, however, still need to be reduced to acceptable proportions.

Improving bureaucracy

5.7 The organisation should have some specific features.

- Small working groups (to promote group loyalty and purpose)
- Small working establishments (for the same reasons)
- As little centralisation as possible (to give junior management more scope)
- A highly developed two-way communication system

5.8 **Culture** may be used to increase the flexibility and humanity of the organisation. A less rule-bound structure/culture may be developed in particular units of the bureaucracy, such as those with direct customer/client contact.

5.9 Opportunities should be created for **individualism and innovation**, if only in certain units of the organisation. The bureaucracy may then be able to attract individuals of a less conforming type, better able to handle change, ambiguity and flexibility.

Bureaucracies and change

5.10 *Burns and Stalker* contrasted the **organic** structure of management (see below), which is more suitable to conditions of change, with a **mechanistic** system of management, which is more suited to stable conditions. A mechanistic structure, which appears very much like a bureaucracy, has the following characteristics.

(a) Authority is delegated through a hierarchical, formal scalar chain, and 'position power' is used in decision-making.

(b) Communication is **vertical** (ie up and down the scalar chain) rather than **lateral**.

(c) Individuals regard their own tasks as specialised and not directly related to the goals of the organisation as a whole.

(d) There is a precise definition of duties in each individual job (rules, procedures, job definitions).

5.11 Mechanistic systems are **unsuitable in conditions of change** because they tend to deal with change by cumbersome methods.

(a) The **ambiguous figure system**: in dealing with unfamiliar problems authority lines are not clear, matters are referred 'higher-up' and the top of the organisation becomes over-burdened by decisions.

(b) **Mechanistic jungle**: jobs and departments are created to deal with the problems caused by change, creating further and greater problems.

(c) **Committee system**: committees are set up to cope with the new problems. The committees can only be a temporary problem-solving device, but the situations which create the problems are not temporary.

However, for certain types of change this might be qualified.

Organic organisations: suitability for change

5.12 In contrast to mechanistic structures, Burns and Stalker identified an **organic structure** (also called an **organismic structure**). They believed organic structures were better suited to conditions of change than mechanistic structures. The mechanistic structures and the organic structure are contrasted in the table below.

Mechanistic	Organic
Tasks are specialised and broken down into subtasks.	Specialist knowledge and expertise is seen to contribute to the 'common task' of the concern.
Each individual task is 'abstract', pursued with techniques and purposes more or less distinct from that of the concern. People are concerned with task efficiency, not with how the task can be made to improve organisational effectiveness	Each task is seen and understood to be set by the total situation of the firm: people are concerned with the task insofar as it contributes to organisational effectiveness.
Managers are responsible for co-ordinating tasks	Each task is adjusted and redefined through interaction with others. This is rather like co-ordination by mutual adjustment
There are precise job descriptions and delineations of responsibility.	Job descriptions are less precise: it is harder to 'pass the buck'
'Doing the job' takes priority over serving the interests of the organisation.	'The spread of commitment to the concern beyond any technical definition'
Hierarchic structure of control. An individual's performance assessment derives from a 'contractual relationship with an impersonal organisation.'	Network structure of control. An individual's job performance and conduct derive from a supposed community of interest between the individual and the organisation, and the individual's colleagues. (Loyalty to the 'team' is an important control mechanism.)
Decision-making is taken at the top, where knowledge is supposed to reside.	Relevant technical and commercial knowledge can be located anywhere 'omniscience is no longer imputed to the head of the concern.'

BPP
PUBLISHING

Mechanistic	Organic
Interaction is mainly vertical (up and down the scalar chain), and takes the form of commands and obedience.	Interaction is lateral and communication between people of different rank represents consultation, rather than command.
Operations and working behaviour are governed by instructions issued by superiors.	Communication consists of information and advice rather than instructions and decisions.
Insistence on loyalty to the concern and obedience to superiors.	Commitment to the concern's task (eg mission) is more highly valued than loyalty as such.
Internal knowledge (eg of the organisation's specific activities) is more highly valued that general knowledge.	'Importance and prestige attach to affiliations and expertise valid in the industrial, technical and commercial milieux external to the firm'

5.13 **Four important points** to note

(a) Although organic systems are not hierarchical in the way that bureaucracies are, there are **differences of status**, determined by people's greater expertise, experience and so forth.

(b) The degree of **commitment to the concern** is more extensive in organic than mechanistic system. This is similar to the idea that an organisation's mission should motivate and inspire employees.

(c) The reduced importance of hierarchy is replaced by 'the development of shared beliefs and values'. In other words, corporate culture becomes very powerful. **Control is cultural rather than bureaucratic**.

(d) The two approaches represent **two ends of a spectrum**: there are intermediate stages between bureaucratic and organic organisations. Different departments of a business may be run on different lines. For example, the payroll department of a firm has a **well defined task** (eg paying salaries at the end of the month) with little variation. **Controls** are needed to ensure processing accuracy and to avoid fraud. A **mechanistic** system might be applied here. On the other hand, the 'creative **department**' of an advertising agency, with a number of professional experts (copywriters, graphic designers, account executives), may be run on an **organic** basis.

5.14 Burns and Stalker recognised **that organic systems would only suit individuals with a high tolerance for ambiguity and the personal stresses involved in being part of such an organisation** - but the freedom of manoeuvre is considered worth this personal cost, for individuals who prize autonomy and flexibility.

Organic structures and innovation: the ambidextrous approach

5.15 A criticism levelled at organic organisations is that whilst they may be **good at creating ideas**, they might be **less good at exploiting** them. Decentralisation and loose structures encourage communication, but also perhaps make employees less likely to comply with a management instruction to exploit an innovation: in other words, there are problems of discipline at a basic level.

5.16 An organic structure might therefore be a drawback when certain types of things need to be done. For example, in warfare, a disciplined 'mechanistic' approach might be needed to fight certain kinds of battle: delays and indecision might be costly. (On the other hand, guerilla warfare might be conducted organically.)

5.17 To get round this problem some organisations employ what might be termed an **ambidextrous approach to organisation structure**. By this is meant that organisations employ the elements of both the organic *and* mechanistic structures in their operations.

(a) **Creative departments** may be developed, to deal with R&D and so forth, often as part of an organisation's support staff in the configuration, possibly to offer new ideas to the technostructure. Their precise location in the structural configuration will obviously depend on circumstances.

(b) Instead of creating a permanent arrangement, a mechanistic company might designate certain occasions for employees to behave as if they were in organic companies. Such occasions include brainstorming sessions and quality circles.

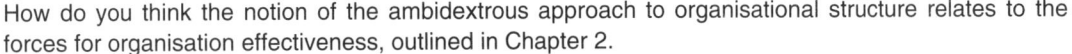

Question 3

How do you think the notion of the ambidextrous approach to organisational structure relates to the forces for organisation effectiveness, outlined in Chapter 2.

Answer

The ambidextrous approach suggests a possible source of conflict between two forces.

- The force for proficiency (whereby the operating core looks for autonomy).
- The forces for efficiency or concentration (in the technostructure and middle line).

Problems may arise where one advances at the expense of another: for example in the UK's NHS doctors might resent suspected interference by managers in clinical (ie treatment) decisions, yet managers might consider such interference to be necessary in order to control costs.

The dual core

5.18 In professional bureaucracies, the operating core is relatively unsupervised, and the professionals doing the work are, in an important sense, in charge of it. However, ensuring certain types of innovation is difficult. Innovation in **technical procedures**, such as experimental surgery, is perhaps best conducted within an **organic structure**, as the free flow of ideas is most important. Innovation might be 'bottom up' in this case.

5.19 However, not all innovation or change refers to technical procedures. Some organisations face the need for frequent administrative change, for example in response to environmental and legal change, whatever its purpose. For this a more 'top-down' **mechanistic approach** is needed to ensure innovations are actually achieved and implemented successfully.

Case example

An example of an administrative change in a professional bureaucracy is the UK's internal market for the National Health service. This is certainly administrative innovation, creating hospitals as autonomous units, and making (some) general practitioners responsible for their own budgets. Although, in theory, the changes were supposed to direct the resources of the NHS more efficiently, there is no doubt that the structure was imposed 'top-down' in a 'mechanistic way'

5.20 This is sometimes referred to as the **dual core approach** which recognises that administrative and technical changes are best effected by different organisation structures, a technical core and an administrative core.

6 INFLUENCES ON ORGANISATION STRUCTURE

6.1 Are there any universally applicable rules governing organisation design?

(a) The **human relations school** held that the key to organisational success was the capacity of the individuals within it. Organisation design should remove impediments to the workforce's natural commitment to work.

(b) The **classical school** was more concerned with the bureaucratic aspects identified earlier in this chapter. All organisations have similar problems which can best be solved by judicious tinkering with management levels, spans of control and so on: the organisation as a machine.

6.2 Both these approaches rested on the assumption that a single key can be found which would unlock the door to success. A **contingency approach** would allow due weight to a **variety** of factors.

- **Personnel** (their talents, skills, attributes, motivation)
- The **task** and the activities which the organisation is involved in
- The **environment**

6.3 This implies that **within the same organisation there may be a number of different structure types**. Some areas will be bureaucratic and role-determined, others will display the features of an organic structure. Take, for example, a theatre. Its accounts department will work in a very different way from the acting troupe. **The contingency approach would hold that the type of structure must be appropriate to task performance and individual/group satisfaction**.

6.4 *Buchanan and Huczynski* classify the activities carried out by an organisation into four main categories in their book *Introduction to Organisational Behaviour*.

(a) **Steady-state activities** are routine and programmable (eg regular account maintenance). This would imply a bureaucratic form.

(b) **Policy-making activities** are concerned with the identification of goals, the allocation of scarce resources and directing people. Policy-making is the job of the strategic apex and technostructure. It is less routine.

(c) **Innovation activities** are concerned with things which change the company's goals or processes (eg new product development, new market investigation). This would imply a less formal structure.

(d) **Breakdown activities** (for emergencies and crises). A bureaucratic system of rules might be best here, if the emergency can be planned for (eg a fire). Otherwise a more fluid structure might be appropriate to guarantee a rapid response.

A contingency approach implies that there are different structures suitable for different activities.

Possible influences on organisation structure

6.5 **Age**

The older the organisation, the more formalised its behaviour. Work is repeated, so is more easily formalised and standardised.

Organisation structure reflects the age of the **industry's** foundation.

6.6 **Size and growth**

- The larger the organisation, the more **elaborate** its structure will be.

- The larger the organisation, the larger the average size of the units within it.

- The larger the organisation, the more formalised is its behaviour (in order to attain **consistency**).

6.7 **Tasks**. Some organisations do simple things, like milk cows. Others do complex things, like design weapons systems or develop new drugs. The **complexity of the task** affects the structure of the organisation.

6.8 **Co-ordination**. Mutual adjustment, direct supervision and standardisation are different methods of co-ordination that are appropriate for different types of work. They all have consequences for organisation structure. They are discussed further in Chapter 7.

6.9 **Skills of managers and workers**. Can people be left alone to do the job, or do they require close supervision? Job design and complexity will influence this.

6.10 **Geographic dispersion**. An organisation with several sites will have a different organisation structure form one located in one place. This affects supervision, as we have seen.

6.11 **Technology**

(a) The stronger the **technical system** (ie the technology) the more formalised the work, and the more bureaucratic the structure of the operating core will tend to be.

(b) The more sophisticated the technology, the more elaborate and professional the support staff will be.

(c) Extensive application of computer and information technology of the **operating core** transforms a bureaucratic administrative structure into an organic one. This is because procedures are incorporated into equipment routines (eg software). It requires specialists to manage the process, and such people tend to communicate informally.

(d) **Information technology** has a profound effect on organisation structure generally.

6.12 **Environment and markets**.

(a) The more **dynamic** the environment the more organic is the structure.

(b) The more complex the environment, the more decentralised is the structure.

(c) The more diversified the markets, the greater the propensity is to split into market based departments/units.

(d) Extreme environmental hostility is a force for centralisation. Direct supervision is fast.

(e) Environmental disparities encourage decentralisation for some activities, centralisation for others. For example, manufacture might be centralised, but marketing might be decentralised.

6.13 **Control**

(a) The more an organisation is subject to **external control** (eg by government, holding company) the more centralised and formalised its structure.

(b) The power needs of organisational members (to control others, or at least to control their own working conditions) can lead to centralisation.

(c) The need for elaborate control systems leads to centralisation and formality.

6.14 **Fashion** favours the structures of the day. For example, although bureaucracies are deeply unfashionable, they are often the best at doing certain kinds of work. Indeed, *Burns and Stalker,* who developed the concept of organic and mechanistic organisations which we discuss in the next chapter, held that neither type of organisation had any intrinsic merits, as the key variables were **product-markets** and **technology**. A company using unchanging technology in familiar markets can work very well with a bureaucracy.

6.15 **Strategy**. The organisation's strategy might influence its structure.

Chapter roundup

- Each constituent part of the organisation exerts an influence on the organisation's configuration.

- The strategic apex exerts a pull to centralise, leading to the simple structure.

- The technostructure exerts a pull to standardise processes, leading to the machine bureaucracy.

- The middle line exerts a pull to balkanise leading to the divisional form.

- The operating core exerts a pull to standardise skills, and leads to a professional bureaucracy.

- The support staff exerts a pull to collaborate, leading to adhocracy.

- An organisation's formal hierarchy can be arranged by territory, function, product, brand, customer/market, staff numbers and work patterns, and equipment specialisation.

- Hybrid structures contain elements of different kinds of departmentation.

- Matrix structures are formal mechanisms to ensure co-ordination across functional lines by the embodiment of dual authority in the organisation structure.

- Mechanistic or bureaucratic organisations are not ideally suited to conditions of change: their strict bureaucratic hierarchies and shallow decision making process do not encourage flexibility. Organic organisations are more flexible structures where roles are less well defined.

- The contingency theory suggests that there is no one best way of designing an organisation, but that there are many influences over organisation structure.

Quick quiz

1 What are the characteristics of the simple structure?

2 Distinguish between machine bureaucracy and professional bureaucracy.

3 What component of the organisation leads a pull to divisionalisation?

4 What are the drawbacks to functional departmentation?

5 Why do many organisations adopt a hybrid structure?

6 What leads to the development of matrix structures?

7 What do you understand by global heterarchy?

8 Why are mechanistic systems unsuitable for conditions of change?

9 Describe the features of organic structures.

10 Why might a dual core approach be needed?

Answers to quick quiz

1   Centralisation, direct supervision, wide span of control, no technostructure

2   The machine bureaucracy works by rules and procedures laid down by the technostructure. It is most effective in a stable environment where tasks are simple and repetitive. The professional bureaucracy depends on the individual skills of the operating core rather than on a technostructure for its standards. It hires trained specialists who control their own work.

3   The middle line seeks to extend its authority.

4   It does not reflect the business processes by which value is created. This means that staff do not appreciate the way the organisation works. Also, it is difficult to identify where profits and losses are made, since traditional cost accounting bundles the costs of most functions together as overheads.

5   Different aspects of the organisation are often best-structured in different ways. For instance, sales may be best organised geographically or by product group, while purchasing and finance may be best centralised to achieve economies of scale.

6   Requirements for flexibility, improved communication, project accountability and interdepartmental co-operation.

7   A global heterarchy is a large multi-national organisation organised in largely autonomous groups. Control is achieved through shared values, bargaining and negotiation.

8   They use cumbersome methods: problems are referred upwards; committees are formed; and new jobs and departments are overlaid on to the existing structure.

9   The structure is fluid and informal with extensive lateral interaction. Control is achieved through individual competence and co-ordination by mutual adjustment. There are few prescribed procedures.

10 The organic approach is appropriate when creativity and responsiveness to changing conditions are required. It depends on individual skill and community of interest. Where work is both routine and important and compliance with standards is required, a more mechanistic approach may be required. We might therefore see an organic structure in a marketing department and a more mechanistic structure in an accounts department.

Now try the questions below from the Exam Question Bank

Number	Level	Marks	Time
Q6	Introductory	20	36 mins
Q7	Introductory	20	36 mins

Chapter 8

BUSINESS FUNCTIONS

Topic List		Syllabus Reference	Ability required
1	Marketing	(i)	Comprehension
2	Research and development	(i)	Comprehension
3	The importance of operations	(i)	Comprehension
4	Production	(i)	Comprehension
5	Service operations	(i)	Comprehension
6	Human resources management	(i)	Comprehension
7	The finance function	(i)	Comprehension
8	The value chain		

Introduction

This chapter looks at the roles of the more important departments in a business and how they fit together. We start with a reasonably full look at marketing as this function is emphasised in the syllabus content. The other functions are covered more briefly. We conclude with a look at the value chain.

Learning outcomes covered in this chapter

- Explain the general characteristics and operation of the main functional areas of an organisation.

- Explain the workings of the marketing function of an organisation and the major tools and techniques used by marketing specialists.

Syllabus content covered in this chapter

- The general operation of the main functional areas of business (ie operations, marketing, human resource management, finance, research and development, information systems management).

- The organisation and activities of the marketing function (ie marketing research, market segmentation, marketing strategy formulation).

- The concept of the marketing mix and the major tools therein (ie branding, product mix, pricing, advertising, sales promotion, public relations, packaging, distribution).

1 MARKETING

1.1 The marketing function manages an organisation's relationships with its customers.

KEY TERM

Marketing is 'the management process which identifies, anticipates and satisfies customer needs profitably'. (Chartered Institute of Marketing)

Marketing orientation

1.2 Organisations have different orientations towards the customer.

Orientation	Description
Production orientation	'Customers will buy whatever we produce - our job is to make as many as we can'. (Demand exceeds available supply.)
Product orientation, a variant of production orientation	'Add more features to the product - demand will pick up'. Such firms do not research what customers actually want.
Sales orientation	Customers are naturally sales resistant so the product must be sold actively and aggressively and customers must be persuaded to buy them.
Marketing orientation	The key task of the organisation is to determine the needs, wants and values of a target market and to adapt the organisation to delivering the desired satisfactions more effectively and efficiently than its competitors.

Identifying customers

1.3 The marketing orientation is focused on the customer so it is appropriate that we deal with the **customer** first.

1.4 A useful distinction is between the household or 'consumer' market and the organisational market in which goods and services are sold to **organisations** (eg businesses, the government) for use in their own activities.

Market segmentation   5/01

1.5 A market is not a mass, homogeneous group of customers, each wanting an **identical** product. Instead it can be analysed into **segments**.

KEY TERM

A **market segment** is a group of customers with common needs, preferences or characteristics who respond in a similar way to a given set of market stimuli.

BPP PUBLISHING

1.6 Marketing activity is more effective if groups can be identified and targeted. This is done by **market segmentation** which groups potential customers according to identifiable characteristics relevant to their purchasing behaviour. The **segmentation approach** recognises that people have different wants and needs and that some are willing to pay more or go to greater lengths to satisfy them. More opportunities are open to organisations which are willing to satisfy needs with a differentiated marketing mix.

1.7 **Important elements of market segmentation**

(a) While the total market consists of varied groups of consumers, each group has **common needs and preferences,** and may well react to market stimuli in the same way. For example, the market for umbrellas might be segmented according to sex. Women might seem to prefer umbrellas of a particular size and weight. The men's market might further be subdivided by age or activity, for example, professionals, commuters, golfers. Each subdivision of the market will show increasingly common traits. Golfers appear to buy large multi-coloured umbrellas.

(b) **Each market segment can become a target market for a firm, requiring a unique marketing mix. Segmentation should enable a company to formulate an effective strategy for selling to a given group.**

1.8 There are many possible characteristics of buyers which could be chosen as segmentation variables and a number of criteria for effective market segmentation.

(a) **Measurability** is the degree to which information exists or is cost effectively obtainable on the characteristics of interest. Whilst a car manufacturer may have access to information about **location** of customers, **personality traits** are more difficult to obtain information about, because the required tests may be impractical to administer.

(b) **Accessibility** is the degree to which the company can identify and communicate with the chosen segments. Thus whilst a car dealer may be able to access potential corporate customers, by direct mail or tele-sales, identifying individual customers with family incomes in excess of £30,000 pa would not be so easy.

(c) **Substantiality** is the degree to which the segments are large enough to offer profitable returns. Thus, whilst a large number of people in social group DE aged over 65 could be identified, their potential profitability to a retailer is likely to be less in the long term than a smaller number of 17-18 year olds. This latter group might be worth cultivating, using a specially devised marketing approach, whereas the former might not be.

Benefits of segmentation

1.9 Segmentation only makes sense if it brings appropriate benefits.

(a) Segmentation should increase benefits to consumers by providing product features more closely matching their needs.

(b) Segmentation enables the firm to identify those groups of customers who are most likely to buy. This ensures that resources will not be wasted, and marketing and sales activity can be highly focused. The result should be lower costs, greater sales and higher profitability.

(c) Across the industry, segmentation will provide greater customer choice by generating a variety of products within a particular class from which consumers can choose.

1.10 **Typical segments for consumer products and services**

Segmentation variable	Comments and examples
Geographical area	Customer preferences (eg for certain types of food) may differ from area to area.
Age	The package holiday market is partly segmented by age: SAGA serve the over 55s; Club 18-30 serve the 18-30 age group.
Sex	The market for cosmetics, perfumes and facial care products is segmented by sex.
Income/wealth	eg luxury goods.
Occupation	eg City suits, white coats for doctors, overalls.
Education	This may be relevant to the marketing of newspapers.
Family	The family life cycle: people go through various life stages which affect their purchasing power and priorities, especially where children are involved.
Religious affiliation	Charities; food products, as some religions have particular dietary laws.
Ethnic background and nationality	Food; cultural products (such as Hindi films).
Social class	Socio-economic groupings can be reliable indicators of purchasing patterns.
Life style	Life style or psychological factors, such as personality and attitudes, can be condensed into categories of life style, eg people have different attitudes to risk.
End use	How a product is used at home can suggest different ways of selling it.
Buyer behaviour	Different customers approach the purchasing process in different ways: some customers are cynical about advertising messages.

1.11 **Segmentation bases of the business market**

Segmentation variable	Comments and examples
Geographical area	A solicitor might offer services to the local business community.
Type of business	Some accountancy firms specialise in serving clients in certain types of business (eg retailing).
Size	The needs of small owner-managed businesses are often very different from those of large companies.

BPP PUBLISHING

Identifying and anticipating customer needs

Marketing research and market research

1.12 While segmentation can give a basis for marketing, any marketing decision is inevitably made under conditions of uncertainty which can be reduced, if not eliminated, by the right **information**.

(a) **Strategic decision-making** requires information such as product life cycle estimates, and potential market size.

(b) **Tactical decisions** are about less important matters such as planning sales territories or setting short-term marketing cost budgets, and need more focused information.

(c) **The information may be used to create a marketing database** used for market share analysis, competitor analysis and analysing customer buying habits. Many loyalty card schemes are designed to get information about customers' buying patterns so their needs can be targeted precisely.

1.13 The information system for marketing is referred to as **marketing research**.

> ### KEY TERMS
>
> **Marketing research** is 'the objective gathering, recording and analysing of all facts about problems relating to the transfer and sales of goods and services from producer to consumer or user.'
>
> **Market research** is finding out information about a particular product or service.

The scope of marketing research

1.14 (a) **Sales research**
   - Analysis of the market potential for existing products
   - Forecasting likely demand for new products
   - Study of market trends
   - Study of the characteristics of the market
   - Analysis of market shares

(b) **Product research**
   - Customer acceptance of proposed new products
   - Comparative studies between competitive products
   - Studies into packaging and design
   - Forecasting new uses for existing products
   - Customer attitudes
   - Research into the development of a product line (range)

(c) **Price research**
   - Analysis of how demand changes with price
   - Analysis of costs and contribution or profit margins
   - The effect of changes in credit policy on demand
   - Customer perceptions of price (and quality)

(d) **Communications research**
   - Motivation research for advertising and sales promotion effectiveness
   - Analysing the effectiveness of advertising on sales demand
   - Analysing the effectiveness of individual aspects of advertising

- Establishing sales territories
- Analysing the effectiveness of salesmen
- Analysing the effectiveness of other sales promotion methods

(e) **Distribution research**
- The location and design of distribution centres
- The analysis of packaging for transportation and shelving
- Dealer supply requirements
- Dealer advertising requirements
- The cost of different methods of transportation and warehousing

Market research

1.15 Two important types of forecast are derived from market research.

(a) **Market forecasts**. These are forecasts for the market **as a whole**. They are mainly involved in the assessment of environmental factors, outside the organisation's control, which will affect the demand for its products/services.

(b) **Sales forecasts** focus on a particular firm. They are estimates of sales expressed in volume, value and profit perhaps by area and product in a future period. It takes into account such aspects as sales to certain categories of customer, promotion activities, the extent of competition, product life cycle, performance of major products.

Satisfying customer needs: the marketing mix

1.16 Before you continue, recall the Chartered Institute of Marketing's definition in Paragraph 1.1. The last word is **profitably**.

1.17 There is thus a balance to be achieved between organisational capacity and customer requirements. This balance is expressed in the **marketing mix,** which is the framework in which the customer and the business deal with each other.

The mix is also known as **the 4 Ps** (product, place, promotion, price).

Product

1.18 The **product** element of the marketing mix is what is being sold, whether this be widgets, power stations, haircuts, holidays or financial advice. (A product, then, could be a service.) Product issues include:

- Design (size, shape)
- Features
- Quality and reliability
- Packaging
- Safety
- Ecological friendliness
- What it does

1.19 The **implication of the marketing orientation** is that the **product or service** is not a thing with features but, from the customer's point of view is a **package of benefits, which meets a need or provides a solution** to a problem.

BPP PUBLISHING

1.20 **Core and augmented product**

(a) The **core product** is a product's essential features. The core product of a credit card is the ability to borrow up to a certain limit and pay off in varied instalments.

(b) **Augmentations** are additional benefits. Most credit cards offer travel insurance.

1.21 Marketing managers make the following distinction.

(a) Product **class**. This is a broad category of product, such as cars, washing machines and so forth. This corresponds to the core or generic product identified above.

(b) Product **form**. This category refers to the different types of product within a product class. The product class 'cars' may have several forms, including five-door hatchbacks, four-wheel drive vehicles, hearses and so forth.

(c) **Brand or make**. This refers to the particular brand or make of the product form. For example, the Nissan Micra, Vauxhall Corsa and Rover 100 are, broadly speaking, examples of the same product form.

The product life cycle

1.22 A product will probably go through the stages of introduction, growth, maturity, decline and senility. A **different marketing approach is appropriate to each stage**, and different levels of sales and profit can be expected. Note that the product life cycle is a **model** of what **might** happen, **not a law** prescribing what **will** happen. In other words, not all products go through these stages or even have a life cycle.

Place: distribution

1.23 **Place** covers two main issues.

(a) **Outlets.** Where products are sold, for instance, in supermarkets and shops

(i) For most consumer goods, this involves one or more **intermediaries**, such as wholesalers, and then retailers.

(ii) Direct distribution is when a firm runs its own shops or, via **mail order,** uses the postal service to bypass intermediaries.

(b) **Logistics.** Even where intermediaries are used, a manufacturer still has to distribute products to wholesalers and retailers. Logistics includes to warehousing, storage, and transportation.

Promotion: marketing communications

1.24 **Promotion** in the marketing mix includes all marketing communications, by which the public knows about the product or service. Promotion is traditionally the main responsibility of marketing personnel, and is their most visible role. The aim of promotion is to generate:

- **Awareness** of the product/service
- **Interest** in the product
- **Desire** to buy
- **Action** (ie an actual purchase)

The mnemonic is **AIDA,** which is widely used in the world of marketing.

1.25 Promotion includes:

(a) **Advertising**: newspapers, TV, cinema, internet web-sites

(b) **Sales promotion**: eg money-off coupons, 'two for the price of one' offers

(c) **Direct selling** by sales personnel. This is often necessary in industrial markets, or where the products are complex or where they have to be tailored precisely to the customer (such as personal pension plans)

(d) **Public relations** (crisis management, obtaining favourable press coverage)

Price

1.26 Products have to be sold at a **price** which meets the organisation's profit objectives.

(a) The **price element of the mix** itself can cover the basic price, as well as discounts, credit terms and interest free credit.

(b) **Price is influenced by demand**. With **penetration** pricing: a low price is charged to persuade as many people as possible to buy the product. With **price skimming**: prices are set to cream off the highest level of profits even though this restricts the number of people able to afford the product. The price is then gradually reduced to skim lower segments one by one.

(c) **Price is also part of the image** of the product: rightly or wrongly, a high-priced product is often assumed to be of better quality than a cheaply priced product. A high price also conveys an image of exclusivity.

(d) Price is also a weapon against **competitors**.

Service marketing

1.27 In addition, for **services** such hospital care or air travel there are **three more Ps.**

- The **people** who deliver the service (eg smiling or surly staff).
- The **processes** by which the service is delivered (eg queuing systems at Disneyworld).
- The **physical evidence** of the service (such as a glossy brochure).

1.28 **All elements of the marketing mix must be consistent with each other.**

Question 1

'An accounts department is not making goods and selling them and so does not need the marketing concept.' Is this a fair comment?

Answer

No.

(a) The accounts department supplies information to various other parts of the organisation. Providing information is its service, and the other parts of the organisation are, effectively, its customers.

(b) An accounts department deals with customers all the time, especially credit customers: after all it sends out the bills and collects the money. As its activities are directly involved with customers, it must take the marketing philosophy on board, too.

BPP PUBLISHING

1.29 **Section summary**
- Marketing deals with a firm's customers.
- Marketing research identifies customer needs.
- Groups of customers with similar needs are a segment.
- A marketing mix (product, place, price, promotion and for services people, processes and physical evidence) is devised to meet the needs of the segment.

2 RESEARCH AND DEVELOPMENT

2.1 Here are some definitions culled from *Statement of Standard Accounting Practice 13*.

> **KEY TERMS**
>
> **Pure research** is original research to obtain new scientific or technical knowledge or understanding. There is no obvious commercial or practical end in view.
>
> **Applied research** is also original research work like (a) above, but it has a specific practical aim or application (eg research on improvements in the effectiveness of medicines etc).
>
> **Development** is the use of existing scientific and technical knowledge to produce new (or substantially improved) products or systems, prior to starting commercial production operations.

2.2 Many organisations employ **specialist staff** to conduct research and development (R&D). They may be organised in a separate functional department of their own. In an organisation run on a product division basis, R&D staff may be employed by each division.

The R&D department

2.3 **Roles of the R&D department**

(a) **Environmental analysis.** Providing the organisation with knowledge of current opportunities and threats presented by developments in the technological environment. This might involve monitoring scientific journals, new patent applications and so forth.

(b) **Position audit.** Identifying technological strengths and weaknesses in the organisation's products and processes.

(c) Developing **new products** (or prolonging the lifespan of old products). **Development** is the function of translating useful research results into production. The development of a product might follow the stages set out below.

Step 1.　Preparing a specification for the new products

Step 2.　Preparing drawings or computer models (in CAD systems) of the product (or components)

Step 3.　Developing and testing prototypes

Step 4.　Preparing methods of assembly and assembly procedures

Step 5.　Supervising first product runs

Step 6.　Field test

Step 7.　Releasing the product for full production and selling to the market

(d) Developing **new production processes**, in response to the need for increased productivity or cost reduction, or to the availability of new technologies.

(e) **Plan and control** R&D work

(f) **Culture.** Ensure that innovation and the exercise of creative imagination are encouraged amongst employees. This clearly is tied in with the marketing orientation of a firm and with its commitment to quality.

Product and process research

2.4 There are two categories of R&D.

> **KEY TERMS**
>
> **Product research** is based on researching new products, in other words the organisation's 'offer' to the market.
>
> **Process research** is based on improving the way in which those products or services are made or delivered, or the efficiency with which they are made or delivered.

Product research

2.5 **Product research** involves developing, testing and prototyping. A proposed new product will go through an extensive **screening process** whereby the idea is assessed for:

(a) Conformance to the firm's strategic objectives (eg it might only be a short-term money spinner but might attract attention).

(b) Attractiveness to enough customers.

(c) Technical feasibility.

(Thus, there will be a lot of marketing research before the product is introduced.)

Process research

2.6 Process research involves attention to how the goods/services are produced. Process research has these rules.

(a) **Processes** are crucial in service industries (eg fast food), where processes are part of the services sold.

(b) **Productivity.** Efficient processes save money and time.

(c) **Planning.** If you know how long certain stages in a project are likely to take, you can plan the most efficient sequence.

(d) **Quality management.**

2.7 **Problems with R&D**

(a) **Organisational.** Problems of authority relationships and integration arise with the management of R&D. The function will have to liase closely with marketing and with production, as well as with senior management responsible for corporate planning: its role is both strategic and technical.

(b) **Financial.** R&D is by nature not easily planned in advance, and financial performance targets are not easily set. Budgeting for long-term, complex development projects with uncertain returns can be a nightmare for management accountants.

BPP PUBLISHING

(c) **Evaluation and control.** Pure research or even applied research may not have an obvious pay off in the short term. Evaluation could be based on successful application of new ideas, ie patents obtained, commercial viability etc.

(d) **Staff problems.** Research staff are usually highly qualified and profession-orientated, with consequences for the style of supervision and level of remuneration offered to them.

(e) **Cultural problems.** Encouraging innovation means trial and error, flexibility, tolerance of mistakes in the interests of experimentation, high incentives etc. If this is merely a subculture in an essentially bureaucratic organisation, it will not only be difficult to sustain, but will become a source of immense 'political' conflict. The R&D department may have an 'academic' or university atmosphere, as opposed to a commercial one.

2.8 **R & D should be closely co-ordinated with marketing.**

(a) Customer needs, as identified by marketers, should be a vital input to new product developments.

(b) The R&D department might identify possible changes to product specifications so that a variety of marketing mixes can be tried out and screened.

Case example

An example of the relationship of R & D to marketing was described in an article in the *Financial Times* (14 July 1992) about the firm Nestlé, which invests £46m a year in research (and approximately £190m on development). Nestlé had a central R & D function, but also regional development centres. The central R & D function was involved in basic research. 'Much of the lab's work was only tenuously connected with the company's business... When scientists joined the lab, they were told "Just work in this or that area. If you work hard enough, we're sure you'll find something"'. The results of this approach were:

(a) The research laboratory was largely cut off from development centres.
(b) Much research never found commercial application.

As part of Nestlé's wider reorganisation, which restructured the business into strategic business units (SBU's), formal links have been established between R & D and the SBUs. This means that research procedures have been changed so that a commercial time horizon is established for some projects.

---

3 THE IMPORTANCE OF OPERATIONS

3.1 **'Operations' are the link between the strategy and the customer.** They appear lower in status than strategy formulation, but are critical in delivering customer satisfaction and profits. In **service industries**, in particular, the operational interface is the **moment of truth** with the customer.

3.2 **Link to mission.** The organisation's **mission** is only really meaningful if, at operational level, the mission is embodied in **policies and behaviour standards.**

3.3 **Link to human resources management**

(a) Operations management is linked to **job design**. Most jobs are designed around tasks to be done or roles to be played.

(b) **Changing** operations management can involve a major risk of process failure. Old ways of doing things have to be unlearnt.

KEY TERM

Operations plans are the fully detailed specifications by which individuals are expected to carry out the predetermined cycles of operations to meet sectoral objectives.

3.4 Operations plans are made for marketing, production, distribution and finance, IT systems and so on. They are **interrelated**.

(a) The **marketing plan** will detail expected selling quantities, and timings, advertising expenditure sales force activities.

(b) From the estimates of selling quantities, the required **production plan** can be formulated, stating what needs to be produced and at what cost, to match the volume and diversity of products that marketing expects to sell. The production programmes should include cost estimates (allowing for inflation) for direct materials, labour, energy and any other major expenditures, as well as overhead recovery.

3.5 There are potential snags in co-ordinating the efforts of the marketing and production departments to produce an optimal plan.

(a) **Marketing staff** are occasionally **over-optimistic** about what they can sell, and so might ask for too much production. This will result in excess stocks.

(b) **Inefficiencies in manufacture** might give rise to unnecessarily high costs, thereby denying the marketing function the chance to sell at a profit the goods for which there is demand at a given price.

(c) Many small companies fail through **over hasty expansion** or **over trading**, for example by:

　(i) **Pursuing volume sales as opposed to profitable sales** (ie selling a lot, at low and unsustainable margins). A large firm might see this as an investment in market share.

　(ii) **Getting one large order, and forsaking others**. A diverse customer base may be a better guarantee of long term success.

3.6 Operations can be divided into production and service operations.

4 PRODUCTION

4.1 The production function plans, organises, directs and controls the necessary activities to provide products and services.

Activity	Example
Obtain **inputs** to the production 'system', such as plant facilities, materials and labour.	Inputs: timber, screws, nails, adhesives, varnish, stain, templates, cutting tools, carpenters
Adding of value The activities below occupy most of the production manager's attention: • Scheduling jobs on machines • Assigning labour to jobs • Controlling the quality of production and/or service delivery • Improving methods of work • Managing materials and equipment, to avoid waste	Operations: sawing, sanding, assembly, finishing
Create **outputs,** ie finished products and Services	Outputs: tables, chairs, cabinets, and so on.

BPP PUBLISHING

Intermediate activities in all three processes include processing, inspection and storage. The linkages in the process are usually provided by information. For example the stock control system will detail movements in and out of the warehouse. To control operations, a variety of records are required.

4.2 Production management decisions

(a) **Longer-term decisions**

These are related to setting up the production organisation.

- Selection of equipment and processes.
- Job design and methods.
- Factory location and layout.
- Ensuring the right number and skills of employees.

(b) **Short-term decisions**

These are concerned with the running and control of the organisation.

- Production and control
- Quality management
- Maintenance
- Labour control and supervision
- Stock control

Relationships with other functions

4.3 Longer term decisions, particularly relating to design and the innovation of improved products, cannot be taken by the production department alone; its activities must be **integrated with other functions** in the firm.

- **Product design** is co-ordinated with **R & D**.

- **Job design** will involve consultation with **human resources** specialists.

- The quantities needed to be produced will be notified by the **sales department**.

- The **human resources department** will be involved in managing the work force.

- The **finance department** might indicate the resources available for new equipment.

5 SERVICE OPERATIONS

5.1 Quality in service industries has two aspects.

(a) **Technical quality** of the service encounter (ie what is received by the customer). For example, a customer is going to a bank about a pension. Service operations depend on the technical product training of the staff and their knowledge of the bank's services.

(b) **Functional quality** of the service encounter (ie how the service is provided). The dimension relates to the psychological interaction between the buyer and seller and is typically perceived in a very subjective way.

- **Relationships between employees**
- **Appearance and personality of service personnel**
- **Service-mindedness of the personnel**
- **Accessibility of the service to the customer**
- **Approachability of service personnel**

5.2 **Dimensions of service operations**

Determinants	Comments
Tangibles	The physical evidence, such as the quality of fixtures and fittings of the company's service area, must be consistent with the desired image.
Reliability	Getting it right first time is very important, not only to ensure repeat business, but, in financial services, as a matter of ethics, if the customer is buying a future benefit.
Responsiveness	The staff's willingness to deal with the customer's queries must be apparent.
Communication	Staff should talk to customers in non-technical language which they can understand.
Credibility	The organisation should be perceived as honest, trustworthy and as acting in the best interests of customers.
Security	This is specially relevant to medical and financial services organisations. The customer needs to feel that the conversations with bank service staff are private and confidential. This factor should influence the design of the service area.
Competence	All the service staff need to appear competent in understanding the product range and interpreting the needs of the customers. In part this can be achieved through training programmes.
Courtesy	Customers (even rude ones) should perceive service staff as polite, respectful and friendly. This basic requirement is often difficult to achieve in practice, although training programmes can help.
Understanding customers' needs	The use of computer-based customer databases can be very impressive in this context. The service personnel can then call up the customer's records and use these data in the service process, thus personalising the process. Service staff need to meet customer needs rather than try to sell products. This is a subtle but important difference.
Access	Minimising queues, having a fair queuing system and speedy but accurate service are all factors which can avoid customers' irritation building up. A pleasant relaxing environment is a useful design factor in this context.

6 HUMAN RESOURCES MANAGEMENT

KEY TERMS

Human resources management (HRM): 'a strategic, coherent and comprehensive approach to the management and development of the organisation's human resources in which every aspect of that process is wholly integrated with the overall management of the organisation'. (Michael Armstrong)

Personnel management: 'That part of human resources management concerned with staffing the enterprise, meeting the needs of people at work and the practical rules and procedures governing relationships between employees and the organisation'.

R Bennett

6.1 **Differences between HRM and personnel management**

Personnel management	HRM
Administration of the employee's legal relationship with the organisation	Mobilising employee commitment to the **mission and values** of the organisation
Specialist activity, concerned with labour relations	Human resources issues and management are integrated with the needs of the business and its customers
Conflict is managed by adversarial negotiation	Aim is to **pre-empt conflict** by developing staff

6.2 HRM promises more flexibility than the traditional, administration emphasis of personnel management. This is because the HRM philosophy and practice is orientated towards forward management.

    (a) The rise of HRM coincided with the **erosion of collective bargaining, employment and trade union rights** in the UK.

    (b) Management thus had more power. The emphasis thus changed from:

        (i) 'Managing labour relations' to

        (ii) Getting the most out of employees

6.3 The **emphases of HRM** are thus:

    The interests of the **organisation**

- A **strategic** approach
- Getting **added value** from people by training
- **Managing employees' performance**
- Gaining **commitment** to the objectives and values of the organisation

6.4 **Objectives of HRM**

    (a) **Develop an effective organisation** which will respond effectively to change.

    (b) **Obtain and develop the human resources** required by the organisation and use and motivate them effectively.

    (c) **Create and maintain a co-operative climate of relationships** within the organisation.

    (d) **Meet the organisation's** social and legal **responsibilities**.

6.5 HRM is dealt with in much more detail in Part C of this Study Text.

7 THE FINANCE FUNCTION 5/01

7.1 **Role of the finance department**

- **Raising money,** and ensuring money is available to those who need it.
- **Recording** and **controlling** what happens to money. This might include sundry tasks such as payroll and credit control
- Providing **information to managers** to help them make decisions.
- **Reporting** to stakeholders such as shareholders and tax authorities

Management accounting information

7.2 The finance function plays a critical role in providing information to management to assist in **planning, decision making and control.**

    (a) **Planning**

        (i) The finance function draws up **budgets** which directs and allocates resources.

(ii) The finance function also produces **forecasts** of anticipated future results.

(b) **Decision making**. The finance function is often involved in assessing and modelling the expenditure and cash flow implications of proposed decisions.

(c) **Control**

(i) **Budgets are also used to monitor performance**. The finance function regularly provides information comparing budgeted revenues and costs for a period, with actual results and with comparisons from previous months.

(ii) **Management accountants** are involved in assessing the contribution which products, services, processes and other operations make to overall profitability.

(iii) **Costing based on predetermined standards** provides the information (variance analysis) which enables managers to identify weaknesses and look for remedies (attention directing) all in a timely manner.

7.3 The success of management accountants in meeting their job objectives will depend upon two things.

- The **quality of the information** they provide.
- Whether the information they provide to other managers is used properly.

Co-ordination with other departments

7.4 Instead of being seen as helpers and advisers to other managers, management accountants are sometimes regarded as an 'enemy' who produce reports on performance that try to **find fault**. However, close co-ordination with other departments is essential.

(a) The **purchase ledger section** relies on the purchasing department to send copies of purchase orders and confirm the validity of invoices received from suppliers, and also to inform the purchase ledger staff about any despatches concerning goods received, or purchases returns. The section also relies on the cashier to inform it of all payments of invoices.

(b) The **sales ledger section** relies on **sales staff** to send copies of sales order or confirmations of goods delivered to customers, and on the cashier to pass on information about payments received.

(c) The sales ledger section must also co-operate with **debt collection staff**, by helping to prepare monthly statements and lists of aged debtors. **Credit control** work and the work of the debt collection staff are also closely interdependent, relying on the free exchange of information between them.

(d) The **financial accounting** staff responsible for the preparation of the annual accounts might rely on the management accounting staff for data about stock records, so as to place a value on closing stocks in the accounts.

(e) As **information providers** to other managers in other departments in the organisation, accountants cannot be fully effective unless they work in co-operation with these other managers.

The finance department and strategic planning

7.5 The role of finance is three-fold.

- Finance is a **resource**, which can be deployed so that objectives are met.
- A firm's **objectives** are often expressed in financial or semi-financial terms.
- **Financial controls** are often used to plan and control the implementation of strategies.

Financial indicators are often used for detailed performance assessment. (Over-reliance on financial performance ignores key long-term issues such as competitors.)

7.6 As a planning medium and tool for monitoring, financial management contributes to the strategy by:

(a) **Ensuring that resources of finance are available** in order to meet the strategy. Issues of raising equity or loan capital are important here. The amount of resources that the strategy will consume needs to be assessed, and the likely cost of those resources. Those resources should be secure and sufficient. Cash flow forecasting will also be necessary to ensure that the strategy does not lead to problems of liquidity (ie the company does not find it suddenly has no money).

(b) **Integrating the strategy into budgets** for revenues, operating costs and capital expenditure over a period. The budgeting process serves both as a planning tool and as a means of financial control and monitoring.

(c) **Establishing the necessary performance measures**, in line with other departments for monitoring strategic objectives.

(d) **Establishing priorities**, if, for example, altered conditions make some aspects of the strategy hard to fulfil.

(e) **Assisting in the modelling process**. Financial models are simplified representations of the business. It is easier to experiment with models, to see the effect on the business of changes in variables, than with the business itself. As finance is a measure of success, it is also a measure of sensitivity.

8 THE VALUE CHAIN

8.1 The **value chain** model of corporate activities, developed by *Michael Porter*, offers a bird's eye view of the firm and what it does. Porter calls it a **theory of the firm**.

Exam focus point

The value chain is not specifically included in the syllabus for Paper 11. However, it is an *extremely valuable model* and worth your attention for two reasons.

(a) It is a very good way of thinking about an organisation as a whole since it emphasises the way the various systems work together.

(b) It is very useful in the exam. You can use it as a basis for analysing the data given in questions and for structuring answers. Use it as a kind of checklist to ensure that you have covered all the angles.

8.2 Competitive advantage, says Porter, arises out of the way in which firms organise and perform **value activities**.

KEY TERM

Value activities are the means by which a firm creates value in its products.

8.3 Activities incur costs, and, in combination with other activities, provide customer satisfactions that generate **margin**.

8.4 EXAMPLE

Let us explain this point by using the example of a **restaurant**. A restaurant's main value activities can be divided into buying food, cooking it, and serving it to customers. There is no reason, in theory, why the customers should not do all these things themselves, at home. The customer however, is not only prepared to **pay for someone else** to do all this but also **pays more than the cost of** the resources (food, wages and so on). The ultimate value a firm creates is measured by the amount customers are willing to pay for its products or services above the cost of carrying out value activities. A firm is profitable if the realised value to customers exceeds the collective cost of performing the activities.

(a) Customers **purchase value**, which they measure by comparing a firm's products and services with similar offerings by competitors.

(b) The business **creates value** by carrying out its activities either more efficiently than other businesses, or by combining them in such a way as to provide a unique product or service.

Question 2

Outline different ways in which the restaurant can create value.

Answer

Here are some ideas. Each of these options is a way of organising the activities of buying, cooking and serving food in a way that customers will value.

(a) It can become more efficient, by automating the production of food, as in a fast food chain.

(b) The chef can develop commercial relationships with growers, so he or she can obtain the best quality fresh produce.

(c) The chef can specialise in a particular type of cuisine.

(d) The restaurant can be styled for those customers who value atmosphere and a sense of occasion, in addition to a restaurant's purely gastronomic pleasures.

(e) The restaurant can serve a particular type of customer, such as holiday-makers or business people.

8.5 According to Porter, the value activities of *any* firm can be divided into nine types. Here is his diagram.

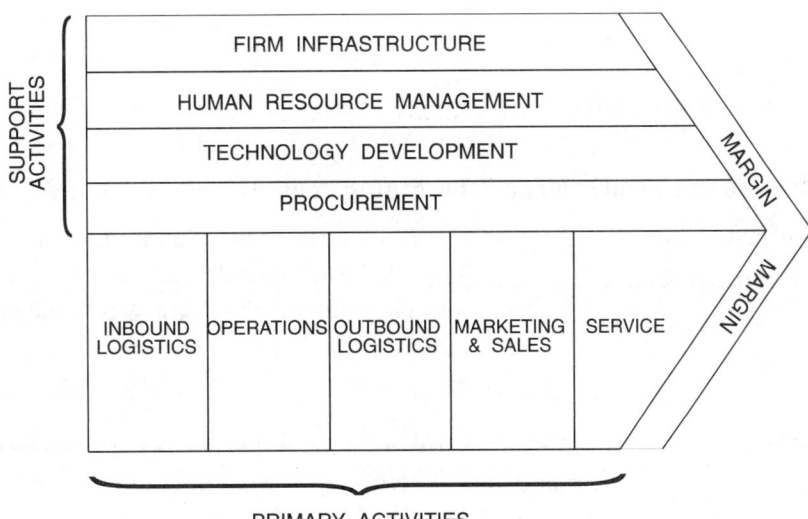

BPP
PUBLISHING

The **margin** is the excess the customer is prepared to **pay** over the **cost** to the firm of obtaining resource inputs and providing value activities. It represents the **value created** by the **value activities** themselves and by the **management of the linkages** between them.

> **Exam focus point**
> This diagram is worth committing to memory as it can be used both to analyse data and to structure answers.

Activity

8.6 **Primary activities** are directly related to production, sales, marketing, delivery and service.

	Comment
Inbound logistics	Receiving, handling and storing inputs to the production system: warehousing, transport, stock control and so on.
Operations	Convert resource inputs into a final product. Resource inputs are not only materials. People are a resource especially in service industries. Note that this is not just applicable to manufacturing firms, hence the careful choice of name. Service companies also have operations.
Outbound logistics	Delivering the product to customers; this may include storage, testing, bulk transport, packaging, delivery and so on.
Marketing and sales	Informing customers about the product, persuading them to buy it, and enabling them to do so: advertising, promotion and so on.
After sales service	Installing products, repairing them, upgrading them, providing spare parts and so forth.

8.7 **Support activities** provide purchased inputs, human resources, technology and infrastructural functions to support the primary activities. The first three tend to provide specific elements of support to the primary activities.

Activity	Comment
Procurement	Acquire the resource inputs to the primary activities (eg purchase of materials, subcomponents equipment).
Technology development	Product design, improving processes and/or resource utilisation.
Human resource management	Recruiting, training, developing and rewarding people.
Firm infrastructure	General management, planning, finance, quality control, public and legal affairs: these activities normally support the chain as a whole rather than individual activities. They are crucially important to an organisation's strategic capability in all primary activities.

8.8 It is important to understand that **activities are not the same as departments**. This is particularly true of support activities, which may be spread across a range of departments. To take a simple example, procurement may be largely the responsibility of the Purchasing Department, but buying machinery might be undertaken by the Production Director in a

manufacturing company, accounting software might be bought by the Chief Accountant and overnight subsistence might be bought by sales people.

8.9 **Linkages** connect the activities of the value chain, wherever they take place.

(a) **Activities in the value chain affect one another**. For example, more costly product design or better quality production might reduce the need for after-sales service.

(b) **Linkages require co-ordination**. For example, Just In Time requires smooth functioning of operations, outbound logistics and service activities such as installation.

8.10 Because activities can be spread across departments, rather than corresponding to neat, organisation chart boundaries, managing them for best effect can be extremely difficult. Cost control can be a particular problem. The dispersion of activities also complicates the management of linkages.

Value system

8.11 Activities and linkages that add value do not stop at the organisation's **boundaries**. For example, when a restaurant serves a meal, the quality of the ingredients - although they are chosen by the cook - is determined by the grower. The grower has added value, and the grower's success in growing produce of good quality is as important to the customer's ultimate satisfaction as the skills of the chef. A firm's value chain is connected to what Porter calls a **value system**.

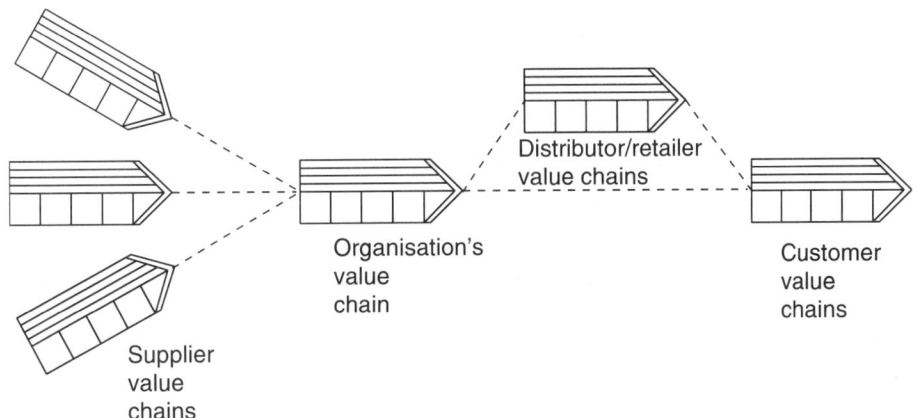

8.12 **Using the value chain.** A firm can secure competitive advantage in several ways.

- Invent new or better ways to do activities
- Combine activities in new or better ways
- Manage the linkages in its own value chain
- Manage the linkages in the value system

Question 3

Sana Sounds is a small record company. Representatives from Sana Sounds scour music clubs for new bands to promote. Once a band has signed a contract (with Sana Sounds) it makes a recording. The recording process is subcontracted to one of a number of recording studio firms which Sana Sounds uses regularly. (At the moment Sana Sounds is not large enough to invest in its own equipment and studios.) Sana Sounds also subcontracts the production of records and CDs to a number of manufacturing companies. Sana Sounds then distributes the disks to selected stores, and engages in any promotional activities required.

What would you say were the activities in Sana Sounds' *value chain*?

Answer

Sana Sounds is involved in the record industry from start to finish. Although recording and CD manufacture are contracted out to external suppliers, this makes no difference to the fact that these activities are part of Sana Sounds' own value chain. Sana Sounds earns its money by managing the whole set of activities. If the company grows then perhaps it will acquire its own recording studios.

8.13 Section summary

- The value chain models how activities can be deployed to add value for the customer.
- Value chains are part of a value system.
- Firms can benefit by performing activities in a unique way and/or exploiting linkages.

> ## Chapter roundup
>
> - The **marketing orientation** places 'the customer' at the heart of a company's decision making process. The marketing organisation identifies and satisfies customer needs profitably.
>
> - The **marketing mix** is described as the 4Ps (product, price, place, promotion). For services add: people, processes, physical evidence.
>
> - **Market and marketing research** identifies the customer's needs. Primary research involves interviewing customers directly, with the specific aim of assessing their tastes and opinions. Secondary research involves reviewing other sources of information (eg government statistics, social trends).
>
> - The **research and development function (R & D)** is sometimes involved in **basic and applied** research although in many cases it will be more appropriate for a company to use the research resources of outside bodies. **Development** of new **products** or **processes** is often carried out in-house.
>
> - There are two aspects to service quality: technical quality and functional quality. Service operations depend very much on the people who deliver the service. They should be willing, trustworthy, discreet, polite, competent technically and good communicators.
>
> - **Human resources management** (HRM) is more than simply **personnel administration**. It involves the effective deployment of skills and personnel to meet the organisation's objectives.
>
> - HRM activities cover the fields of remuneration, job design, motivation, employee participation, and management structure and style. HRM uses people as a resource both of labour power and of problem solving ability and creativity.
>
> - The **finance** function records financial transactions, reports to shareholders (financial accounts staff), plans and controls how funds are obtained and deployed (treasury) and provides internal information to management for planning, decision-making and control (management accounting). Other tasks include working capital management and credit control. As finance is a 'common language' it is used in planning and implementing strategies.
>
> - The value chain is an important and useful model that shows how value activities are integrated within the firm.

Quick quiz

1   Distinguish a marketing orientated firm from a sales orientated firm.

2   What is the scope of marketing research?

3   What are the 4 P's?

4   Distinguish between product research and process research.

5   What is the role of the production function?

6   What is HRM?

7   What are HRM's main emphases?

8   How can HRM enhance organisational effectiveness?

9   How does the finance function relate to strategy?

Answers to quick quiz

1   A sales oriented firm works hard to sell its existing products. A marketing oriented firm finds out what the market wants and tries to provide it.

2   Marketing research includes research relating to sales, products, pricing, communications and distribution.

3   Product, place, price and promotion

4   Product research is about developing new products, while process research is about developing new methods of production.

5   The production function plans, organises and controls the central value adding activities of the organisation.

6   A strategic approach to the management and development of human resources.

7   A strategic approach; the needs of the organisation; training for added value; performance management; gaining commitment.

8   By obtaining, developing and motivating the human resources needed by the organisation.

9   Strategic objectives are normally expressed in financial, or at least numerical, terms. Finance is a major resource and particularly flexible in the ways in which it can be deployed. Financial controls are used in the implementation of strategies.

Now try the question below from the Exam Question Bank

Number	Level	Marks	Time
Q8	Exam	20	36 mins

Chapter 9

THE MANAGEMENT ACCOUNTANT AND THE ORGANISATION

Topic List	Syllabus Reference	Ability required
1 The role of the management accountant	(ii)	Comprehension
2 Departmental performance measures	(ii)	Comprehension
3 Modern developments	(ii)	Comprehension

Introduction

In this chapter we look at the way the work of the management accountant contributes to the management of the organisation. Management accountancy is largely concerned with the provision of accurate, usable information that is relevant to control and decision-making. The nature of that information will vary from organisation to organisation and from department to department. In the first two sections of the chapter we discuss some general principles that may be applied by management accountants to their work.

The role of the management accountant is constantly developing. In Section 3 we examine some of the new techniques management accountants are using and the changing demands that are made of them

Learning outcomes covered in this chapter

- Explain the relationship between the work of the Management Accountant and the functional areas of an organisation.

- Analyse the information needs of managers in each of the main functional areas of an organisation.

Syllabus content covered in this chapter

- The information required by managers in the various functional areas of a business organisational and the role of the Management Accountant in identifying and satisfying those information needs.

1   THE ROLE OF THE MANAGEMENT ACCOUNTANT

1.1   The broad division of accountancy into financial accountancy and management accountancy reflects the two main purposes to which accounting information is put.

(a)   Financial accountants provide information that is mostly of use to those **outside the organisation.**

(b)   Management accountants provide information that is useful **within the organisation**: that is, information that can be used by managers, to assist them in their work.

1.2 Most management accounting information is used for three purposes.

- Planning
- Controlling
- Decision-making

1.3 In 1955, *Simon* identified three typical attributes of management accounting information.

(a) It should be useful for **scorekeeping** - seeing how well the organisation is doing overall.

(b) It should be **attention-directing** - indicating problem areas that need to be investigated.

(c) It should be useful for **problem-solving** - providing a means of evaluating alternative responses to the situations in which the organisation finds itself.

These qualities are still relevant to the management accountant's output.

Decision-making

1.4 Most of the rest of this chapter is concerned with various informational aspects of the management accountant's role in planning and controlling routine operations. However, we will first deal with **decision making**. Clearly, decisions should be made as rationally as possible and in the light of as much information as can be made available. It will often be the task of the management accountant to assemble, collate, present and interpret the information needed. Several techniques are available for this purpose.

(a) Discounted cash flow methods

(b) Decision-relevant costs

(c) Operational research and management science techniques such as queuing theory, regression analysis and linear programming

Other, more specialised techniques exist, particularly in the field of strategic financial management.

1.5 You will be aware from your mainstream accounting studies that using these techniques properly is one of the most demanding tasks you can be called on to perform. Management accountants will be expected to deploy them at whatever level they work. For instance, regression analysis may be useful to make sense of raw data at the level of an individual machine on a factory floor, while discounting may assist strategic investment decisions at board level.

Budgetary control

1.6 The management accountant's input into the processes of organisational planning and control usually takes the form of a system of **budgetary control**.

> **KEY TERM**
>
> **Budgetary control** is the establishment of budgets relating the responsibilities of executives to the requirements of a policy, and the continuous comparison of actual with budgeted results, either to secure by individual action the objectives of that policy or to provide a basis for its revision .

1.7 A budget is a plan, usually expressed in money terms, and it forms the basis of a **control system.**

Control System

The essence of control is the measurement of results and comparison of them with the original plan. Any deviation from plan indicates that control action is required to make the results conform more closely with plan.

> **KEY TERM**
>
> **Feedback** occurs when the results (outputs) of a system are used to control it, by adjusting the input or behaviour of the system. Businesses use feedback information to control their performance.
>
> **Single loop feedback** results in the system's behaviour being altered to meet the plan.
>
> **Double loop feedback** can result in changes to the plan itself.

1.8 **Double loop feedback** is control information transmitted to a higher level in the system. Whereas single loop feedback is concerned with immediate task control, higher level feedback is concerned with overall control. The term double loop feedback indicates that feedback is used to indicate both divergence between the observed and expected results where control action might be required, and also the need for adjustments to the plan itself.

1.9 **Feedforward control**

(a) **Control delay.** A timelag may exist between the actual results and the corrective action. However, results can be anticipated.

(b) **Feedforward control** uses **anticipated** or forecast results, and compares them with the plan. **Corrective action** is thus taken **in advance**, before it is too late to do anything effective. Control is exercised before the results, rather than after the event.

1.10 **Main uses of budgetary control**

- To define the objectives of the organisation as a whole.
- To reveal the extent by which actual results have exceeded or fallen short of the budget.
- To indicate why actual results differ from those budgeted.
- As a basis for the revision of the current budget, or the preparation of future budgets.
- To ensure that resources are used as efficiently as possible.
- To see how well the activities of the organisation have been co-ordinated.
- To provide some central control where activities are decentralised.

1.11 *Emmanuel et al* describe **four necessary conditions that must be satisfied before any process can be said to be controlled.** These will help us to put control into a wider context still.

(a) **Objectives** for the process being controlled must exist, for without an aim or purpose control has no meaning.

(b) The **output of** the process must be **measurable** in terms of the dimensions defined by the objectives.

(c) A **predictive model** of the process being controlled is required so that causes for the non-attainment of objectives can be determined and proposed corrective actions evaluated.

(d) There must be a **capability of taking action** so that deviations of attainment from objectives can be reduced.

1.12 It is important to understand that this concept of control involves more than just measuring results and taking corrective action. Control in the broad sense embraces **the formulation of objectives** - deciding what are the things that need to be done - as well as monitoring their attainment by way of feedback. Management accountants working in senior management will be major contributors to the objective-setting process for two reasons.

(a) As *Drucker* pointed out, the most crucial aspect of management performance in business is economic success; that is, **financial targets are the vital ones**.

(b) Targets are only useful if performance can be **measured**: performance measurement is a major aspect of management accountancy.

Budget centres and organisation structure

1.13 The budget is normally broken down into elements, each of which concerns a **budget centre**. Budget centres will generally reflect the structure of the organisation. This means that the selection of budget centres will be influenced by issues such as size, task, staff, environment, age and culture. Possible **bases** for budget centres are **different activities** or **functions**, different **products**, different **geographical areas**, different **customers** and so on. Budget centres may overlap in the case of a matrix organisation.

1.14 Each budget centre will have a manager responsible for it, who will be extremely interested in the budgetary control information relating to it. The management accountant is therefore at the hub of the organisation's management information system and must liase closely with managers to ensure that they get the information they need in order to discharge their responsibilities.

Performance measurement

1.15 **Performance measurement aims to establish how well something or somebody is doing in relation to previous or expected activity or in comparison with another thing or body.** The 'thing' may be a machine, a factory, a branch, a subsidiary company or an organisation as a whole. The 'body' may be an individual employee, a manager, or a group of people.

Critical success factors

1.16 As long ago as 1955 *Lewis* made a study of *GEC's* management reporting system and found that it produced reports on the following factors.

- Profitability
- Market share
- Productivity
- Product leadership

- Personnel development
- Employee attitudes
- Public responsibility
- Balance between short-range and long-range goals

These are examples of 'critical success factors'.

> **KEY TERM**
>
> **A critical success factor** is an element of organisational activity that is central to its future success.

1.17 There are usually **fewer than ten** of these factors that any one executive should monitor. Furthermore, they are very time dependent so they should be **re-examined** as often as necessary to keep abreast of the current business climate.

1.18 Critical success factors can be set and used by **identifying objectives and goals, determining which factors are critical for accomplishing each objective** and then determining a small number of performance measures for each factor. For example, if next day delivery were an objective, an employee attitude survey that revealed indifference (or over-defensiveness) towards customer complaints about late deliveries would be an indication of failure.

Question 1

How could product leadership be measured, besides considering market share?

Answer

Qualitative measures ought to be available in the form of reviews by consumer magazines, newspapers, and trade press, awards, endorsement by public figures, and direct comment from customers.

The balanced scorecard

1.19 Another approach, originally developed by *Kaplan and Norton*, is the use of a **balanced scorecard** consisting of a variety of indicators both financial and non-financial. This was mentioned briefly in Chapter 2.

> **KEY TERM**
>
> The **balanced scorecard approach** is an approach to the provision of information to management to assist strategic policy formulation and achievement. It emphasises the need to provide the user with a set of information which addresses all relevant areas of performance in an objective and unbiased fashion. The information provided may include both financial and non-financial elements, and cover areas such as profitability, customer satisfaction, internal efficiency and innovation.

1.20 The balanced scorecard focuses on **four different perspectives**.

Perspective	Question	Explanation
Customer	What do existing and new customers value from us?	Gives rise to targets that matter to customers: cost, quality, delivery, inspection, handling and so on.
Internal	What processes must we excel at to achieve our financial and customer objectives?	Aims to improve internal processes and decision making.
Innovation and learning	Can we continue to improve and create future value?	Considers the business's capacity to maintain its competitive position through the acquisition of new skills and the development of new products.
Financial	How do we create value for our shareholders?	Covers traditional measures such as growth, profitability and shareholder value but set through talking to the shareholder or shareholders direct.

Performance targets are set once the key areas for improvement have been identified, and the balanced scorecard is the **main monthly report**.

1.21 The scorecard is **balanced** in the sense that managers are required to **think in terms of all four perspectives**, to **prevent improvements being made in one area at the expense of** another.

Problems with the balanced scorecard

1.22 As with all techniques, problems of application can arise.

Problem	Explanation
Conflicting measures	Some measures in the scorecard such as research funding and cost reduction may naturally conflict. It is often difficult to determine the balance which will achieve the best results.
Selecting measures	Not only do appropriate measures have to be devised but the number of measures used must be agreed. Care must be taken that the impact of the results is not lost in a sea of information.
Expertise	Measurement is only useful if it initiates appropriate action. Non-financial managers may have difficulty with the usual profit measures. With more measures to consider this problem will be compounded.

Interpretation	Even a financially-trained manager may have difficulty in putting the figures into an overall perspective.

2 DEPARTMENTAL PERFORMANCE MEASURES

Deciding what measures to use

2.1 Clearly different measures are appropriate for different departments. Determining which measures are used in a particular case will require **preliminary investigations** along the following lines.

(a) The **objectives/mission** of the department must be **clearly formulated** so that when the factors critical to the success of the mission have been identified they can be translated into performance indicators.

(b) **Measures** must be **relevant** to the way the department operates. Managers themselves must believe the indicators are useful.

(c) **The costs and benefits of providing resources** (people, equipment and time to collect and analyse information) to produce a performance indicator must be carefully **weighed up**.

(d) **Performance must be measured in relation to something**, otherwise measurement is meaningless.

Profitability, activity and Productivity

2.2 In general, there are three possible **points of reference for measurement**.

(a) **Profitability**

Profit has two components: **cost and income**. All parts of an organisation and all activities within it incur costs, and so their success needs to be judged in relation to cost. Only some parts of an organisation receive income, and their success should be judged in terms of both cost and income.

(b) **Activity**

All parts of an organisation are also engaged in activities (activities cause costs). Activity measures could include the following.

(i) Number of orders received from customers, a measure of the effectiveness of marketing

(ii) Number of machine breakdowns attended to by the repairs and maintenance department.

Each of these items could be measured in terms of **physical numbers, monetary value**, or **time spent**.

(c) **Productivity**

This is the **quantity of the product or service produced in relation to the resources put in**, for example so many units produced per hour or per employee. It defines **how efficiently resources are being used**.

The **dividing line between productivity and activity is thin**, because every activity could be said to have some 'product', or if not can be measured in terms of lost units of product or service.

Financial performance measures

2.3 Financial measures (or **monetary measures**) are very familiar to you. Here are some examples, accompanied by comments from a single page of the *Financial Times*.

Measure	Comment
Profit	The commonest measure of all. Profit maximisation is usually cited as the main objective of most business organisations: 'ICI increased pre-tax profits to £233m'; 'General Motors... yesterday reported better-than-expected first-quarter net income of $513 (£333m) ...
Revenue	'the US businesses contributed £113.9m of total group turnover of £409m'
Costs	'Sterling's fall benefited pre-tax profits by about £50m while savings from the cost-cutting programme instituted in 1991 were running at around £100m a quarter'; 'The group interest charge rose from £48m to £61m'.
Share price	'The group's shares rose 31p to 1278p despite the market's fall'.
Cash flow	'Cash flow was also continuing to improve, with cash and marketable securities totalling $8.4bn on March 31, up from $8bn at December 31'.

2.4 The important point to note here is that the monetary amounts stated **are only given meaning in relation to something else**. Profits are higher than last year's; cashflow has improved compared with last quarter's.

2.5 We can generalise the above and give a list of **yard-sticks against which financial results are usually placed so as to become measures.**

- **Budgeted** sales, costs and profits
- **Standards** in a standard costing system
- The **trend** over time (last year/this year, say)
- The **results of other parts** of the business
- The **results of other businesses**
- The **economy** in general
- **Future potential** (eg a new business in terms of nearness to breaking even)

2.6 More sophisticated measures such as **return on investment** and **residual income** have their place in the measurement of overall performance.

Quantitative and qualitative performance measures

2.7 It is possible to distinguish between **quantitative information**, which is **capable of being expressed in numbers**, and **qualitative information**, which **can only be expressed in numerical terms with difficulty.**

2.8 An example of a **quantitative performance measure** is '**You have been late for work twice this week and it's only Tuesday!**'. An example of a **qualitative performance measure is 'My bed is very comfortable'.**

2.9 The first measure is likely to find its way into a staff appraisal report. The second would feature in a bed manufacturer's customer satisfaction survey. Both are indicators of whether their subjects are doing as good a job as they are required to do.

2.10 **Qualitative measures** are by nature **subjective and judgmental** but this does not mean that they are not valuable. They are especially valuable when they are derived from several different sources because then they can be expressed in a mixture of quantitative and qualitative terms, which is more meaningful overall. 'Seven out of ten customers think our beds are very comfortable' is a **quantitative** measure of customer satisfaction as well as a **qualitative** measure of the perceived performance of the beds.

Operational performance indicators

2.11 **Financial measures do not convey the full picture of a company's performance**, especially in a modern manufacturing environment. Increasingly therefore companies are discovering the usefulness of quantitative and qualitative **non-financial performance measures** such as quality, machine down time, and so on.

Sales

2.12 Traditionally sales performance is measured in terms of **price and volume variances**, and also perhaps a **sales mix variance**. Other possible measures include **revenue targets** and **target market share**. These are all highly valid measures and there is no reason to suppose that they will not remain the principal measures for sales. They may, of course, be **analysed in some detail:** by country, by region, by individual products, by salesperson and so on.

2.13 However, in a **customer-focused organisation** the basic information 'Turnover is up by 14%' can be supplemented by a host of other indicators.

Indicator	Detail
Customer rejects/returns: total sales	This ratio helps to monitor customer satisfaction, providing a check on the efficiency of quality control procedures.
Deliveries late: deliveries on schedule	This ratio can be applied both to sales made to customers and to receipts from suppliers. When applied to customers it provides an indication of the efficiency of production and production scheduling. The term **'cycle time'** is used in this context (the length of time between receipt of an order and delivery of the product).
Flexibility measures	These indicate how well able a company is to respond to customers' requirements, both in terms of delivering the goods on time, and in terms of speed of launching new products and changing old procedures to meet market needs.
Number of people served and speed of service	This is particular relevant in a shop or bank. If it takes too long to reach the point of sale, future sales are liable to be lost.
Customer satisfaction	You have probably filled in customer attitude surveys in fast-food restaurants or on aeroplanes for input to the organisation's management information system.
Marketing measures	These might include number of sales per enquiry, amount of new business brought in per sales rep and so on.

Customer profitability analysis

2.14 In certain circumstances a useful approach to performance evaluation may be the **analysis of profitability by customer or customer group**. Profitability can vary widely between different customers because **various overhead costs are, to some extent, variable and customer-driven.**

- Discounts
- Sales force (eg telesales are cheaper and more time-efficient than a field sales force)
- Quality control (some customers demand higher quality)
- Merchandising
- Distribution (full-pallet transactions are cheaper than breaking bulk)
- Promotions
- Financing costs
- Enquiries

> **KEY TERM**
>
> **Customer profitability analysis (CPA)** is an analysis of the revenue streams and service costs associated with specific customers or customer groups.

2.15 The task of customer profitability analysis is to **relate these variabilities in cost to individual customers or customer groups.** Managers can use this information to **check whether individual customers are actually profitable** to sell to, and to **assess whether profitability can be improved for any customer** by switching effort from one type of overhead activity to another, or by reducing spending on some overhead activities.

2.16 Customer profitability analysis can **provide valuable management accounting information.**

(a) It helps a firm to **identify unprofitable customers** as well as unprofitable products.

(b) It draws attention to the **three ways of improving profitability**, both for individual customers and so for products in total.

    (i) Productivity improvements to reduce product costs
    (ii) Higher sales volumes to customers, to increase total contribution
    (iii) More efficient use of overhead resources to improve customer profitability

Costs

2.17 Improving performance in the area of costs means **making them as low as possible.** Some possible approaches are **setting a target which is an ideal standard** and measuring progress towards the ideal by comparing actual costs with the standard over time, or **setting a target for periodic improvement of costs** (for example, 'reduce costs by 3% per annum') and comparing actual performance against this. This is **kaizen costing** or **continuous improvement.**

Materials

2.18 Traditional measures are **standard costs** for materials, and price and particularly **usage variances.** Many traditional systems also analyse **wastage**, although as we have seen elsewhere, wastage is **to some extent encouraged** by systems that regard a certain level of loss as normal and acceptable.

2.19 Measures in modern manufacturing environments such as number of rejects in materials supplied, and the timing and reliability of deliveries of materials are discussed later in the context of quality and total quality management.

2.20 Other relevant measures include the following.

(a) **Stock turnover.** This is a traditional measure, but a particularly relevant one in a Just-in-Time production environment, where the aim is to minimise all stocks.

(b) **Physical qualities** of materials may be crucially important to the final product, and if so the performance of materials should be measured. They may have to demonstrate a certain degree of smoothness, hardness, pliability, or stickiness; they may have to be a consistent shade of a certain colour or a consistent smell. Do they retain their shape, or do some get misshapen in transit or during production?

Labour

2.21 Labour costs are traditionally measured in terms of **standard performance** and **rate and efficiency variances.**

2.22 Many other **staff-related measures may be established,** such as sales per salesperson; almost any aspect of a business's performance can be measured in terms of the different individuals or groups who actually do the job.

2.23 **Qualitative measures** of labour performance concentrate on matters such as ability to communicate, interpersonal relationships with colleagues, customers' impressions ('so and so was extremely helpful/rude'), and levels of skills attained.

2.24 Some matters are extremely **difficult to measure,** notably **staff morale,** but attempts can be made. British Telecom, for example, carries out an annual staff attitude survey amongst at least a quarter of its staff and measures the responses to 25 questions. BT also uses 'harder' measures like the rate of labour turnover, levels of absenteeism and evidence of industrial action.

2.25 *Drury* makes the additional point that **employee-based measures are very important when assessing the performance of the employees' manager.** High profitability or tight cost control should not be accompanied by 100% labour turnover!

Overheads

2.26 Apart from **standards for variable overheads and efficiency variances**, a variety of **time-based measures** are available. Here are just two examples.

(a) **Machine down time: total machine hours.** This ratio could be used to monitor machine availability and can provide a measure of machine usage and efficiency.

(b) **Value added time: production cycle time.** Value added time is the direct production time during which the product is being made and value is therefore being added. The production cycle time includes non-value-added times such as set-up time, downtime, idle time etc. The **optimum ratio is 100%,** but in practice this optimum will not be achieved. A high ratio will help a company to satisfy customer orders more quickly.

2.27 Overhead expenses may also be measurable in **qualitative terms**: is the light adequate? Is the office or factory warm enough? Does the general state of cleanliness detract from workers' performance?

Activity-based management and overheads

2.28 When a business introduces a system of **Activity based costing (ABC)** (discussed in Section 3 of this Chapter) it is forced to reanalyse its overheads in term of their underlying causes or **cost drivers**. The **implications for performance measurement are highly significant.**

2.29 For example, if a large part of production overheads used to be known as 'warehousing', but are now recognised as 'materials handling costs' that are incurred in relation to the number of production runs, then a materials handling rate per production run can be established. Many such insights will become possible using ABC and they are useful not only for costing products but also as **a measurement that will help in the management of costs.**

Non-financial performance measures

> **KEY TERM**
>
> **Non-financial performance measures** are 'Measures of performance based on non-financial information which may originate in and be used by operating departments to monitor and control their activities without any accounting input. Non-financial performance measures may give a more timely indication of the levels of performance achieved than do financial ratios, and may be less susceptible to distortion by factors such as uncontrollable variations in the effect of market forces on operations.'

2.30 The beauty of non-financial performance measures is that **anything can be compared if it is meaningful to do so**. The measures should be tailored to the circumstances so that, for example, number of coffee breaks per 20 pages of Study Text might indicate to you how hard you are studying!

2.31 However, many of the measures that are suggested combine elements from the chart shown below. The chart is not intended to be prescriptive or exhaustive, merely to encourage you to think creatively.

Errors/failure	Time	Quantity	People
Defects	Second	Parts/components	Employees
Equipment failures	Minute	Units produced	Employee skills
Complaints	Hour	Units sold	Customers
Returns	Shift	Services performed	Competitors
Stockouts	Cycle	kg/litres/metres	Suppliers
Lateness/waiting	Day	Documents	
Miscalculation	Month	Deliveries	
Absenteeism	Year	Enquiries	

2.32 Traditional measures derived from these lists like 'kg (of material) per unit produced' or 'units produced per hour' are fairly obvious, but what may at first seem a fairly unlikely combination may also be very revealing. 'Miscalculations per 1,000 invoices' would show how accurately the invoicing clerk was working. 'Defects per return' may show that customers are very fussy about quality or (if there are no defects in returned goods) that their real needs are not being properly identified.

The advantages and disadvantages of non-financial measures

2.33 Unlike traditional variance reports, they can be provided **quickly** for managers, per shift or on a daily or hourly basis as required. They are likely to be **easy to calculate**, and **easier for non-financial managers to understand** and therefore to use effectively.

2.34 There are problems associated with choosing the measures and there is a danger that **too many such measures could be reported**, overloading managers with information that is not truly useful, or that sends conflicting signals. There is clearly a need for the management accountant to work more closely with the managers who will be using the information to make sure that their needs are properly understood. The measures used are likely to be developed and refined over time. It may be that some will serve the purpose of drawing attention to areas in need of improvement but will be of no further relevance once remedial action has been taken. A flexible, responsive approach is essential.

2.35 Arguably, they are **less likely to be manipulated** than traditional profit-related measures and they should, therefore, **offer a means of counteracting short-termism**, since short-term profit at any (non-monetary) expense is rarely an advisable goal. However, the ultimate goal of commercial organisations in the long run is likely to remain the maximisation of profit and so the **financial aspect cannot be ignored**. A further danger is that they might lead managers to pursue **detailed operational goals** and become **blind to the overall strategy** in which those goals are set. A **combination** of financial and non-financial measures is likely to be most successful.

3 MODERN DEVELOPMENTS 5/01

> **Exam focus point**
> The first exam under the new syllabus included a part question based on this topic. This is a good example of the way the Examiner requires you to think outside the strict limits of the syllabus content and learning outcomes. The impact of modern developments such as environmental reporting is nowhere specified in the syllabus. Nevertheless, as a student at this level, you should both be keeping abreast of new ideas generally and be able to discuss them within the context of the syllabus. Thus, while the relevant part of the syllabus content merely talks about the 'information needs of managers', a question on how those needs are changing is quite fair.

3.1 The modern world is changing rapidly and the world of business is particularly dynamic. While many traditional aspects of management accounting practice continue largely unchanged, developments both in the way organisations are run and in wider society have had their impact. The purpose of this section is to discuss some of the recent developments.

Management accounting techniques

3.2 Developments in manufacturing such as JIT have led to the adoption of new techniques, particularly in the field of cost accounting. The detail of the way these techniques are applied in practice is not relevant to Paper 11; we will be more concerned with the reasons why they have been developed and their implications for the organisation.

Activity based costing

3.3 Traditional overhead absorption costing using absorption rates based on labour hours has become unsatisfactory for several reasons.

(a) Overheads have been growing as a proportion of total costs, because of increasing use of sophisticated machinery in production and increasing costs of marketing.

(b) Manufacturing labour costs have been falling absolutely, not just as a proportion of total cost.

(c) The structure of overheads has become more complex, reflecting the increased complexity of manufacturing systems and growing attention to quality management.

3.4 The first two of the points above taken together mean that labour hour overhead absorption rates have become several times larger than the labour rates themselves. In turn, this means that the accuracy of overhead absorption is very sensitive to the accuracy with which labour cost is measured. This, taken with point (c) above has led to a search for a better way to absorb overheads into product cost.

3.5 **Activity based costing** (ABC) has come to prominence as a solution to this problem. The principle is that resources consumed indirectly as overheads when products are made pass through an intermediate stage. Previously, labour hours was used as a proxy for this intermediate stage. The ABC approach is that this intermediate stage consists of the performance of necessary **activities** (such as supervision, maintenance and procurement) and the cost of these activities can be allocated to products with great accuracy. **Activities consume resources and products consume activities**.

3.6 The use of ABC requires the identification of the factors that determine the magnitude of the costs associated with each salient activity. These factors are known as **cost drivers**. In the case of the procurement activity, for example, the cost driver might be the number of purchase orders raised.

3.7 The costs associated with an activity are pooled and used to establish a **cost driver rate**, such as a cost per purchase order. Cost driver rates are then applied to the cost card for each product on the basis of the demands it makes on the various activities. A product incorporating a wide range of components purchased in small batches from a number of different suppliers would absorb more of the cost of the purchasing activity than would a product with simpler procurement requirements, for example.

3.8 **Advantages of ABC**

   (a) Direct labour absorption rates are abolished.

   (b) The use of multiple cost drivers recognises the complexity of modern processes in the cost of products.

   (c) Management attention is drawn forcefully to the **causes** of costs, which eases the problems of cost control and reduction.

   (d) Cost related decisions such as setting prices can be taken on the basis of more accurate information.

JIT and backflush costing

3.9 The *Toyota* system of production management has a number of important features that extend well beyond JIT delivery and lean production. However, the drive to eliminate inventory has made possible a significant simplification of the cost accounting process.

3.10 One of the main reasons for undertaking the effort of accounting for costs has been the need to value stocks of raw materials and components, work in progress and finished goods. Traditionally, cost book keeping has tracked factory production as output has moved from process to process, faithfully reflecting inputs of materials, labour and overheads. When manufacturing involved lengthy waiting and queuing times, this was essential if control was to be maintained.

3.11 JIT manufacturing has two effects that upset this system.

   (a) A very short period of time elapses from the delivery of raw materials to the despatch of a finished product. Work in progress is not in existence long enough for its value to be an issue.

   (b) There is very little inventory at any stage of manufacturing: the value of stock is unlikely to be material to the accounts.

3.12 **Backflush costing** simplifies the process of cost accounting. In its simplest form, no accounting entries are made until an item of production is complete. At that point a debit entry is made in the factory operating statement to reflect the standard manufacturing cost of the item. This is balanced by a credit for the cost of materials and a further single credit for **conversion cost**, which includes both labour and overheads.

3.13 Backflush costing thus reduces the cost of cost accounting itself.

Management information systems

> **KEY TERM**
>
> A **management information system** can be defined as a system 'which collects and presents management information to a business in order to facilitate its control'.

3.14 The rapid advance of information technology has led to the development of sophisticated computer based management information systems (MIS). These have revolutionised the collection, analysis and presentation of data of all types. Managers no longer have to choose between information overload and working by hunch. Relevant data is rapidly available in a usable form. Such systems have been particularly useful for controlling operations at all levels, even though, as the diagram below illustrates, there are significant contrasts between information needs at the different levels of management.

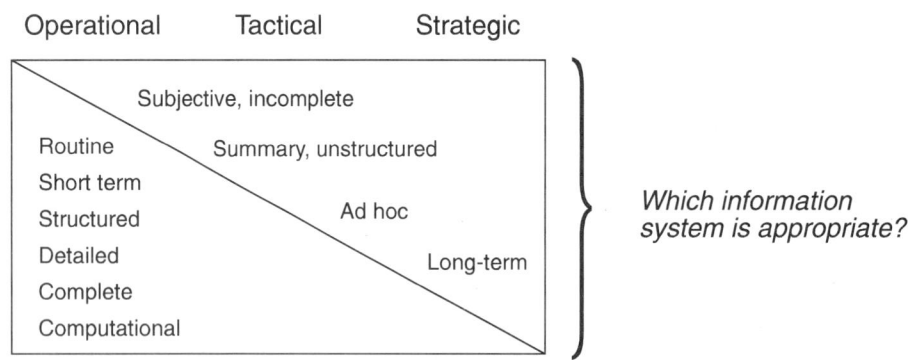

3.15 The scope of an MIS, potentially, is to satisfy all the informational needs of management. A good MIS will provide good information to those who need it. It is thus an important adjunct to management accountancy, and it will often fall to the management accountant to specify the outputs that are required.

3.16 An MIS is good at providing regular formal information gleaned from normal commercial data. For example, an MIS relating to sales could provide managers with information about matters such as those below.

   • Gross profit margins of particular products
   • Success in particular markets
   • Credit control information (eg payments)

It may be less efficient at presenting information which is relatively unpredictable, or informal, or unstructured. So, for example, an MIS could not provide information relating to the sudden emergence of a new competitor into the market.

3.17   While an MIS may not, in principle, be able to provide all the information used by management, it should however be sufficiently flexible to enable management to incorporate unpredictable, informal or unstructured information into decision-making processes. For example, many decisions are made with the help of financial models (eg spreadsheets) so that the effect of new situations can be estimated easily.

Operational level MIS

3.18   **Operational decisions are essentially small-scale and procedural**. Operational information is often highly formal and quantitative. This is time of manufacturing especially. Many operational decisions can, in fact, be incorporated into computer processing.

3.19   Most MIS at operational level, however, are essentially used for processing transactions, updating files and so forth.

Tactical level MIS

3.20   A variety of systems can be used at tactical level, and there may be a greater reliance than at operational level on information produced from the sources below.

- Exception reporting
- Informal systems
- Investigation and analysis of data acquired at operational level
- Externally generated data

3.21   The MIS at tactical level will interact with the same systems as that at operational level, and in fact tactical information may be generated in the same processing operation as operational level information. For example, tactical level information comparing actual costs incurred to budget can be produced by a system in which those costs are recorded. Functional MIS at tactical level are typically related to other functional MIS. Information from the sales MIS will affect the financial accounting system, for example.

Strategic level MIS

3.22   At strategic level the information system is likely to be informal, in the sense that it is not possible always to quantify or program strategic information, and much of the information might come from environmental sources. The MIS will provide summary level data from transactions processing. Human judgement is used more often at this level, as many strategic decisions cannot be programmed.

Comparisons

3.23   In a **finance subsystem,** the operational level would deal with cash receipts and payments, bank reconciliations and so forth. The tactical level would deal with cash flow forecasts and working capital management. Strategic level financial issues are likely to be integrated with the organisation's commercial strategy, but may relate to the most appropriate source of finance (eg long-term debt, or equity).

	Inputs	*Process*	*Outputs*
Strategic	Plans, competitor information, overall market information	Summarise Investigate Compare Forecast	Key ratios, ad hoc market analysis, strategic plans
Management/tactical	Historical and budget data	Compare Classify Summarise	Variance analyses Exception reports
Operational	Customer orders, Programmed stock control levels, cash receipts/payments	Update files Output reports	Updated files listings, invoices

Executive information system (EIS)

3.24 An **executive information system** is a type of DSS which gives the executive, normally a senior executive easy access to key internal and external data. An EIS is likely to have the following features.

- Provision of summary-level data, captured from the organisation's main systems.

- A facility which allows the executive to 'drill-down' easily from higher levels of information to lower.

- Data manipulation facilities (eg comparison with budget or prior year data).

- Graphics and other aids, for user-friendly presentation of data.

- A template system. (ie the same type of data eg sales figures is presented in the same format, irrespective of changes in the volume of information required.

- Ease of use ('idiot-proof' not just user friendly).

- Tools for analysis (including ratio analysis, forecasts, what-if analysis, trends).

Corporate governance and social responsibility

3.25 Ethics and social responsibility are discussed in Chapter 5 and all of that discussion applies here. However, there are some other related matters that are particularly relevant to the role of the management accountant.

3.26 **Corporate governance**. Financial wrongdoing by senior managers is of particular interest to management accountants who are themselves in senior positions. They are likely to be responsible for the internal control systems that are a principal line of defence against such wrongdoing and so may well be among the first to suspect that something is amiss. The dilemma of the potential whistleblower, discussed at the end of Chapter 5, may or may not apply, but a heavy responsibility will inevitably exist.

3.27 **Environmental reporting**. Large organisations are coming under increasing pressure to conform to environmentally sound practices in their operations. In many advanced countries there are stringent legal requirements, which, obviously, must be respected. There is also a further range of requirements promoted by the green lobby, some more reasonable than others. Large organisations must have a settled policy on these matters if they are not to be embarrassed. It is becoming accepted that it is appropriate for such organisations to demonstrate their compliance with the law and their own principles through the mechanism of environmental reporting.

3.28 **Social responsibility.** Where the stakeholder view is accepted, and where the political climate makes it appropriate, a similar approach may be taken in respect of social responsibility actions.

Chapter roundup

- An organisation's information systems are a vital part of its control system at strategic, tactical and operational level.

- Budgets are part of the organisation's control system, but cannot be the only controls.

- Budgets and accounting controls generally replicate the structure of the organisation hierarchy and the allocation of tasks and resources to responsibility centres (eg cost and profit centres). However, using profit centres can be dangerous if there is high interdependence between departments.

- Performance measures will vary from department to department and may be based on quantitative or qualitative data, or both.

- There have been a number of developments in cost accounting in recent years, driven by the changes in production techniques. Activity based costing gives more accurate product costs than the labour hour absorption rate method. The elimination of stocks and rapidity of production associated with JIT makes the simplified method of backflush costing possible.

- There is a growing requirement for awareness of ethical, environmental and socially responsible conduct.

Quick quiz

1   Draw a model of a control system.

2   What attributes did Simon look for in management accounting information?

3   Give three possible bases for organising budget centres.

4   What is a critical success factor?

5   What are the three most common references for performance measurement?

6   What are likely to be the outputs from a finance IT system at the management / tactical level?

7   What is a cost driver?

Answers to quick quiz

1

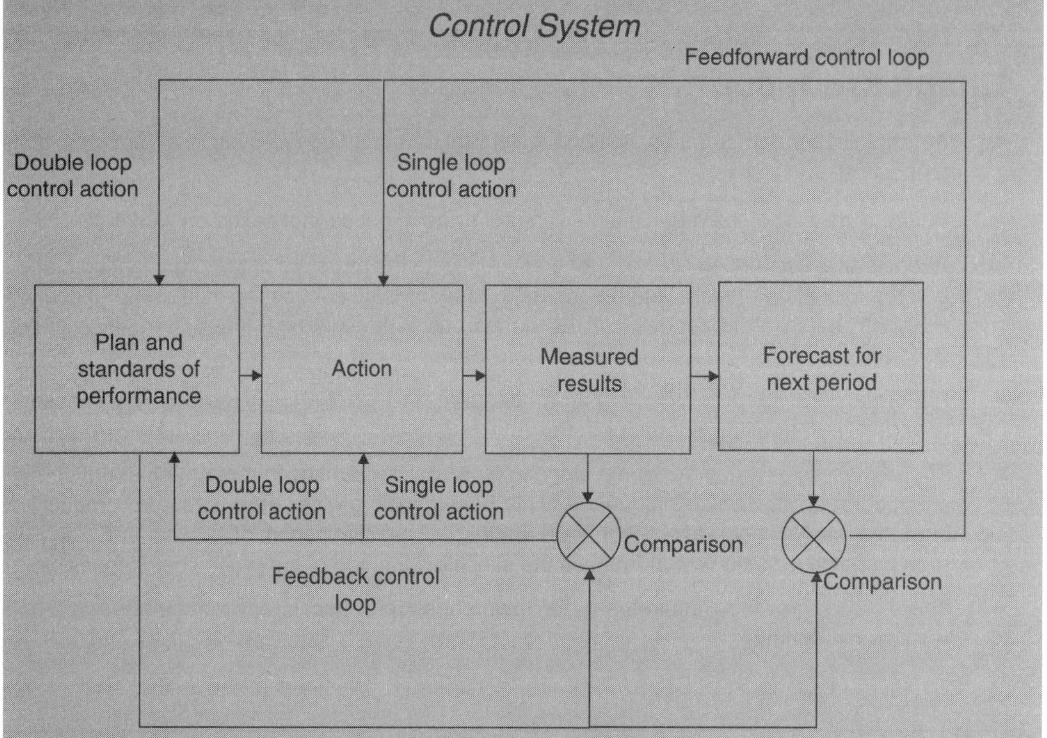

Control System

Feedforward control loop

Double loop control action

Single loop control action

| Plan and standards of performance | → | Action | → | Measured results | → | Forecast for next period |

Double loop control action — Single loop control action

⊗ Comparison

⊗ Comparison

Feedback control loop

2   Usefulness for score-keeping, usefulness for problem solving and potential for directing attention

3   Department, geography, function, product, customer

4   An element of organisational activity that is central to its future success

5   Profitability, activity and productivity

6   Exception reports; routine performance summaries, analysis of operational data.

7   The aspect of an activity that determines its total cost

Now try the question below from the Exam Question Bank

Number	Level	Marks	Time
Q9	Introductory	11	20 mins

Part C
Human resource management

Chapter 10

HUMAN RESOURCES

Topic List	Syllabus Reference	Ability required
1　What is human resource management?	(iii)	Analysis
2　Assessing human resource needs: the HR plan	(iii)	Analysis
3　Recruitment	(iii)	Analysis
4　Selection	(iii)	Analysis
5　Induction training	(iii)	Analysis

Introduction

In this chapter we start our coverage of human resource management (HRM).

By way of introduction, we note that HRM is different from traditional personnel management. Be sceptical. A recent report suggested that firms which employed specialist personnel or HRM staff were *more* likely to have industrial relations problems than those which did not (perhaps these would have been worse without them). There is also no evidence that employees are in any way happier in HRM environments. The ultimate purpose of HRM is strategic success.

By the end of this chapter you should have learned that human resources management takes a **strategic** approach to an organisation's recruitment, training and appraisal systems, in addition to personnel administration.

Any requirement for human resources revealed in the strategy-making process can be met by a mix of recruitment from outside or promotion from within (depending on the demography of the organisation and its internal labour markets).

Organisations are looking for a flexible and versatile workforce, leading to a growth in part-time working, teleworking and so on. This is discussed in the context of personal planning.

Recruitment is a major HRM activity which has its own procedures and skills. It is often associated with induction training.

Learning outcomes covered in this chapter

- Explain the process of human resource planning and its relationship to other types of business plan.

- Produce and explain a human resource plan for an organisation.

- Produce a plan for the recruitment, selection and induction of finance department staff.

- Produce a plan for the induction of new staff into the finance department of an organisation.

Syllabus content covered in this chapter

- The relationship of the human resource plan to other types of business plan.

- The determinants and content of a human resource plan (i.e. organisational growth rate, skills, training, development, strategy, technologies, natural wastage).

- The problems which may be encountered in the implementation of a human resource plan and the ways in which such problems can be avoided or solved.

- The human issues relating to recruitment, dismissal and redundancy and how to manage them.

- The process of recruitment and selection of staff using different recruitment channels (ie advertisement, agencies, consultants, executive search).

- The content and format of job descriptions, candidate specifications and job advertisements.

- The techniques that can be used in the selection of the most suitable applicant for a job (ie interviews, assessment centres, intelligence tests, aptitude tests, psychometric tests).

- The importance of negotiation during the offer and acceptance of a job.

- The process of induction and the importance thereof.

1 WHAT IS HUMAN RESOURCE MANAGEMENT?

Scope of HRM

1.1 Human resource management (HRM) is concerned with people at work and their relationships as they arise in the working environment.

1.2 It is possible to identify **four main objectives of HRM**.

(a) To develop an effective human component for the organisation which will respond effectively to change.

(b) To obtain and develop the human resources required by the organisation and to use and motivate them effectively.

(c) To create and maintain a co-operative climate of relationships within the organisation.

(d) To meet the organisation's social and legal responsibilities relating to the human resource.

1.3 These can be implemented in various activities, as in the diagram on the next page.

1.4 The phrase 'human resources' implies that managing labour is more than a case of supervising staff and agreeing their pay rates. Effective human resource management and employee development are necessary for the following reasons.

(a) To **increase productivity**. Developing employee skills might make employees more productive, hence the recent emphasis on public debate on the value of training.

(b) To **enhance group learning**. Employees work more and more in multi-skilled teams. Each employee has to be competent at several tasks. Some employees have to be trained to work together (ie in teamworking skills).

(c) To **reduce staff turnover**. Reducing staff turnover, apart from cutting recruitment costs, can also increase the effectiveness of operations. In service businesses, such as hotels, or retail outlets, reductions in staff turnover can be linked with repeat visits by customers. As it is cheaper to keep existing customers than to find new ones, this can have a significant effect on profitability.

(d) To **encourage initiative**. Organisations can gain significant advantage from encouraging and exploiting the present and potential abilities of the people within them.

HR Activities	HR Objectives	Responsibility	Relationships	Human resource	Organisation
		To meet the organisation's social and legal responsibilities	To create and maintain a co-operative climate of relationships within the organisation	To obtain and develop the human resources required by the organisation and to use and motivate them effectively	To design and develop an effective organisation which will respond appropriately to change
Organisation	Organisation design			•	•
	Organisation development		•	•	•
Manpower	Manpower planning			•	•
	Recruitment	•		•	
	Employment	•		•	
	Training		•	•	•
	Performance review			•	
	Management development			•	•
Motivation	Job design	•		•	•
	Remuneration	•		•	
Employee relations	Industrial relations	•	•		
	Consultation and participation	•	•		•
	Communications		•		•
Employee services	Health and safety	•			
	Welfare	•		•	
	Personnel records and information systems			•	

BPP PUBLISHING

Views of HRM

Personnel management: the old view

1.5 The **traditional view** of personnel management has been essentially **task-**, **activity-** or **technique**-based.

(a) Setting general and specific management policy for employment relationships and establishing and maintaining a suitable organisation for leadership and co-operation

(b) Collective bargaining

(c) Staffing and organisation: finding, getting and holding prescribed types and numbers of workers

(d) Aiding the self-development of employees at all levels, providing opportunities for personal development and growth as well as requisite skills and experience

(e) Incentivising: developing and maintaining the motivation in work

(f) Reviewing and auditing manpower and management in the organisation

(g) Industrial relations research, carrying out studies designed to explain employment behaviour, and thereby improve manpower management

1.6 In 1968, *Crichton* (*Personnel Management in Context*) complained that personnel work was often a matter of 'collecting together such odd jobs from management as they are prepared to give up.' Other writers shared this view, notably *Peter Drucker*, who - while recognising the importance of human resources in the organisation - saw the personnel function of the time as 'a collection of incidental techniques without much internal cohesion'. According to Drucker, the personnel manager saw his role as 'partly a file clerk's job, partly a housekeeping job, partly a social worker's job and partly 'fire fighting' to head off union trouble or to settle it.' (*The Practice of Management*, 1955).

1.7 The status and contribution of the personnel function is still often limited by its being perceived as having an essentially reactive and defensive role. The personnel manager is judged according to his effectiveness in avoiding or settling industrial disputes, preventing accidents and ill-health (and their associated costs), filling vacancies and so on.

1.8 This is a vicious circle. As long as personnel policy and practice is divorced from the strategy of the business, and fails to be proactive and constructive, it will be perceived by line management to have little to do with the real world of business management, or profitability: personnel specialists therefore command scant respect as business managers, and their activities continue to be limited to areas of little strategic impact.

Human Resource Management

1.9 The situation has, however, been changing, and a new approach has emerged which has been labelled *Human Resource Management (HRM)*.

> 'The real requirement is proactive and constructive rather than defensive and reactive. To discharge their true role, personnel managers must anticipate the needs of the organisation in the short and the long term. They must develop the policies to produce solutions to anticipated problems resulting from the external and internal environment, whilst influencing and creating the attitudes amongst employees needed for the enterprise's survival and success.'
>
> *Livy, Corporate Personnel Management*

'HRM' is a recently fashionable term, which some personnel specialists have seized upon and applied to themselves, whether or not they are in fact doing anything more than staff administration, in the interests of their status and self-esteem.

1.10 However, a precise and positive interpretation of HRM centres on the following notions.

(a) Personnel management has been changing in various ways in recent years. Many of its activities have become more complex and sophisticated and, particularly with the accelerating pace of change in the business environment, less narrowly concerned with areas previously thought of as personnel's sole preserve (hiring and firing, training, and industrial relations. **The personnel function has become centrally concerned with issues of broader relevance to the business and its objectives, such as change management, the introduction of technology, and the implications of falling birthrates and skill shortages for the resourcing of the business.**

(b) Personnel management should be integrated with strategic planning, that is, with management at the broadest and highest level. The objectives of the personnel function should be directly related to achieving the organisation's goals for growth, competitive gain and improvement of 'bottom line' performance.

(c) Personnel managers should be businessmen or women - even entrepreneurs.

1.11 *S Tyson* and *A Fell* (*Evaluating the Personnel Function*) suggest **four major roles** for personnel/human resource management which illustrate the shift in emphasis from the odd job to the strategic viewpoint.

(a) To represent the organisation's **central value system** (or culture)

(b) To **maintain the boundaries of the organisation** (its identity and the flow of people in and out of it)

(c) To provide **stability and continuity** (through planned succession, flexibility and so on)

(d) To adapt the organisation to **change**

The role of departmental managers

1.12 Some companies will have a separate human resource function with staff authority over other departments. Smaller companies may not be able to afford the luxury of such a function.

1.13 HRM is thus a set of activities that may or may not have a separate department in the technostructure to manage it. The existence of a separate function depends on the following factors.

(a) **Size of the organisation.** An organisation with only a few employees will not have even the most basic separate personnel function. Recruitment for the accounts department, for example, will be the job of the Chief Accountant or Finance Director. A single individual in the organisation (eg the company secretary) might be delegated to co-ordinate the advertising, draw up standard employment contracts and so forth.

(b) **The activities of the organisation.** In an organisation with, say, trade union representation, human resource specialists may be required. An organisation with people employed in different activities might need some central way to ensure fair and equal treatment in wages and conditions. Equal pay for equal work is the law, but how do you assess which different jobs are of equal value to the organisation?

1.14 Let us assume that we are dealing with a large organisation, with a separate staff department dealing with human resources. What would be the relative roles of line and staff management in the various activities identified in the preceding diagram?

1.15 **Organisation**

(a) **Organisation design** determines the structure of **reporting relationships** (whether, for example, matrix or functional structures are to be used). Organisation design can be a **strategic** issue but HRM may make an advisory input.

(b) **Organisation development** is, according to *Bennis*, 'a complex education strategy designed to change the beliefs, attitudes, values and structure of organisation so that they can better adapt to new technologies, markets and challenges and to the dizzying rate of change itself.' Human resources expertise might be needed as such a strategy of change needs careful handling. Line managers will obviously be involved, however, as they will be implementing these changes in their own departments. The human resources department will possess **expert power**, but little more.

1.16 **Manpower**

(a) **Planning.** Line managers have the best idea of what their activities are going to be. They might also have some idea of the necessary skills needed. However, they are likely to be less well acquainted than the specialists with **labour market conditions**, **pay rates** in other firms and so forth. Line managers' demands may be unrealistic, and HR specialists might have to reach a suitable compromise.

(b) **Recruitment.** In many large organisations recruitment is a combined activity. Obviously, line managers will be involved in designing skills specifications and personnel specifications to guide the HR department's recruitment drive. However, in most cases the HR department will advertise any vacancies, design application forms, review early applications, select candidates for interview, design and arrange aptitude tests and so forth. The HR department will weed out **unsuitable** candidates (eg people whose skills are not appropriate or whose values and attitudes are not suited to the organisation culture). For some jobs, line managers have no say whatsoever in the final outcome. For others, the HR specialists might present line managers with a **shortlist of suitable candidates** for the final decision.

(c) **Employment.** Once the new recruit has arrived, he or she probably signs an employment contract, and, as part of the induction process, completes other formalities. The employee's boss now takes over and (unless, of course, the employee is to work as an HR specialist) the HR department's role is minimal, in the **day to day** management of the employee. **Line managers therefore are responsible for the effective use of human resources on an operational basis**.

(d) **Training.** Training is often provided **on the job** by the line managers, as the new employee will have to learn the ropes somehow. The line manager will also identify the department's **training needs**. The actual courses, however, are likely to be run by training specialists. The HR department, if this is in line with corporate strategy, may require that each employee receives a certain amount of training each year.

(e) **Performance review.** Line managers are responsible in the first instance for **assessing** the performance of employees under their charge. However, the performance review is often related to pay rises and promotions. It is probable that there will have been involvement by human resources professionals in the **design** of the appraisal system, especially as a major purpose of performance review is staff development. In a unionised organisation, pay policy will be arrived at by agreement.

(f) **Management development.** Developing the skills of managers is a **functional responsibility of line managers,** but might be likely to be part of an overall strategy especially if the organisation recruits 'fast track' candidates. Human resources are almost certain to be involved.

1.17 **Motivation**

(a) **Job design** is the integration of various tasks into a **single job.** Line managers will know about the tasks, but might be less able to match these successfully with the skills available and with labour market conditions.

(b) **Remuneration.** The aggregate amount of remuneration might be set as part of the company's overall strategy to earn profits. The line manager will have limited discretion over any pay rise other than a performance related element. Of course remuneration consists of much more than salary. An appropriate package of benefits now forms an important part of the individual's total reward. It is necessary to establish policy on such benefits as cars, soft loans and travel, both in order to maintain differentials and to control cost. Some employers operate a **cafeteria system** under which employees may select benefits and salary within a total package cost.

(c) **Culture.** For HRM, **motivation** is an important weapon, as employees' commitment is supposed to replace techniques of control imposed by management. HR specialists must be involved in the development of this new approach.

1.18 **Employee relations**

(a) Human resources professionals have a major role in **negotiating** with different trade unions in the annual wage round, to come up with an appropriate agreement. Line and functional managers will be involved (eg to suggest changes in working practices).

(b) **Consultation and participation** might also be a feature of the company's practice if, for example, it has quality circles. In short, the size of the work unit (eg team) as well as the culture of the company determines the degree of participation. Employee participation implies participation in decisions at work unit level. Participation will thus be an overall policy of the company, but will be implemented at the work place.

1.19 **Employee services**

(a) **Health and safety** activities are a **legal requirement.** The HR department should ensure that line managers know what is required, even to the extent of arranging inspections.

(b) **Individual employee welfare,** too, is primarily the responsibility of the line manager, but HR personnel might be involved in the negotiation of company policy for all workers. Certain aspects of employee welfare, such as flexitime, maternity leave, or creches for example, might best be planned centrally, so that there is **consistency of treatment.** As such benefits invariably cost money, it is best to have a company-wide policy to deal with them.

(c) **Personnel records** are generally maintained in the HR function. This is because some of the detail is confidential. Records might contain salary details, sickness records, attendance and so forth.

Case example

London bus drivers

The pressures faced by recruiters and indeed human resources managers in general is exemplified by recruiting for the bus industry. Here, problems of staff turnover, reward, recruitment catchment areas and pools, labour market trends and key stakeholder pressures are thrown into sharp focus, as described in the Financial Times (20 August 1997).

London bus drivers tend not to say in a job for more than a few months. The capital's bus companies are facing the highest levels of staff turnover since the 1950s. A combination of the reviving economy and the expanding London bus network means that some bus companies are having to replace up to 40 per cent of drivers a year.

Pay is one issue, shift work is another. A number of bus drivers, for instance, are skilled workers for whom the job was a welcome safety net during the recession of the early 1990s. But the pay, at £230 to £300 for a 40 hour week, is not enough to keep them now.

But the bus companies, competing in a deregulated market, are under pressure to match their services to commuter needs, rather than the body clocks of their drivers.

The squeeze on numbers of these semi-skilled workers - it takes six weeks to train a bus driver - is now so acute that some bus companies are looking outside London for staff. Go Ahead Group, which owns London General Transport with 1,400 drivers, has launched a scheme to recruit drivers from the provinces.

Some argue that what is really needed is a fundamental change of culture at London Transport. This is the authority that puts out to tender the coveted 400 London bus routes. The companies with the lowest cost base scoop the best routes as they require less public subsidy.

CentreWest, owed by FirstBus, believes that recruiting drivers from outside their local area spells trouble. Instead, it has broadened its recruitment policy to include significantly older and younger drivers, as well as more women.

Metroline hopes to keep its drivers by offering the prospect of 'virtually a job for life and very high staff share ownership as well as good pension schemes'.

Bus bosses agree that the work has got tougher, with congestion now blocking London's roads from 7am to midnight.

2 ASSESSING HUMAN RESOURCE NEEDS: THE HR PLAN

2.1 The human resources plan might arise out of a strategic plan.

(a) **The work to be done will largely result from the business plan**. The production management might determine **how** the work will be done. If, for example, the company is introducing new machinery, then the human resource requirements (eg training, possible redundancy, safety measures) need to be thought out.

(b) **The skills base** includes technical skills, interpersonal skills, and management skills. The need for **technical** and **management** skills are obvious enough. **Interpersonal skills** are important, as they deal with the service offered to customers and affect teamwork. Training can include issues of body language such as eye contact and or how to interpret customer behaviour.

2.2 Human resources are hard to predict and control.

(a) **Demand.** Environmental factors (eg government decisions or the state of the markets) create uncertainties in the demand for labour.

(b) **Supply.** Factors such as education or the demands of competitors for labour create uncertainties in the supply of labour.

(c) **Goals**. Employees as individuals have their own personal goals, and make their own decisions about, for example, whether to undertake further training. When large numbers of individuals are involved, the pattern of behaviour which emerges in response to any change in strategy may be hard to predict.

(d) **Constraints**. Legislation as well as social and ethical values constrain the ways in which human resources are used, controlled, replaced and paid.

2.3 Human resource planning concerns the acquisition, utilisation, improvement and return of an enterprise's human resources. Human resource planning deals with:

- Recruitment
- Retention (company loyalty, to retain skills and reduce staff turnover)
- Downsizing (reducing staff numbers)
- Training and retraining to enhance the skills base

2.4 **The process of human resources planning**

```
┌─────────────────────────────────────────────────┐
│              1. STRATEGIC ANALYSIS               │
│   •  of the environment                          │
│   •  of the organisation's manpower strengths    │
│      and weaknesses, opportunities and threats   │
│   •  of the organisation's use of manpower       │
│   •  of the organisation's objectives            │
└─────────────────────────────────────────────────┘
                        ↓
┌─────────────────────────────────────────────────┐
│              2. FORECASTING                      │
│   •  of internal demand and supply               │
│   •  of external supply                          │
└─────────────────────────────────────────────────┘
```

Strategic analysis

2.5 The current and future position should constantly be kept under review.

(a) **The environment**: population and education trends, policies on the employment of women and on pension ages and trends generally in the employment market must be monitored.

(b) The organisation's HR **strengths, weaknesses, opportunities and threats** need to be analysed so as to identify skills and competence gaps and the level of innovation. Threats may involve competitors 'poaching' staff.

(c) **Human resource utilisation**. An assessment should be made of how effectively the organisation is currently utilising its staff .

(d) **Objectives**. Core and subsidiary corporate objectives should be analysed to identify the manpower implications. New products, technology, sites, 'culture' and structure will all make demands on staff.

2.6 **Timescales** are very important. An immediate gap may prompt instant recruitment while long-term corporate objectives will allow long-term plans for updating existing staff and providing them with the skills required.

BPP PUBLISHING

Forecasting

2.7 **Estimating demand**. Planning future HR needs requires accurate forecasts of turnover and productivity (eg if fewer staff are required for the same output). The demand can be estimated from:

- New venture details
- New markets (need new staff)
- New products/services
- New technology (new skills)

- Divestments
- Organisational restructuring (eg relocation)
- Cost reduction plans

2.8 **Estimating supply**

(a) **Current workers. A stocks and flows analysis** will define the **internal labour market**. It describes, not just aggregate quantities, but movements in and out of certain grades, by occupation and grade and according to length and service. This can be used in **modelling**.

(b) The **external labour market**. Labour **market research** does four things.

- It measures potential employees' awareness of the organisation.
- It discerns attitudes of potential employees towards the organisation.
- It suggests possible segments for advertising purposes.
- It provides analysis of population trends for long-term forecasting.

2.9 A **position survey** compares demand and supply. Discrepancies between them in the numbers required/available, their grade, skills or location can be removed through the application of an integrated manpower strategy.

Closing the gap between demand and supply: the HR plan

2.10 The HR plan is prepared on the basis of personnel requirements, and the implications for productivity and costs. The HR plan breaks down into subsidiary plans.

Plan	Comment
Recruitment plan	Numbers; types of people; when required; recruitment programme.
Training plan	Numbers of trainees required and/or existing staff needing training; training programme.
Redevelopment plan	Programmes for transferring, retraining employees.
Productivity plan	Programmes for improving productivity, or reducing manpower costs; setting productivity targets.
Redundancy plan	Where and when redundancies are to occur; policies for selection and declaration of redundancies; re-development, re-training or re-location of redundant employees; policy on redundancy payments, union consultation etc.
Retention plan	Actions to reduce avoidable labour wastage.

The plan should include budgets, targets and standards. It should allocate responsibilities for implementation and control (reporting, monitoring achievement against plan).

2.11 **Tactical plans** can then be made, within this integrated framework, to cover all aspects of the HRM task.

- Pay and productivity bargaining

- Physical conditions of employment
- Management and technical development and career development
- Organisation and job specifications
- Recruitment and redundancies
- Training and retraining
- Manpower costs

2.12 Shortages or surpluses of labour which emerge in the process of formulating the position survey must be dealt with.

(a) Meeting a **shortage**

- Internal transfers and promotions, training etc
- External recruitment
- Reducing labour turnover, by reviewing possible causes
- Overtime
- New equipment and training to improve productivity so reducing the need for more people

(b) Meeting a **surplus**

- Running down manning levels by natural wastage
- Restricting recruitment
- Part-time working
- Redundancies - as a last resort, and with careful planning

Control over human resources

2.13 Once the HR plan has been established, regular control reports should be produced.

(a) Actual numbers recruited, leaving and being promoted should be compared with planned numbers. If actual levels seem too high, action can be taken by stopping recruitment temporarily. If levels seem too low recruitment, promotions or retraining activity should be stepped up.

(b) Actual pay, conditions of employment and training should be compared with assumptions in the manpower plan. Do divergences explain any excessive staff turnover?

(c) **Periodically the manpower plan itself should be reviewed and brought up to date.**

Question 1

'Productivity through people'. In other words, enthusiastic and committed employees are essential for business success. Do you agree?

Answer

Here are a few suggestions. You may have different views. Like any set of ideas which pretends to give businesses an elixir of immortality, the grandiose claims of HRM should be taken with a small pinch of salt. Why?

(a) No matter how good, loyal, committed and enthusiastic the people are, if the basic commercial strategy is wrong, the company will fail.

(b) A strong culture can inhibit the recognition of information that does not conform with its assumptions. Even flexibility may not be enough.

(c) Some organisations can be run without commitment. 'Tapping employees' creativity and insight' might result in disagreement and conflict in some cases.

3 RECRUITMENT

> **KEY TERMS**
>
> **Recruitment** is the part of the process concerned with finding the applicants: it is a 'positive' action by management, going out into the labour market, communicating opportunities and information and generating interest.
>
> **Selection** is the part of the employee recruiting process which involves choosing between applications for jobs: it is largely a 'negative' process, eliminating unsuitable applicants.

3.1 **A systematic approach to recruitment and selection**

Step 1. Detailed personnel **planning**.

Step 2. **Job analysis**, so that for any given job there are three things.

   (a) A statement of the component tasks, duties, objectives and standards (**a job description**).

   (b) A specification of the skills, knowledge and qualities required to perform the job (**a job specification**).

   (c) A reworking of the job specification in terms of the kind of person needed to perform the job (**a person specification**).

   Note that the phrases 'job description' and 'job specification' are often used interchangeably.

Step 3. **Identification of vacancies**, by way of the personnel plan (if vacancies are created by demand for new labour) or requisitions for replacement staff by a department which has 'lost' a current job-holder.

Step 4. Evaluation of the **sources** of labour, again by way of the personnel plan, which should outline personnel supply and availability, at macro- and micro-levels. Internal and external sources, and media for reaching both, will be considered.

Step 5. Review of **applications**, assessing the relative merits of broadly suitable candidates.

Step 6. **Notifying** applicants of the results of the selection process.

Step 7. Preparing employment contracts, induction, training programmes and so on.

Job analysis, job design and competences

3.2 Procedures for recruitment should only be carried out in the context of a recruitment policy, which might cover issues such as internal/external applications of post, non-discrimination and so forth, courteous processing of applicants, the type of tests favoured.

> **Exam focus point**
>
> The best answered question in December 1997 dealt with recruitment and selection, in the context of a job analysis exercise.

Job analysis

3.3   The management of the organisation needs to analyse the sort of work needed to be done in order to recruit effectively. The type of information needed is outlined below.

Type of information	Comments
Purpose of the job	This might seem obvious. As an accountant, you will be expected to analyse, prepare or provide financial information; but this has to be set in the context of the organisation as a whole.
Content of the job	The tasks you are expected to do. If the purpose of the job is to ensure, for example, that people get paid on time, the tasks involve include many activities related to payroll.
Accountabilities	These are the results for which you are responsible. In practice they might be phrased in the same way as a description of a task.
Performance criteria	These are the criteria which measure how good you are at the job. These are largely taste related.
Responsibility	This denotes the importance of the job. For example, a person running a department and taking decisions involving large amounts of money is more responsible that someone who only does what he or she is told.
Organisational factors	Who does the jobholder report to directly (line manager)?
Developmental factors	Likely promotion paths, if any, career prospects and so forth. Some jobs are 'dead-end' if they lead nowhere.
Environmental factors	Working conditions, security and safety issues, equipment etc.

Case example

Chase Manhattan Bank has clear procedures.

The competency definition and the scale are used to assess to what extent the individual has developed the competency, through seven points ranging from 'minimal knowledge' to 'recognisable ability' (representing a firm professional standard) and up to 'advisory level' (related to the best in the external market). This range is positioned as an external, absolute scale, not an internal relative measure. As such, it is used for individuals (always starting with self-analysis) to agree with their manager their individual competency profile, or for managers to specify the competency demands of given roles or specific job vacancies, or for the business to profile the differing requirements of customers.

It reaches the strategic needs of the organisation at its most macro level, but equally - and vitally, as a prerequisite for a successful corporate agenda - it supports a stream of products which get to the individual's agenda of professional development, career opportunity ad performance-related reward.

Conventionally, people see themselves are hired - and hopefully empowered - to do a job, and increasingly they are also expected to combine in cohesive teams.

Competences

3.4 A current approach to job design is the development and outlining of **competences**.

> **KEY TERM**
>
> A person's **competence** is 'a capacity that leads to behaviour that meets the job demands within the parameters of the organisational environment and that, in turn, brings about desired results'. (Boyzatis)

3.5 Some take this further and suggest that a competence embodies the ability to **transfer** skills and knowledge to new situations within the occupational area.

3.6 **Different sorts of competences**

(a) **Behavioural/personal** competences are underlying personal characteristics and behaviour required for successful performance, for example, 'ability to relate well to others'. Most jobs require people to be good communicators.

(b) **Work-based/occupational competences** are 'expectations of workplace performance and the outputs and standards people in specific roles are expected to obtain'. This approach is used in NVQ systems (see below). They cover what people have to do to achieve the results of the job. For example, a competence for a Chartered Management Accountant might be to 'produce financial and other statements and report to management'.

(c) **Generic competences** can apply to all people in an occupation.

3.7 **Some competences for managers**

Competence area	Competence
Intellectual	• Strategic perspective
	• Analytical judgement
	• Planning and organising
Interpersonal	• Managing staff
	• Persuasiveness
	• Assertiveness and decisiveness
	• Interpersonal sensitivity
	• Oral communication
Adaptability	
Results	• Initiative
	• Motivation to achievement
	• Business sense

These competences can be elaborated by identifying **positive** and **negative** indicators.

Job design

3.8 Parameters of job design (Mintzberg)

(a) **Job specialisation**

(i) **How many different tasks** are contained in the jobs and how broad and narrow are these tasks? **The task may be determined by operations management.** Until recently, there has been a trend towards narrow specialisation, reinforced, perhaps by demarcations laid down by trade unions. On the production line, a worker did the same task all the time. Modern techniques, however, require workers to be **multi-skilled**.

(ii) **To what extent does the worker have control over the work?** At one extreme ('scientific management') the worker has little control over the work. At the other extreme (eg an electrician) the worker controls the task.

(b) **Regulation of behaviour.** Co-ordination requires that organisations formalise behaviour so as to predict and control it.

(c) **Training in skills and indoctrination in organisational values.**

3.9 *Belbin* (People Management, 6 March 1997) describes a way of **tailoring job design to delayered, team based structures and flexible working systems.**

(a) Flattened delayered hierarchies lead to greater uncertainty as to how jobs are performed and there is the added problem of **locus of control**.

(b) Old hierarchies had the merit of **clarity** in that people knew exactly what was expected of them.

3.10 Belbin et al developed *Workset*, which uses colour coding to classify work and working time into seven types.

1	Blue: tasks the job holder carries out in a prescribed manner to an approved standard
2	Yellow: individual responsibility to meet an objective (results, not means)
3	Green: tasks that vary according to the reactions and needs of others
4	Orange: shared rather than individual responsibility for meeting an objective
5	Grey: work incidental to the job, not relevant to the four core categories
6	White: new or creative undertaking outside normal duties
7	Pink: demands the presence of the job holder but leads to no useful results

3.11 The manager gives an outline of the proportion of time spent on each 'colour' of work. The job holder then briefs the manager on what has actually been done. This highlights differences between managers' and job-holders' **perceptions of jobs,** and indeed different **jobholders had widely different ideas as to what they were supposed** to do. Important issues arise when there is a gap in perception. Underperformance in different kinds of work can be identified, and people can be steered to the sort of work which suits them best.

Job description

> **KEY TERM**
>
> A **job description** sets out the purpose of the job, where it fits in the organisation structure, the context of the job, the accountabilities of the job and the main tasks the holder carries out.

BPP
PUBLISHING

3.12 **Purposes of job descriptions**

Purpose	Comment
Organisational	Defines the job's place in the organisational structure
Recruitment	Provides information for identifying the sort of person needed (person specification)
Legal	Provides the basis for a contract of employment
Performance	Performance objectives can be set around the job description

3.13 **Contents of a job description**

(a) **Job title** (eg Assistant Financial Controller). This indicates the function/department in which the job is performed, and the level of job within that function.

(b) **Reporting to** (eg the Assistant Financial controller reports to the Financial Controller), in other words the person's immediate boss. (No other relationships are suggested here.)

(c) **Subordinates** directly reporting to the job holder.

(d) **Overall purpose** of the job, distinguishing it from other jobs.

(e) **Principal accountabilities or main tasks**

(i) Group the main activities into a number of broad areas.

(ii) Define each activity as a statement of accountability: what the job holder is expected to achieve (eg **tests** new system to ensure they meet agreed systems specifications).

(f) The current fashion for multi-skilling means that **flexibility** is expected.

Alternatives to job descriptions

3.14 **Detailed** job descriptions are perhaps only suited for jobs where the work is largely repetitive and therefore performed by low-grade employees: once the element of **judgement** comes into a job description it becomes a straitjacket. Many of the difficulties that arise where people adhere strictly to the contents of the job description, rather than responding flexibly to task or organisational requirements.

3.15 Perhaps job descriptions should be written in terms of the **outputs and performance levels** expected. Some firms are moving towards **accountability profiles** in which outputs and performance are identified explicitly.

3.16 **Role definitions**. Whereas a **job** is a group of tasks, a role is more than this. A **role** is a part played by people in meeting their objectives by working competently and flexibly within the context of the organisation's objectives, structures and processes. A **role definition** is wider than a job description. It is less concerned with the details of the job content, but how people interpret the job.

Case example

Guinness

According to *People Management* (11 September 1997) in May 1996 Guinness Brewing Great Britain introduced a new pay system based on competences.

Restrictive job definitions, lengthy job descriptions and a 24-grade structure were replaced by broad role profiles and three pay bands. Roles are now specified in terms of 'need to do' (primary accountabilities), 'need to know' (experience and knowledge requirements) and 'need to be' (levels of competence).

Competences are defined as 'the skill, knowledge and behaviours that need to be applied for effective performance'. There are seven of them, including commitment to results and interpersonal effectiveness. Roles are profiled against each relevant competence and individuals' actual competences are compared with the requirements through the performance management process.

Person specification

3.17 A person specification identifies the **type of person** the organisation should be trying to recruit - character, aptitudes, educational or other qualifications, aspirations. It is an interpretation of the job specification in terms of the kind of person suitable for the job.

Question 2

Do you have a job description? Does it include everything listed in paragraph 5.8? How well do you think it describes what you actually do on a day to day basis? If you do not have a job description, draw one up, and then draw up a job and personnel specification. How well do *you* match?

3.18 Research has been carried out into what a personnel specification ought to assess. J *Munro Fraser's Five Point Pattern of Personality* directs the selector's attention to specific aspects of the candidate's character.

- Impact on others
- Acquired knowledge or qualifications
- Innate ability
- Motivation
- Adjustment and emotional balance.

Advertising job vacancies

3.19 After a job description and a personnel specification have been prepared, the organisation should advertise the job vacancy.

3.20 The job description and personnel specification can be used as guidelines for the wording of any advertisement or careers prospectus pamphlet.

3.21 The choice of advertising medium will depend on **cost, frequency,** the frequency with which the organisation wants to advertise the job vacancy and its **suitability** to the target audience.

3.22 **Advertising media for recruitment**

- In-house magazines
- Professional journals
- National newspapers
- Local newspapers
- Local radio
- Job centres
- Recruitment agencies
- Schools careers officers
- University careers officers
- Careers/job fairs
- Open days
- The internet

BPP PUBLISHING

4 SELECTION

Application forms

4.1 Job advertisements usually ask for a CV (resumé) or require an application form to be completed. The CV is more usual in applications for executive posts, except in the public sector. Application forms are usual for jobs below executive level, and at all levels in the public sector.

4.2 The application form should therefore help the selection officer(s) to **sift through the applicants**, and to reject some at once so as to avoid the time and costs of unnecessary interviews. It should therefore:

(a) **Obtain relevant information** about the applicant and which can be compared with the requirements (education and other qualifications, experience relevant to the job, age, interests even) of the job.

(b) Give applicants the opportunity to write about himself or herself, his or her career ambitions or why he or she wants the job.

The interview

4.3 **Aims of the interview** (often the deciding factor)

- Finding the best person for the job, through direct assessment
- Giving the applicant the chance to learn about the firm

4.4 **Preparation.** The interviewer should study three things.

(a) The **job description** (and specification if separate), to review the major demands of the job

(b) The **personnel specification**, to make relevant assessments of the applicant's character and qualifications

(c) The **application form**, to decide on questions or question areas for each applicant

4.5 **Conduct of the interview**

(a) The **layout** of the room and the number of interviewers should be planned carefully.

(b) The **manner** of the interviewers, their tone of voice, and the way their early questions are phrased can all be significant in establishing the tone of the interview.

(c) Questions should be put carefully. The interviewers should not be trying to confuse the candidate, but should be trying to obtain the information they need.

(d) Candidates should be encouraged to talk.

(e) The candidate should be given the opportunity to ask questions.

4.6 **Limitations of interviews**

(a) **Unreliable assessments**. Interviewers may disagree. A suitable candidate might be rejected or an unsuitable candidate offered a job.

(b) **They fail to provide accurate predictions** of how a person will perform in the job. Research has shown this time and again.

(c) The **interviewers are likely to make errors** of judgement even when they agree about a candidate.

(i) A **halo effect**: a **general** judgement based on a **single** attribute.

(ii) **Contagious bias**. Interviewers might change the behaviour of the applicant by suggestion. The wording of questions or non-verbal clues might lead the applicant to tell the interviewers more of what they wanted to hear.

(iii) Interviewers sometimes **stereotype** candidates on the basis of insufficient evidence, eg on the basis of dress, hair style, accent of voice etc.

(iv) **Incorrect assessment** of qualitative factors such as motivation, honesty or integrity. Abstract qualities are very difficult to assess in an interview.

(v) **Logical error**. An interviewer might draw conclusions about a candidate from what he or she says without logical justification for those conclusions.

(vi) **Incorrectly used rating scales**. For example, if interviewers are required to rate a candidate on a scale of 1-5 for a number of different attributes, there might be a tendency to mark candidates inconsistently.

4.7 Interviewers should be **trained** to conduct and assess interviews.

Testing

4.8 Tests are used supplement interviews or select applicants for interview.

4.9 **Types of test**

(a) **Psychological tests and personality tests**. An individual may be required to answer a long series of questions or score a variety of statements which indicate basic attitude profiles.

(b) **Intelligence tests** measure the applicant's general intellectual ability.

(c) **Proficiency tests** are perhaps the most closely related to an assessor's objectives, because they measure ability to do the **work involved.**

(d) **Aptitude tests** aim to provide information about the candidate's abilities. Aptitude tests can test mental ability (IQ tests, tests in mathematics, general knowledge or use of English) and physical dexterity.

(e) **Psychometric tests** contain features of all of the above. They are selection tests that seek to **quantify** psychological dimensions of job applicants, for example intelligence, personality and motivation. Candidates might be required to answer a list of questions. Those answers are then marked and the candidate is given a score.

Case example

The *Myers-Briggs Type Indicator* is used to categorise people as to whether they are introvert/extrovert, objective/intuitive, logical/emotional, decisive/ hesitant, and so forth. These tests may be used:

(a) in the initial selection of new recruits
(b) in the allocation of new entrants to different branches of work
(c) as part of the process of transfer or promotion.

4.10 **Advantage of tests**

- A test can be a sensitive measuring instrument.
- Tests are standardised, so that all candidates are assessed by the same yardstick.

- Tests always measure the same thing (eg IQ).

4.11 **Disadvantages**

(a) They give a spurious accuracy to complex issues.

(b) They are culturally-specific. Many tests for managers were developed in the US. The cultures in the UK and US differ in many respects (eg attitudes to 'hunting').

4.12 The use of **biodata** involves obtaining, analysing and scoring **biographical information** (eg age gender, education, leisure). Items of information are weighted according to their proven ability to predict job performance. A person's biodata is scored and a mark is given. A cut-off score would be a required minimum for the candidate to be considered for further assessment.

4.13 **Group selection methods** might be used by an organisation as the final stage of a selection process for management jobs. They consist of a series of tests, interviews and group situations over a period of two days or so, involving a small number (eg six to eight) of candidates for a job. After an introductory chat to make the candidates feel at home, they will be given one or two tests, one or two individual interviews, and several group situations in which the candidates are invited to discuss problems together and arrive at solutions as a management team.

(a) **Advantages**

- Selectors have more time to study the candidates.
- They test interpersonal skills.
- They reveal more about the candidates' personalities.
- They are suitable for selection of potential managers.

(b) **Disadvantages**

- Time and cost
- The lack of experience of interviewers/selectors
- Candidates might behave atypically in a contrived situation.

Question 3

Some schools careers officers give tuition in interview techniques to young people looking for jobs. What do you think this says about interviewing, as opposed to testing, as a means of selection?

Answer

If interview techniques are taught, it might imply that, in the absence of any other selection criteria, your success at interview will have more to do with your ability to present yourself in an interview situation than your ability to do the job. On the other hand, an interview is a test of how well you perform under pressure, in an unfamiliar environment and with strangers. This might reflect some of the interpersonal skills required for a job.

References

4.14 It is common to obtain references from the candidate's previous employers and other people the candidate is acquainted with. **A reference does enable an employer to check the basic accuracy of the candidate's CV** but little more than this.

5 INDUCTION TRAINING

5.1 On the first day, a manager or personnel officer should welcome the new recruit. He/she should then introduce the new recruit to the person who will be their **immediate supervisor.**

5.2 The immediate supervisor should commence the **process of induction**.

Step 1. Pinpoint the areas that the recruit will have to learn about in order to **start the job**. Some things (such as detailed technical knowledge) may be identified as areas for later study or training.

Step 2. Explain first of all the nature of the job, and the goals of each task, both of the recruit's job and of the department as a whole.

Step 3. Explain about hours of work, and stress the importance of time-keeping. If flexitime is operated, the supervisor should explain how it works.

Step 4. Explain the structure of the department: to whom the recruit will report, to whom he/she can go with complaints or queries and so on.

Step 5. Introduce the recruit to the people in the office. One particular colleague may be assigned to the recruit as a **mentor**, to keep an eye on them, answer routine queries, 'show them the ropes'.

Step 6. Plan and implement an appropriate **training programmes** for whatever technical or practical knowledge is required. Again, the programme should have a clear schedule and set of goals so that the recruit has a sense of purpose, and so that the programme can be efficiently organised to fit in with the activities of the department.

Step 7. Coach and/or train the recruit; and check regularly on their progress, as demonstrated by performance, as reported by the recruit's mentor, and as perceived by the recruit him or herself.

5.3 After three months, six months or one year the performance of a new recruit should be formally appraised and discussed with them. Indeed, when the process of induction has been finished, a recruit should continue to receive periodic appraisals, just like every other employee in the organisation.

Question 4

'Joining an organisation with around 8,500 staff, based on two sites over a mile apart and in the throes of major restructuring, can be confusing for any recruit. This is the situation facing the 20 to 30 new employees recruited each month by the Guy's and St Thomas' Hospital Trust, which was formed by the merger of the two hospitals in April.

In a climate of change, new employees joining the NHS can be influenced by the negative attitudes of other staff who may oppose the current changes. So it has become increasingly important for the trust's management executive to get across their view of the future and to understand the feelings of confusion new staff may be experiencing.'

Personnel Management Plus, August 1993

See if you can design a 9-5 induction programme for these new recruits, in the light of the above. The programme is to be available to **all** new recruits, from doctors and radiographers to accountants, catering and cleaning staff and secretaries.

BPP PUBLISHING

Chapter roundup

- **Personnel management** in the past was never perceived to have a strategic role, dealing as it did with issues of hiring and firing, industrial relations and so forth.

- HRM is concerned with the most effective use of human resources. It deals with organisation, manpower, motivation, employee relations and employee services.

- **Human resource management (HRM)** is based on the assumption that the management and deployment of staff is a key **strategic** factor in an organisation's competitive performance. HRM requires top management involvement and the promotion of culture and **values,** so that employees' **commitment**, as opposed merely to their consent, is obtained.

- Personnel/manpower planning should be based on the organisation's strategic planning processes, with relation to analysis of the labour market, forecasting of the external supply and internal demand for labour, job analysis and plan implementation.

- HRM also pays attention to the organisation's value systems.

- Recruitment is a means by which people from outside the organisation are brought in. Selection is when a suitable employee is chosen.

- **Job analysis** determines the requirements for a job. The job's tasks are set out in a job description. A job specification describes the skills or competences required for the job. A **person specification** describes the sort of person suitable for a job.

- Selection involves a filtering process, by reviewing application forms, interviewing and testing.

- **Interviews** are a widely used selection method. Many firms prefer to use tests as, for large numbers of candidates, they provide am more reliable prediction of performance on the job than interviews. **Tests** can assess intelligence, personality etc. Interviews are flawed because of bias and difficulties people have in interpreting a candidate's behaviour.

- New recruits need time to learn the job and settle in. Many organisations have formal procedures for **induction.**

Quick quiz

1. What are the objectives of human resource management?

2. How can HRM affect organisation effectiveness?

3. What four areas are dealt with by human resources planning?

4. What are the contents of the HR plan?

5. What are the three parameters of job design?

6. Distinguish between recruitment and selection.

7. What is a job description?

Answers to quick quiz

1   To develop an effective human component for the organisation, which will respond well to change; to obtain, develop and motivate the human resources needed by the organisation; to satisfy the social and legal responsibilities relating to the human resource.

2   By increasing productivity, enhancing group learning, reducing staff turnover and encouraging initiative.

3   Tyson and Fell suggest: to represent the organisation's central value system; to maintain the boundaries of the organisation; to provide stability and continuity; and to adapt the organisation to change.

4   The HR plan breaks down into subsidiary plans for recruitment, training, redundancy, retention, productivity and redevelopment.

5   Mintzberg suggests: job specialisation; regulation of behaviour; and training in skills and indoctrination in organisational values.

6   Recruitment is about finding applicants while selection is about choosing the right applicants.

7   A job description sets out the purpose of the job, where it fits into the organisation, its context, accountabilities and main tasks.

Now try the question below from the Exam Question Bank

Number	Level	Marks	Time
Q10	Introductory	18	32 mins

BPP PUBLISHING

Chapter 11

INDIVIDUALS

Topic List	Syllabus Reference	Ability required
1 Performance and productivity	(iii)	Evaluation
2 Individuals	(iii)	Evaluation
3 Motivation	(iii)	Evaluation
4 Pay and job satisfaction	(iii)	Evaluation

Introduction

This chapter concentrates on the human element in organisations: all the structures and systems described in earlier chapters depend for their success on the involvement of individual managers and workers and the relationships between them. This chapter is an important grounding, as it puts into context some of the issues about human resource management discussed in Chapter 18. Also, the organisation's management information system is only one aspect of communication in organisations. In this chapter we discuss how individuals communicate and solve problems in a group context: you can probably see how this applies to techniques such as TQM.

(a) We discuss the complex interaction between the individual and the organisation, particularly so far as personality variables are concerned (Section 1) and (Section 2) and consider some psychological aspects.

(b) In Sections 3 and 4, we describe the likely relationships between needs and wants on the one hand, motivation and incentives on the other, and the resultant behaviour patterns displayed by individuals at work. We analyse and appraise the relevance and practical utility of some of the major theories of motivation developed by writers like Maslow, McGregor, Herzberg, Vroom and Lawler and Porter. We also describe the concept of a psychological contract between the individual and the organisation.

Learning outcome covered in this chapter

- Evaluate the tools which can be used to influence the behaviour of staff within a business, particularly within the finance department.

Syllabus content covered in this chapter

- A range of models of human behaviour and motivation and their application in a business context (eg Taylor, Schein, McGregor, Maslow, Herzberg, Handy, Lawrence and Lorsch).

- The design of reward systems.

1 PERFORMANCE AND PRODUCTIVITY

1.1 Organisations are pre-occupied with performance. Many of the control systems we discussed earlier mentioned actual performance and instituted corrective action:

individuals, however, do not work in quite such a mechanical way, and it helps managers to have a fairly broad view as to the influences on labour productivity.

1.2 Many factors will influence job performance, as demonstrated by the diagram below.

Variables affecting performance

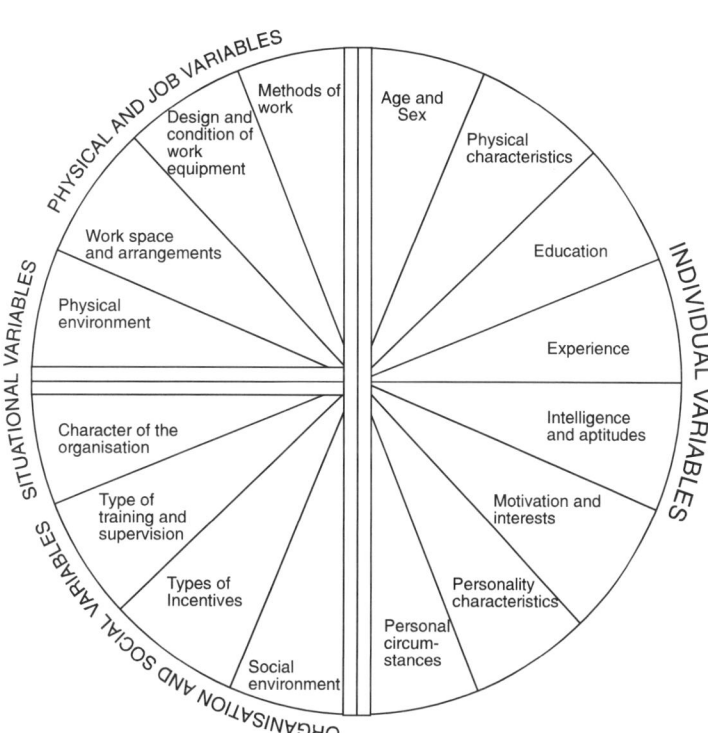

1.3 **The diagram emphasises individual characteristics, but you should remember that these exist in an organisation context.** People respond to the signals and controls issued by management, and management policies, both personally (in a manager's own personal approach to managing) and collectively (in control systems and reward systems etc) are critical influences on individual performance. In the following sections of this chapter we therefore discuss characteristics of individuals and management responses of motivation and leadership.

2 INDIVIDUALS

Personality

2.1 Individuals are unique. In order to explain, describe and identify the differences between people, psychologists use the concept of personality.

2.2 Personality has been defined as 'the total pattern of characteristic ways of thinking, feeling and behaving that constitute the individual's distinctive method of relating to the environment.'

2.3 **People possess a self-image,** a subjective picture of themselves and their behaviour, and what they desire to be. Psychological adjustment depends on the flexibility of the self-image in relation to experience and environment. If an individual's perception of his own qualities, abilities and attitudes is accurate, coherent and consistent with his experience, and adaptable to change as it occurs, the individual will be well-adjusted.

BPP PUBLISHING

Individual development

2.4 According to most accepted theories, personality is made up of various parts which combine and interact with external influences to shape the behaviour of the whole person. The general trend over time is towards increasing diversity and complexity, and usually therefore an increasing sense of selfhood, and the need to develop that personal potential.

2.5 According to *Chris Argyris*, psychologist and management writer, as people mature they display certain characteristics.

(a) **An increasing tendency to activity, rather than passivity**. This is partly because of the widening scope for action, with learning and experience, and partly to do with a growing sense of self.

(b) **Diversification of behaviour patterns**. The personality progresses to a wider and more subtle range of responses.

(c) **A tendency to move from dependence towards independence**

(d) **Acceptance of equal or superior relationship to others**. Generally, as we mature, we feel that a certain position is due to our self image, our age and experience.

(e) **Lengthening perspectives**. A person's sense of time is highly subjective. Increasingly the pressures of responsibility lengthen the time-scales with which we are prepared to work.

(f) **Deepening and more stable interests**. Experience generally provides a wider range of potential interests; priorities are altered as personality develops.

(g) **Increasing self-awareness**. Our self-image - and therefore our personality - is formed by experience over time, and is constantly adjusted.

2.6 Argyris suggests that there are 'basic incongruities' between what the formal business organisation **requires** of individuals, and the psychological needs of the individual striving to reach maturity, **which individuals themselves can recognise.**

2.7 In an organisation, especially a **bureaucracy** or one run on principles of **scientific management**, individuals tend to become content - or at least submissive - within the framework of organisation and control. They become largely passive, limited in their perspective of the overall purpose and value of their work for example, and willing to utilise only a few of their abilities (usually not the most important ones).

2.8 This can be blamed on the typical approach to management of organisations. The immature outlook thus created merely perpetuates the assumption that the workers (and even lower managers) are short-sighted, petty, incapable of initiative and responsibility: the structure of authority and control from the higher levels of the hierarchy is further reinforced: it is a vicious circle.

The organisation's interest in personal development

2.9 Frustration, conflict, feelings of failure and low prospects tend to show themselves in such effects as high labour turnover, absenteeism or preoccupation with financial rewards (in compensation for lack of other satisfactions) - which can be as self-defeating for the organisation as they are unhealthy for the individual.

2.10 We should also note that there are a great many other work and non-work variables in the equation. A happy workforce will not necessarily make the organisation profitable (if the

market is unfavourable): they will not necessarily be more productive (if the task itself is badly designed or resources scarce) nor even more highly motivated.

Question 1

Do you think an assessment of personality should form part of an organisation's recruitment process? Does your answer apply equally whatever the job in question may be? How can an organisation assess a candidate's personality in any case?

Answer

There is room for you to have your own opinions on this topic. In practice of course job advertisements frequently do specify that they are looking for an 'outgoing personality', 'the ability to work in teams', 'a sense of humour' and so on. Sometimes, especially if certain skills are in short supply, the organisation has to accommodate the personality of the person who is otherwise best qualified for the job. Where social interaction is incidental to, rather than an actual part of, the job in question a variety of different personalities might fit the bill equally well. Techniques for assessing personality include interviews, personality tests, psychometric tests, role-playing and even graphology (hand writing analysis).

Personality differences and work behaviour

2.11 What difference does personality make to behaviour at work, and to the management of individuals? In general terms, organisations will make certain generalised assumptions about the personalities of the individuals they employ, about the type of individuals they would wish to employ and to whom they would wish to allocate various tasks and responsibilities.

2.12 It has not been possible to prove frequent organisational assumptions that extrovert or stable personalities are more successful in particular occupations than any other type of individual.

(a) The extrovert may be active, cheerful, social and not averse to risk, but may also be unreliable, easily bored, irresponsible and fickle.

(b) Neurotics tend to be depressive, anxious, obsessive and emotional, but they may also be conscientious and highly disciplined, and they do not fret under authority.

2.13 Nonetheless, if we assume broad consistency in traits or types of personality, we *can* make some useful observations about individual differences and work behaviour - at least enough to be going on with in the real world. Three examples are **authoritarianism,** the **need for achievement,** and **self esteem.**

Authoritarianism

2.14 People might **want to be controlled** in a work situation because of the benefits of control processes.

(a) Control **provides feedback** on the individual's performance, which may be essential for learning, satisfaction, motivation and the confirmation or adjustment of self-image;

(b) Control gives the task itself **definition and structure,** standard methods and levels of performance. This is reassuring to most individuals, and essential to those with high security needs;

(c) Control encourages **dependency,** which is particularly welcome to a personality type known as the **authoritarian personality.**

BPP PUBLISHING

It has been argued that such traits lead individuals to large, highly structured organisations, such as the armed services, which provide secure, ordered, controlled environments.

Need for achievement

2.15 *McClelland* identified the **need for achievement as a prime motivator for people who have a strong desire for success** (in relation to standards of excellence, and in competition with others) and a strong fear of failure. Such people tend to want work which offers the features they value.

(a) Personal responsibility

(b) Moderately difficult tasks and goals that present a challenge and an opportunity to display ability but are not excessively difficult, since that might increase the possibility of failure

(c) Acceptable, realistic levels of risk-taking, but not gambles, again because of the fear of failure

(d) Cear, frequent feedback on performance, so that they can improve their performance, or have their success confirmed

2.16 McClelland's researches led to certain suggestions.

(a) Entrepreneurs tend to rank high on need for achievement.

(b) Chief executives of large companies, having fulfilled their ambitions, tend to rank low on need for achievement.

(c) Successful 'up and coming' managers rank high on need for achievement.

(d) A need for achievement can be taught to managers on training courses, by getting them into the habit of thinking in achievement terms, and using achievement imagery.

Self esteem

2.17 Argyris, among others, has suggested that **individuals continually seek to increase their self esteem**. The experience of **psychological success** is one aspect of this, making the individual feel more competent and more secure. Psychological success is experienced when an individual sets himself a challenging goal which is in some way related to his self-concept, and determines his own methods of achieving it.

2.18 Self-esteem affects behaviour at work.

(a) An individual's confidence in his competence contributes to the successful demonstration of that competence or ability.

(b) A sense of competence is a secure basis for risk-taking in important personal areas.

(c) Self-esteem is also an important factor in the success of training and appraisal schemes at work.

Attitudes

2.19 An **attitude** is the position that an individual has adopted in response to a theory or belief, an object, event or other person. Attitudes are subjective, in other words dependent on perception and personal experience, rather than wholly objective, although reasoned opinions may be part of the individual's attitudinal position.

2.20 A positive attitude to work might lead to particular behaviour.

(a) Commitment to the **objectives** of the organisation, or adoption personal objectives that are compatible with those of the organisation.

(b) Acknowledgement of the right of the organisation to set standards of **acceptable behaviour.**

(c) A willingness to contribute to the development and improvement of work **practices** and **performance.**

(d) **Belief** that a fair day's pay is received for a fair day's work.

(e) Taking advantage of opportunities for **personal development.**

2.21 There are several **non-work** factors that might influence attitudes to work.

(a) **Class and class-consciousness**: attitudes about the superiority or inferiority of others, attitudes to money, as well as attitudes to work itself.

(b) **Age**. Attitudes to sexual equality, morality and education for example have varied from one generation to the next. Attitudes also tend to become less flexible with age.

(c) **Race, culture or religion**. Attitudes about these areas will again affect the way in which people regard each other - with tolerance, suspicion or hostility - and their willingness to co-operate in work situations.

(d) **Lifestyle and interests**. Again, attitudes about these areas affect interpersonal relations, and the self concept of each individual.

(e) **Sex**. Attitudes to the equality of the sexes, and their various roles at work and in society, may be influential. Women at work may be made to feel inferior, incompetent or simply unwelcome, while men working for female managers might feel their masculinity threatened.

3 MOTIVATION

3.1 It is in an organisation's interests to know the reasons or motives behind people's behaviour. In particular, if the organisation finds reasons why people might perform well at work, it can utilise that knowledge to encourage them.

3.2 Motivating employees to work hard and well is a perennial problem for managers, and some management practices are based on quite crude assumptions of how people are motivated. *Douglas McGregor* categorises **managers' assumptions** into two types.

> **KEY TERM**
>
> **Theory X and Theory Y:** Two contrasting managerial approaches to motivation described by Douglas McGregor.

(a) **Theory X. This is the theory that most people dislike work and responsibility and will avoid both if possible**. Because of this, most people must be coerced, controlled, directed and threatened with punishment to get them to make an adequate effort towards the achievement of the organisation's objectives.

(b) **Theory Y. This theory holds that the expenditure of physical and mental effort in work is as natural as play or rest**. The ordinary person does not inherently dislike work: according to the conditions, it may be a source of satisfaction or punishment. The average human being can learn not only to accept but to seek responsibility. At

present the potentialities of the average person are not being fully used. A manager with this sort of attitude to his staff is likely to be a democratic, consultative type.

Motivation theories

3.3 (a) **Content theories** assume that human beings have a package of motives which they pursue: they have a set of needs or desired outcomes. *Maslow's* need hierarchy theory and *Herzberg's* two-factor theory are two of the most important approaches of this type.

(b) **Process theories** explore the process through which outcomes become desirable and are pursued by individuals. This approach assumes that man is able to select his goals and choose the paths towards them, by a conscious or unconscious process of calculation. Expectancy theory is an example of this type.

Maslow's hierarchy of needs

> ### KEY TERM
>
> **Hierarchy of needs**: a ranked structure of behavioural stimuli within the individual, which explain motivation.

3.4 Apart from 'biogenic needs' or 'drives', that is, biological determinants of behaviour, activated by deprivation, there are **psychogenic needs** - emotional or psychological needs. The American psychologist Abraham Maslow argued that man has seven innate needs, and put forward certain propositions about the motivating power of these needs.

He described two higher order needs.

(a) The need for freedom of inquiry and expression: for social conditions permitting free speech and encouraging justice, fairness and honesty.

(b) The need for knowledge and understanding: to gain and order knowledge of the environment, to explore, learn, experiment. These are essential pre-requisites for the satisfaction of the remainder.

The other five needs can be arranged in a 'hierarchy of relative pre-potency'. Each level of need is **dominant until satisfied**; only then does the next level of need become a motivating factor. A need which has been satisfied no longer motivates an individual's behaviour. The need for self-actualisation can never be satisfied.

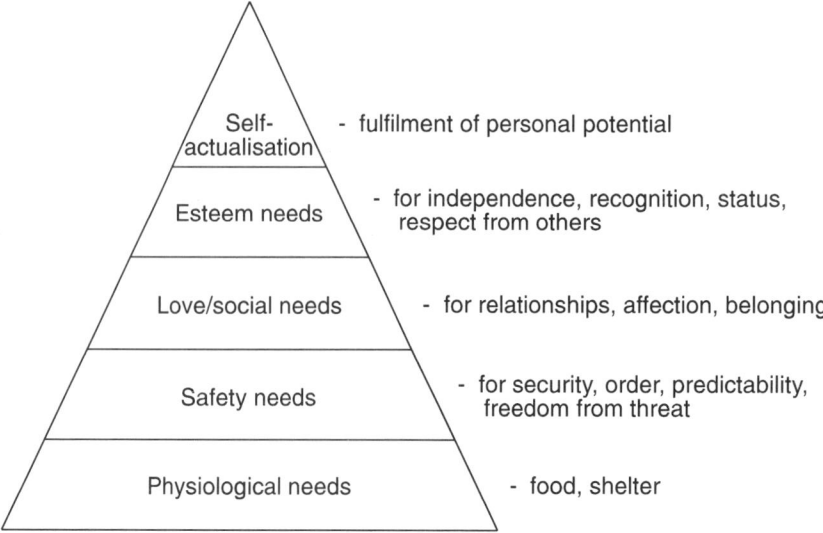

3.5 There is a certain intuitive appeal to Maslow's theory. After all, you are unlikely to be concerned with status or recognition while you are hungry or thirsty because primary survival needs will take precedence. Likewise, once your hunger is satisfied, the need for food is unlikely to be a motivating factor.

3.6 It is also worth noting that Maslow did *not* intend his views to be applied to the specific context of behaviour at work: needs can be satisfied by aspects of a person's life outside work. However, since work provides a livelihood and takes up such a large part of a person's life, it is obviously going to play an important part in the satisfaction of his needs.

3.7 There are various problems associated with Maslow's theory.

(a) Empirical verification for the hierarchy is hard to come by. Physiological and safety needs are not always uppermost in the determination of human behaviour.

(b) Research does not bear out the proposition that needs become less powerful as they are satisfied, except at the very primitive level of primary needs like hunger and thirst.

(c) It is difficult to predict behaviour using the hierarchy: the theory is too vague.

(d) Application of the theory in work contexts presents various difficulties. For example, the role of money or pay is problematic, since it arguably represents other rewards like status, recognition or independence.

(e) The ethnocentricity of Maslow's hierarchy has also been noted - it does seem broadly applicable to Western English-speaking cultures, but it is less relevant elsewhere.

ERG

3.8 *Alderfer* simplified Maslow's need hierarchy down to three categories.

- The need for existence
- The need to relate to others
- The need for personal growth

He called this the 'existence-relatedness-growth' (ERG) model.

3.9 ERG is also a hierarchical model, but Alderfer points out that each individual may have different levels of each kind of need: thus avoiding the difficulties associated with Maslow's idea that needs become less powerful as they are satisfied.

McClelland

3.10 *David McClelland* also proposed a needs-based theory. It is not as wide ranging as Maslow's in that it does not take Maslow's very basic needs into account. McClelland identified three needs. They are not in any hierarchy.

Affiliation	*Power*	*Achievement*
People who need a sense of belonging and membership of a group tend to be concerned with maintaining personal relationships.	People who need power seek a leadership position to influence and control.	People have a strong desire for success and a fear of failure.

3.11 McClelland suggested three things about these needs.

(a) Top managers have a strong need for power and a low need for affiliation.

(b) Entrepreneurs have a high need for achievement.

(c) It is possible to 'teach' these needs in some cases (by teaching people to think with the right imagery so that they develop the needs).

A two-factor content theory: Herzberg

3.12 The American psychologist Frederick Herzberg interviewed 203 Pittsburgh engineers and accountants. The subjects were asked to recall **events which had made them feel good about their work, and others which made them feel bad about it**. Analysis revealed that the factors which created satisfaction were different from those which created dissatisfaction.

> **KEY TERMS**
>
> Frederick Herzberg identified two groups of work related factors which caused satisfaction and dissatisfaction respectively.
>
> **Motivators** produced satisfaction when present and were capable of motivating the individual.
>
> **Hygiene factors** (or **maintenance factors**) could not give satisfaction or provide motivation when present. Their absence, however, caused dissatisfaction.

3.13 In his book *Work and the Nature of Man*, Herzberg distinguished between **hygiene factors** and **motivator factors**, based on what he saw as two separate 'need systems' of individuals.

(a) There is a **need to avoid unpleasantness**. This need is satisfied at work by hygiene factors. Hygiene satisfactions are short-lived: individuals come back for more, in the nature of drug addicts.

(b) There is a **need for personal growth**, which is satisfied by motivator factors, and not by hygiene factors.

3.14 **A lack of motivators at work will encourage employees to concentrate on bad hygiene** (real or imagined) and to demand more pay for example. Some individuals are not mature enough to want personal growth: these are 'hygiene seekers' because they can only be satisfied by hygiene factors.

3.15 **Hygiene** or **maintenance** factors.

- Company policy and administration
- Salary
- The quality of supervision
- Interpersonal relations
- Working conditions
- Job security

3.16 Herzberg calls such factors **hygiene factors** because they are essentially preventative. They prevent or minimise **dissatisfaction** but do not give **satisfaction**, in the same way that sanitation minimises threats to health, but does not give 'good' health. They are called 'maintenance' factors because they have to be continually renewed. Satisfaction with environmental factors is not lasting. In time dissatisfaction will occur.

3.17 **Motivator factors create job satisfaction** and are effective in motivating an individual to superior performance and effort. These factors give the individual a sense of self-fulfilment or personal growth.

- Status (although this may be a hygiene factor as well as a motivator factor)
- Advancement
- Gaining recognition
- Being given responsibility
- Challenging work
- Achievement
- Growth in the job

3.18 Herzberg suggested means by which motivator satisfactions could be supplied. Stemming from his fundamental division of motivator and hygiene factors, he encouraged managers to study **the job itself** (the type of work done, the nature of tasks, levels of responsibility) rather than **conditions of work**. If there is sufficient challenge, scope and interest in the job, there will be a lasting increase in satisfaction and the employee will work well; productivity will be above normal levels. The extent to which a job must be challenging or creative to a motivator-seeker will depend on each individual ability and his tolerance for delayed success.

Expectancy theory: a process theory

3.19 The expectancy theory of motivation is a process theory, based on the assumptions of cognitive psychology that human beings are purposive and rational, aware of their goals and behaviour. Essentially, the theory states that **the strength of an individual's motivation to do something will depend on the extent to which he expects the results of his efforts, if successfully achieved, to contribute towards his personal needs or goals**.

3.20 In 1964 *Victor Vroom*, another American psychologist, worked out a formula by which human motivation could actually be assessed and measured, based on an expectancy theory of work motivation. Vroom suggested that the strength of an individual's motivation is the product of two factors.

(a) The strength of his preference for a certain outcome. Vroom called this **valence**. It may be represented as a positive or negative number, or zero - since outcomes may be desired, avoided or considered with indifference.

(b) The individual's expectation that the outcome will result from a certain behaviour. Vroom called this **subjective probability**: it is only the individual's 'expectation', and depends on his perception of the probable relationship between behaviour and outcome. As a probability, it may be represented by any number between 0 (no chance) and 1 (certainty). It is also called **expectancy**.

3.21 In its simplest form, the expectancy equation therefore looks like this.

Force or strength of motivation to do something	=	**V**alence ie strength of his preference for a certain outcome	×	**E**xpectation that behaviour will result in desired outcome

3.22 This is what you would expect: if either valence or expectation have a value of zero, there will be no motivation.

(a) If an employee has a high expectation that productivity will result in a certain outcome (say, promotion), but he is indifferent to that outcome (doesn't want the responsibility), V = 0, and he will not be motivated to productive behaviour.

(b) If the employee has a great desire for promotion - but does not believe that productive behaviour will secure it for him, E = 0, and he will still not be highly motivated.

(c) If V = -1, (perhaps because the employee fears responsibility and does not want to leave his work group), the value for motivation will be negative, and the employee may deliberately under-produce.

3.23 Are human beings really so predictable, however? Are we as **rational** as expectancy theory implies? The expectancy theory has been useful in organisational practice because it does make room for the subjectivity of human perceptions. In its most complex form, where a number of alternative expected outcomes are taken into account, the expectancy equation can be a fair reflection of the various influences on behaviour.

3.24 Experience within the organisation is the main influence on the 'E' and 'V' values of the equation. The particular factors which influence valence and expectation will be those which management will want to identify and change, in order to increase 'F' or motivation in employees.

(a) The value attached to an outcome will partly reflect what is valued generally (and especially by the individual's colleagues or career models) in a particular organisation.

(b) The expectancy will reflect the individual's experience of what can be achieved in the organisation, what rewards he and others like him have received in the past for certain behaviours.

Porter and Lawler

3.25 A variant on expectancy theory was provided by *Porter and Lawler*. Whilst maintaining the crucial distinction between valence and expectancy, more elements are added to the model. This is because the revised model aims to predict not just **motivation** as such but **performance**.

3.26 So as well as valence, expectancy and force of motivation, other variables influence performance.

(a) Basic managerial skills

    (i) The ability to do the job
    (ii) The ability to identify jobs which need to be done

(b) The past record of performance: this obviously has an impact on expectancy, and so can be considered as part of a feedback system.

(c) Influences on **valence** include the differing values of *intrinsic* satisfactions (interest in the job, a sense of accomplishment, enjoyment) and *extrinsic* satisfactions (eg pay), as well as the rewards which seem to be **fair** (or equitable). These satisfactions return to affect valence, again in a feedback system. The diagram below summarises the theory, and relates it to expectancy theory.

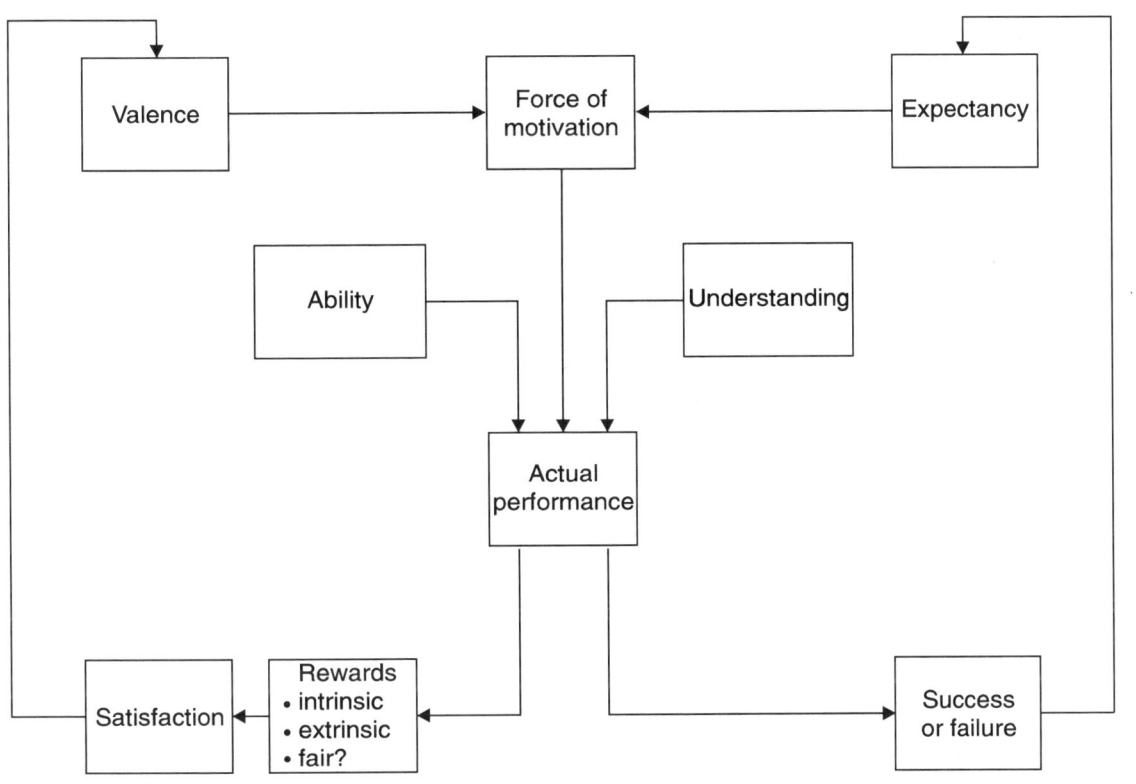

Question 2

What factors in yourself or your organisation motivate you:

(a)   to turn up to work at all?
(b)   to do an average day's work?
(c)   to work particularly hard?

Other process theories

Equity theory

3.27   Equity theory deals with issues of fairness, in other words that people seek a fair return for their efforts, not necessarily the maximum reward. *Adams* makes these suggestions.

(a)   People compare what they receive with what others receive, for a perceived level of effort.

(b)   **Inequity** exists if another person gets more for a given level of input.

(c)   People get more upset the more inequity there is.

(d)   The more upset someone is, the harder he or she will work to restore 'equity'.

3.28   Equity theory was backed up in the laboratory but hard to apply in the real world.

Goal-setting theory

3.29   Goal-setting theory suggests that **goals** can motivate.

(a)   Challenging goals, providing they have been accepted, lead to better performance than easy goals.

(b)   The best goals are specific as they focus people's attention.

(c)   Knowledge of results is essential.

3.30 Goal theory has the most empirical support of any motivation, but there are some limits to how it applies.

    (a) Research has concentrated on quantity not quality of output.

    (b) At work, people pursue several goals consecutively; achieving one may mean neglecting another. This is particularly a problem for organisations where trade offs have to be made.

Psychological contracts

3.31 A **psychological contract** exists between individuals in an organisation and the organisation itself.

    (a) The individual expects to derive certain benefits from membership of the organisation and is prepared to expend a certain amount of effort in return.

    (b) The organisation expects the individual to fulfil certain requirements and is prepared to offer certain rewards in return.

3.32 Three types of psychological contract can be identified.

    (a) **Coercive contract.** This is a contract in which the individual considers that he or she is being forced to contribute his efforts and energies involuntarily, and that the rewards he receives in return are inadequate compensation.

    (b) **Calculative contract.** This is a contract, accepted **voluntarily** by the individual, in which he expects to do his job in exchange for a readily identifiable set of rewards. With such psychological contracts, motivation can only be increased if the rewards to the individual are improved. If the organisation attempts to demand greater efforts without increasing the rewards, the psychological contract will revert to a coercive one, and motivation may become negative.

    (c) **Co-operative contract.** This is a contract in which the individual identifies himself with the organisation and its goals, so that he/she actively seeks to contribute further to the achievement of those goals. Motivation comes out of success at work, a sense of achievement, and self-fulfilment. The individual will probably want to share in the planning and control decisions which affect his work, and **co-operative contracts are therefore likely to occur where employees participate in decision-making.**

3.33 Motivation happens when the psychological contract, within which the individual's motivation calculus operates for new decisions, is viewed in the same way by the organisation and by the individual, and when both parties are able to fulfil their side of the bargain - the individual agrees to work, or work well, in return for whatever rewards or satisfactions are understood as the terms of the 'contract'.

4   PAY AND JOB SATISFACTION   5/01

4.1 You may have noticed that none of the well-known catalogues of human needs mentions money - yet it is often assumed to be a means of satisfying any or all of the other needs. The value of money as a motivator will therefore depend on its **perceived value** for the individual, but, on the other hand, it can usefully be offered as an incentive because it is instrumental in satisfying so many different needs.

4.2 We must remember, however, that an employee needs income to live. Employees probably have two basic concerns: to earn **enough** pay and that the pay should be **fair**. This can be assessed in two ways.

(a) **Equity** - a fair rate for the job

(b) **Relativity**, or fair differentials, ie justified differences between the pay of different individuals

4.3 The assumption behind most payment systems is that pay is the prime motivating factor. As Herzberg, among others, suggested, however, it is more likely to be a cause of dissatisfaction.

4.4 Herzberg himself admitted that pay is the most important of all the hygiene factors. *Goldthorpe, Lockwood et al*, in their *Affluent Worker* study of the Luton car industry, suggested that workers may have a purely **instrumental** orientation to work - deriving satisfaction not from the work itself but from the rewards obtainable with the money earned by working. The Luton workers experienced their work as routine and dead-end, but had made a rational decision to enter employment which offered high monetary reward rather than intrinsic interest.

4.5 As expectancy theory indicates, pay is only likely to motivate a worker to improved performance if there is a clear and consistent link between performance and monetary reward and if monetary reward is valued. Salary structures do not always allow enough leeway to reward individual performance in a job (since fairness usually dictates a rate for the job itself, in relation to others): **incentive schemes**, however, are often used to re-establish the link between effort and reward.

Incentive schemes

4.6 The purpose of incentive schemes is to **improve performance by linking it to reward**. It is believed that performance incentives take effect in several ways.

(a) Staff members' effort and attention are **directed to where they are most needed**; the need for performance is emphasised.

(b) **Commitment and motivation are enhanced**. This is particularly important when there are cultural obstacles to improvement.

(c) **Achievement** can be rewarded separately from **effort**, with advantages for the recruitment and retention of high quality employees.

A further advantage is that labour costs are linked to organisational performance.

4.7 Schemes may be based on individual performance or on group performance. Individual schemes are common when the work is essentially individualistic and the output of a single person is easy to specify and measure. However, much work is performed by teams and it is impossible to identify each person's output. Such work calls for a group incentive scheme. The main problem with team incentive payments is that there is unlikely to be a single consistent standard of effort or achievement within the group. Inevitably there will be those who perform better than others and they are likely to be aggrieved if all group members are rewarded equally.

4.8 The ultimate group incentive scheme is the organisation wide scheme, in which all employees are rewarded in accordance with overall performance, usually as measured by profit . This tends to be very popular in good times and the cause of disappointment and resentment when the firm is doing badly. The value of such schemes is questionable.

4.9 **Types of incentive scheme**

- Performance related pay (PRP)
- Bonus schemes
- Profit-sharing

Performance related pay

4.10 The most common individual PRP scheme for wage earners is straight **piecework**: payment of a fixed amount per unit produced, or operation completed.

4.11 For managerial and other salaried jobs, however, a form of **management by objectives** will probably be applied.

(a) Key results will be identified and specified, for which merit awards (on top of basic salary) will be paid.

(b) There will be a clear model for evaluating performance and knowing when, or if, targets have been reached and payments earned.

(c) The exact conditions and amounts of awards can be made clear to the employee, to avoid uncertainty and later resentment.

4.12 For service and other departments, a PRP scheme may involve bonuses for achievement of key results, or points schemes, where points are awarded for performance on various criteria (efficiency, cost savings, quality of service and so on). Certain points totals (or the highest points total in the unit, if a competitive system is used) then win cash or other awards.

Bonus schemes

4.13 **Bonus schemes** are supplementary to basic salary, and have been found to be popular with entrepreneurial types, usually in marketing and sales. Bonuses are both incentives and rewards.

4.14 **Group incentive schemes** typically offer a bonus for a group (equally, or proportionately to the earnings or status of individuals) which achieves or exceeds specified targets. Typically, bonuses would be calculated monthly on the basis of improvements in output per man per hour against standard, or value added (to the cost of raw materials and parts by the production process).

4.15 **Value added schemes** work on the basis that improvements in productivity (indicated by a fall in the ratio of employment costs to sales revenue) increases value added, and the benefit can be shared between employers and employees on an agreed formula. So if sales revenue increases and labour costs (after charges for materials, utilities and depreciation have been deducted) stay the same, or sales revenue remains constant but labour costs decrease, the balance becomes available. There has been an increase in such schemes in recent years (for example, at ICI).

Profit sharing schemes and employee shareholders

4.16 **Profit sharing schemes** offer employees (or selected groups of them) bonuses, perhaps in the form of shares in the company, related directly to profits. The formula for determining the amounts may vary, but in recent years a straightforward distribution of a percentage of profits above a given target has given way to a value added related concept.

4.17 Profit sharing is in general based on the belief that all employees can contribute to profitability, and that that contribution should be recognised. If it is, the argument runs, the effects may include profit-consciousness and motivation in employees, commitment to the future prosperity of the organisation and so on.

4.18 The actual incentive value and effect on productivity may be wasted, however, if the scheme is badly designed.

(a) A **perceivably significant sum** should be made available to employees - once shareholders have received appropriate return on their investment - say, 10% of basic pay.

(b) There should be a clear, and not overly delayed, **link between performance and reward**. Profit shares should be distributed as frequently as possible - consistent with the need for reliable information on profit forecasts and targets and the need to amass a significant pool for distribution.

(c) The scheme should only be introduced if profit forecasts indicate a reasonable chance of achieving the target: profit sharing is welcome when profits are high, but the potential for disappointment is great.

(d) The greatest effect on productivity arising from the scheme may in fact arise from its use as a focal point for discussion with employees, about the relationship between their performance and results, and areas and targets for improvement. Management must be seen to be committed to the principle.

4.19 **Difficulties associated with incentive schemes**

(a) Increased earnings simply may not be an incentive to some individuals. An individual who already enjoys a good income may be more concerned with increasing his leisure time, for example.

(b) Workers are unlikely to be in complete control of results. External factors, such as the general economic climate, interest rates and exchange rates may play a part in **profitability** in particular. In these cases, the relationship between an individual's efforts and his reward may be indistinct.

(c) Greater specialisation in production processes means that particular employees cannot be specifically credited with the success of particular products. This may lead to frustration amongst employees who think their own profitable work is being adversely affected by inefficiencies elsewhere in the organisation.

(d) Even if employees are motivated by money, the effects may not be altogether desirable. An instrumental orientation may encourage self-interested performance at the expense of teamwork: it may encourage attention to output at the expense of quality, and the lowering of standards and targets (in order to make bonuses more accessible).

(e) It is often all too easy to manipulate the rules of the inventive scheme, especially where there are allowances for waiting time, when production is held up by factors beyond the control of the people concerned. Special allowances, guaranteed earnings and changes in methods also undermine incentive schemes.

(f) Poorly designed schemes can produce labour cost increases out of proportion to output improvements.

Case example

Personnel Management, November 1990, reported research into the benefits and problems of performance-related pay.

	Black & Decker	Komatsu UK	Birds Eye Walls	Co. A	Co. B	Co. C	Co. D	Co. E
1 Benefits of PRP cited								
Improves commitment and capability	Yes	Yes	Yes	Yes	Yes	Yes	Yes	Yes
Complements other HR initiatives	Yes	Yes	Yes	Yes	Yes	Yes		Yes
Improves business awareness	Yes	Yes	Yes		Yes	Yes		
Better two-way communications	Yes	Yes	Yes		Yes	Yes		Yes
Greater supervisory responsibility		Yes	Yes	Yes	Yes			Yes

	Black & Decker	Komatsu UK	Birds Eye Walls	Co. A	Co. B	Co. C	Co. D	Co. E
2 Potential problems cited								
Subjectivity			Yes			Yes	Yes	Yes
Supervisors' commitment and ability	Yes	Yes	Yes		Yes	Yes	Yes	Yes
Translating appraisals into pay	Yes	Yes	Yes	Yes		Yes		Yes
Divisive/against team working			Yes	Yes		Yes	Yes	Yes
Union acceptance/employee attitudes			Yes	Yes	Yes		Yes	Yes

'In the wrong hands, PRP can do more harm than good, so organisations considering PRP should consider carefully whether it is appropriate for them ... Other payment systems which do not seek to directly link individual performance and reward may be more suited to the aims of the business.'

4.20 All such schemes are based on the principle that people are willing to work harder to obtain more money. However, the work of *Elton Mayo* and *Tom Lupton* has shown that there are several constraints which prevent most people from seeking to maximise their earnings.

(a) Workers are generally capable of influencing the timings and control systems used by management.

(b) Workers remain suspicious that if they achieved high levels of output and earnings then management would alter the basis of the incentive rates to reduce future earnings. Work groups therefore tend to restrict output to a level that they feel is **fair** and **safe**.

(c) Generally, the workers conform to a group output norm. The need to have the approval of their fellow workers by conforming to that norm is more important than the money urge.

4.21 In the *Affluent Worker* study referred to above, Goldthorpe and Lockwood recognised that people do not, by and large, seek to maximise their earnings. Instead, a person will work as hard as necessary to earn the money he wants - but not past the point at which the deprivations demanded of him (in terms of long hours or danger or antisocial conditions) are greater than he feels are worthwhile.

The assessment of satisfaction and morale

4.22 Morale is a kind of collective self-confidence. It tends to reflect success, job satisfaction, trust in leaders and balanced conditions of work. It is common to hear the phrase **low morale** in industrial relations, in connection with undesirable effects such as poor productivity, absenteeism and high labour turnover. However, the signs by which morale is often gauged are by no means clear cut.

(a) **Low productivity is not invariably a sign of low morale**. It is possible to envisage situations where a group experiences high satisfaction and sense of success, precisely because output is low: if the group is deliberately attempting to sabotage management objectives, or control incentive systems, for example.

(b) **High labour turnover is not a reliable indicator of low morale**: the age structure of the workforce and other factors in natural wastage will need to be taken into account. Low turnover, likewise, is no evidence of high morale: people may be staying because of lack of other opportunities in the local job market, for example.

(c) There is some evidence that **satisfaction correlates with mental health** - so that symptoms of stress or psychological failure may be a signal to management that all is not well, although again, a range of non-work factors may be contributing.

(d) Attitude surveys may indicate workers' perception of their job satisfaction, by way of interview or questionnaire. They are, however, likely to be fraught with ambiguity, and inhibitions due to considerations of job security. A confidential semi-structured interview may be used - but will be costly in time and manpower.

Alleviating dissatisfaction and low morale

4.23 If evidence of low morale is found it will need to be analysed. A 'hard nosed' approach may be justified if the problem is traced to subversion or conflict in the group. In such cases, the removal of certain individuals - from the group, or from the organisation if necessary - may be effective in at least restoring conditions of equilibrium, in which efforts to build morale may be possible. Otherwise, it should be recognised that low morale implies a state of unhappiness, frustration, perhaps alienation: punishment, dismissals and threats are more likely to aggravate than alleviate such a situation.

4.24 If particular causes of dissatisfaction have been identified, they should be addressed. The problem may be fairly easily solved by cultural or managerial means, if, for example, morale is low because the workers feel unappreciated, do not feel part of a team or do not get enough information to commit themselves to organisational goals.

Exam focus point

Motivation is an ideal topic for a scenario question. You might be introduced to a situation and asked to explain why the people in the organisation are, say, demotivated. You could be asked to comment on the motivational impact of changes proposed by management.

Chapter roundup

- Personality is the totality of an individual's thoughts, feelings and behaviours, which integrate the person, are consistent and distinguish the person from someone else.

- Personality is shaped by a variety of factors, both inherited and environmental.

- In the work environment, people can assume different roles according to their personality. In judging individuals:

  ° perceptual selectivity leads to the halo effect whereby some characteristics, in the perceiver's viewpoint, dominate others

  ° stereotyping organises perceptions and assumes that people who share one characteristic share a set of others.

  People develop views of themselves through interaction with others. Social influences include: role models, peer groups and the variety of roles the individual is expected to play.

- Individuals have attitudes. These affect an individual's response to situations. Behaviour at work is formed by attitudes at work and attitudes to work. Attitudes to work can be set by the wider social and cultural influences on the individual, and how that individual is motivated.

- A group has certain attributes that a crowd does not possess; groups have many important functions in organisations. Group norms may work to raise or to lower the standard rate of unit production.

- Motivation directs individual behaviour. It is in the interests of an employer to know how to motivate employees' behaviour for the employer's benefit. Maslow's hierarchy of needs and Herzberg's theory assume that individuals have a set of needs. Process theories, such as expectancy theory, assume that different outcomes *become* desirable, and that desirable outcomes are not 'given' in advance.

- Individuals have legal contracts with an employer, but there is also a set of expectations which can form a psychological contract.

- Pay can be a motivator in certain circumstances. However these depend on the value individuals ascribe to pay, the way in which incentive schemes are implemented.

- There is no proven link between job satisfaction and performance, but participation can sometimes enhance both.

Quick quiz

1 What variables affect job performance?

2 How would you expect people to develop as they age?

3 What needs are satisfied by hygiene factors and motivator factors?

4 Why might you prefer expectancy theory to the ideas of Maslow or Herzberg?

5 What are the limitations of pay as a motivator?

Answers to quick quiz

1 Organisational and social variables: social environment, incentives, training and supervision; situational variables: The character of the organisation, physical environment; physical and job variables: working conditions, equipment and methods; individual variables: age, sex, physique, education, experience, intelligence, aptitude, motivation, personality, circumstances.

2 Argyris suggested that mature people become more active and less passive; diversify their behaviour patterns; become more independent; expect more respect; consider longer time scales; develop deeper and more stable interests; and become increasingly self-aware.

3 Hygiene factors satisfy the need to avoid unpleasantness, while motivators satisfy the need for personal growth.

4 Expectancy theory is based on the assumption that human behaviour is purposive and rational. The theories of Maslow and Herzberg emphasise innate drives.

5 Pay is a classic hygiene factor: to the extent that it influences motivation, it can have only a negative effect, when it is inadequate.

Now try the question below from the Exam Question Bank

Number	Level	Marks	Time
Q11	Exam	18	32 mins

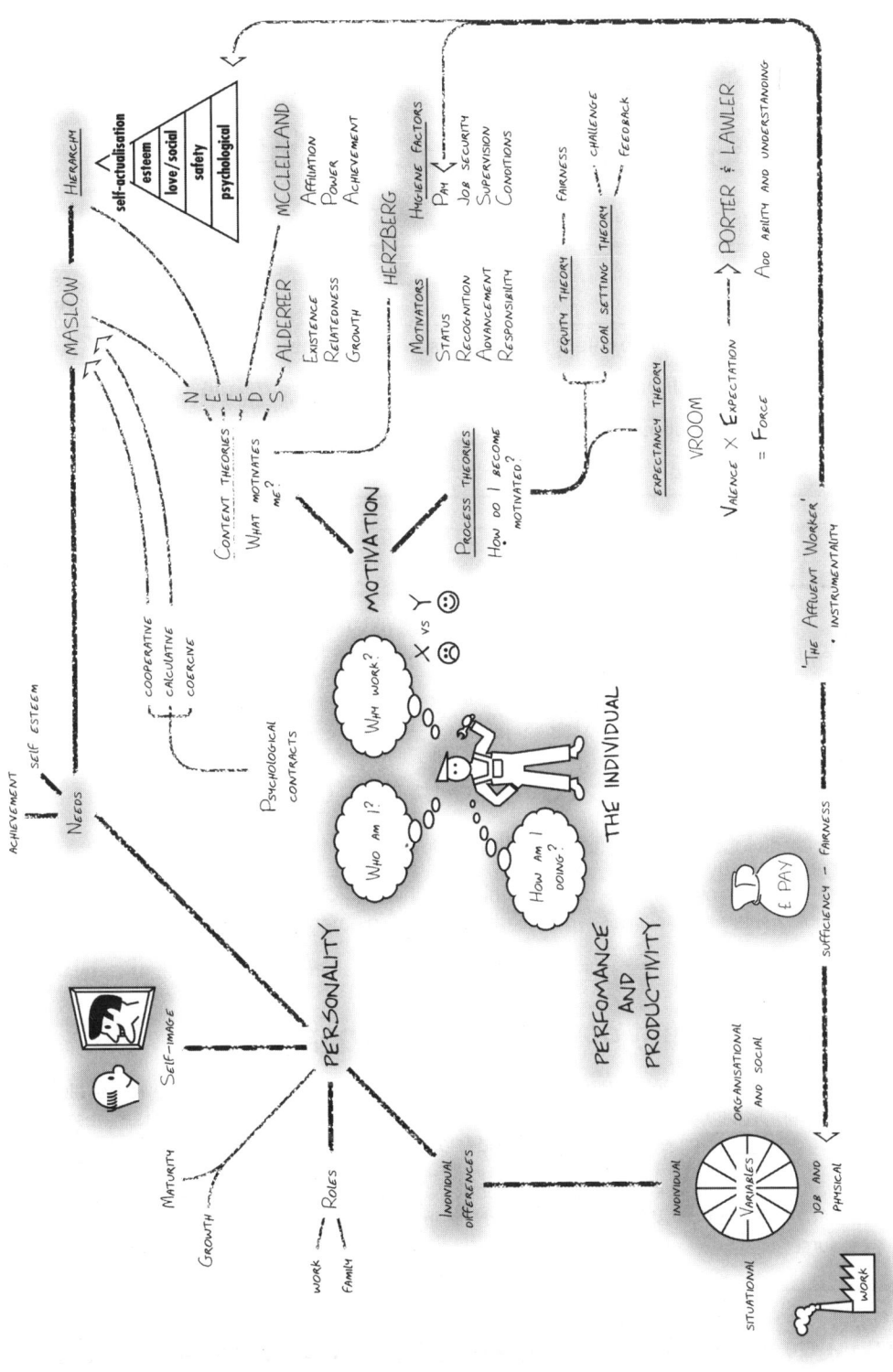

Chapter 12

TRAINING AND DEVELOPMENT

Topic list		Syllabus Reference	Ability required
1	Human resource development and organisational learning	(iii)	Analysis
2	Training and development needs	(iii)	Analysis
3	Methods of development and training	(iii)	Analysis
4	Evaluating training	(iii)	Analysis

Introduction

Training is widely recognised as a means to render employees efficient and productive, but it is no panacea for bad work organisation, personal incompetence or poor management.

The strategic purpose of training is to raise the overall skills level of the organisation. This should increase efficiency and responsiveness.

Learning outcomes covered in this chapter

- Explain the importance of human resource development planning.

- Produce a training and development plan for the staff of a finance department and analyse the major problems associated with the design and implementation of such a plan.

- Produce and explain the planning and delivery of a training course on a finance related topic.

Syllabus content covered in this chapter

- The distinction between development and training and the tools available to develop and train staff (ie education, training methods, management development programmes, promotion, succession and career planning, job redesign).

- The stages in the planning and conduct of a training course, the features and benefits of the various tools and visual aids used and the importance of feedback during and after a training course.

1 HUMAN RESOURCE DEVELOPMENT AND ORGANISATIONAL LEARNING

1.1 Resourcing an organisation (in HRM jargon) is about building and maintaining the **skills and knowledge base** of the organisation.

> **KEY TERM**
>
> **Human resource development** (HRD). The process of extending personal abilities and qualities by means of education, training and other learning experiences.

What is development?

> **KEY TERMS**
>
> **Development** is 'the growth or realisation of a person's ability and potential through the provision of learning and educational experiences'.
>
> **Training** is 'the planned and systematic modification of behaviour through learning events, programmes and instruction which enable individuals to achieve the level of knowledge, skills and competence to carry out their work effectively'.
>
> (Armstrong, *Handbook of Personnel Management Practice*)

1.2 **Overall purpose of employee and management development**

- **Ensure** the firm meets current and future performance objectives by...
- **Continuous improvement** of the performance of individuals and teams, and by...
- **Maximising people's** potential for growth (and promotion).

1.3 **Development activities**

- Training, both on and off the job
- Career planning
- Job rotation
- Appraisal (see previous chapter)
- Other learning opportunities

1.4 Organisations often have a **training and development strategy**, based on the overall strategy for the business. We can list the following steps.

Step 1. Identify the skills and competences are needed by the **business plan**

Step 2. Draw up the **development strategy** to show how training and development activities will assist in meeting the targets of the corporate plan.

Step 3. **Implement** the training and development strategy.

This approach produces training with the right qialities.
- Relevance
- Problem-based (ie corrects a real lack of skills)
- Action-oriented
- Performance-related

HRD and the organisation

1.5   Benefits for the organisation of training and development programmes

Benefit	Comment
Minimise the learning costs of obtaining the skills the organisation needs	Training supports the business strategy.
Lower costs and **increased productivity**, thereby improving performance	Some people suggest that higher levels of training explain the higher productivity of German as opposed to many British manufacturers
Fewer accidents, and better health and safety	EU health and safety directives require a certain level of training. Employees can take employers to court if accidents occur or if unhealthy work practices persist.
Less need for detailed supervision	If people are trained they can get on with the job, and managers can concentrate on other things. Training is an aspect of **empowerment**.
Flexibility	Training ensures that people have the **variety** of skills needed – multi-skilling is only possible if people are properly trained.
Recruitment and succession planning	Training and development attracts new recruits and ensures that the organisation has a supply of suitable managerial and technical staff to take over when people retire.
Change management	Training helps organisations manage change by letting people know why the change is happening and giving them the skills to cope with it.
Corporate culture	Training programmes can be used to build the corporate culture or to direct it in certain ways, by indicating that certain **values** are espoused.
	Training programmes can **build relationships** between staff and managers in different areas of the business
Motivation	Training programmes can increase commitment to the organisation's goals

1.6   These benefits are real – but training cannot do everything. Training only really covers:

Aspect of performance	Areas covered
Individual	Education; Experience; possibly Personal Circumstances (if successful completion of training is accompanied by a higher salary
Physical and job	Methods of work
Organisational and social	Type of training and supervision

1.7 Training **cannot** improve performance problems arising from factors other than training needs.

- Bad management
- Poor job design
- Poor equipment, factory layout and work organisation
- Other characteristics of the employee (eg intelligence)
- Motivation – training gives the ability (but not necessarily the willingness) to improve
- Poor recruitment

Training and the individual

1.8 For the individual employee, the benefits of training and development are more clear-cut, and few refuse it if it is offered.

Benefit	Comment
Enhances portfolio of **skills**	Even if not specifically related to the current job, training can be useful in other contexts, and the employee becomes more attractive to employers and more promotable
Psychological benefits	The trainee might feel reassured that he/she is of continuing value to the organisation
Social benefit	People's social needs can be met by training courses – they can also develop networks of contacts
The job	Training can help people do their job better, thereby increasing job satisfaction

Developing skills and knowledge: the learning organisation

1.9 Managers can try to develop a **learning organisation.** The learning organisation has a number of facets.

- It encourages continuous learning and knowledge generation at all levels.
- It has the processes to move knowledge around the organisation.
- It can transform knowledge into actual behaviour.

The justification for this is that **knowledge can be created and exploited**. Training is one part of this.

> **KEY TERM**
>
> In their book *The Learning Company: A Strategy for Sustainable Development*, Pedler, Burgoyne and Boydell suggest the following might be a good description of a **learning organisation**:
>
> 'An organisation that facilitates the learning of all its members *and* continuously transforms itself.'

1.10   **Characteristics of the learning organisation**

Characteristics	Comments
Learning approach to strategy	Experimentation and feedback built into a system. As much information as possible is brought to bear on a problem.
Participative policy making	All members of a learning company have the chance to participate in the learning process.
Informating	This is the use of information not as a control mechanism, but as a resource for the whole organisation to exploit in order to develop new insights.
Formative accounting	Accounting and budgeting systems should be structured to assist learning. Such systems might encourage individuals to act as 'small businesses treating internal users as **customers'**.
Internal exchange	Internal exchange develops the idea of the **internal customer**. Each unit regards the other units as customers, whose needs must be identified and satisfied, in the context of the company as a whole.
Reward flexibility	In a learning company, there is a flexible approach to reward and remuneration.
Enabling structures	Organisation structures are *temporary* arrangements that must respond to changed conditions and opportunities.
Boundary workers as environmental scanners	In a learning organisation, environmental monitoring is not restricted to specialists or managers. All employees dealing with the boundary should try and monitor the environment.
Inter-company learning	Learn from other firms.
Learning climate	Functions of management in a learning organisation • Encourage continuous learning. • Create processes to move knowledge around. • Transform knowledge into behaviour

Case example

Servicing Xerox copiers

Our story begins with researchers working on artificial intelligence who wanted to see if they could replace the paper documentation that Xerox technicians used on the road with an expert system.

The team found that it was indeed possible to build software that could do just that. But when they showed their first efforts to technicians, the response was underwhelming.

What kept technicians from finding fixes was not that the documentation was paper-based but that it didn't address all the potential problems. And not all problems were predictable. Machines in certain regions could react to extreme temperatures in different ways. A can of Mountain Dew overturned in one part of a machine could wreak havoc in another seemingly unconnected part. Technicians could handle these mishaps quickly only if they had seen them before or if another technician had run into a similar problem and shared the results.

Once the conversations with technicians revealed this gap in information sharing, the researchers realised that AI was the wrong approach. What Xerox needed instead was knowledge management. It wasn't a smart computer program that was going to fix these things, it was sharing the best ways to make these repairs.

When the researchers realised they needed to look at the way technicians work, they spent time in the field, following the technicians from call to call. What they observed proved invaluable – knowledge sharing was already unofficially ingrained in the organisation. Most striking was not how technicians solved common problems, but what they did when they came up against a tricky, intermittent one. Often they called one another on radios provided by the company. And in informal gatherings they shared vexing problems and their fixes.

Meanwhile, another researcher was busy comparing the way French and U.S. technicians worked. He discovered that, while French technicians appeared to work from immaculate, uniform documentation put out by headquarters, their real solutions also came from a second set of documentation – notes they carried with them detailing what they'd learned. It was from that database that researchers started building the first laptop-based knowledge-sharing system.

The researchers took the first iteration to France and began a series of exhaustive sessions with the French experts in the Xerox headquarters outside Paris. In those sessions, something magical happened: The system took on the shape of the people working on it, evolving with each suggestion from the actual users.

But the worldwide customer service group didn't take the project seriously. Nobody believed that the knowledge of the technicians was really valuable. So, working stealthily, outside the realm of worldwide management, the research team gave laptops and the fledging program to 40 technicians and matched them with a control group of technicians who relied solely on their own knowledge when fixing machines. After two months, the group with the laptops had 10 percent lower costs and 10 percent lower service time than those without – and the control group was jealous of those with the system.

By 1998, the system was officially deployed in the United States and began to make its way around the globe. Today it has more than 15,000 user tips, with more being added every day. The hope is that by 2002 it will be distributed worldwide to the company's 25,000 technicians. And already success stories abound. One technician in Montreal authored a tip about a 50-cent fuse-holder replacement that caused a chronic problem with a high-speed colour copier. A Brazilian technician had the same problem, and his customer wanted the $40,000 machine replaced. When he found the tip from Montreal, he fixed the machine in minutes. Current estimates have the system saving Xerox at least $7 million in time and replacement costs. It's tales like those that make senior management happy.

Adapted from Meg Mitchell, www.darwinmag.com February 2001.

1.11 Training has a role in creating the learning organisation.

- Training enables skills to be disseminated.
- Training courses are an opportunity for people to get together.

Training and performance management

1.12 Training is no panacea for many problems of performance.

(a) It is irrelevant to problems caused by faulty organisation, layout, methods, equipment, employee selection and placement and so on.

(b) Cost, time, inconvenience, apathy and an unrealistic expectations of training in the past may restrict its effectiveness.

(c) Limitations imposed by intelligence, poor motivation and the psychological restrictions of the learning process also restrict its effectiveness.

Case example

Training and IT

A study by the DTI suggests about half of UK companies believe that their employees do not have sufficient understanding of IT to use the technologies to their full competitive advantage. Not surprisingly, then, the study says that a third of UK companies provide no training.

BPP PUBLISHING

2 TRAINING AND DEVELOPMENT NEEDS

The training process in outline

2.1 In order to ensure that training meets the real needs of the organisation, large firms adopt a planned approach to training. This has the following steps.

Step 1. Identify and define the **organisation's training needs**. It may be the case that recruitment might be a better solution to a problem than training.

Step 2. **Define the learning required** – in other words, specify the knowledge, skills or competences that have to be acquired. For technical training, this is not difficult: for example all finance department staff will have to become conversant with the new accounting system.

Step 3. **Define training objectives** – what must be learnt and what trainees must be able to do after the training exercise.

Step 4. **Plan training programmes** – training and development can be planned in a number of ways, employing a number of techniques, as we shall learn about in Section 3. (Also, people have different approaches to learning, which have to be considered.) This covers three things.

- Who provides the training
- Where the training takes place
- Divisions of responsibilities between trainers, line managers or team leaders, the individual personally.

Step 5. **Implement the training**

Step 6. **Evaluate** the training: has it been successful in achieving learning objectives.

Step 7. Go back to Step 2 if more training is needed.

Training needs analysis

Case example

Training for quality

The British Standards for Quality Systems (BS EN ISO 9000: formerly BS 5750) which many UK organisations are working towards (often at the request of customers, who perceive it to be a 'guarantee' that high standards of quality control are being achieved) includes training requirements. As the following extract shows, the Standard identifies training needs for those organisations registering for assessment, and also shows the importance of a systematic approach to ensure adequate control.

The training, both by specific training to perform assigned tasks and general training to heighten quality awareness and t0 mould attitudes of all personnel in an organisation, is central to the achievement of quality.

The comprehensiveness of such training varies with the complexity of the organisation.

The following steps should be taken:

1   Identifying the way tasks and operations influence quality in total

2   Identifying individuals; training needs against those required for satisfactory performance of the task

3   Planning and carrying out appropriate specific training

4   Planning and organising general quality awareness programmes

5   Recording training and achievement in an easily retrievable form so that records can be updated and taps in training can be readily identified

BSI, 1990

2.2 From the example above, you should see that training needs analysis covers three issues.

Current state	Desired state
Organisation's current results	Desired results, standards
Existing knowledge and skill	Knowledge and skill needed
Individual performance	Required standards

The difference between the two columns is the **training gap**. Training programmes are designed to improve individual performance, thereby improving the performance of the organisation.

2.3 **Training surveys** combine information from a variety of sources to discern what the training needs of the organisation actually are.

(a) The **business strategy** at corporate level.

(b) **Appraisal and performance reviews:** the purpose of a performance management system is to improve performance, and training maybe recommended as a remedy.

(c) **Attitude surveys** of employees, asking them what training they think they need or would like.

(d) **Evaluation of existing training** programmes.

(e) **Job analysis,** which deals with three things.

- Reported difficulties people have in meeting the skills requirement of the job

- Existing performance weaknesses that could be remedied by training

- Future changes in the job

The job analysis can be used to generate a training specification covering the knowledge needed for the job, the skills required to achieve the result, attitudinal changes required.

Setting training objectives

2.4 The **training manager** will have to make an initial investigation into the problem of the gap between job or competence *requirements* and current performance of *competence*.

2.5 If training would improve work performance, training **objectives** can then be defined. They should be clear, specific and related to observable, measurable targets.

- Behaviour - what the trainee should be able to do
- Standard - to what level of performance
- Environment - under what conditions (so that the performance level is realistic)

2.6 EXAMPLE

'At the end of the course the trainee should be able to describe ... or identify ... or distinguish x from y ... or calculate ... or assemble ...' and so on. It is insufficient to define the objectives of training as 'to give trainees a grounding in ...' or 'to encourage trainees in a better appreciation of ...': this offers no target achievement which can be quantifiably measured.

2.7 Training objectives link the identification of training needs with the content, methods and technology of training.

Training needs	Learning objectives
To know more about the Data Protection Act	The employee will be able to answer four out of every five queries about the Data Protection Act without having to search for details.
To establish a better rapport with customers	The employee will immediately attend to a customer unless already engaged with another customers.
	The employee will greet each customer using the customer's name where known.
	The employee will apologise to every customer who has had to wait to be attended to.
To assemble clocks more quickly	The employee will be able to assemble each clock correctly within thirty minutes.

Having identified training needs and objectives, the manager will have to decide on the best way to approach training: there are a number of types and techniques of training, which we will discuss below.

3   METHODS OF DEVELOPMENT AND TRAINING

Incorporating training needs into an individual development programme

KEY TERM

A **personal development plan** is a 'clear developmental action plan for an individual which incorporates a wide set of developmental opportunities including formal training.'

3.1   The purpose of a personal development plan will vary.

- Improving performance in the existing job
- Developing skills for future career moves within and outside the organisation.

KEY TERM

Skills: what the individual needs to be able to do if results are to be achieved. Skills are built up progressively by repeated training. They may be manual, intellectual or mental, perceptual or social.

3.2   Preparing a personal development plan involves these steps.

Step 1.   Analyse the current position. You could do a personal SWOT analysis. The supervisor can have an input into this by categorising the skills use of employees on a grid as follows, in a **skills analysis**.

		Performance	
		High	*Low*
Liking of skills	*High*	Likes and does well	Likes but doesn't do well
	Low	Dislikes but does well	Dislikes and doesn't do well

The aim is to try to incorporate more of the employees' interests into their actual roles.

Step 2. **Set goals to cover performance in the existing job,** future changes in the current role, moving elsewhere in the organisations, developing specialist expertise. Naturally, such goals should have the characteristic, as far as possible of SMART objectives (ie specific, measurable, attainable, realistic and time-bounded).

Step 3. **Draw up action plan** to achieve the goals, covering the developmental activities listed in paragraph 3.1.

Formal training

3.3 **Formal training**

(a) **Internal courses** are run by the organisation's training department or may be provided by external suppliers.

(b) **Types of course**

  (i) **Day release**: the employee works in the organisation and on one day per week attends a local college or training centre for theoretical learning.

  (ii) **Distance learning, evening classes and correspondence courses,** which make demands on the individual's time outside work. This is commonly used, for example, by typists wishing to develop or 'refresh' shorthand skills.

  (iii) **Revision courses** for examinations of professional bodies.

  (iv) **Block release** courses which may involve four weeks at a college or training centre followed by a period back at work.

  (v) **Sandwich courses,** usually involve six months at college then six months at work, in rotation, for two or three years.

  (vi) A **sponsored full-time course** at a university for one or two years.

(c) **Computer-based training** involves interactive training via PC. The typing program, Mavis Beacon, is a good example.

(d) **Techniques** used on the course might include:

  • Lectures
  • Seminars, in which participation is encouraged
  • Simulation. For example, you may have been sent on an audit training course.

3.4 **Course training methods**

(a) **Lectures**. Lectures are suitable for large audiences and can be an efficient way of putting across information. However lack of participation may lead to lack of interest from, and failure to understand by most of the audience.

(b) **Discussions.** Discussions aim to impart information but allow much greater opportunities to audience participation. They are often suitable for groups up to 20 and can be a good means of maintaining interest.

(c) **Exercises.** An exercise involves a particular task being undertaken with pre-set results following guidance laid down. They are a very active form of learning and are a good means of checking whether trainees have assimilated information.

(d) **Role plays.** Trainees act out roles in a typical work situation. They are useful practice for face-to-face situations. However, they may embarrass and may not be taken seriously.

(e) **Case studies.** Case studies identify causes and/or suggest solutions. They are a good means of exchanging ideas and thinking out solutions. However trainees may see the case study as divorced from their real work experience.

3.5 **Programmed learning** can be provided on a computer terminal, but it is still associated with printed booklets which provide information in easy-to-learn steps. The booklet asks simple questions which the trainee must answer. If they are answered correctly, the trainee is instructed to carry on with more learning. If the questions are answered wrongly, the booklet gives an alternative set of instructions to go back and learn again. Programmed learning has several advantages.

(a) A trainee can work through the course in simple stages with frequent checks of understanding. Misunderstandings are quickly put right.

(b) A trainee is kept actively involved in the learning process because he must keep answering questions put to him in the booklet.

(c) Giving correct answers immediately reinforces the learning process.

(d) The trainee can work at his or her own pace.

3.6 **Disadvantages of formal training**

(a) An individual will not benefit from formal training unless he or she **wants to learn**. The individual's superior may need to provide encouragement in this respect.

(b) If the **subject matter** of the training course does not **relate to an individual's job**, the learning will quickly be forgotten.

(c) Individuals may not be able to carry over what they have learned to their own particular job.

On the job training

3.7 **Successful on the job training**

(a) The assignments should have a **specific purpose** from which the trainee can learn and gain experience.

(b) The organisation must **tolerate any mistakes** which the trainee makes. Mistakes are an inevitable part of on the job learning.

(c) The work should **not be too complex**.

3.8   **Methods of on the job training**

(a)   **Demonstration/instruction:** show the trainee how to do the job and let them get on with it. It should combine **telling** a person what to do and **showing** them how, using appropriate media. The trainee imitates the instructor, and asks questions.

(b)   **Coaching:** the trainee is put under the guidance of an experienced employee who shows the trainee how to do the job.

- **Establish learning targets.**
- **Plan a systematic learning and development programme.**
- **Identify opportunities for broadening the trainee's knowledge and experience.**
- **Take into account the strengths and limitations of the trainee.**
- **Exchange feedback.**

(c)   **Job rotation:** the trainee is given several jobs in succession, to gain experience of a wide range of activities.

(d)   **Temporary promotion:** an individual is promoted into his/her superior's position whilst the superior is absent due to illness.

(e)   **'Assistant to' positions:** a junior manager with good potential may be appointed as assistant to the managing director or another executive director.

(f)   **Action learning:** a group of managers are brought together to solve a real problem with the help of an advisor who explains the management process that actually happens.

(g)   **Committees:** trainees might be included in the membership of committees, in order to obtain an understanding of inter-departmental relationships.

(h)   **Project work.** Work on a project with other people can expose the trainee to other parts of the organisation.

Learning styles

3.9   The way in which people learn best will differ according to the type of person. That is, there are **learning styles** which suit different individuals. *Honey and Mumford* have drawn up a popular classification of four learning styles.

(a)   **Theorists** seek to understand underlying concepts and to take an intellectual, 'hands-off' approach based on logical argument. They prefer training with a clear programme and structure and which allows time for analysis. They like teachers who share their preference for concepts and analysis.

(b)   **Reflectors**
- Observe phenomena, think about them and then choose how to act.
- Need to work at their own pace
- Find learning difficult if forced into a hurried programme.
- Produce carefully thought-out conclusions after research and reflection
- Tend to be fairly slow, non-participative (unless to ask questions) and cautious.

(c)   **Activists**
- Deal with practical, active problems. No patience with theory.
- Require training based on hands-on experience.
- Excited by participation and pressure, such as new projects.
- Flexible and optimistic, but tend to rush at something without due preparation, take risks and then get bored.

(d) **Pragmatists**

- Only like to study if they can see its direct link to practical implications.
- Good at learning new techniques in on-the-job training.
- Aim is to implement action plans and/or do the task better.
- May discard as impractical good ideas which require development.

The learning cycle (Kolb)

3.10 Kolb suggested that classroom-type learning is 'a specialist activity cut off from the real world and unrelated to one's life': a teacher or trainer directs the learning process on behalf of a passive learner. Experiential learning involves **doing**, however, and puts the learners in an active problem-solving role: a form of **self-learning** which encourages the learners to formulate and commit themselves to their own learning objectives.

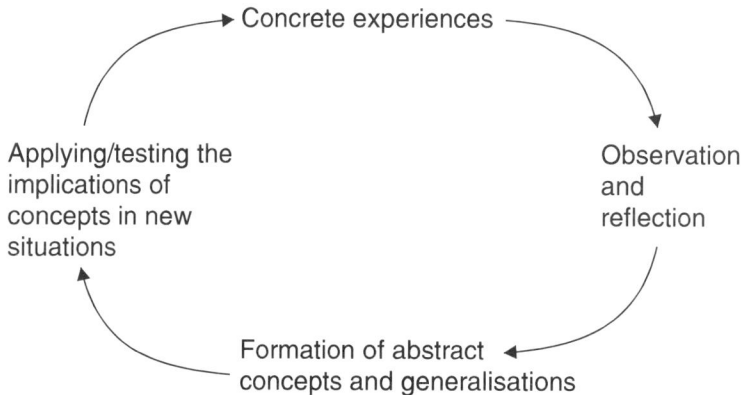

4 EVALUATING TRAINING

KEY TERMS

Validation of training means observing the results of the course and measuring whether the training objectives have bee achieved.

Evaluation of training means comparing the actual costs of the scheme against the assessed benefits which are being obtained. If the costs exceed the benefits, the scheme will need to be redesigned or withdrawn.

4.1 **Ways of validating and evaluating a training scheme**

(a) **Trainees' reactions to the experience:** asking the trainees whether they thought the training programme was relevant to their work, and whether they found it useful.

(b) **Trainee learning:** measuring what the trainees have learned on the course by means of a test at the end of it.

(c) **Changes in job behaviour following training.** This is relevant where the aim of the training was to learn a skill.

(d) **Organisational change as a result of training:** finding out whether the training has affected the work or behaviour of other employees not on the course.

(e) **Impact of training on organisational goals:** seeing whether the training scheme (and overall programme) has contributed to the overall objectives of the organisation.

Case example

People Management in April 1996 reported that a number of Whitbread pubs had improved performance as a result of a change in the company's training scheme. Previously the company's training scheme had aimed to improve the service standards of individuals, and there were also discussions with staff on business developments. It was felt however that other companies in the same sector had overtaken Whitbread in these respects.

Whitbread therefore introduced an integrated approach to assessment of the performance of pubs. Assessment is by four criteria; training (a certain percentage of staff have to have achieved a training award), standards (suggested by working parties of staff), team meetings and customer satisfaction. Managers are trained in training skills and they in turn train staff, using a set of structured notes to ensure a consistent training process.

Pubs that fulfil all the criteria win a team hospitality award, consisting of a plaque, a visit from a senior executive, and a party or points for goods scheme. To retain the award and achieve further points, pubs have then to pass further assessments which take place every six months.

The scheme seemed to improve standards. Significantly staff turnover was down and a survey suggested morale had improved, with a greater sense of belonging particularly by part-time staff. A major cause of these improvements may well be the involvement of staff and management in the design process.

Chapter roundup

- **Human resource development (HRD)** means **training**. Training is one way of providing an organisation with the skills that it needs. It contributes to improved economic performance and results in the development of corporate culture.

- **Training** can be **on-the-job** or at a different site. **Formal** training courses are useful if the subject is relevant to the job, and if the course involves interaction with other members of the company. Background knowledge is then imparted through one on the job training. The learning organisation values training as a source of desirable improvement and uses it to faster innovation.

- The management of training and development is an iterative, rational process that includes several different aspects.
    - Identification of training **needs**
    - Definition of training **objectives**
    - **Planning** of training
    - **Delivery** of training
    - **Evaluation** of training

Quick quiz

1   Define human resource development.

2   What are the advantages of training to an organisation?

3   What is the learning organisation?

4   What are the steps in a training programme?

5   What are the steps in a personal development plan?

6   Describe the methods of on the job training.

7   How can learning theory assist training?

8   What is the learning cycle?

Answers to quick quiz

1   The process of extending personal abilities and qualities by means of education, training and other learning experiences.

2   Less need for supervision; personal flexibility; recruitment and succession planning; change management; development of corporate culture; improved motivation.

3   An organisation that facilitates learning by all of its members and continuously transforms itself.

4   Identify training needs; define learning requirements; define training objectives; plan training programmes; implement the training; evaluate the training.

5   A personal SWOT analysis; goal setting; plan formulation.

6   Demonstration: showing how followed by imitation; coaching: a more focussed form of personal instruction with targets, a programme and feedback; job rotation: a sequence of different jobs to broaden experience; temporary promotion: during the superior's absence; 'assistant to' positions: staff work at a high level; action learning: a problem solving task force is set up under supervision; Committee membership; project work: interdepartmental co-operation.

7   Research indicates that different people learn best under different circumstances; if individuals' learning styles can be established, more effective training can be devised for them.

8   Kolb suggested that the learning experience was iterative, with four main stages: concrete experience; observation and reflection; abstract conceptualisation and generalisation; and practical application.

Now try the question below from the Exam Question Bank

Number	Level	Marks	Time
Q12	Exam	20 marks	36 mins

Chapter 13

APPRAISAL AND CAREER MANAGEMENT

Topic List		Syllabus Reference	Ability required
1	Appraisal	(iii)	Evaluation
2	Problems with appraisal	(iii)	Evaluation
3	Managing careers	(iii)	Evaluation

Introduction

Appraisal is part of the job of line management, though it is usually *administered* by HR staff. It forms an important channel of two-way communication. Most people like to be told how they are progressing. Appraisal can be used for a number of purposes.

- Setting targets for improvement

- Determining training needs

- Considering potential for promotion

- Reviewing remuneration

There are several new approaches to the appraisal process which improve upon review by a supervisor. This include upward appraisal and 360° appraisal.

Career management is found in larger organisations, especially those which tend to promote from within. It identifies a cadre of managers with potential for promotion and gives them the training and experience they need to do well in more senior positions.

Learning outcomes covered in this chapter

- Explain the process of succession and career planning.

- Evaluate a typical appraisal process.

Syllabus content covered in this chapter

- The importance of appraisals, their conduct and the problems often associated with them

- The relationship between performance appraisal and the reward system

1 APPRAISAL 5/01

KEY TERM

Appraisal: the systematic review and assessment of an employee's performance, potential and training needs.

Appraisal: review past performance to establish the current position

1.1 The process of appraisal is part of the system of **performance management**. Whilst performance management as a whole is forward looking, the process of appraisal is designed to review performance over the past period, with a view to identifying any deficiencies, and improving it in the future.

The purpose of appraisal

1.2 The general purpose of any appraisal system is to improve the efficiency of the organisation by ensuring that the individuals within it are performing to the best of their ability and developing their potential for improvement. It has a number of aspects.

(a) **Reward review**. The appraisal should assess whether employees are deserving of a bonuses or pay increases as compared with their peers.

(b) **Performance review.** The appraisal can be used for planning and following-up training and development programmes by identifying training needs and validating training methods.

(c) **Potential review**. This is an aid to planning career development and succession which attempts to predict the level and type of work the individual will be capable of in the future.

1.3 **Objectives of appraisals**

(a) **Establishing what the individual has to do** in a job in order that the objectives for the section or department are realised

(b) **Establishing the key or main results** which the individual will be expected to achieve in the course of his or her work over a period of time

(c) **Comparing the individual's level of performance against a standard**, to provide a basis for remuneration above the basic pay rate

(d) **Identifying the individual's training and development needs** in the light of actual performance

(e) **Identifying potential candidates for promotion**

(f) **Identifying areas for improvement**

(g) **Establishing an inventory of actual and potential performance within the undertaking** to provide a basis for manpower planning

(h) **Monitoring the undertaking's initial selection procedures** against the subsequent performance of recruits, relative to the organisation's expectations

(i) **Improving communication** about work tasks between different levels in the hierarchy

1.4 **The need for appraisal**

(a) Managers and supervisors may obtain **random impressions** of subordinates' performance (perhaps from their more noticeable successes and failures), but **rarely form a coherent, complete and objective picture.**

(b) They may have a fair idea of their subordinates' **shortcomings** - but may not have devoted time and attention to the matter of **improvement and development.**

(c) **Judgements are easy to make, but less easy to justify** in detail, in writing, or to the subject's face.

(d) **Different assessors may be applying a different set of criteria, and varying standards of objectivity and judgement.** This undermines the value of appraisal for comparison, as well as its credibility in the eyes of the appraisees.

(e) Unless stimulated to do so, **managers rarely give their subordinates adequate feedback on their performance.**

1.5 **Three basic problems in appraisal**

(a) The **formulation of desired traits and standards** against which individuals can be consistently and objectively assessed.

(b) **Recording assessments.** Managers should be encouraged to utilise a standard and understood framework, but still allowed to express what they consider important, and without too much form-filling.

(c) **Getting the appraiser and appraisee together**, so that both contribute to the assessment and plans for improvement and/or development.

The process of appraisal

1.6 **A typical appraisal system**

Step 1. **Identify criteria for assessment**, perhaps based on job analysis, performance standards, person specifications and so on.

Step 2. **Prepare an appraisal report.** In some systems both the appraisee and appraiser prepare a report. These reports are then compared.

Step 3. **Carry out an appraisal interview**, for an exchange of views about the appraisal report, targets for improvement, solutions to problems and so on.

Step 4. **The assessor's superior reviews the assessment**, so that the appraisee does not feel subject to one person's prejudices. Formal appeals may be allowed, if necessary to establish the fairness of the procedure.

Step 5. **Prepare and implement an action plan** to achieve improvements and changes agreed.

Step 6. **Follow-up** the progress of the action plan.

BPP PUBLISHING

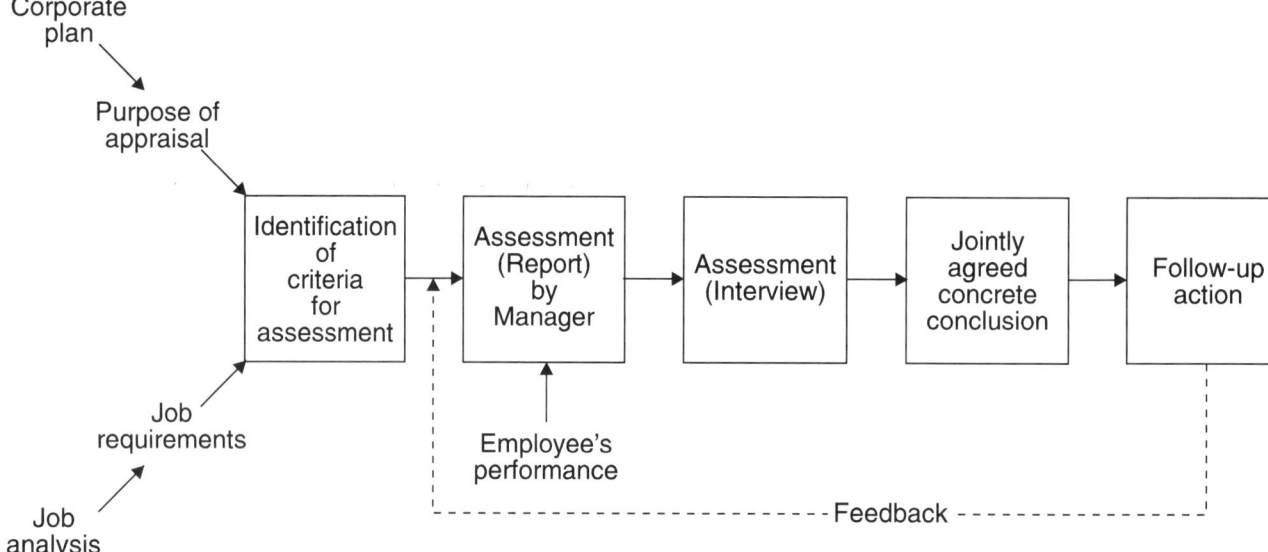

1.7 Most systems provide for appraisals to be recorded, and report forms of various lengths and complexity may be designed.

The appraisal report: self appraisal

What is appraised?

1.8 **Appraisal standard**. Assessments must be related to a common standard, in order for comparisons to be made between individuals: on the other hand, they should be related to meaningful performance criteria, which take account of the critical variables in each different job.

1.9 An appraisal report is written before the interview.

(a) Key performance issues relate to the **job description**.

(b) **Personality** is not relevant unless specifically related to performance.

(c) A **competence** is an observable skill or ability to complete a particular task successfully. It can include the ability to transfer skills and knowledge to new situations.

1.10 **Appraisal techniques**

(a) **Overall assessment**. Managers write in narrative form their judgements about the appraisees. There will be no guaranteed consistency of the criteria and areas of assessment, however, and managers may not be able to convey clear, effective judgements in writing.

(b) **Guided assessment**. Assessors are required to comment on a number of specified characteristics and performance elements, with guidelines as to how terms such as 'application', 'integrity' and 'adaptability' are to be interpreted in the work context. This is more precise, but still rather vague.

(c) **Grading**. Grading adds a comparative frame of reference to the general guidelines, whereby managers are asked to select one of a number of levels or degrees to which the individual in question displays the given characteristic. These are also known as **rating scales**. Numerical values may be added to ratings to give rating scores. Alternatively a less precise **graphic scale** may be used to indicate general position on a plus/minus scale.

Factor: job knowledge

High _____√_____ Average _____ Low

(d) **Behavioural incident methods**. These concentrate on **employee behaviour**, which is measured against typical behaviour in each job, as defined by common **critical incidents** of successful and unsuccessful job behaviour reported by managers.

(e) **Results-orientated schemes**. This reviews performance against specific targets and standards of performance agreed in advance by manager and subordinate together. As a result, the subordinate is more involved in appraisal and evaluates success or progress in achieving specific, jointly-agreed targets. The manager becomes a counsellor. Learning and motivation theories suggest that clear and known targets are important in modifying and determining behaviour. The effectiveness of the scheme will still, however, depend on the **targets set** (are they clearly defined and realistic?) and the **commitment** of both parties to make it work.

Self-appraisals

1.11 Individuals may carry out their own self-evaluation as a major input into the appraisal process. This has the advantage that the system is clearly aimed at the needs of the individual. Such a scheme has several **advantages.**

(a) It **saves the manager time** as the employee identifies the areas of competence which are relevant to the job and his/her relative strengths in these competences.

(b) It offers **increased responsibility** to the individual which may improve motivation.

(c) This may be a way of reconciling the goals of both the individual and the organisation.

(d) It may overcome the problem of needing skilled appraisers, thus cutting training costs and reducing the managerial role in appraisal.

(e) In giving the responsibility to an individual, the scheme may offer more **flexibility** in terms of timing, with individuals undertaking ongoing self-evaluation.

However, people are often not the best judges of their own performance.

1.12 Many schemes combine the two - manager and subordinate fill out a report and compare notes.

Interviews and counselling

1.13 The extent to which any discussion or counselling interview is based on the written appraisal report varies in practice. Some appraisees see the report in advance.

1.14 *Maier (The Appraisal Interview)* identifies three types of approach to appraisal interviews.

(a) **The tell and sell method**. The manager tells the subordinate how he or she has been assessed, and then tries to sell (gain acceptance of) the evaluation and the improvement plan. This requires unusual human relations skills in order to convey constructive criticism in an acceptable manner, and to motivate the appraisee.

(b) **The tell and listen method**. The manager tells the subordinate how he or she has been assessed, and then invites the subordinate to respond. Moreover, this method does not assume that a change in the employee will be the sole key to improvement: the manager may receive helpful feedback about how job design, methods, environment or supervision might be improved.

(c) **The problem-solving approach**. The manager abandons the role of critic altogether, and becomes a counsellor and helper. The discussion is centred not on the assessment, but on the employee's work problems. The employee is encouraged to think solutions through, and to make a commitment to personal improvement.

Follow-up

1.15 After the appraisal interview, the manager may complete the report, with an overall assessment, assessment of potential and/or the jointly-reached conclusion of the interview, with recommendations for follow-up action. The manager should then discuss the report with the counter-signing manager (usually his or her own superior), resolving any problems that have arisen in making the appraisal or report, and agreeing on action to be taken. The report form may then go to the management development adviser, training officer or other relevant people as appropriate for follow-up.

1.16 **Follow-up procedures**

(a) Informing appraisees of the results of the appraisal, if this has not been central to the review interview.

(b) Carrying out agreed actions on training, promotion and so on.

(c) Monitoring the appraisee's progress and checking that he has carried out agreed actions or improvements.

(d) Taking necessary steps to help the appraisee to attain improvement objectives, by guidance, providing feedback, upgrading equipment, altering work methods or whatever.

1.17 'Any appraisal scheme can only be understood within the organisation structure of which it is a part' (*Buchanan and Huczynski*). Appraisal schemes reflect the **values** an organisation seeks to promote.

1.18 A problem with many appraisal schemes in practice is that they concentrate exclusively on the **individual subordinate**. In other words they **reinforce hierarchy**, and are perhaps unsuitable to organisations where the relationship between management and workers is **fluid** or participatory. Upward, customer and 360° appraisals address this, but they are not widely adopted.

1.19 Appraisal systems, because they target the individual's performance, concentrate on the **lowest level of performance feedback.** They ignore the organisational and systems context of that performance. (For example, if any army is badly led, no matter how brave the troops, it will be defeated.) Appraisal schemes would seem to regard most **organisation problems** as a function of the **personal characteristics** of its members, rather than the **systemic problem** of its overall design.

1.20 A performance appraisal system is **designed by specialists** in the technostructure and **operated by managers** in the middle line. Its effectiveness depends on a number of factors.

(a) The **effort** line managers are prepared to put into the appraisal process

(b) The **integrity** of line managers

(c) The **ability** of line managers to do more than just give good appraisals to people who have a similar personality and background

(d) The congruence between what the organisation **actually wants** and the behaviours it is **prepared to reward**

1.21 If appraisal systems operate **successfully** as feedback control systems (in other words, if they do alter employees' performance) and identify behaviours to be encouraged, then, assuming organisational success is to some measure based on individual performance, they will influence the success of strategy.

2 PROBLEMS WITH APPRAISAL 5/01

2.1 In theory, such appraisal schemes may seem very fair to the individual and very worthwhile for the organisation, but **in practice the appraisal system often goes wrong.** *Lockett* (in *Effective Performance Management*) suggests that these **appraisal barriers** can be identified as follows.

Appraisal barriers	Comment
Appraisal as confrontation	Many people dread appraisals, or use them 'as a sort of show down, a good sorting out or a clearing of the air.'
	(a) There is a lack of agreement on performance levels.
	(b) The feedback is subjective - in other words the manager is biased, allows personality differences to get in the way of actual performance etc.
	(c) The feedback is badly delivered.
	(d) Appraisals are 'based on yesterday's performance not on the whole year'.
	(e) Disagreement on long-term prospects.
Appraisal as judgement	The appraisal 'is seen as a one-sided process in which the manager acts as judge, jury and counsel for the prosecution'. However, the process of performance management 'needs to be jointly operated in order to retain the commitment and develop the self-awareness of the individual.'
Appraisal as chat	The other extreme is that the appraisal is a friendly chat 'without ... purpose or outcome ... Many managers, embarrassed by the need to give feedback and set stretching targets, reduce the appraisal to a few mumbled "well dones!" and leave the interview with a briefcase of unresolved issues.'
Appraisal as bureaucracy	Appraisal is a form-filling exercise, to satisfy the personnel department. Its underlying purpose, improving individual and organisational performance, is forgotten.
Appraisal as unfinished business	Appraisal should be part of a continuing process of performance management.
Appraisal as annual event	Many targets set at annual appraisal meetings become irrelevant or out-of-date.

Appraisal and pay

2.2 **Another problem is the extent to which the appraisal system is related to the pay and reward system.** Many employees consider that the appraisal system should be definitely linked with the reward system, on the ground that extra effort should be rewarded. Although this appears fair view, there are major drawbacks to it.

(a) **Funds available** for pay rises rarely depend on one individual's performance alone - the whole company has to do well.

(b) **Continuous improvement** is always necessary - many firms have 'to run to stand still'. Continuous improvement should perhaps be expected of employees as part of their work, not rewarded as extra.

(c) In low-inflation environments, **cash pay rises are fairly small**.

(d) **Comparisons between individuals** are hard to make, as many smaller firms cannot afford the rigour of a job evaluation scheme.

(e) Performance management is about a lot more than pay for *past* performance - it is often **forward looking** with regard to future performance.

Appraisal, management expertise and empowerment

2.3 In 2.1 above, we suggested that appraisals could be subverted by managers who were biased, badly briefed or who only looked at yesterday's performance.

2.4 There can be problems in organisations where **empowerment** is practised and employees are given more responsibility.

(a) Many **managers may not have the time** to keep a sufficiently close eye on individual workers to make a fair judgement.

(b) In some jobs, **managers do not have the technical expertise to judge** an employee's output.

(c) **Employees depend on other people** in the workplace/organisation to be effective - in other words, **an individual's results may not be entirely under his/her control**.

2.5 A person's performance is often indirectly or directly influenced by the **management style** of the person doing the appraisal. However, given the disparity of power between the manager and the appraisee, key issues may not get raised. (An article in the Harvard Business Review was entitled 'Managing Your Boss': this suggests that an appraiser's own behaviour may be a factor in the appraisee's performance, but that such two-way discussions may not be appreciated.)

2.6 Even the best objective and systematic appraisal scheme is subject to **personal** and **interpersonal problems**.

(a) Appraisal is often **defensive on the part of the subordinate**, who believes that criticism may mean a low bonus or pay rise, or lost promotion opportunity.

(b) Appraisal is often **defensive on the part of the superior**, who cannot reconcile the role of judge and critic with the human relations aspect of interviewing and management. Managers may in any case feel uncomfortable about 'playing God' with employee's futures.

(c) The superior might show **conscious or unconscious bias** in the appraisal or may be influenced by rapport (or lack of it) with the interviewee. Systems without clearly defined standard criteria will be particular prone to the subjectivity of the assessor's judgement.

(d) The manager and subordinate may both **be reluctant to devote time and attention to appraisal**. Their experience in the organisation may indicate that the exercise is a waste of time (especially if there is a lot of form-filling) with no relevance to the job, and no reliable follow-up action.

(e) The organisational culture may **simply not take appraisal seriously**: Interviewers are not trained or given time to prepare, appraisees are not encouraged to contribute, or the exercise is perceived as a 'nod' to Human Relations with no practical results.

Exam focus point

The first exam under the new syllabus, in May 2001, included a question on appraisal in Section B. It was an unusual question in that it was not set in a short scenario, so an answer could be entirely theoretical. There were only two questions of this type out of several on the paper. Both were in Section B.

The appraisal question came in two parts. Part (a), worth 6 marks, asked for a description of the most common objectives of an appraisal system. Part (b), worth 14 marks, required a discussion of the **effectiveness** of appraisal systems: a rather more demanding topic.

New approaches to appraisal

Improving the system

2.7 The appraisal scheme should itself be assessed (and regularly re-assessed) according to the following general criteria for evaluating appraisal schemes.

Criteria	Comment
Relevance	• Does the system have a useful purpose, relevant to the needs of the organisation and the individual? • Is the purpose clearly expressed and widely understood by all concerned, both appraisers and appraisees? • Are the appraisal criteria relevant to the purposes of the system?
Fairness	• Is there reasonable standardisation of criteria and objectivity throughout the organisation? • Is it reasonably objective?
Serious intent	• Are the managers concerned committed to the system - or is it just something the personnel department thrusts upon them? • Who does the interviewing, and are they properly trained in interviewing and assessment techniques? • Is reasonable time and attention given to the interviews - or is it a question of 'getting them over with'? • Is there a genuine demonstrable link between performance and reward or opportunity for development?
Co-operation	• Is the appraisal a participative, problem-solving activity - or a tool of management control? • Is the appraisee given time and encouragement to prepare for the appraisal, so that he can make a constructive contribution? • Does a jointly-agreed, concrete conclusion emerge from the process? • Are appraisals held regularly?
Efficiency	• Does the system seem overly time-consuming compared to the value of its outcome? • Is it difficult and costly to administer?

Upward appraisal

2.8 A notable modern trend, adopted in the UK by companies such as BP and British Airways and others, is **upward appraisal,** whereby employees are not rated by their superiors but by their subordinates. The followers appraise the leader.

2.9 **Advantages of upward appraisal.**

(a) Subordinates tend to know their superior better than superiors know their subordinates.

(b) As all subordinates rate their managers statistically, these ratings tend to be more reliable - the more subordinates the better. Instead of the biases of individual managers' ratings, the various ratings of the employees can be converted into a representative view.

(c) Subordinates' ratings have more impact because it is more unusual to receive ratings from subordinates. It is also surprising to bosses because, despite protestations to the contrary, information often flows down organisations more smoothly and comfortably than it flows up. When it flows up it is qualitatively and quantitatively different. It is this difference that makes it valuable.

2.10 **Problems with the method** include fear of reprisals, vindictiveness, and extra form processing. Some bosses in strong positions might refuse to act, even if a consensus of staff suggested that they should change their ways.

Customer appraisal

2.11 In some companies part of the employee's appraisal process must take the form of **feedback from 'customers' (whether internal or external).** This may be taken further into an influence on remuneration (at *Rank-Xerox*, 30% of a manager's annual bonus is conditional upon satisfactory levels of 'customer' feedback). This is a valuable development in that customers are the best judges of customer service, which the appraisee's boss may not see.

360 degree appraisal

2.12 Taking downwards, upwards and customer appraisals together, some firms have instituted **360 degree appraisal** (or multi-source appraisal) by collecting feedback on an individual's performance from the following sources (outlined by *Peter Ward* in *People Management*, 9 February 1995).

(a) The person's immediate manager.

(b) People who report to the appraisee, perhaps divided into groups.

(c) Peers and co-workers: most people interact with others within an organisation, either as members of a team or as the receivers or providers of services. They can offer useful feedback.

(d) Customers: if sales people know what customers thought of them, they might be able to improve their technique.

(e) The manager personally: all forms of 360 degree appraisal require people to rate themselves. Those 'who see themselves as others see them will get fewer surprises.'

2.13 Sometimes the appraisal results in a counselling session, especially when the result of the appraisals are conflicting. For example, an appraisee's manager may have a quite different view of the appraisee's skills than subordinates.

3 MANAGING CAREERS

3.1 **Career management** is an aspect of HRM. It is a technique whereby the progress of individuals within an organisation from job to job is planned with organisational needs and individual capacity in mind. Large organisations have traditionally offered planned career progression.

3.2 Career management is both an individual and an organisational issue.

(a) It ensures that the organisation has a reserve of managers-in-waiting. In flat or delayered organisations this is particularly important, as the jump in responsibility from junior to senior positions is much wider than in organisations with extensive hierarchies.

(b) It ensures people get the right training to enable them to develop the right abilities for the job.

3.3 For the organisation, career management also determines whether, as a matter of policy, the organisation will only promote from **within**, as opposed to hiring **outsiders** for some or all of its management positions.

3.4 To what extent are careers supposed to cross functional boundaries? Two models can be suggested here.

Model A

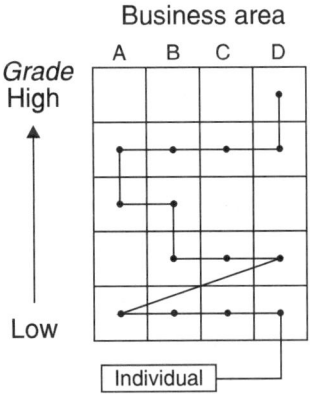

In this case, the individual is given a great degree of experience in different business areas in order to get to know the business. Some Japanese companies, for example, are happy to allocate production executives to marketing departments on their slow way up. Promotion has, in the past, largely been based on seniority. An individual is assessed **on experience**. This should help organisational learning by giving the individual an experience of many different parts of the business.

Model B

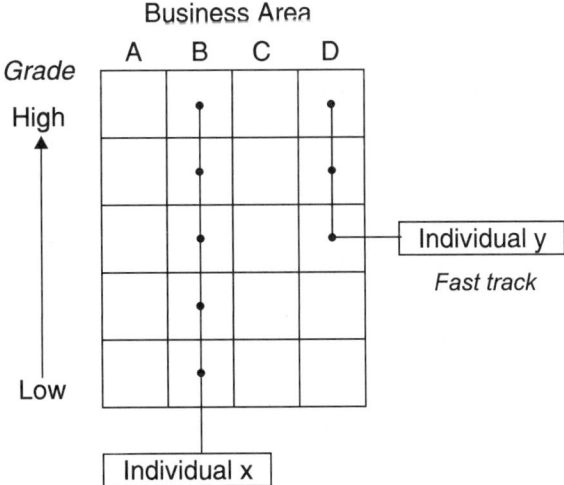

In the case of individual X, promotion is entirely within one business area. This may enhance specialist skills, but creates a narrowing of outlook. This line of promotion might be particularly true of professional functions in the **technostructure**. This model also allows a 'fast-track' for individuals brought in at intermediate levels.

3.5 Career management timescales will vary according to organisation priorities.

(a) Organisations might recruit on the basis of current performance with little regard to the future. The assumption is that deliberate grooming of managers is unnecessary. This approach is characteristic of small organisations.

(b) Long-term planners take a great deal of time structuring employees' careers, in order to develop employees' potential. Bureaucracies, which are able to predict future needs, are able to plan in this way.

(c) Another approach tries to assess a person's long-term ability on the basis of his or her current performance. Flexibility is valued. However, a career path is not predictable.

3.6 Where an organisation's needs are likely to change, it is not always possible to take a too rigid approach to career planning.

Question 1

What sort of career management system do you think is operated in the following cases?

(a) 'People join us at Junior Trainee level. Within one year they are promoted to Senior Trainee, and the year after that Assistant Accountant. Their titles denote the sort of skills and experience they are expected to have. After qualification, they are promoted to Senior Accountant, then Supervisor. Promotion above Supervisor level is not guaranteed, but a successful candidate would certainly reach Manager grade, dealing with larger clients, and running more staff. Exceptional candidates become Partners of the firm'.

(b) 'As a fashion design firm we recruit directly from art schools, but the way the market goes we have to be flexible. People who work with us have to show a willingness to get involved, and a talent for bright ideas which combine flair with a real-world understanding of the people that like our clothes. But the sky's the limit for the talented'.

Answer

(a) Long-range planning at the lower levels, but this tapers off at the higher levels.

(b) The fashion firm combines a policy of recruitment as and when it is needed, with an assumption that people can 'create' their own career structure. People can get on, but this cannot be planned.

3.7 Career management issues are especially relevant to professional staff such as management accountants for a number of reasons.

(a) They need to retain and develop their technical specialism. A successful management accountant should be able to keep up to date so that his or her knowledge is of continued use to the organisation. An accountant is a member, perhaps, of the organisation's technostructure.

(b) On the other hand, the management accountant may view his or her qualification as a springboard into general management: in which case the right considerations should be given to easing the path from functional to general management.

The difference between management education, training and development

3.8 A useful distinction between management education, training and development was given in the report *The Making of British Managers*, prepared for the BIM and CBI in 1987 by *Constable and McCormick*. The report gave the following definitions.

'Education is that process which results in formal qualifications up to and including post-graduate degrees.'

Training is 'the formal learning activities which may not lead to qualifications, and which may be received at any time in a working career.'

'Development is broader again: job experience and learning from other managers, particularly one's immediate superior, are integral parts of the development process.'

Development could include a variety of features:

- Career planning for individual managers
- Job rotation
- Standing in for the boss while he is away on holiday
- On-the-job training
- Counselling, perhaps by means of regular appraisal reports
- Guidance from superiors or colleagues
- Education and training

3.9 Education is therefore an element of training, which is an aspect of development.

The relationship of education, training and development

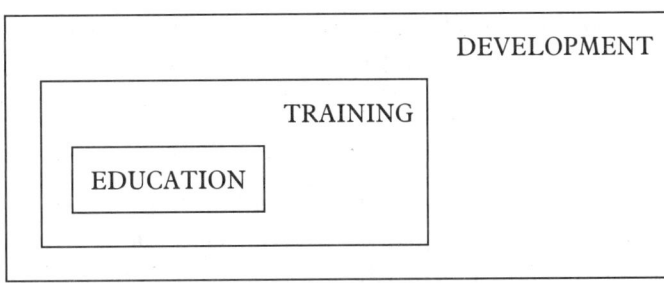

3.10 It is worth getting clear in your mind at the beginning why management education, training and development are needed.

(a) Without training and development, managers are unlikely to be ready for promotion when the time comes, and they will not do their new job well until they have learnt by mistakes.

(b) The selection of individuals for promotion is unlikely to be reliable, and the wrong people might be selected for senior jobs. Individuals will rise to their level of incompetence!

(c) Vacancies will often have to be filled by recruitment from outside the organisation, because not enough in-house managers will be good enough or sufficiently ready for promotion.

(d) An organisation should show an interest in the career development of its staff, so as to motivate them and encourage them to stay with the firm. Management development programmes are an important feature of being a good employer.

Management education

3.11 Education, for successful students, leads on to a formal qualification. For managers in the UK there is a wide variety of possible qualifications.

- Undergraduate business and management degrees
- Undergraduate degrees in related subjects such and Economics and Accountancy
- Postgraduate business and management degrees

- The postgraduate Diploma in Management Studies
- Qualifications from professional institutes

Management training

3.12 Formal training which does *not* lead on to a qualification has two main aspects.

(a) Post-experience management courses, provided by training companies or colleges and polytechnics

(b) In-company management training, using the company's own training staff and/or consultants brought in from outside

3.13 The 1987 report by Constable and McCormick, referred to earlier, reported these findings from a survey of UK employers.

(a) Most employers regard innate ability and experience as the two key ingredients of an effective manager. But education and training help, especially in broadening the outlook of managers with only functional experience previously, and without experience of general management.

(b) There was agreement that it would be both inappropriate and impossible to make management a controlled profession similar to accountancy and law. **However, making a managerial career more similar to the professions and having managers acquire specific competences appropriate to each stage of their careers** were seen as beneficial.

3.14 Skills training is concerned with teaching a person how to do a particular job, or how to do it better. Functional managers, especially supervisors and junior managers, should be given skills training to help them to do their job better.

3.15 In addition to **technical** skills training, an organisation should provide training to potential managers or existing managers in **management** techniques and skills. It has already been suggested that employees might want promotion, but cannot be offered it yet, either because there are not enough vacancies and they must wait their turn, or because they are not yet good enough, or even because they might never be good enough for further advancement. Large organisations therefore have two problems.

(a) **Motivating** their existing staff and keeping them where they might be expected to wait for further promotion

(b) Providing **training** to ensure that sufficient staff are available to fill management positions capably when vacancies do arise.

3.16 **Training** follows on from **recruitment** and **selection**, and also **appraisal** of performance.

(a) Potential managers can be given training in management skills, either on internal courses or on courses with external organisations such as business schools.

(b) Existing managers can be given training in new skills required for their existing job (eg the technological changes in organisations and the development of computer usage suggest the need for training in computer applications and software for management work).

(c) Existing managers can be given training in the skills required for higher, general management (eg with discussions of organisation policy, and lectures given by directors).

3.17 Designing appropriate in-house courses and encouraging some managers to obtain a professional qualification should be two key features of an education and training programme for managers.

3.18 The time given to managers for education could take a variety of forms.

(a) A full year off to study for a qualification

(b) Block release to attend study courses or revision courses

(c) Day release, perhaps to attend courses at a local college

(d) Reducing the workload on individuals, so that they don't have to work long hours and overtime, to give them time to attend evening classes or study at home

Time off for studying should be paid for by the employer, who might also contribute towards the cost of text books and courses for professional examinations.

Management development

3.19

> **KEY TERM**
>
> **Management development** is the process of improving the effectiveness of an individual manager by developing the necessary skills and understanding of organisational goals.

Although management development is in some respects a natural process, the term is generally used to refer to **a conscious policy** within an organisation to provide a programme of individual development. A variety of techniques could be used.

- Formal education and training
- On-the-job training
- Group learning sessions
- Conferences
- Counselling

3.20 The principle behind management development is that by giving an individual time to study the techniques of being a good manager, and by counselling him about his achievements in these respects, the individual will realise his full potential. The time required to bring a manager to this potential is *possibly* fairly short.

The transition from functional to general management

3.21 There is one particular aspect of management development and training that organisations should look at closely - **the transition from functional to general management**. At some stage in his or her career, a management accountant might be promoted from a job which is concentrated mainly on functional expertise (eg accountancy skills) into a job where the requirement is for **broader** and **more general management** skills, - such as organising, staffing, controlling, dealing with other departments or organisations, long-term planning and so on.

3.22 The change in a manager's work caused by moving from a functional to a general management position can be seen by highlighting some of the important differences in the two types of role.

BPP PUBLISHING

	Functional manager	*General manager*
Orientation	• task orientated - focus on the functional tasks in hand	• goal orientated - focus on achievement of organisational (and divisional) goals and objectives
Role	• organiser	• facilitator - co-ordinating interdepartmental activities; obtaining and allocating resources
Information	• defined sources • usually through formal channels	• poorly defined sources • often acquired by informal contacts
Goals	• short term	• long term

3.23 The transition from functional to general manager is usually accompanied by promotion to a more senior position in the management hierarchy and therefore the contrast in roles between functional and general management is also found between junior and middle/senior management. But this comparison must not be overstated; much depends on the structure of the organisation concerned.

(a) The traditional, **functional structure** tends to keep managers in functional roles until they reach very senior levels and sometimes for their entire careers.

(b) A **divisional structure**, however, gives relatively junior managers experience of general management roles, usually as the chief executive of small business units. Organisational structure can therefore have a significant impact on the age and seniority of managers making the transition from functional to general management and therefore the extent of the difficulties it may create.

3.24 Recent research has brought to light the difficulties which managers face in changing from one role to another and these are often particularly acute when the change involves moving from a functional to a general management position. In addition to the normal problems of switching jobs, the manager taking up a general management post has to deal with an abrupt change in the skills needed to perform his role effectively.

3.25 **Technical skills** are concerned with an ability to cope with large quantities of data and information and to select the appropriate key points to form the basis for decision-taking. **Interpersonal skills** involve inspiring, motivating, leading and controlling people to achieve goals which are often poorly defined. For the general manager, the latter are more important.

The transition curve

3.26 The transition from functional to general manager is a complex process and the time taken to complete it varies according to the degree of perceived change involved. Since a move from functional to general management is correctly viewed as a major change, transitions of this sort take longer than average to complete.

3.27 No two people face and deal with managerial transition in exactly the same way. Recognition of the complex nature of transition, however, has important implications for management development in general and training in particular.

(a) Transition takes time; research indicates that, on average, people feel in control only after a period of 24-30 months.

(b) Changes which involve considerable adaptation, such as moving from a functional to a general management position, take longer than the average.

(c) Because transition is often a lengthy process, management should avoid moving people from position to position too frequently.

(d) For succession planning and training to be successful, it needs to go beyond the point of entry to the new job.

(e) People in transition often have more severe entry problems than newcomers, since they are frequently not given a breathing space before being expected to perform adequately. This increases the pressures on them and may ultimately reduce their performance and that of the organisation as a whole.

3.28 **To help with the transition from technical to general management, an organisation should have a planned management development programme**. This could have several aspects.

(a) Individuals should be encouraged to acquire suitable **educational qualifications** for senior management. 'High-fliers' for example might be encouraged to study for an MBA or a DMS early on in their career. Senior finance managers ought to have an accountancy qualification.

(b) **In-house training programmes** might be provided for senior managers and individuals who are being groomed for senior management. Formal training in general management skills can be very helpful.

(c) **Careful promotion procedures** should aim to ensure that only managers with the potential to do well are promoted into senior management positions.

(d) There should be a system of **regular performance appraisal**, in which individuals are interviewed and counselled by their managers on what they have done well, what they have not done so well, how to improve their performance in their current job and how to develop their skills for a more senior job.

(e) **Opportunities to gain suitable experience** should be provided to managers who are candidates for more senior positions. There are several possibilities.

   (i) Allowing subordinates to stand in for their boss whenever the boss is away

   (ii) Using staff officer positions to groom future high fliers

   (iii) Using a divisionalised organisation structure to delegate general management responsibilities further down the management hierarchy.

Chapter roundup

- Appraisal reviews rewards, performance and potential. It is part of performance management and can be used to establish areas for improvement and training needs. Appraisal techniques include overall assessment, grading and results-oriented schemes.

- The appraisal interview may be conducted as tell and sell, tell and listen or in a problem solving manner.

- There are disadvantages to appraisal schemes. It is a very bureaucratic process and may be discussed as an annual ritual. It is easy for appraisal to become confrontational, with the manager taking a judgmental line, or for it to degenerate into a purposeless chat.

- Upward appraisal obtains a new perspective on managers by using information from their subordinates. 360° appraisal extends this process co-workers, customers and suppliers.

- Career management affects both the individual and the organisation. It is particularly relevant to managers and professionals and most developed in bureaucracies. It provides the organisation with a pool of promotable managers and the individual with appropriate training and experience.

- Management development includes general education, specific learning and wider experience. It is essential if managers are to make the leap from functional to general management.

Quick quiz

1. State 3 purposes of appraisal?

2. What are the six steps in a typical appraisal system?

3. What is guided assessment?

4. How does Maier analyse approaches to appraisal interviews?

5. Why might appraisal be confrontational?

6. What is 360° appraisal?

7. What is career management?

8. What is the difference between the roles of the functional manager and the general manager?

Answers to quick quiz

1   Reward review; performance review; potential review.

2   Identify assessment criteria; prepare a report; assessment interview; moderation by next level up; prepare action plan; implement action plan.

3   Guidelines are provided for comment on specified performance areas.

4   Tell and sell; tell and listen; problem solving.

5   Lack of agreement on performance levels; subjective assessment; badly conducted interviews; superficial performance assessment; disagreement on long-term prospects.

6   Appraisal from all sides including peers, subordinates, superiors, other departments and business contacts.

7   The planning and control of individual progression with individual and organisational requirements in mind.

8

	Functional manager	*General manager*
Orientation	• task orientated - focus on the functional tasks in hand	• goal orientated - focus on achievement of organisational (and divisional) goals and objectives
Role	• organiser	• facilitator-co-ordinating interdepartmental activities; obtaining and allocating resources
Information	• defined sources • usually through formal channels	• poorly defined sources • often acquired by informal contacts
Goals	• short term	• long term

Now try the question below in the Exam Question bank

Number	Level	Marks	Time
Q13	Exam	20	36 mins

Part D
Management of relationships

Chapter 14

MANAGEMENT AND THE HUMAN RESOURCE

Topic List	Syllabus Reference	Ability required
1 Leadership	(iv)	Analysis
2 Discipline	(iv)	Analysis
3 Retirement, resignation and redundancy	(iii)	Analysis
4 Maternity	(iv)	Comprehension
5 Discrimination and equal opportunities	(iv)	Comprehension
6 Health and safety	(iv)	Comprehension

Introduction

The quality of management is a major determinant of organisational success, and the ability to deal properly with subordinates is an important aspect of the manager's work. In this chapter we examine ideas about leadership and management style before going on to look at the legal framework which impinges on the relationship between management and worker.

There is no universally applicable style of management, though we can make some widely accepted points about authority and responsibility.

The legal framework has been created in response to a perceived exploitation of work people and a concern that all organisations should behave in a humane way to their staff.

Learning outcomes covered in this chapter

- Analyse the issues involved in managing the dismissal, retirement and redundancy of individual staff.

- Explain the concepts of authority, power, responsibility and delegation.

- Analyse the relationships between managers and subordinates.

- Analyse situations where problems have been caused by the adoption of an ineffective or inappropriate management style and recommend remedial action.

- Explain the problems of maintaining discipline and evaluate the tools available to help a manager achieve this.

- Explain how the legal environment influences the relationship between the organisation and its employees, and between the employees of an organisation.

- Explain the responsibilities of the organisation, its managers and staff in relation to health and safety and advise how a manager can ensure the health and safety of subordinates.

- Explain the various ways in which fair treatment of employees can be achieved, and the role of government in ensuring this.

BPP
PUBLISHING

Syllabus content covered in this chapter

- The concepts of power, authority, responsibility and delegation and their application to organisational relationships.

- The characteristics of leaders and managers.

- Management style theories (eg Likert, Tannenbaum and Schmidt, Blake and Mouton).

- The advantages and disadvantages of different styles of management.

- Contingency approaches to management style (eg Adair, Fiedler).

- Disciplinary procedures and their operation, including the form and process of formal disciplinary action and dismissal.

- The nature and effect of legal issues affecting work and employment, including the application of appropriate employment law (ie relating to health, safety, discrimination, fair treatment, childcare, contracts of employment, working time).

---

1 LEADERSHIP 5/01

Exam focus point

Leadership featured prominently under the old syllabus. Like many topics in this paper, it can be linked with theories of motivation and also with change. In May 1999 it appeared in a question alongside the organisational life cycle.

1.1 Two important variables in managerial effectiveness are **style** and a **capacity to motivate** subordinates.

1.2 **A manager's style is the way in which the manager handles his or her relationship with the task and with subordinates.** This is sometimes referred to as leadership which is the process of **influencing others** to work willingly and to the best of their capabilities.

Trait theories

1.3 **Early theories suggested that there are certain qualities, personality characteristics or 'traits' which make a good leader.** These might be aggressiveness, self-assurance, intelligence, initiative, energy, a drive for achievement or power, appearance, interpersonal skills, administrative ability, imagination, a certain upbringing and education, the 'helicopter factor' (the ability to rise above a situation and analyse it objectively).

1.4 Trait theory has now been superseded as it ignored the complexities of the leadership situation. Moreover, not everybody with leadership traits turns out to be a good leader! Alternative approaches to leadership theory have been developed over the years, and some of these are described below.

Style theories

1.5 Four different styles of leadership were identified by *Huneryager and Heckman* (1967): **dictatorial, autocratic, democratic and laissez faire**. These four divisions or 'compartments' of management style are really a simplification of a continuum of styles, from the most dictatorial to the most laissez-faire.

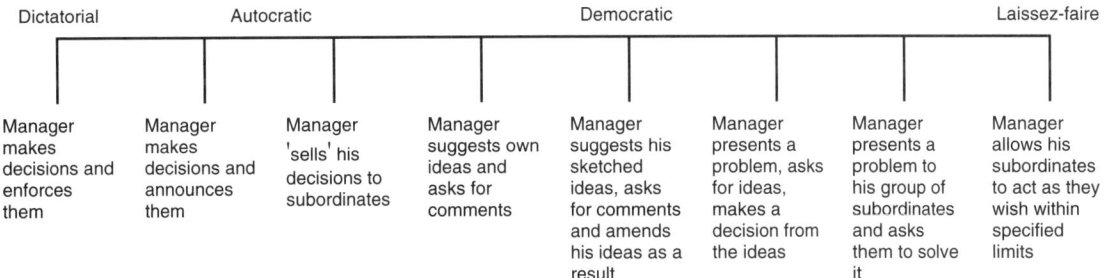

This continuum of leadership styles was first described by *Tannenbaum and Schmidt* in 1958.

Tells/sells/consults/joins

1.6 A slightly different analysis of leadership styles, based on this continuum, was made by the Research Unit at *Ashridge Management College*, based on research in several industries in the UK (reported 1966). This research distinguished four different management styles. They are outlined, with their strengths and weaknesses, in the table on the following page. Note that the Ashridge model has not included any real equivalent of the laissez-faire style. The findings of the Ashridge studies included the following two important points.

(a) Subordinates preferred the **consults** style of leadership. Those managed in that way had the most favourable attitude to work, but managers were most commonly thought to be exercising the **tells** or **sells** style.

(b) The least favourable attitudes were found amongst subordinates who were **unable to perceive a consistent style** of leadership in their boss.

Style and effectiveness

1.7 In his books *New Patterns of Management* and *The Human Organisation, Rensis Likert* attempted through research to answer the question 'what do effective managers have in common?' His research showed that **four main elements are normally present in effective managers**.

(a) **They expect high levels of performance from subordinates, other departments and themselves.**

(b) **They are employee-centred.** They spend time getting to know their workers and develop a situation of trust whereby their employees feel able to bring their problems to them. When necessary, their actions can be hard but fair. Such managers try to face unpleasant facts in a constructive manner and help their staff to do the same.

(c) **They do not practise close supervision.** The truly effective manager knows performance levels that can be expected from each individual and has helped them to define their own targets. The manager judges results and does not closely supervise the actions of subordinates.

(d) **They operate the participative style of management as a natural style.** If a job problem arises they do not impose a favoured solution. Instead, they pose the problem and ask the staff member involved to find the best solution. Having then agreed their solution the participative manager would assist his staff in implementing it.

The Ashridge College management style analysis

Style	Characteristics	Strengths	Weaknesses
Tells (autocratic)	The manager makes all the decisions, and issues instructions which must be obeyed without question.	(1) Quick decisions can be made when speed is required. (2) It is the most efficient type of leadership for highly-programmed routine work.	(1) It does not encourage the sub-ordinates to give their opinions when these might be useful. (2) Communications between the manager and sub-ordinate will be one-way and the manager will not know until afterwards whether the orders have been properly understood. (3) It does not encourage initiative and commitment from subordinates.
Sells (persuasive)	The manager still makes all the decisions, but believes that subordinates have to be motivated to accept them in order to carry them out properly.	(1) Employees are made aware of the reasons for decisions. (2) Selling decisions to staff might make them more committed. (3) Staff will have a better idea of what to do when unforeseen events arise in their work because the manager will have explained his intentions.	(1) Communications are still largely one-way. Subordinates might not accept the decisions. (2) It does not encourage initiative and commitment from subordinates.
Consults	The manager confers with subordinates and takes their views into account, but has the final say.	(1) Employees are involved in decisions before they are made. This encourages motivation through greater interest and involvement. (2) An agreed consensus of opinion can be reached and for some decisions consensus can be an advantage rather than a weak compromise. (3) Employees can contribute their knowledge and experience to help in solving more complex problems.	(1) It might take much longer to reach decisions. (2) Subordinates might be too inexperienced to formulate mature opinions and give practical advice. (3) Consultation can too easily turn into a facade concealing, basically, a sells style.
Joins (democratic)	Leader and followers make the decision on the basis of consensus.	(1) It can provide high motivation and commitment from employees. (2) It shares the other advantages of the consultative style (especially where subordinates have expert power).	(1) The authority of the manager might be undermined. (2) Decision-making might become a very long process, and clear decisions might be difficult to reach. (3) Subordinates might lack enough experience.

1.8 Likert emphasises that all four features must be present for a manager to be truly effective. **A manager's concern for people must be matched by his concern for achieving results.**

1.9 Likert also identified 4 different management styles.

    (a) **Exploitative autoeratic**

- No confidence or trust in subordinates
- Decisions imposed
- No delegation of decision-making
- Threats used to motivate
- Little communication or teamwork with subordinates

(b) **Benevolent authoritative**

- Superficial, condescending confidence and trust
- Decisions imposed
- Rewards used to motivate
- Paternalistic involvement of subordinates

(c) **Participative**

- Some confidence and trust in subordinates
- Consults but controls decision-making
- Some motivation by involvement
- Uses subordinates ideas

(d) **Democratic**

- Subordinates trusted completely
- Delegation of decision-making
- Goals set participatively, achievement rewarded
- Ideas and opinions shared.

1.10 Likert's research in *New Patterns of Management* was into supervision of clerical staff in an insurance company. He found that the most productive departments were supervised using a participative or democratic style.

1.11 Note two things about these findings.

(a) The staff were, by definition, reasonably well educated and intelligent.

(b) The clerical work of an insurance company is highly procedural and lends itself to delegated decision-making in accordance with established rules and guidelines.

It is therefore inappropriate to draw too many sweeping conclusions from Likert's findings.

1.12 *Blake and Mouton* designed the management grid (1964). It is based on two fundamental ingredients of managerial behaviour, namely **concern for production** (or the task) and **concern for people**.

1.13 The extreme cases shown on the grid are defined below.

(a) 1.1 **impoverished**: the manager is lazy, showing little interest in either staff or work.

(b) 1.9 **country club**: the manager is attentive to staff needs and has developed satisfying relationships. However, there is little attention paid to achieving results.

(c) 9.1 **task management**: almost total concentration on achieving results. People's needs are virtually ignored.

(d) 5.5 **middle of the road or the dampened pendulum**: adequate performance through balancing the necessity to get out work while maintaining morale of people at a satisfactory level.

(e) 9.9 **team**: high performance manager who achieves high work accomplishment through 'leading' committed people who identify themselves with the organisational aims.

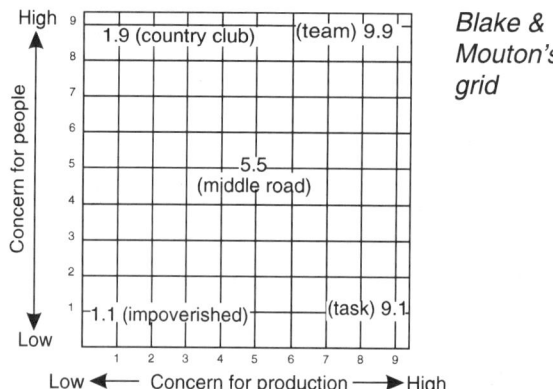

Blake & Mouton's grid

1.14 *Hersey and Blanchard* developed a model of leadership which appears to **map style theories on to the grid** suggested by Blake and Mouton.

(a) First, the leader should determine what he or she wishes to **accomplish**.

(b) Then, the leader should determine the **maturity** of the followers. Maturity has three components.

- **Achievement motivation** (can the followers set high but realistic goals?).

- **Responsibility** (willingness and ability to assume it).

- **Education/experience**. Maturity in practice is divided into psychological maturity (eg attitude to work) and job maturity (eg problem solving ability).

1.15 Similar to Blake and Mouton's concern for tasks and people, Hersey and Blanchard identify two axes of behaviour.

(a) **Task behaviour,** concerned with getting the job cone. This can be directive, in that the leader issues instructions

(b) **Relationship behaviour** is equivalent to concern for people.

The diagram below identifies the different leadership styles associated with followers of different maturity.

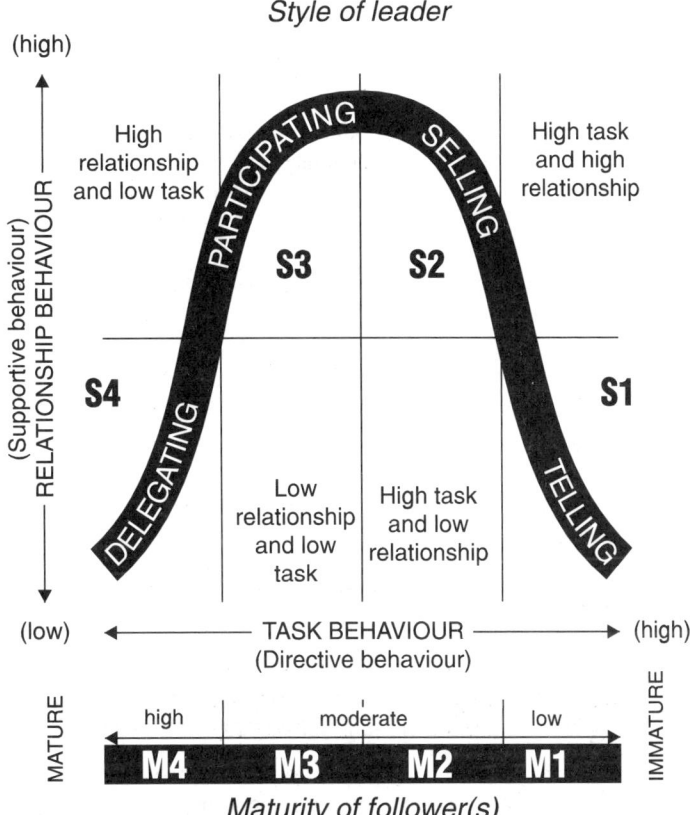

Style of leader

Reasonably enough, the need for managerial direction reduces as maturity increases. Higher levels of supportive behaviour are appropriate for moderate maturity. Where maturity is low, subordinates may be unable to respond properly to supportive behaviour; where maturity is high it is unnecessary.

A contingency approach to leadership

1.16 A contingency approach to leadership is one which argues that the ability of a manager to be a leader, and to influence his subordinate work group, depends on the **particular situation**, and will **vary from case to case**. *Charles Handy* suggested factors which contribute to a leader's effectiveness in any situation. This approach is linked to the contingency approach to designing organisations, which rejects the notion of universally applicable principles and proceeds via a consideration of the dominant factors in a given situation. These will vary from case to case. In particular, the nature of the group and its needs and desires are critical.

1.17 *J Adair's* action-centred, or situational model sees the leadership process in a context made up of three main variables, all of which are interrelated and must be examined in the light of the whole situation. These are **task needs**, the **individual needs** of group members, and the **needs of the group** as a whole. The total situation dictates the relative priority that must be given to each of the three sets of needs. Effective leadership is identifying and acting on that priority to create a balance between the needs. Meeting of the various needs can be expressed as specific management roles, as in the diagram below.

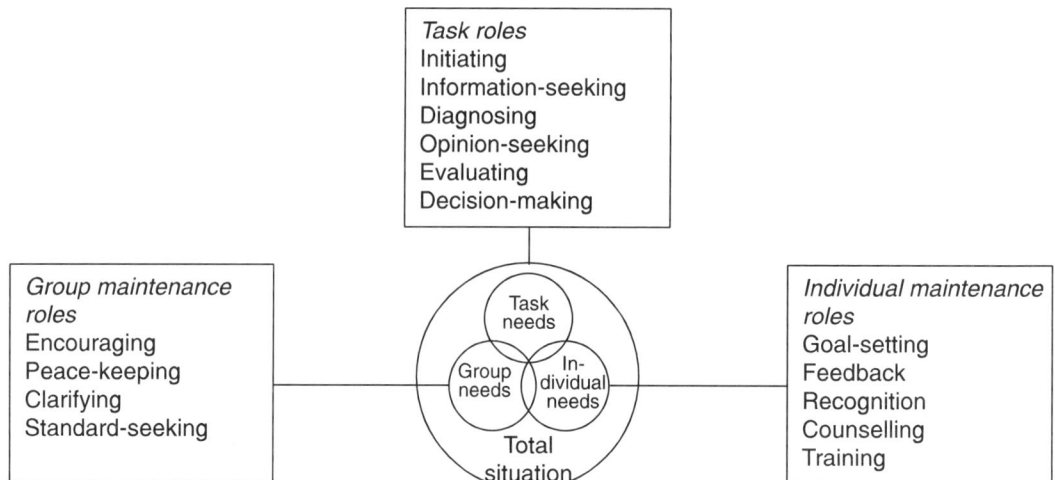

Adair's model is unusual in that it integrates both the needs of the individual and the dynamics of the group.

Question 1

In your career so far, you might have worked for a number of managers. Jot down the following features of each situation on a scale of 1-5 for comparative purposes.

(a)   The degree to which you had control over your own work.
(b)   The degree to which you were consulted on decisions which affected you.
(c)   The degree to which your advice was sought about decisions affecting your section.

If you worked for managers who had different approaches to these issues, do you think these approaches influenced *your* effectiveness? What score to questions (a), (b) and (c) would you give your *ideal boss*? and your *current boss*?

1.18   *Fiedler* carried out extensive research on the nature of leadership and found that people become leaders partly because of their own attributes and partly because of the nature of the situation they find themselves in.

1.19   **Critical dimensions.** He found 3 'critical dimensions' of the situation that influence leadership effectiveness.

(a)   **Position power**. This was discussed in Chapter 6. It is the same thing as organisational authority.

(b)   **Task structure**. Work is easier to organise and accountability easier to determine when the task is clear, well defined and unambiguous. The quality of performance is difficult to control when the task is vague and unstructured.

(c)   **Leader-subordinate relations**. The leader's task is eased when subordinates have trust and confidence in him or her.

1.20   The three critical dimensions are measures of the extent to which **the situation** provides the leader with **influence over subordinates**. Fiedler found that a **task-oriented** approach was most productive when the situation was either very favourable to the leader or very unfavourable. In less extreme cases, a more people-centred approach was more effective. This is summed up in the diagram below.

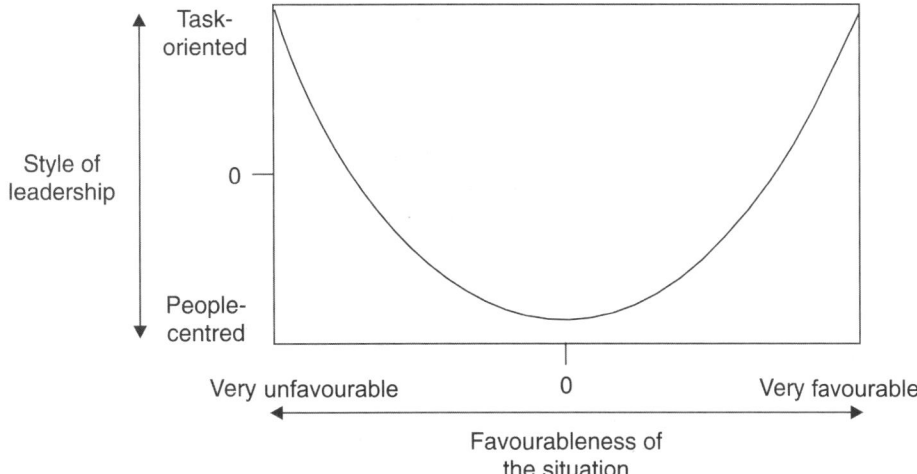

2 DISCIPLINE

2.1 Discipline in the workplace is subject to extensive legal regulation. Disciplinary systems must be fair and applied consistently. Any manager contemplating disciplinary action would be well advised to take expert advice. In particular, the law on dismissal is complex and weighted towards the employee.

> **KEY TERM**
>
> **Discipline** promotes good order and behaviour in an organisation by enforcing acceptable standards of conduct. It can be enforced by sanctions, encouraged by example or created by individuals' own sense of what is fitting and proper.

2.2 Another approach makes a the distinction between methods of maintaining sensible conduct and orderliness which are essentially co-operative, and those based on warnings, threats and punishments.

(a) **Positive** (or constructive) **discipline** relates to procedures, systems and equipment in the work place which have been designed specifically so that the employee has **no option** but to act in the desired manner to complete a task safely and successfully. A machine may, for example, shut off automatically if its safety guard is not in place.

(b) **Negative discipline** is then the promise of **sanctions** designed to make people choose to behave in a desirable way. Disciplinary action may be punitive (punishing an offence), deterrent (warning people not to behave in that way) or reformative (calling attention to the nature of the offence, so that it will not happen again).

2.3 The best discipline is **self discipline**. Even before they start to work, most mature people accept the idea that following instructions and fair rules of conduct are normal responsibilities that are part of any job. Most team members can therefore be counted on to exercise self discipline.

Types of disciplinary situations

2.4 There are many types of disciplinary situations which require attention by the manager. Internally, the most frequently occurring are these.

- Excessive absenteeism
- Poor timekeeping

- Defective and/or inadequate work performance
- Poor attitudes which influence the work of others or reflect on the image of the firm
- Breaking rules regarding rest periods and other time schedules
- Improper personal appearance
- Breaking safety rules
- Other violations of rules, regulations and procedures
- Open insubordination such as the refusal to carry out a work assignment.

2.5 Managers might be confronted with disciplinary problems stemming from employee behaviour *off* the job. These may be an excessive drinking problem, the use of drugs or some form of narcotics, or involvement in some form of law breaking activity. In such circumstances, whenever an employee's off-the-job conduct has an impact upon performance on the job, the manager must be prepared to deal with such a problem within the scope of the disciplinary process.

Disciplinary action

2.6 The purpose of discipline is not punishment or retribution. Disciplinary action must have as its goal the improvement of the future behaviour of the employee and other members of the organisation. The purpose obviously is the avoidance of similar occurrences in the future.

2.7 In the UK, discipline in civilian organisations is governed by the ACAS Code of Practice on disciplinary and grievance procedures. As far as disciplinary procedures are concerned, the code of practice lays down certain essential features.

...good disciplinary procedures should:

- be in writing
- specify to whom they apply
- be non-discriminatory
- provide for matters to be dealt with without undue delay
- provide for proceedings, witness statements and records to be kept confidential
- indicate the disciplinary actions which may be taken
- specify the levels of management which have the authority to take the various forms of disciplinary action
- provide for workers to be informed of the complaints against them and where possible all relevant evidence before any hearing
- provide workers with an opportunity to state their case before decisions are reached
- provide workers with the right to be accompanied
- ensure that, except for gross misconduct, no worker is dismissed for a first breach of discipline
- ensure that disciplinary action is not taken until the case has been carefully investigated
- ensure that workers are given an explanation for any penalty imposed
- provide a right of appeal – normally to a more senior manager – and specify the procedure to be followed

---

2.8 The Code goes on to discuss how disciplinary matters should be dealt with. All disciplinary incidents should be thoroughly investigated and a written record made by the appropriate manager. It will then be necessary to decide how to proceed. Many minor cases of poor performance or misconduct are best dealt with by informal advice, coaching or counselling. An informal oral warning may be issued. None of this forms part of the formal disciplinary procedure, but workers should be informed clearly what is expected and what action will be taken if they fail to improve.

2.9 In cases involving gross misconduct, breakdowns in relationships or risk to persons or property, a brief suspension on pay may be ordered while the case is investigated. Such a suspension is not in itself a disciplinary sanction.

2.10 Any **disciplinary action** must be preceded by a **disciplinary hearing** at which the worker must be told of the allegations made and allowed to answer them. Any rights under the organisation's own disciplinary procedure should be explained at this stage.

2.11 When the facts of the case have been established, it may be decided that formal disciplinary action is needed. The Code of Practice divides this into three stages. These are usually thought of as consecutive, reflecting a progressive response. However, it may be appropriate to miss out one of the earlier stages when there have been serious infringements.

2.12 **First warning**. A first warning could be either oral or written depending on the seriousness of the case.

(a) An **oral warning** should include the reason for issuing it, notice that it constitutes the first step of the disciplinary procedure and details of the right of appeal. A note of the warning should be kept on file but disregarded after a specified period, such as 6 months.

(b) A **first written warning** is appropriate in more serious cases. It should inform the worker of the improvement required and state that a final written warning may be considered if there is no satisfactory improvement. A copy of the first written warning should be kept on file but disregarded after a specified period such as 12 months.

A first written warning may also be appropriate if there has not been satisfactory improvement after an oral warning has been issued.

2.13 **Final written warning**. If an earlier warning is still current and there is no satisfactory improvement, a final written warning may be appropriate. Also, sufficiently serious infringements may lead directly to the issue of a final written warning.

2.14 A final written warning should give details of the offence, state that failure to improve may lead to dismissal or a lesser sanction and explain the appeals procedure. Despite its name, a final written warning is not necessarily final, since the ACAS Code of Practice requires that it should be disregarded for disciplinary purposes after a specified period such as 12 months.

2.15 Note that, depending on the offence, it is not necessary to progress through all of these levels of warning. One could go straight to the final written warning. This is thus a very flexible system, capable of dealing with disciplinary problems in a measured and proportionate way. It is however **always** necessary to investigate the allegations and to give the worker opportunity to reply to them.

Disciplinary sanctions

2.16 The final stage in the disciplinary process is the imposition of sanctions.

(a) **Suspension without pay**

This course of action would be next in order if the employee has committed repeated offences and previous steps were of no avail. Disciplinary lay-offs usually extend over

several days or weeks. Some employees may not be very impressed with oral or written warnings, but they will find a disciplinary lay-off without pay a rude awakening. This penalty is only available if it is provided for in the contract of employment

(b) **Demotion**

This course of action is likely to bring about dissatisfaction and discouragement, since losing pay and status over an extended period of time is a form of constant punishment. This dissatisfaction of the demoted employee may easily spread to co-workers, so most enterprises avoid downgrading as a disciplinary measure like suspension without pay, this sanction may only be imposed if it is provided for in the contract of employment.

(c) **Discharge**

Discharge is a drastic form of disciplinary action, and should be reserved for the most serious offences. For the organisation, it involves waste of a labour resource, the expense of training a new employee, and disruption caused by changing the make-up of the work team. There also may be damage to the morale of the group.

Question 2

How (a) accessible and (b) clear are the rules and policies of your organisation/office: do people really know what they are and are not supposed to do? Have a look at the rule book or procedures manual in your office. How easy is it to see - or did you get referred elsewhere? is the rule book well-indexed and cross-referenced, and in language that all employees will understand?

How (a) accessible and (b) clear are the disciplinary procedures in your office? Are the employees' rights of investigation and appeal clearly set out, with ACAS guidelines? Who is responsible for discipline?

Relationship management in disciplinary situations

2.17 Even if the manager uses sensitivity and judgement, imposing disciplinary action tends to generate **resentment** because it is an unpleasant experience. The challenge is to apply the necessary disciplinary action so that it will be least resented.

(a) **Immediacy**

Immediacy means that after noticing the offence, the manager proceeds to take disciplinary action as *speedily* as possible, subject to investigations while at the same time avoiding haste and on-the-spot emotions which might lead to unwarranted actions.

(b) **Advance warning**

Employees should know in advance (eg in a Staff Handbook) what is expected of them and what the rules and regulations are.

(c) **Consistency**

Consistency of discipline means that each time an infraction occurs appropriate disciplinary action is taken. Inconsistency in application of discipline lowers the morale of employees and diminishes their respect for the manager.

(d) **Impersonality**

Penalties should be connected with the act and not based upon the personality involved, and once disciplinary action has been taken, no grudges should be borne.

(e) **Privacy**

As a general rule (unless the manager's authority is challenged directly and in public) disciplinary action should be taken in private, to avoid the spread of conflict and the humiliation or martyrdom of the employee concerned.

Disciplinary interviews

2.18 **Preparation for the disciplinary interview**

(a) **Gathering the facts** about the alleged infringement

(b) **Determination of the organisation's position:** how valuable is the employee, potentially? How serious are his offences/lack of progress? How far is the organisation prepared to go to help him improve or discipline him further?

(c) **Identification of the aims of the interview**: punishment? deterrent to others? improvement? Specific standards of future behaviour/performance required need to be determined.

(d) **Ensure that the organisation's disciplinary procedures have been followed**

(i) Informal oral warnings (at least) have been given.

(ii) The employee has been given adequate notice of the interview for his own preparation.

(iii) The employee has been informed of the complaint against his right to be accompanied by a colleague or representative and so on.

2.19 **The content of the disciplinary interview**

Step 1. The manager will explain the purpose of the interview.

Step 2. The charges against the employee will be delivered, clearly, unambiguously and without personal emotion.

Step 3. The manager will explain the organisation's position with regard to the issues involved: disappointment, concern, need for improvement, impact on others. This can be done frankly - but tactfully, with as positive an emphasis as possible on the employee's capacity and responsibility to improve.

Step 4. The organisation's expectations with regard to future behaviour/performance should be made clear.

Step 5. The employee should be given the opportunity to comment, explain, justify or deny. If he is to approach the following stage of the interview in a positive way, he must not be made to feel 'hounded' or hard done by.

Step 6. The organisation's expectations should be reiterated, or new standards of behaviour set for the employee.

(i) They should be specific and quantifiable, performance related and realistic.

(ii) They should be related to a practical but reasonably short time period. A date should be set to review his progress.

(iii) The manager agrees on measures to help the employee should that be necessary. It would demonstrate a positive approach if, for example, a mentor were appointed from his work group to help him check his work. If his poor performance is genuinely the result of some difficulty or distress

BPP PUBLISHING

outside work, other help (temporary leave, counselling or financial aid) may be appropriate.

Step 7. The manager should explain the reasons behind any penalties imposed on the employee, including the entry in his personnel record of the formal warning. He should also explain how the warning can be removed from the record, and what standards must be achieved within a specified timescale. There should be a clear warning of the consequences of failure to meet improvement targets.

Step 8. The manager should explain the organisation's appeals procedures: if the employee feels he has been unfairly treated, there should be a right of appeal to a higher manager.

Step 9. Once it has been established that the employee understands all the above, the manager should summarise the proceedings briefly.

Records of the interview will be kept for the employee's personnel file, and for the formal follow-up review and any further action necessary.

Question 3

Outline the steps involved in a formal disciplinary procedure (for an organisation with unionised employees) and show how the procedure would operate in a case of:

(a) Persistent absenteeism

(b) Theft of envelopes from the organisation's offices

Answer

Apart from the outline of the steps involved - which can be drawn from the chapter, this question raises an interesting point about the nature of different offences, and the flexibility required in the handling of complex disciplinary matters.

There is clearly a difference in kind and scale between

o unsatisfactory conduct (eg absenteeism)
o misconduct (eg insulting behaviour, persistent absenteeism, insubordination) and
o 'gross misconduct' (eg theft or assault).

The attitude of the organisation towards the purpose of disciplinary action will to a large extent dictate the severity of the punishment.

o If it is punitive it will 'fit the crime'.
o If it is reformative, it may be a warning only, and less severe than the offence warrants.
o If it is deterrent, it may be more severe than is warranted (ie to 'make an example').

The absenteeism question assumes that counselling etc. has failed, and that some sanction has to be applied, to preserve credibility. The theft technically deserves summary dismissal (as gross misconduct), but it depends on the scale and value of the theft, the attitude of the organisation to use of stationery for personal purposes (ie is it theft?) etc. Communicating the situations given might best be done as follows.

(a) Telephone, confirmed in writing (order form, letter)

(b) Noticeboard or general meeting

(c) Fact-to-face conversation. it would be a good idea to confirm the outcome of the meeting in writing so that records can be maintained.

(d) Either telephone or face-to-face.

3   RETIREMENT, RESIGNATION AND REDUNDANCY

Retirement

3.1   In the UK, many employees are taking **early retirement** perhaps as a result of corporate downsizing, but many people still search for work at an older age and there are pressure groups seeking to ban **ageism** in recruitment. Retirement ages for men and women are being **equalised**.

3.2   Organisations **encourage retirement** for a variety of reasons.

- Promotion opportunities for younger workers
- Early retirement is an alternative to redundancy
- The age structure of an organisation may become unbalanced
- The cost of providing pensions rises with age

Resignation

3.3   People resign for many reasons, personal and occupational. Employees who are particularly valuable should be encouraged to stay. Particular problems the employee has been experiencing (eg salary) may be solvable, though not always in the short term.

3.4   In any case, an **exit interview**, when the leaver explains the decision to go, is a valuable source of information.

3.5   The **period of notice** required for the employee to leave should be set out in the contract of employment, but some leeway may be negotiated on this.

Dismissal

3.6   Dismissal has three important aspects.

(a)   The termination of an employee's contract **by the employer**

(b)   The ending of a fixed-term contract **without renewal** on the same terms

(c)   Resignation by the **employee** where the **employer's conduct** breaches the contract of employment. This is **constructive dismissal**

3.7   The **statutory minimum** period of notice to be given is determined by the employee's length of continuous service in the employer's service. Longer periods may be written into the contract, at the employer's discretion, and by agreement. Either party may waive his right to notice, or accept payment in lieu of notice. An employee is entitled to a written statement of the **reasons** for dismissal.

Unfair dismissal

3.8   An employee might protest about being dismissed and there are various legal remedies available, subject to the employee's age and employment history. Under employment protection legislation, the employee has to **prove** that he has been dismissed. The onus is then on the **employer to prove** that the dismissal was **fair**.

3.9   **Potentially fair grounds for dismissal.**

(a)   **Redundancy,** provided that the selection for redundancy was fair.

(b) **Legal impediment:** the employee could not continue to work in his present position without breaking a legal duty or restriction.

(c) **Non-capability,** provided adequate training and warnings had been given.

(d) **Misconduct,** provided warnings suitable to the offence have been given.

(e) **Other substantial reason:** for example, the employee is married to a competitor.

3.10 **Automatically unfair dismissal**

- Unfair selection for redundancy
- Membership and involvement in a trade union
- Pregnancy
- Insisting on documented payslips and employment particulars
- Carrying out certain activities in connection with health and safety at work

3.11 The Conciliation Officer or Industrial Tribunal to whom a complaint of unfair dismissal is made may order various **remedies**, subject to the circumstances of the case.

- **Re-instatement**: giving the employee the old job back.

- **Re-engagement**: giving the employee a job comparable to the old one.

- **Compensation**: which may include redundancy pay, breach of contract and punitive award.

3.12 **Incompetence or misconduct**

(a) **Incompetence** means that the employee's best efforts have not reached the standard required.

(b) If the employee has **deliberately not** done his best, however, this is **misconduct**.

3.13 The solution to these difficulties lies partly in the hands of the HRM function, which as a number of responsibilities.

(a) Ensuring that **standards of performance and conduct** are set, clearly defined and communicated to all employees

(b) **Warning** employees where a gap is perceived between standard and performance

(c) Giving a clearly defined and reasonable **period for improvement** - with help and advice where necessary, and clear improvement targets

(d) Ensuring that **disciplinary procedures** and the ultimate consequences of continued failure are made clear

If such procedures are formulated, the employer will not only feel that the employee has been given every chance to redeem the situation, but will also be in a strong position at a tribunal in rebutting a complaint of unfair dismissal.

Disciplinary procedures

3.14 The use of a disciplinary system can be evidence in certain situations that an employee has not been dismissed unfairly.

Redundancy

3.15 **Redundancy** is dismissal under two circumstances.

(a) The employer has ceased to carry on the business at all or in the place where the employee was employed.

(b) The requirements of the business for employees to carry out work of a particular kind have ceased or diminished or are expected to.

3.16 **Compensation** is a legal entitlement, and encourages employees to accept redundancy without damage to industrial relations.

3.17 The employee is **not entitled** to compensation in three circumstances.

(a) The employer has made offer of suitable alternative employment and the employee has **unreasonably** rejected it.

(b) The employee is of pensionable age or over, or has less than two years' continuous employment.

(c) The employee's conduct merits **dismissal without notice**.

There are certain legal minima for compensation offered, based on age and length of service.

Procedure for handling redundancies

3.18 From a purely humane point of view, it is obviously desirable to consult with employees or their representatives. Notice of impending redundancies is a legal duty for redundancies over a certain number.

3.19 **The impact of a redundancy programme can be reduced in several ways.**

- Retirement of staff over the normal retirement age
- Early retirement to staff approaching normal retirement age
- Restrictions on recruitment to reduce the workforce over time by natural wastage
- Dismissal of part-time or short-term contract staff
- Offering retraining and/or redeployment within the organisation
- Seeking voluntary redundancies

3.20 Where management have to choose between individuals doing the same work, they may dismiss the less competent or require people to re-apply for the job. The LIFO principle may be applied. Newcomers are dismissed before long-serving employees.

3.21 Many large organisations provide benefits in excess of the statutory minimum, with regard to consultation periods, terms, notice periods, counselling and aid with job search, training in job-search skills and so on.

3.22 Many firms provide advice and **outplacement** counselling, to help redundant employees find work elsewhere.

Question 4

Will HRM become increasingly involved in getting rid of people instead of recruiting them?

Answer

(a) John Hunt *(The Shifting Focus of the Personnel Function)* 'In sharp contrast to the search for talent is the dramatic shift in the personnel function from people resourcing to people exiting.'

(b) Pressures on intensive use of manpower, contraction of workforce (plus expansion in unemployment in UK), viz:

    (i)   competition

    (ii) new technology

    (iii) recession and decline in world trade.

(c) But it is not necessarily a trend which will continue in future. Technology does not always 'replace' human operation and lead to manpower savings. It also creates jobs.

(d) There are alternatives to redundancy: job-sharing, use of manpower agencies, part-time or temporary assignments, networking.

4 MATERNITY

4.1 Because of increased attention to the implications of equal opportunities and because of the need to recruit more women returnees to the labour force, many organisations are improving their maternity and child care arrangements. A woman has several entitlements.

(a) **Leave of absence** for maternity, return to her own job afterwards, subject to least 21 days' notice in writing of her intention and reconfirmation that she is to return to work.

(b) **Return to her old job** or suitable alternative after maternity leave (subject to certain qualification requirements), proper notice having been given.

(c) **14 weeks maternity leave,** or more subject to employment history.

(d) Time off for **ante-natal care**.

(e) **Statutory Maternity Pay**, subject to certain qualification requirements.

4.2 Many employers have introduced more generous maternity agreements. It is possible that time off for fathers upon the birth of a child may be allowed - the right exists in some EU countries.

5 DISCRIMINATION AND EQUAL OPPORTUNITIES

Legal rights to equal opportunity

5.1 In Britain, two main Acts have been passed to deal with inequality of opportunity.

(a) The **Sex Discrimination Act 1975,** outlawed certain types of discrimination on the grounds of sex or marital status.

(b) The **Race Relations Act 1976** outlawed certain types of discrimination on grounds of colour, race, nationality, or ethnic or national origin.

In both Acts, the obligation of **non-discrimination applies to all aspects of employment,** including advertisements, recruitment and selection programmes, access to training, promotion, disciplinary procedures, redundancy and dismissal.

5.2 **Types of discrimination**

(a) **Direct discrimination:** one interested group is treated less favourably than another (except for exempted cases). This is illegal in the UK.

(b) **Indirect discrimination:** requirements or conditions are imposed, with which a substantial proportion of the interested group could not comply, to their detriment.

(c) **Positive discrimination** gives give **preference** to a protected person, regardless of comparative suitability and qualification for the job. British legislation does **not** (except with regard to training) **permit positive discrimination**. In particular, there is no quota scheme (except for registered disabled persons). The organisation may, however, set itself **targets** for the number of such persons that they will aim to employ - *if* the required number of *eligible* and *suitably qualified* people can be recruited.

(d) A number of countries in the world use **positive discrimination as an aspect of social policy to correct perceived disadvantages** endured by various ethnic and other groups in society. (For example, in India **scheduled castes** are entitled to a proportion of government jobs.)

5.3 **Equal pay legislation** is intended 'to prevent discrimination as regards terms and conditions of employment between men and women' and covers equal pay for the same work and for work of equal value.

5.4 The **Disability Discrimination Act 1995** gives disabled people similar rights against discrimination to these already established in relation to sex and race. However, failure to make 'reasonable adjustments' can be justified on grounds of cost or disruption to the organisation.

Rehabilitation of Offenders

5.5 **Rehabilitation of Offenders Act 1974**. A conviction for most criminal offences (earning less than 30 months in prison) is 'spent' after a period of time that varies according to the severity of the offence. After this period offenders (other than doctors, lawyers, teachers, accountants and police officers) are 'rehabilitated' and are not obliged to disclose the nature of their offences or details of their convictions.

Management practice

5.6 The practical implications of the legislation for employers are set out in **Codes of Practice**, issued by the Commission for Racial Equality and the Equal Opportunities Commission. These do not have the force of law, but may be taken into account by Employment Tribunals, where discrimination cases are brought before them.

5.7 Organisations make minimal efforts to avoid discrimination, paying lip-service to the idea to the extent of claiming 'We are an Equal Opportunities Employer' on advertising literature! To turn such a claim into reality involves several processes.

(a) **Support from the top** of the organisation for the formulation of a practical policy.

(b) A **working party** drawn from, for example, management, unions, minority groups, the HRM department and staff representatives.

(c) **Action plans and resources** including staff, to implement and monitor the policy, publicise it to staff, arrange training and so on.

(d) **Monitoring**. The numbers of women and ethnic minority staff can be monitored when applying to, entering and leaving the organisation, and when applying for transfers, promotions or training schemes.

(e) **Positive action,** which is the process of taking active steps to **encourage** people from disadvantaged groups to apply for jobs and training, and to compete for vacancies.

5.8 **Implications for recruitment and selection.** There is always a risk that a disappointed job applicant, for example, will attribute his or her lack of success to discrimination, especially if the recruiting organisation's workforce is conspicuously lacking in representatives of the same ethnic minority, sex or group. Steps must be taken to **ensure** that this is not the case and to **demonstrate** that it is not so.

   (a) **Advertising**

      (i) Avoid wording that suggests preference for a particular group.

      (ii) Employers must not indicate or imply any 'intention to discriminate'.

      (iii) Recruitment literature should state that the organisation is an Equal Opportunities employer.

      (iv) The placing of advertisements only where the readership is predominantly of one race or sex is construed as indirect discrimination.

   (b) **Recruitment agencies.** Instructions to an agency should not suggest any preference.

   (c) **Application forms.** These should include no questions which are not work-related (such as domestic details) and which only one group is asked to complete.

   (d) **Interviews**

      (i) Any non-work-related question must be asked of **all** interviewees.

      (ii) It may be advisable to have a witness at interviews, or at least to take detailed notes, in the event that a claim of discrimination is made.

   (e) **Selection tests.** These must be wholly relevant, and should not favour any particular group. Even personality tests have been shown to favour white male applicants.

   (f) **Records.** Reasons for rejection, and interview notes, should be carefully recorded, so that in the event of investigation the details will be available.

Question 5

Find the policy statement of your organisation related to equal opportunities. Is it being carried out in practice? How many women and racial minority groups are represented in your own office in managerial positions? Do you think the position is improving or not?

Ask your personnel or training department, if necessary, about special programmes and opportunities for women in your organisation. What more do you think (a) could and (b) should be done.

5.9 **Measures to address the underlying problems of equal opportunities**

- Appointing **Equal Opportunities Managers**.
- **Flexible hours** or part-time work, 'term-time' or annual hours contracts.
- **Career-break** or return-to-work schemes for women.
- Training for **women returnees**.
- **Awareness training** for managers.
- The provision of **workplace nurseries** for working mothers.
- **Positive action** to encourage job and training applications from minority groups.
- Alteration of **premises** to accommodate wheelchair users.

Sexual harassment

5.10 **Sexual harassment** may be defined as any **unwanted** conduct with sexual connotations, physical or verbal. Rulings in a number of high profile court cases suggest that sexual harassment is **unlawful sex discrimination**, under the Sex Discrimination Act.

6 HEALTH AND SAFETY

6.1 **Importance of maintaining health and safety at work**

- An employer has **legal obligations** under UK and EU law.
- Accidents and illness **cost the employer money**.
- The company's **image** in the marketplace and society may suffer.

6.2 The **major legislation in the UK** covers a number of Acts of Parliament. EU law will become more important.

Management practices

6.3 **Employers' duties**

(a) All **work practices** must be safe.

(b) The work **environment** must be safe and healthy.

(c) All plant and equipment must be maintained to the necessary standard.

(d) Information, instruction, training and supervision should **encourage safe working practices**. Employers must provide training and information to all staff.

(e) The safety policy should be clearly **communicated** to all staff.

(f) They must carry out **risk assessments**, generally in writing, of all work hazards. Assessment should be continuous. They must **assess the risks to anyone else affected by their work activities.**

(g) They must **share hazard and risk information** with other employers, including those on adjoining premises, other site occupiers and all subcontractors coming onto the premises.

(h) They must **introduce controls** to reduce risks.

(i) They should **revise safety policies** in the light of the above, or initiate safety policies if none were in place previously.

(j) They must **identify employees** who are especially at risk.

(k) They must employ competent safety and health **advisers**.

6.4 The Safety Representative Regulations provide A **safety representative** may be appointed by a recognised trade union, and for **Safety Committees** to be set up at the request of employee representatives.

Employees

6.5 **Employees' duties**

(a) Take reasonable care of themselves and others

(b) Allow the employer to carry out his or her duties (including enforcing safety rules)

(c) Not interfere intentionally or recklessly with any machinery or equipment

(d) Inform the employer of any situation which may be a danger (this does not reduce the employer's responsibilities in any way)

(e) Use all equipment properly

Question 6

What aspects of your own work environment (if any) do you think are:

* a hindrance to your work?
* a source of dissatisfaction?
* a hazard to your health or safety?

Health and safety (display screen equipment) regulation, 1992

6.6 If you have ever worked for a long period at a VDU you may personally have experienced some discomfort. Back ache, eye strain and stiffness or muscular problems of the neck, shoulders, arms or hands are frequent complaints. RSI (repetitive strain injury) is cited as causing permanent disability in some occupations.

6.7 Following the implementation of the EU directive on workstations any new workstations put into service now have to meet new requirements and existing workstations must be adapted to comply or be replaced by the end of 1996. Those cover VDU screens, glare, radiation, breaks and free eyesight testing.

Accident and safety policies

6.8 Accidents are **expensive.**

(a) Time is lost by the injured employee and other staff.

(b) Direct costs are incurred by disruption to operations at work; damage and repairs and modification to the equipment; compensation payments or fines resulting from legal action; increased insurance premiums.

(c) Output from the injured employee on return to work is often reduced.

(d) Recruiting and training a replacement for the injured worker will have its own cost.

6.9 An employee who is injured as a result of either the **employer's failure to take reasonable care** or a **statutory duty** can **sue.**

(a) An employee is not deemed to consent to the risk of injury because he or she is aware of the risk. It is the employer's duty to provide a safe working system.

(b) Employees can become inattentive or careless in doing work which is monotonous or imposes stress. This factor too must be allowed for in the employer's safety precautions.

(c) The employer should encourage and insist on its proper use of safety equipment.

(d) Many dangers can be caused by carelessness or other fault of an otherwise competent employee, possibly by his mere thoughtlessness.

6.10 **Reducing the frequency and severity of accidents**

* Develop **safety consciousness** among staff.
* Develop effective consultative **participation.**

- Give adequate **instruction** in safety rules and measures.
- **Materials handling should be minimised.**
- **Good maintenance** pays dividends.
- Implement in full the **code of practice** for the industry.
- **Safety inspections** should be carried out regularly.

6.11 Accident reporting systems

(a) Accidents should be reported on an **accident report form**.

(b) **Statistical trends** should be monitored to reveal areas where recurring accidents suggest the need for special investigation, but only more serious incidents will have to be followed-up in depth.

(c) **Follow-up** should be clearly aimed at preventing recurrence - not placing blame.

6.12 There are other specific rules covering fire escapes, fire equipment and risks.

Health and safety policy

6.13 In order to enhance safety awareness, promote good practice and comply with legal obligations, many employers have a **health and safety policy** for their staff. Such a policy will have a number of features.

- Statement of **principles**
- Detail of **safety procedures**
- **Compliance with the law**
- **Detailed instructions** on how to use equipment
- **Training requirements**

6.14 Senior managers **must set a good example**.

(a) **Visibly reacting to breaches** of the policy (eg if the fire doors are blocked open, remove the blockage).

(b) **Ensuring that the policy is communicated** to staff (eg memoranda, newsletters).

(c) **Setting priorities for operations.**

(d) **Involving staff in the health and safety process.**

Case example

Charles Hampden-Turner (in his book *Corporate Culture*) notes that attitudes to safety can be part of a corporate *culture*. He quotes the example of a firm called (for reasons of confidentiality) *Western Oil*.

(a) Western Oil had a bad safety record. 'Initially, safety was totally at odds with the main cultural values of productivity (management's interests) and maintenance of a macho image (the worker's culture) ... Western Oil had a culture which put safety in conflict with other corporate values.' In particular, the problem was with its long-distance truck drivers (who in the US have a culture of solitary independence and self reliance) who drove sometimes recklessly with loads large enough to inundate a small town. The company instituted *Operation Integrity* to improve safety, in a lasting way, changing the policies and drawing on the existing features of the culture but using them in a different way.

(b) The culture had five dilemmas.

(i) *Safety-first vs macho-individualism*. Truckers see themselves as 'fearless pioneers of the unconventional lifestyle ... "Be careful boys!" is hardly a plea likely to go down well with this particular group'. Instead of trying to control the drivers, the firm recommended that they become *road safety consultants* (or design consultants). Their advice was sought on improving the system. This had the advantage that 'by making drivers critics of the system their roles as outsiders were preserved and promoted'. It tried to tap their heroism as promoters of public safety.

(ii) *Safety everywhere vs safety specialists*. Western Oil could have hired more specialist staff. However, instead, the company promoted cross functional safety teams from existing parts of the business, for example, to help in designing depots and thinking of ways to reduce hazards.

(iii) *Safety as cost vs productivity as benefit*. 'If the drivers raced from station to station to win their bonus, accidents were bound to occur ... . The safety engineers rarely spoke to the line manager in charge of the delivery schedules. The unreconciled dilemma between safety and productivity had been evaded at management level and passed down the hierarchy until drivers were subjected to two incompatible injunctions, work fast and work safely.' To deal with this problem, safety would be built into the reward system.

(iv) *Long-term safety vs short-term steering*. The device of recording 'unsafe' acts in operations enabled them to be monitored by cross-functional teams, so that the causes of accidents could be identified and be reduced.

(v) *Personal responsibility vs collective protection*. It was felt that if 'safety' was seen as a form of management policing it would never be accepted. The habit of management 'blaming the victim' had to stop. Instead, if an employee reported another to the safety teams, the person who was reported would be free of *official* sanction. Peer presence was seen to be a better enforcer of safety than the management hierarchy.

6.15 The diagram below shows a systematic approach to health and safety.

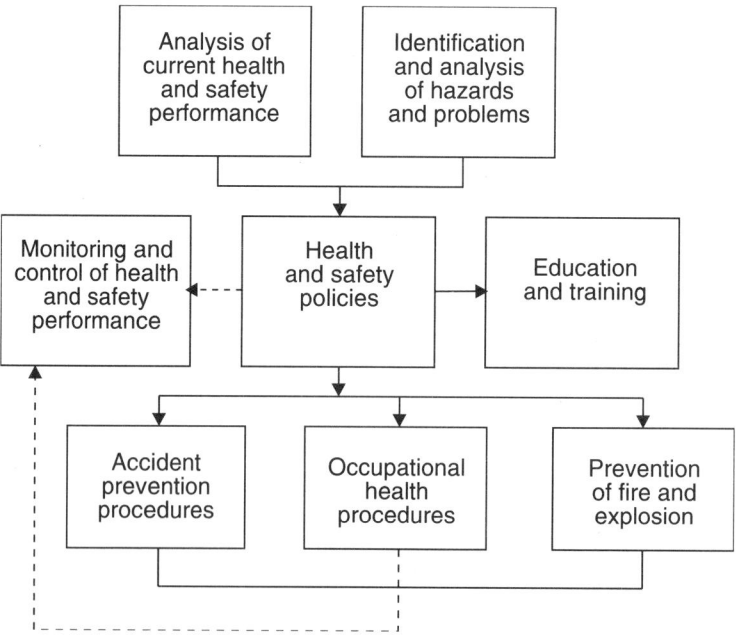

Chapter roundup

- Early leadership theories concentrated upon the **qualities** of the leader. More recent work has concentrated on what leaders **do** and **how they do it.**

- Most analyses of leadership are based on a **spectrum of styles** ranging from dictatorial through democratic to laissez-faire. *Likert* found that effective managers have high expectations, use participation naturally but do not supervise closely and know their staff well. *Blake and Mouton* considered manager's performance in terms of concern for **task** and concern for **people**. *Adair's* analysis was similar but added **group** needs. It is unlikely that a single style will work everywhere, so a **contingency approach** is advisable.

- **Authority** is the decision making discretion given to a manager, while **responsibility** is the obligation to perform duties. Sufficient authority should be granted to permit the efficient discharge of the appointed responsibility. **Delegation** is essential wherever there is a hierarchy of management. **Power** is the **ability** to do something whereas authority; expert power is possessed by those acknowledged as experts.

- Disciplinary systems are needed in all organisations to deal with human failings. Discipline is legally regulated and the ACAS code of practice is an essential framework.

- Retirement, resignation, redundancy and, especially, dismissed are also heavily regulated by law, as are maternity, discrimination and health and safety.

Quick quiz

1   What did Likert find characteristic of effective managers?

2   What are the axes of Blake and Mouton's grid?

3   What three areas of activity did Adair feel a manager should address?

4   What is the difference between power and authority?

5   Why is delegation necessary?

6   What is expert power?

7   Outline a disciplinary procedure.

8   What are potentially fair grounds for dismissal?

9   What is redundancy?

10   What is the difference between direct and indirect discrimination?

11   What duties has the employee under health and safety law?

Answers to quick quiz

1 Expectation of high levels of performance; employee-centredness; avoidance of close supervision; a naturally participative style

2 Concern for production and concern for people

3 Task needs, individual needs and group needs

4 Authority is the right to do something; power is the ability to do it

5 No-one can do everything: delegation is a natural consequence of organisation.

6 Power based on the acknowledgement of expertise

7 Informal talk; oral reprimand; written warning; disciplinary sanction; disciplinary cases should be handled in conformance with the ACAS Code

8 Redundancy; legal impediment; non-capability; misconduct; other substantial reasons

9 Dismissal when the business has ceased or when employees are no longer required to carry out particular work

10 Direct discrimination occurs when one group is treated less favourably than another; indirect discrimination occurs when conditions are imposed which disadvantage a group

11 Take reasonable care; allow employers to carry out their H&S duties; use machinery properly; inform employer of dangers

Now try the question below from the Exam Question Bank

Number	Level	Marks	Time
Q14	Exam	20	36 mins

Chapter 15

GROUPS IN ORGANISATIONS

Topic List	Syllabus Reference	Ability required
1 Creating effective teams	(iv)	Analysis
2 Conflict in organisations	(iv)	Analysis
3 Conflict: groups and departments	(iv)	Analysis
4 Political behaviour	(iv)	Analysis
5 Managerial response to conflict	(iv)	Analysis

Introduction

People rarely work alone; often they work in groups co-operating on a task. Work groups or teams are becoming increasingly popular as a means of organising work. In section 1, we describe the issues behind teambuilding. Multi-skilled or multi-disciplinary teams enable the organisation to deploy resources flexibly.

Organisations are collections of groups which have their own interests and agendas, and there are many tensions between them.

Some believe that conflict is a problem that has to be fixed. Others believe that conflict is inevitable, and can produce desirable outcomes for the organisation.

Conflict often focuses on the distribution of power between individuals and departments, and can be manifested in political behaviour.

Learning outcomes covered in this chapter

- Explain the formation of groups and the way in which groups and their members behave.

- Identify the different roles adopted by members of a group, and explain the relevance of this to the management of the group.

- Analyse the causes of inter-group and interpersonal conflict in an organisation and recommend ways in which such conflict might be managed.

Syllabus content covered in this chapter

- Theories of group development, behaviour and roles (eg Tuckman, Belbin).

- The sources of conflict in organisations and the ways in which conflict can be managed to ensure working relationships are productive and effective.

1   CREATING EFFECTIVE TEAMS

1.1   In your working life, though, you will generally find yourself working as part of a group or **team**; or, if you are a supervisor or a manager, you may direct a team. A team is more than just a collection of individuals - it has a specific purpose and even a sense of an identity, and in a work context it has a task to perform.

Groups

> **KEY TERM**
>
> A **group** is 'any collection of people who perceive themselves to be a group'.

1.2 Unlike a random collection of individuals, a group of individuals share a common sense of identity and belonging. They have certain attributes that a random crowd does not possess.

   (a) A **sense of identity**. There is awareness of membership and acknowledged boundaries to the group which define it.

   (b) **Loyalty to the group,** and acceptance within the group. This generally expresses itself as conformity or the acceptance of the norms of behaviour and attitudes that bind the group together and exclude others from it.

   (c) **Purpose and leadership**. Most groups have an express purpose, whatever field they are in: most will, spontaneously or formally, choose individuals or sub-groups to lead them towards the fulfilment of those goals.

1.3 A **primary working group** is the immediate social environment of the individual worker. A formal group used for particular objectives in the work place is called a team. Although many people enjoy working in teams, their popularity in the work place arises because of their effectiveness in fulfilling the organisation's work.

Teams

1.4 **Aspects of terms**

> **KEY TERM**
>
> A **team** is a 'small number of people with complementary skills who are committed to a common purpose, performance goals and approach for which they hold themselves basically accountable'.

   (a) **Work organisation.** Teams combine the skills of different individuals and avoid complex communication between different business functions.

   (b) **Control.** Fear of letting down the team can be a powerful motivator, hence teams can be used to control the performance and behaviour of individuals. Teams can also be used to resolve conflict.

   (c) **Knowledge generation**. Teams can generate ideas.

   (d) **Decision-making.** Teams can be set up to investigate new developments and decisions can be evaluated from more than one viewpoint.

Teamworking

1.5 The basic work units of organisations have traditionally been specialised functional departments. In more recent times, organisations are adopting small, flexible teams. Teamworking allows work to be shared among a number of individuals, so it gets done faster without people losing sight of their whole tasks or having to co-ordinate their efforts through lengthy channels of communication.

1.6 A team may be called together temporarily, to achieve specific task objectives (**project team**), or may be more or less permanent, with responsibilities for a particular product, product group or stage of the production process (a **product or process team**). There are two basic approaches to the organisation of team work: multi-skilled teams and multi-disciplinary teams.

> **Exam focus point**
> Multi-skilled and multi-disciplinary teams contribute to a *flexible* workforce, the topic of a question set in May 1998.

Multi-disciplinary teams

1.7 Multi-disciplinary teams bring together individuals with **different skills** and specialisms, so that their skills, experience and knowledge can be **pooled or exchanged**. Teamworking of this kind encourages freer and faster communication between disciplines in the organisation.

(a) Teamworking increases workers' **awareness of their overall objectives** and targets.

(b) Teamworking **aids co-ordination**.

(c) Teamworking **helps to generate solutions to problems**, and suggestions for improvements, since a multi-disciplinary team has access to more 'pieces of the jigsaw'.

Multi skilled teams

1.8 A team may simply bring together a number of individuals who have **several skills** and can perform **any** of the group's tasks. These tasks can then be shared out in a more flexible way between group members, according to who is available and best placed to do a given job at the time it is required.

Development of the team

> **Exam focus point**
> Tuckman's work is clearly identified in the learning outcomes for this part of the syllabus. This is fairly easy to learn as an essay topic. A scenario might require you to identify the stage a team is at, or to suggest ways to move the team through each stage.

1.9 Four stages in team development were identified by *Tuckman*.

Step 1. **Forming**

The team is just coming together, and may still be seen as a collection of individuals. Each member wishes to impress his or her personality on the group. The individuals will be trying to find out about each other, and about the aims and norms of the team. There will at this stage probably be a wariness about introducing new ideas. The objectives being pursued may as yet be unclear and a leader may not yet have emerged. This period is essential, but may be time wasting: the team as a unit will not be used to being autonomous, and will probably not be an efficient agent in the planning of its activities or the activities of others.

Step 2. **Storming**

This frequently involves more or less open conflict between team members. There may be changes agreed in the original objectives, procedures and norms established for the group. If the team is developing successfully this may be a fruitful phase as more **realistic targets are set and trust between the group members increases.**

Step 3. **Norming**

A period of settling down: there will be agreements about work sharing, individual requirements and expectations of output. Norms and procedures may evolve which enable methodical working to be introduced and maintained.

Step 4. **Performing**

The team sets to work to execute its task. The difficulties of growth and development no longer hinder the group's objectives.

The ideal team

1.10 **Characteristics of the ideal functioning team**

(a) Each individual gets the support of the team, a sense of identity and belonging which encourages loyalty and hard work on the group's behalf.

(b) Skills, information and ideas are shared, so that the team's capabilities are greater than those of the individuals.

(c) New ideas can be tested, reactions taken into account and persuasive skills brought into play in group discussion for decision making and problem solving.

(d) Each individual is encouraged to participate and contribute and thus becomes personally involved in and committed to the team's activities.

(e) Goodwill, trust and respect can be built up between individuals, so that communication is encouraged and potential problems more easily overcome.

Problems with teams

1.11 Unfortunately, team working is rarely such an undiluted success. There are certain constraints involved in working with others.

(a) Awareness of **group norms** and the desire to be acceptable to the group may **restrict individual personality** and flair.

(b) **Too much discord. Conflicting roles and relationships** (where an individual is a member of more than one group) can cause difficulties in communicating effectively.

(c) **Personality problems,** and will suffer if one member dislikes or distrusts another; is too dominant or so timid that the value of his ideas is lost; or is so negative in attitude that constructive communication is rendered impossible.

(d) **Rigid leadership** and procedures may stifle initiative and creativity in individuals.

(e) **Differences of opinion** and political conflicts of interest are always likely.

(f) **Too much harmony.** Teams work best when there is room for disagreement. They can become dangerously blinkered to what is going on around it, and may confidently forge ahead in a completely **wrong** direction. *I L Janis* describes this as **group think**. The cosy consensus of the group prevents consideration of alternatives, constructive

criticism or conflict. Alternatively, efforts to paper over differences may lead to bland recommendations without meaning.

(g) **Corporate culture and reward systems.** Teams will fail if the company promotes and rewards the individual at the expense of the group.

(h) **Too many meetings.** Teams should not try to do everything together. Not only does this waste time in meetings, but team members are exposed to less diversity of thought.

(i) **Powerlessness.** People will not bother to work in a team or on a task force if its recommendations are ignored.

(j) **Suitability.** Teamworking does not suit all jobs.

Question 1

What might be the strategic impact of group think?

Answer

Group think characterises the behaviour of managers in early corporate decline. It also applies to *Johnson and Scholes'* concept of the *recipe*, the tried and trusted formula for success.

Creating an effective work team

1.12 The management problem is how to create effective, efficient work teams. *Handy* takes a contingency approach to the problem of team effectiveness.

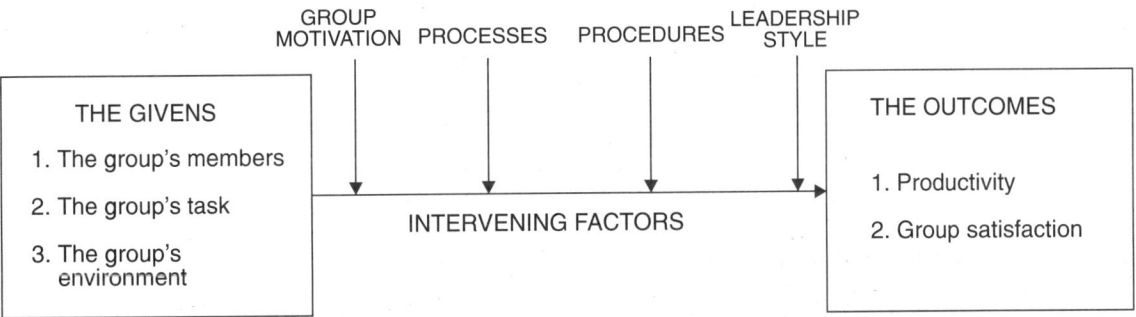

Management can operate on both 'givens' and 'intervening factors' to affect the 'outcomes'.

Givens

1.13 **Members.** Belbin, in a study of business-game teams at Carnegie Institute of Technology in 1981, drew up a list of the most effective character-mix in a team. This involves eight necessary roles which should ideally be balanced and evenly 'spread' in the team.

Member	Role
Co-ordinator	Presides and co-ordinates; balanced, disciplined, good at working through others.
Shaper	Highly strung, dominant, extrovert, passionate about the task itself, a spur to action.
Plant	Introverted, but intellectually dominant and imaginative; source of ideas and proposals but with disadvantages of introversion.

BPP PUBLISHING

Member	Role
Monitor-evaluator	Analytically (rather than creatively) intelligent; dissects ideas, spots flaws; possibly aloof, tactless - but necessary.
Resource-investigator	Popular, sociable, extrovert, relaxed; source of new contacts, but not an originator; needs to be made use of.
Implementer	Practical organiser, turning ideas into tasks; scheduling, planning and so on; trustworthy and efficient, but not excited; not a leader, but an administrator.
Team worker	Most concerned with team maintenance - supportive, understanding, diplomatic; popular but uncompetitive - contribution noticed only in absence.
Finisher	Chivvies the team to meet deadlines, attend to details; urgency and follow-through important, though not always popular.

The **specialist** joins the group to offer expert advice when needed. Notice that one team member may play two or more roles.

1.14 **The task.** The nature of the task must have some bearing on how a group should be managed.

(a) If a job must be done urgently, it is often necessary to dictate how things should be done, rather than to encourage a participatory style of working.

(b) Jobs which are routine, unimportant and undemanding will be insufficient to motivate either individuals or the group as a whole.

The environment

1.15 The team's environment relates to factors such as the physical surroundings at work and to inter-group relations.

Intervening factors and outcomes

1.16 **Processes and procedures.** Research indicates that a team which tackles its work systematically will be more effective than one which lives from hand to mouth, and muddles through.

1.17 **Motivation and leadership style.** High productivity outcomes may be achieved if work is so arranged that satisfaction of individuals' needs coincides with high output. Where teams are, for example, allowed to set their own improvement goals and methods and to measure their own progress towards those goals, it has been observed (by *Peters and Waterman* among others) that they regularly exceed their targets. The **style of leadership** adopted by the team leader can also affect its outcome. This depends on the circumstances.

1.18 Individuals may bring their own **hidden agendas** to groups for satisfaction - goals which may have nothing to do with the declared aims of the team - such as protection of a sub-group, impressing the boss, inter-personal rivalry etc.

Effective teams

1.19 Some teams work more effectively than others, for a variety of reasons, and we can identify ways of evaluating whether a team is effective.

Factor	Effective team	Ineffective team
	Quantifiable factors	
Labour turnover	Low	High
Accident rate	Low	High
Absenteeism	Low	High
Output and productivity	High	Low
Quality of output	High	Low
Individual targets	Achieved	Not achieved
Stoppages and interruptions to the work flow	Low	High (eg because of misunderstandings, disagreements)
	Qualitative factors	
Commitment to targets and organisational goals	High	Low
Understanding of team's work and why it exists	High	Low
Understanding of individual roles	High	Low
Communication between team members	Free and open	Mistrust
Ideas	Shared for the team's benefit	'Owned' (and hidden) by individuals for their own benefit
Feedback	Constructive criticism	Point scoring, undermining
Problem-solving	Addresses causes	Only looks at symptoms
Interest in work decisions	Active	Passive acceptance
Opinions	Consensus	Imposed solutions
Job satisfaction	High	Low
Motivation in leader's absence	High	'When the cat's away...'

Case example

(Adapted from *People Management* October 1997)

The annual staff survey at *Nationwide Building Society* usually places its customer service teams for mortgages and insurance at mid-table in terms of employee satisfaction. This year the teams are at the top. At the same time their productivity has increased by half, sickness absence has fallen by 75 percent and overtime is down to zero.

In the early 1990s Nationwide began to abandon traditional management hierarchies in the non-retail part of its business. In customer service, they were looking for an approach that would further develop multi-skilling while supporting a flatter structure. Self managed teamworking seemed the obvious answer, as it also addressed issues such as morale and job satisfaction.

They work on the premise that the people who know how best to carry out and improve their own work are the teams themselves. Members have shared authority and responsibility to plan, implement and control how their targets are achieved.

In 1995 the Nationwide began a project in the Northampton administrative centre, revolutionising the basis under which the 12 teams in the mortgage and insurance customer service department operated. They increased the level of training and worked on their decision-making, conflict management and team-building skills. Each team had between nine and 18 members, including a leader, but he or she had a coaching, rather than directing, role.

When work comes in, the team decides who is the most appropriate person to take it on, depending on skills and existing workloads. While teams are encouraged to share recourses with each other when necessary, there is also a competitive element. But this is never allowed to detract from the performance of the department - you are only as good as your worst-performing team.

The results of each team are charted, allowing comparative league tables to be created. Initially, one team finished consistently at the foot of the productivity table. Its members consulted colleagues in the more successful teams and altered their work processes accordingly.

Members compared their sickness and overtime figures with those of other teams, and then took responsibility for controlling these elements. Often this was done using a sense of ownership and pride which, could with peer pressure, reduce the need for managerial intervention.

There are several aspects of implementation to be addressed if self-managed teams are to be successful.

- First, there must be clear business reasons for the move.

- There also needs to be recognition by all involved parties that self-managed teams are not a quick fix.

- Another primary issue is that of buy-in and gaining commitment at all levels, while communicating effectively.

- Another important prerequisite is to assess the organisation's existing systems and procedures within which the new teams may have to work.

The value of groups as work units

1.20 **Teams are not the solution to all problems**

(a) Some decisions and tasks are better reached by individuals working alone or having the final say.

(b) Group norms *may* work to lower effectiveness.

(c) Seeing people as a team - or expecting to work as one - is completely unrealistic in many cases (eg if they work in different countries) and more formal co-ordination methods may be necessary.

(d) Groups have been shown to produce fewer ideas - though better evaluated - than the individuals of the group working separately. A group will often produce a better solution to a quiz than its best individual, since 'missing pieces' can be added to his or her performance.

Group norms

1.21 A work group establishes **norms** or acceptable levels and methods of behaviour, to which all members of the group are expected to conform. This group attitude will have a negative effect on an organisation if it sets unreasonably low production norms. Groups often apply unfair treatment or discrimination against others who break their rules.

1.22 Norms are partly the product of rôles and rôle expectations of how people in certain positions behave, as conceived by people in related positions.

Case example

In a classic experiment by Sherif, participants were asked to look at a fixed point of light in a black box in a darkroom. Although the point of light is fixed, it so happens that in the darkness, it *appears* to

move. Each participant was asked to say how far the light moved, and their individual estimates were recorded.

They were next put into a small group where each member of the group gave their own estimates to the others. From this interchange of opinions, individuals began to change their minds about how far the light had moved, and a group 'norm' estimate emerged.

When the groups were broken up, each individual was again asked to re-state his estimate; significantly, they retained the group norm estimate and rejected their previous individual estimate.

The experiment showed the effect of group psychology on establishing norms for the individual himself; even when, as in the case of the experiment, there is no factual basis for the group norm.

1.23 The general nature of group pressure is to require the individual to share in the group's own identity, and individuals may react to group norms and customs in a variety of ways.

- **Compliance** - toeing the line without real commitment
- **Internalisation** - full acceptance and identification
- **Counter-conformity** - rejecting the group and/or its norms

1.24 There are some circumstances which put strong pressure on the individual.

- The issue is not clear-cut.
- The individual lacks support for his own attitude or behaviour.
- The individual is exposed to other members of the group for a length of time.

1.25 Norms may be reinforced in various ways by the group.

(a) **Identification**: the use of badges, symbols, perhaps special modes of speech, in-jokes and so on - the marks of belonging, prestige and acceptance. There may even be initiation rites which mark the boundaries of membership.

(b) **Sanctions** of various kinds. Deviant behaviour may be dealt with by ostracising or ignoring the member concerned ('sending him to Coventry'), by ridicule or reprimand, even by physical hostility. The threat of expulsion is the final sanction.

In other words the group's power to induce conformity depends on the degree to which the individual values his membership of the group and the rewards it may offer, or wishes to avoid the negative sanctions at its disposal.

The Hawthorne Studies

1.26 The work of the **human relations school** of management theory sheds light on the importance of groups within an organisation. Interesting findings emerged from studies conducted at the Hawthorne plant of the *Western Electric Company*.

Case example

The experiments arose from an attempt by Western Electric to find out the effects of lighting standards on worker *productivity*. As a test, it moved a group of girls into a special room with variable lighting, and moved another group of girls into a room where the lighting was kept at normal standards. To the astonishment of the company management, productivity shot up in both rooms. When the lighting was then reduced in the first room, as a continuation of the test, not only did productivity continue to rise in the first room, but it also rose still further in the second room.

The conclusions of the studies were that individual members must be seen as part of a group, and that *informal* groups exercise a powerful influence in the workplace: supervisors and managers need to take account of social needs if they wish to secure commitment to organisational goals.

The Hawthorne studies were the first major attempt to undertake genuine social research, and to redirect attention to human factors at work. They are enduringly popular with managers, not least because they have an apparent simplicity and a straightforward, enthusiastically 'sold' message that 'happy workers are more productive', without over-attention to academic rigour, cautious qualification etc.

By modern standards of research, however, the methodology was 'less than rigorous in many respects' (G A Cole, *Personnel Management*). Human relations ideas were applied throughout the Western Electric Company - but didn't work. The programme was time-costly, as well as expensive; enthusiasm waned as the founders left. The conditions which made the initial experiments a success (the sense of status enjoyed by the girls in the Relay Assembly Test Room, because of their participation in the research) were no longer present when the experimental situation (the counselling service) was made available organisation-wide.

2 CONFLICT IN ORGANISATIONS

2.1 Some people consider that conflict is **avoidable**, caused by disruptive elements (troublemakers) and detrimental to organisational effectiveness. Others take the view that conflict is **inevitable**, part of change, caused by structural factors, for example the class system, and is useful (in small doses) if constructively handled.

The 'happy family' view

2.2 The happy family view presents organisations as **essentially harmonious**.

(a) They are co-operative structures, designed to achieve agreed common objectives, with no systematic conflict of interest.

(b) Management power is legitimate.

(c) Conflicts are **exceptional** and arise from aberrant incidents, such as misunderstandings, clashes of personality and external influences.

2.3 This kind of view is reasonably common in managerial literature, which attempts to come up with training and motivational techniques for dealing with conflicts which arise in what are seen as potentially conflict-free organisations. Conflict is thus blamed on bad management, lack of leadership, poor communication, or bloody-mindedness on the part of individuals or interest groups that impinge on the organisation. The theory is that a strong culture, good two-way communication, co-operation and motivational leadership will eliminate conflict. **Co-operation is assumed to be desirable and achievable.**

The conflict view

2.4 In contrast, there is the view of organisations as **arenas for conflict on individual and group levels**. Members battle for limited resources, status, rewards and professional values. Organisational politics involve constant struggles for control, and choices of structure, technology and organisational goals are part of this process. Individual and organisational interests will not always coincide.

2.5 Organisations may be seen as **political coalitions** of individuals and groups which have their own interests. Management has to create a workable structure for collaboration, taking into account the objectives of all the stakeholders in the organisation. A **mutual survival** strategy, involving the control of conflict through compromise, can be made acceptable in varying degrees to all concerned.

The evolutionary view

2.6 Conflict may be seen as a useful basis for **evolutionary** rather than revolutionary **change**. Conflict keeps the organisation **sensitive to the need to change**, while reinforcing its essential framework of control. The legitimate pursuit of competing interests can balance and preserve social and organisational arrangements. A flexible society benefits from conflict because such behaviour, by helping to create and modify norms, assumes its continuance under changed conditions.

2.7 This **constructive conflict** view may be the most useful for managers. It neither attempts to dodge the issues of conflict, which is an observable fact of life in most organisations; nor seeks to pull down existing organisational structures altogether.

Managers have to get on with the job of managing and upholding organisational goals with the co-operation of other members. We will therefore look more closely at the idea of **managing conflict**.

Constructive and destructive conflict

2.8 Given that conflict is inevitable, and assuming that organisational goals are broadly desirable, there are two aspects of conflict which are relevant in practice to the manager or administrator.

2.9 **Conflict can be highly desirable**. It can energise relationships and clarify issues. Hunt suggests that conflict can have constructive effects.

- It can introduce different solutions to problems.

- Power relationships can be defined more clearly.

- It may encourage creativity and the testing of ideas.

- It focuses attention on individual contributions.

- It brings emotions out into the open.

- It can release hostile feelings.

2.10 Conflict can also be **destructive**.

- It may distract attention from the task.
- It can polarise views and dislocate the group.
- Objectives may be subverted in favour of secondary goals.
- It encourages defensive or spoiling behaviour.
- It may result in disintegration of the group
- Emotional, win-lose conflicts may be stimulated.

Case example

Tjosvold and Deerner researched conflict in different contexts. They allocated to 66 student volunteers the roles of foremen and workers at an assembly plant, with a scenario of conflict over job rotation schemes. Foremen were against, workers for.

One group was told that the organisational norm was to 'avoid controversy'; another was told that the norm was 'co-operative controversy', *trying* to agree; a third was told that groups were out to win any arguments that arose, 'competitive controversy'. The students were offered rewards for complying with their given norms. Their decisions, and attitudes to the discussions, were then monitored.

(a) Where controversy was avoided, the foremen's views dominated.

(b) Competitive controversy brought no agreement - but brought out feelings of hostility and suspicion.

(c) Co-operative controversy brought out differences in an atmosphere of curiosity, trust and openness: the decisions reached seemed to integrate the views of both parties.

But can real managers and workers be motivated to comply with useful organisational 'norms' in this way?

2.11 Handy redefined conflict to offer a useful way of thinking about destructive and constructive conflict and how it might be managed. He observed that organisations are political systems within which resources are scarce and influence unequal. The resulting differences between people emerge in three ways.

- Argument
- Competition
- Conflict

Only **conflict** is considered harmful. **Argument** and **competition** are potentially beneficial and fruitful; both may **degenerate** into conflict if badly managed.

2.12 **Argument** means resolving differences by discussion; this can encourage integration of a number of viewpoints into a better solution. Handy suggests two prerequisites for argument to be effective.

(a) The arguing group must have shared leadership, mutual trust, and a challenging task.

(b) The logic of the argument must be preserved - the issues under discussion must be classified, the discussion must concentrate on available information, and the values of the individuals must be expressed openly and taken into account.

Otherwise, argument will be frustrated. If this is so, or if the argument itself is merely the symptom of an underlying, unexpressed conflict, then conflict will be the result.

2.13 **Competition** can be constructive.

- It sets standards, by establishing best performance through comparison.
- It motivates individuals to better efforts.
- 'It sorts out the men from the boys'.

2.14 In order to be fruitful, competition must be perceived by the participants to be **open,** rather than **closed.** 'Closed' competition is a win-lose (or 'zero-sum') situation, where one party's gain will be another party's loss. 'Open' competition exists where all participants can increase their gains - for example productivity bargaining.

2.15 If competition is perceived to be open, the rules are seen to be fair, and the determinants of success are within the competitors' control, competition can be extremely fruitful. The observations of Peters and Waterman on the motivational effect of comparative performance information supports this view. If these preconditions are not met, competition may again degenerate into conflict.

3   CONFLICT: GROUPS AND DEPARTMENTS

3.1 Much of the work of the organisation is carried out in groups of one sort of another. There are particular problems in how groups work. Research into group dynamics indicates some of the underlying issues of groups and how they behave.

Group cohesion, competition and conflict

Conflict within groups

3.2 In an experiment reported by *Deutsch* (1949), psychology students were given puzzles and human relation problems to work at in discussion groups. Some groups ('co-operative' ones) were told that the grade each individual got at the end of the course would depend on the performance of his group. Other groups ('competitive' ones) were told that each student would receive a grade according to his own contributions.

3.3 No significant differences were found between the two kinds of group in the amount of interest and involvement in the tasks, or in the amount of learning. But the co-operative groups, compared with the competitive ones, had greater productivity per unit time, better quality of product and discussion, greater co-ordination of effort and sub-division of activity, more diversity in amount of contribution per member, more attentiveness to fellow members and more friendliness during discussion.

Conflict between groups

3.4 *Sherif and Sherif* conducted a number of experiments into groups and competing groups.

(a) People tend to identify with a group.

(b) New members of a group quickly learn the norms and attitudes of the others, no matter whether these are positive or negative, friendly or hostile. It is also suggested that inter-group competition may have a positive effect on group cohesion and performance.

3.5 **Within a group** the following effects might be found when the group is competing with another group.

(a) Members close ranks, and submerge their differences; loyalty and conformity are demanded.

(b) The climate changes from informal and sociable to work and task-oriented; individual needs are subordinated to achievement.

(c) Leadership moves from democratic to autocratic, with the group's acceptance.

(d) The group tends to become more structured and organised.

3.6 **Between competing groups** the following effects occur.

(a) The opposing group begins to be perceived as the enemy.

(b) Perception is distorted, presenting an idealised picture of 'us' and a negative stereotype of 'them'.

(c) Inter-group communication decreases.

3.7 In a win-lose situation, where competition is not perceived to result in benefits for both sides, **the winning group will display the following characteristics.**

- Cohesion
- Relaxation into a complacent, playful state
- Return to group maintenance and concern for members' needs
- Assertion of its group self-concept with little re-evaluation

3.8 **The losing group will behave differently**.

(a) It may deny defeat if possible, or place the blame on the arbitrator, or the system.

(b) It may lose its cohesion and splinter into conflict, as blame is apportioned.

(c) It may be keyed-up, fighting mad.

(d) It might turn towards work-orientation to regroup, rather than members' needs or group maintenance.

(e) It will tend to learn by re-evaluating its perceptions of itself and the other group. It is more likely to become a cohesive and effective unit once the defeat has been accepted.

3.9 Members of a group will act in unison if the group's existence or patterns of behaviour are threatened from outside. Cohesion is naturally assumed to be the result of positive factors such as communication, agreement and mutual trust - but in the face of a common enemy (competition, crisis or emergency) cohesion and productivity benefit. *Lipitt and White* indicated that the degree of aggression displayed by a group can also be related to **leadership style**. Groups led in an **authoritarian** way tended to be aggressive.

Cohesion and 'group think'

3.10 It is possible for groups to be *too* cohesive, too all-absorbing. If a group is completely absorbed with its own maintenance, members and priorities, it can become dangerously blinkered to what is going on around it, and may confidently forge ahead in a completely wrong direction. *I L Janis* describes this as **group think**: 'the psychological drive for consensus at any cost, that suppresses dissent and appraisal of alternatives in cohesive decision-making groups.'

3.11 The cosy consensus of the group prevents consideration of alternatives, constructive criticism or conflict. Group think displays a number of symptons.

- A sense of invulnerability - blindness to the risk involved in pet strategies
- Rationalisations for inconsistent facts
- Moral blindness - 'might is right'
- A tendency to stereotype outsiders and enemies
- Strong group pressure to quell dissent
- Self-censorship by members - not rocking the boat
- Perception of unanimity - filtering out divergent views
- Mutual support and solidarity to guard the decision

3.12 Highly political organisations and areas of the organisation structure - for example the top and centre - also tend to put pressure on individuals to 'avoid rocking the boat' - whether this be expressed as cultural control (through tradition and shared values) or as more overt rules and sanctions.

3.13 Since by definition a group suffering from group think is highly resistant to criticism, recognition of failure and unpalatable information, it is not easy to break such a group out of its vicious circle.

- Self-criticism must be actively encouraged.
- Outside ideas and evaluation must be welcomed.
- The group must be encouraged to respond positively to conflicting evidence.

Group sub-cultures and conflict

3.14 Sub-cultures are cultures which exist in a context otherwise dominated by the decisions, values and attitudes of others. *AK Cohen*, among other sociologists, defines sub-cultures as 'cultures which exist within cultures', with three major characteristics.

(a) The group shares a distinctive way of life, knowledge, beliefs, codes, tastes and prejudices.

(b) These are learned from others in the group who already exhibit these characteristics.

(c) Their way of life has 'somehow become traditional' among those who inherit and share the social conditions to which the subcultural characteristics are a response.

3.15 If managers wish to integrate divisionalised structures or geographically dispersed branches, for example, by promoting a strong central culture, they may encounter resistance among the sub-units.

3.16 In any organisation which adopts **cultural control** as its means of control, the issue of sub-cultures is important if they are a threat to the powerful organisation cultures to which all must adhere. This is why recruitment processes are interested in personality as much as technical skills.

Causes and tactics of conflict between departments

3.17 Conflict behaviour in which group dynamics might be evident comes to the fore in the rivalry between individual departments. It is possible to identify several **causes of conflict** between departments.

(a) **Operative goal incompatibility**. Conflict may be caused by differences in the goals of different groups (or individuals). It is a function of management to create a system of planning whereby individual or group goals are formulated within the framework of a strategic plan and to provide leadership, and to encourage individuals to accept the goals of the organisation as being compatible with their personal goals.

(b) **Differentiation. People in different business functions often differ in personality** from those in other functions (eg sales staff and accountants). Personal differences, as regards goals, attitudes and feelings, are also bound to crop up.

(c) **Task interdependence**. The dependence of one department on another (eg for resources or information) may be a cause of conflict if the relationship is badly managed.

(d) **Scarcity of resources**. Resources are a source of power: managers fight for them. Departments may be given excessive targets given limited resources.

(e) **Power distribution. Conflict may also be caused by disputes about the boundaries of authority**. Staff managers may attempt to encroach on the roles of line managers and usurp some of their authority, while departments might start empire building and try to take over the work previously done by other departments.

(f) **Uncertainty**. Conflict can arise in times of change, where new problems arise.

(g) The **reward system** can encourage conflict, for instance, if incentives are designed in a way that rewards one department whilst penalising another.

Exam focus point
Interdepartmental conflict was covered as an essay question in May 1996 and again in May 1999.

4 POLITICAL BEHAVIOUR

4.1 One of the main spheres in which reality disrupts the rational ideal of organisations is politics. Political behaviour is broadly concerned with competition, conflict, rivalry and power relationships in organisations. Organisations are political systems in the sense that they are composed of individuals and groups who have their own interests, priorities and goals: there is competition for finite resources, power and influence; there are cliques, alliances, pressure groups and blocking groups, centred around values, opinions and objectives which may be opposed by others.

4.2 **Aspects of organisational politics**

(a) Individuals wish to experience victory and avoid defeat. They have their own objectives which are not always reconcilable with those of the organisation.

(b) There are inevitable disparities of power and influence in hierarchical organisations - and despite rational organisation designs, events are in reality decided by dominant individuals or coalitions within and/or outside the organisation. Other individuals tend to want to influence, join or overthrow the dominant coalition.

(c) Organisations are constantly involved in compromise, reconciling or controlling differences, and settling for reality rather than the ideal.

(d) **Territory** is a useful analogy for the jealousies and rivalries over boundaries of authority, specialisms and spheres of influence.

(e) Political behaviour might be characteristic of the **informal organisation,** where mangers do each other favours in search of influence.

4.3 *Mintzberg (Power In and Around Organisations)* identifies various **political games**, which can be stimulating for the organisation, but can also degenerate into harmful, all-absorbing conflict.

(a) Games to resist authority - to sabotage the aims of superiors

(b) Games to counter this resistance - the imposition of rules and controls by superiors

(c) Games to build power bases - associating with useful superiors, forming alliances among colleagues, gaining the support of subordinates, getting control of information or resources

(d) Games to defeat rivals - inter-group or inter-departmental conflict

(e) Games to change the organisation - higher power struggles, or rebellion

4.4 **The advantage of political activity is that it is a way of achieving some sort of consensus when there is great uncertainty**. Political activities at senior levels can be said to occur in the following cases.

(a) **Structural change**. Structural changes strike at the heart of the relationships of power and authority in an organisation and are thus intensely political, as people jockey for position in the new order.

(b) **Interdepartmental co-ordination**. In functionally organised businesses, different parts of the organisation do very different jobs and co-ordination between them may be poor. This might lead to turf wars. In a geographically organised business, strong area managements may try to assume for themselves some of the power of the corporate centre: given that the middle line exerts a pull to balkanise (embodying a force for concentration) we should expect political behaviour.

(c) **Management succession**. This involves hire and fire and promotion decisions.

(d) **Allocation of resources**. Departments in organisations compete for scarce resources. These can be allocated **rationally** (eg by investment appraisal methods) or **politically** by bargaining.

Political tactics

4.5 There are a number of approaches an individual manager of department can take in an organisation characterised by political behaviour.

(a) **Increase the power base**, for example by creating and exploiting resource power (dependency), reducing uncertainties or satisfying strategic contingencies. The meaning of these terms was described in the previous section of this chapter.

(b) **Build coalitions** with other internal groups, or with powerful external groups. This technique is used in boardroom 'coups' where executives will try to muster the support of shareholders to be rid of an unpopular or ineffective chief executive.

(c) **Expand networks** with other managers. This means effectively exploiting the informal organisation.

(d) **Constrain the decisions**. In other words, set the agenda for decision-making by posing 'problems' and suggesting 'solutions'.

(e) **Withhold information**. A manager who lacks some important information will be in a weak position for making decisions or urging his own views.

(f) **Present information in a distorted manner**. This will enable the group or manager presenting the information to get their own way more easily. For example, if the engineering department wants to introduce a new item of equipment into service, they might give biased information about likely teething troubles with the equipment's technology or the expected costs of maintenance, or breakdown times.

(g) A group (especially a specialist group such as accounting) which considers its influence to be neglected **might seek to impose rules, procedures, restrictions or official requirements** on other groups, in order to bolster up their own importance.

(h) **By-pass formal channels of communication** and decision-making by establishing informal contacts and friendships with people in a position of importance.

5 MANAGERIAL RESPONSE TO CONFLICT

5.1 *Hunt* identifies five different initial management responses to the handling of conflict - not all of which are effective.

(a) **Denial/withdrawal**. If the conflict is very trivial, it may indeed 'blow over' without an issue being made of it, but if the causes are not identified, the conflict may grow to unmanageable proportions.

(b) **Suppression** - smoothing over, to preserve working relationships despite minor conflicts. As Hunt remarks, however: 'Some cracks cannot be papered over'.

(c) **Dominance** - the application of power or influence to settle the conflict. The disadvantage of this is that it creates all the lingering resentment and hostility of 'win-lose' situations.

(d) **Compromise** - bargaining, negotiating, conciliating. To some extent, this will be inevitable in any organisation made up of different individuals. However, individuals tend to exaggerate their positions to allow for compromise, and compromise itself is seen to weaken the value of the decision, perhaps reducing commitment.

(e) **Integration/collaboration**. Emphasis must be put on the task, individuals must accept the need to modify their views for its sake, and group effort must be seen to be superior to individual effort.

5.2 Often the problem might be firstly to deal with the symptoms, by reducing conflict behaviour, and then deal with the causes of the conflict by encouraging co-operative attitudes.

5.3 The conflict behaviour might be reduced in the following ways.

(a) **Structural separation**. Design the organisation structure so that individuals, groups or departments in conflict have no dealings with each other. This is hardly a long-term solution: in most organisations people need to work together.

(b) **Bureaucratic authority**. Conflict is controlled from above, by people with position power. Again this is a short-term solution, as it will merely encourage political behaviour by the departments in conflict with each other.

(c) **Limited communication**. Again, this is a short-term solution in which inter-departmental communications are restricted.

5.4 Co-operative behaviour might be encouraged in the following ways.

(a) **Integration devices,** such as joint problem-solving teams, force people to work together, and, it is hoped, will encourage co-operative attitudes. A co-ordinator may be appointed.

(b) **Confrontation and negotiation** requires that the members in conflict are forced to hammer out a solution. It is important how the situation is presented to the conflicting parties. A **win-lose strategy** implies that there will be one winner and one loser. Each negotiating party will pursue solely its own interest, will be unwilling to negotiate and will be deceitful and manipulative. A **win-win strategy** presents the conflict as a problem to be solved, not a battle to be won by one of the parties.

(c) **Consultants** can be brought in, as objective arbitrators or catalysts for improving communications, exposing group think and stereotyping and acting as an 'honest broker'. In the UK, the government-sponsored *Advisory Conciliation and Arbitration Service* (ACAS) has played this role.

(d) **Job rotation**. Personnel are swapped between the conflicting departments.

(e) **Super-ordinate goals**. Here senior managers set goals which require the conflicting departments to co-operate in a meaningful way.

(f) **Intergroup training**. People from conflicting departments can be sent on joint training courses to break down barriers and encourage communication.

5.5 **Conflict between management and organised labour** is more problematic. **Collective bargaining** between management and labour has been the traditional way in which pay has been negotiated. Joint management-union committees can help on certain issues. Works

councils with employee representatives are compulsory in most of the EU (except the UK). Union attitudes have also changed, with single-union agreements and no strike agreements.

Chapter roundup

- Groups are central to organisation life. Teams have a 'sense of identity' which a random crowd of individuals does not possess.

- Organisations are using teams increasingly often. Multi-skilled teams contain people who, as individuals, possess many skills. A multi-disciplinary team brings together specialists in different areas.

- The stages of team development are forming, storming, norming and performing. There needs to be a suitable mix of people.

- Conflict can be viewed as inevitable owing to the class system; a continuation of organisation politics by other means; something to be welcomed as it avoids complacency; something resulting from poor management, or something which should be avoided at all costs.

- Conflict is possible owing to the different degrees of power, influence and authority that different groups have. Negative power, for example, is the power to disrupt. Position power derives from formal authority. Resource power can be used to enforce dependency.

- Conflict can be constructive, if it introduces new information into a problem, if it defines a problem, or if it encourages creativity. It can be destructive if it distracts attention from the task or inhibits communication.

- Causes of conflict include operative goal incompatibility, differentiation, interdependence, resource scarcity, power, uncertainty and rewards.

- Conflict can be managed by separating the conflicting parties, restricting communication or imposing a solution. A number of techniques are available actively to promote cooperative behaviour.

- Some conflicts at work arise out of stress, frustration and alienation endured by the individual for a number of reasons. Such behaviour might be a response to management style.

- A symptom of suppressed conflict perhaps results in the existence of counter-cultures, distinct from the official corporate culture, in the workplace.

Quick quiz

1   What is the function of groups and teams?

2   Distinguish between multi-skilled and multi-disciplinary teams.

3   What are the stages of team formation?

4   List typical roles in a team.

5   What is the 'happy family' view of conflict?

6   Why might conflict be desirable?

7   What causes conflict between departments?

8   Give some examples of political behaviour.

9   How should managers respond to conflict?

Answers to quick quiz

1   Working in teams allows connected tasks to be shared and hence completed more quickly. It also allows for specialisation and the division of labour.

2   Members of multi-skilled teams each have more than one skill. Members of multi-disciplinary teams each bring different expertise to the group task.

3   Forming, norming, storming and performing, according to Belbin.

4   Chair, shaper, plant, monitor-evaluator, resource investigator, implementer, team worker and finisher.

5   Organisations are essentially harmonious and conflict is an aberration to be cured.

6   It can encourage creativity and produce new solutions; power relationships and individual contributions are made clear; it may discharge emotional tension.

7   Incompatibility of goals; character differences between typical group members; task interdependence; scarcity of resources; encroachment; uncertainty; the reward system.

8   Building a power base; building coalitions; withholding information; setting agenda; distorting information; imposing authority; by-passing formal channels.

9   Denial, suppression, dominance, compromise and integration are all possible approaches and each has its uses.

Now try the question below from the Exam Question Bank

Number	Level	Marks	Time
Q15	Exam	18	32 mins

Part E
Management of change

Chapter 16

STRATEGIES FOR CRITICAL PERIODS

Topic list	Syllabus reference	Ability required
1 Maintaining effectiveness in times of change	(v)	Evaluation
2 Models of growth and development	(v)	Evaluation
3 Issues of size	(v)	Evaluation
4 Contraction and decline	(v)	Evaluation
5 Structural reorganisation and divestment	(v)	Evaluation

Introduction

Change is a feature of the organisation's environment and requires the organisation to change as well in many different ways. This chapter explores some of these issues. It integrates many of the topics discussed elsewhere in the text, including organisation structure, culture, learning and innovation.

- In Section 1 we describe the circumstances in which organisations typically have to introduce change or react to environmental turbulence. Effectiveness, as discussed in Chapter 2, is has to be maintained over time (Section 1). Organisations must therefore continually *adjust* their activities to cope with this.

- Some people suggest organisations might pass through a life cycle. Evolution and revolution feature together. Greiner's model (Section 2) suggests that the *size* and *range* of a business's activities create problems which have to be solved.

- Change can cause growth and also organisational decline (environmental entropy, vulnerability, organisational atrophy). Many firms fail to accommodate themselves to the necessity for continuous change. Both growth and decline can require structural change (Section 5).

Learning outcomes covered in this chapter

- Evaluate the determinants of change in organisations and the different levels at which change must be managed.

- Explain the process of organisational development and the problems associated with it.

- Evaluate how the organisation and its managers might deal with major critical periods in the development of the organisation.

Syllabus content covered in this chapter

- The impact on the organisation of external and internal change triggers (eg environment factors, mergers and acquisitions, re-organisation and rationalisation)

- The importance of managing critical periods of change (start-up, rapid expansion, re-organisation, merger, redundancy programmes, close-down) and the ways in which these periods can be managed effectively

- Approaches to the management of organisational development and major cultural and structural change (eg Kanter, Lewin, Peters)

BPP PUBLISHING

1   MAINTAINING EFFECTIVENESS IN TIMES OF CHANGE

1.1   Change, in the context of organisation and management, could relate to a number of matters.

    (a) **Changes in the environment**. These could be changes in what competitors are doing, what customers are buying, how they spend their money, changes in the law, changes in social behaviour and attitudes, economic changes, and so on.

    (b) **Changes in the products the organisation makes, or the services it provides**. These are made in response to changes in customer demands, competitors' actions, new technology, and so on.

    (c) **Changes in technology and changes in working methods**. These changes are also in response to environmental change such as the advent of new technology and new laws on safety at work.

    (d) **Changes in management and working relationships**. For example, changes in leadership style, and in the way that employees are encouraged to work together. Also changes in training and development.

    (e) **Changes in organisation structure or size**. These might involve creating new departments and divisions, greater delegation of authority or more centralisation, changes in the way that plans are made, management information is provided and control is exercised, and so on. Organisation re-structuring will be made in response to changes of the types discussed above.

1.2   **Organisational change thus has two aspects.**

    • The original **source** of change - usually, an **environmental change**.
    • A **change within the organisation**, made in response to another change.

1.3   *Buckley and Perkins* made a distinction between **change** and **transformation**. **Change** is gradual and small, whereas **transformation** is change on a significant scale.

    (a) **Organisational transformation** includes major changes in structure, procedures and jobs.

    (b) **Transformation in the way the system operates** involves major changes in communication patterns and working relationships and processes.

    (c) **Transformation in employee consciousness** involves major changes in the way that things are viewed, involving shifts in attitudes, beliefs and myths.

The nature of change

1.4   **New technology**

    • Computerisation
    • New products
    • New working methods
    • Better management information systems

1.5   **Reorganisation**

    (a) A company is taken over, and so has to adopt the organisation policies of the new parent company

    (b) Growth causes reorganisation into divisions, or more specialist functional departments

    (c) Divestment of businesses

(d)   A drive to keep costs down leads to cost cutting measures such as job losses

1.6   Working conditions

- New offices
- Shorter working week
- More varied work times
- More outsourcing, ie giving work to outsiders
- Greater emphasis on occupational health

1.7   Personnel policies

(a)   Changes in rules and procedures - for instance, about smoking at work

(b)   Promotions, transfers, separation of employees, training and development, problems perhaps growing in complexity

1.8   Philosophy of management (relations between management and employees)

(a)   A new senior manager may introduce new style of leadership.

(b)   The attitudes of managers and employees may change over time, perhaps leading to greater participation of subordinates in decision-making.

(c)   Communications with employees may become more open.

(d)   There may be greater collaboration between management and trade unions in labour relations.

1.9   At this point you should refer back to at *Burns and Stalker's* theories on mechanistic and organic organisations. Clearly the nature of the organisation in this sense will affect its success or failure when dealing with change.

Effectiveness over time

1.10   Organisations develop over time and a problem for managers is to maintain the organisation's effectiveness in the face of changes in the environment, the availability of resources and competition for them, and the changed expectations of stakeholders.

1.11   Some people suggest that there is an **organisational life cycle**, with four broad stages.

- The organisation is established.
- There is a period of expansion, as the organisation grows in size and scope.
- A period of maturity ensues, when expansion slackens off.
- The organisation begins to decline.

1.12   **Such a life cycle is not inevitable, providing the organisation shows it is able to adapt.** A useful way of visualising this concept is *Handy's* **Sigmoid Curve**.

BPP PUBLISHING

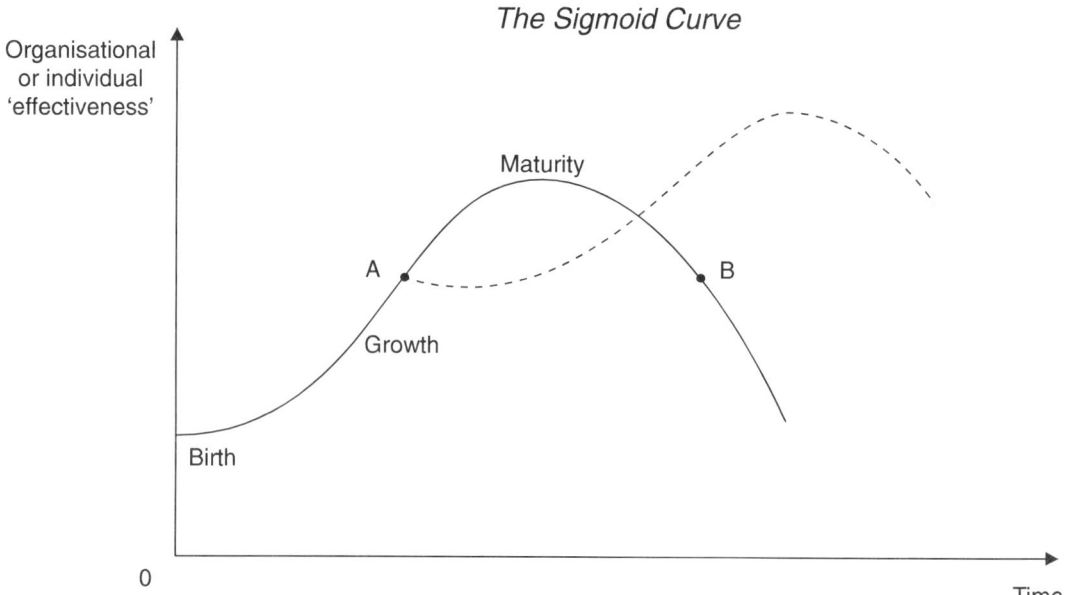

The Sigmoid Curve

1.13 Corporate (or individual) readiness to change and adapt often only occurs at point B on the sigmoid curve, **when the entity is already in crisis** through sustained losses (if it is an organisation) or enforced redundancy or early retirement (if an individual). Rare is the organisation/individual who begins to prepare for change at point A, while still on the upward growth phase in the cycle - yet that it exactly what is necessary nowadays so that, from point A, another sigmoid curve can begin - and survival/prosperity becomes more probable.

Case example

Apple Computers invented the first popular PC and, with the Macintosh, the first widely available user-friendly interface. It did not license its technology to other manufacturers for many years, which meant that it failed to set the 'industry standard'. Microsoft won by avoiding hardware and licensing its operating system (MS DOS and now Windows) to many manufacturers. Apple has now decided to devote itself to a niche and to make it easier for software firms to write programmes for its operating system.

1.14 Undoubtedly, the sigmoid curve has resonance with our experience of organisations and individuals.

(a) Many people remain unemployed for long periods when made redundant because they have not kept their skills and knowledge up to date with changing requirements; large numbers, perhaps less excusably, are more or less totally unprepared for retirement and the sudden change from activity to enforced inactivity which this represents.

(b) Equally, organisations can be very resistant to changes suggested while they are still in the growth phase of the sigmoid curve, their collective attitude perhaps being epitomised by the colloquial phrase, 'If it ain't broke, don't fix it'.

Case example

When Paul Chambers was head of ICI in the 1970s, he proposed organisational changes which were rejected by the ICI board at a time when the company was still enjoying impressive profits; John Harvey-Jones was able to implement similar changes in the 1980s when ICI, in effect, was at point B in the sigmoid curve, having registered its first losses for many years.

Organisational department

> ### KEY TERM
>
> 'Organisational development is a generic term embracing a wide range of intervention strategies into the social processes of an organisation.' *Mullins, Management and Organisational Behaviour*

1.15 **Organisation development (OD)** is an integrated process that attempts to improve the overall performance and effectiveness of an organisation by developing the individuals and groups it is composed of. It has a number of elements, each of which will have different relevance to any given organisational situation.

1.16 A number of processes may be regarded as central to OD.

    (a) **Change management** is dealt with in the next chapter.

    (b) **Management development** is a holistic process, both responding to the organisation's needs and promoting individual personal development. The aim is to develop management skills *throughout* the organisation, not just among those labelled 'manager' so that everything encompassed in the management of the organisation is improved.

    (c) Development of **organisational culture** where required, so that if supports and aims and processes involved in developing the organisation.

    (d) Improvement of the **motivational element**, which includes employee attitudes, commitment and morale.

    (e) Resolution of **conflict** within the organisation.

1.17 OD makes use of a range of intervention strategies, including those listed below.

    (a) Management training based on the *Blake and Mouton Managerial Grid* discussed in Chapter 14. The aim is to promote a 9, 9 orientation: that is, maximum concern for both people and production. This type of management development is called **grid training**.

    (b) **Sensitivity training**. Small, unstructured group meetings (called T-groups) are used to increase sensitivity to emotional reactions in others and in oneself.

    (c) **Team building** attempts to improve work group performance by attention to task procedures, interpersonal relationships and patterns of interaction within the group.

    (d) **Attitudes** are investigated by the use of **survey questionnaires**. Work groups are involved in the interpretation of the data and the development of action plans.

1.18 Mullins sums up OD like this.

> 'OD is action-oriented and tailored to suit specific needs. It takes a number of forms with varying levels of intervention. OD concerns itself with the examination of organisational health and the implementation of planned change. This may include training in interpersonal skills, sensitivity training, and methods and techniques relating to motivational processes, patterns of communication, styles of leadership and managerial behaviour.
>
> Although an OD programme is legitimised by the formal system it focuses on both the formal and the informal system. The initial intervention strategy is usually though the informal system, which includes feelings, informal actions and interactions, group norms and values, and which forms part of the culture of an organisation'

2   MODELS OF GROWTH AND DEVELOPMENT

Growth

2.1   **Organisations grow in a number of ways**.

- Sales revenue (a growth in the number of markets served)
- Profitability (in absolute terms, and as a return on capital)
- Number of goods/services sold
- Number of outlets/sites
- Number of employees
- Number of countries

2.2   **Reasons for growth**

(a) **A genuine increasing demand for the products/services**. For example, there is likely to be a growth in the number of UK hospitals specialising in geriatric illnesses, simply because the number of elderly people in the population is expected to rise.

(b) **Growth can be necessary for an organisation to compete effectively. Economies of scale** can arise from producing in bulk, as high fixed costs can be spread over more units of output.

(c) **The managers of the organisation like growth**, as it increases their power and rewards.

(d) **Shareholders can see growth as a means of increasing their wealth**, in many cases.

(e) Companies take over in order to gain **control over resources**, or the value added at different stages of the supply chain.

2.3   Organisational growth in size can occur by **acquisition** or **organically** (ie generated by an expansion of the organisation's activities). It is to **organic growth** that we shall now turn.

Greiner's model

2.4   An **organisation life cycle model** was suggested by *Greiner*. It assumes that, as an organisation **ages**, it grows in **size**, measured, perhaps by the **number of employees** and **diversity** of activities. This growth takes place in discrete phases. Each phase is characterised by two things.

(a) **Evolution**. This is a distinctive factor that **directs** the organisation's growth.

(b) **Revolution**. There may be a **crisis**, through which the organisation must pass before starting the next phase.

2.5   Greiner identified five phases.

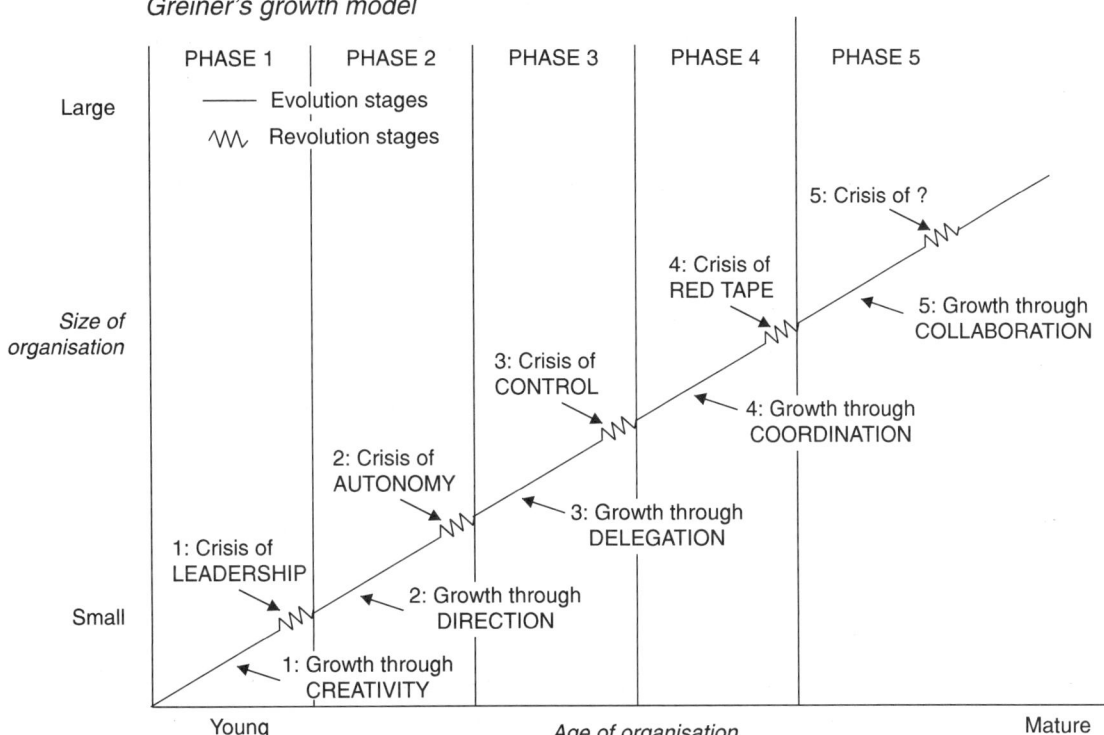

Greiner's growth model

Phase 1

(a) **Growth through creativity**. The organisation is small, and is managed in a personal and informal way. The founders of the business are actively involved in operations, personnel issues and innovation. Apple Computers, for example, started up in a garage. The product range is probably limited. A key goal is survival.

(b) **Crisis of leadership**. Sooner or later there comes a need for distinct **management skills**, relating less to products and marketing issues and more to the co-ordination of the organisation's activities.

Phase 2

(a) **Growth through direction**. Clear direction is provided in response to the crisis of leadership by **professionalising** the management. At the same time, there are more employees. Their initial enthusiasm might be tempered by loss of autonomy and the growth of hierarchy.

(b) **Crisis of autonomy**. Delegation becomes a problem. The top finds it harder and harder to keep in detailed control as there are too many activities, and it is easy to lose a sense of the wider picture. **Employees resent the lack of initiative and their performance falters**.

Phase 3

(a) **Growth through delegation**. The response to the crisis of autonomy in Phase 2 is delegation. This has the advantage of decentralising decision-making and giving confidence to junior managers.

(b) **Crisis of control**. Delegation leads to additional problems of co-ordination and control. **Over-delegation can result in different departments acting sub-optimally**, in other words pursuing their own departmental goals to the detriment of the organisation as a whole.

Phase 4

(a) **Growth through co-ordination**. The addition of internal systems, procedures and so forth aims to ensure co-ordination of activities and optimal use of resources, without reverting to the detailed hands-on methods in Phase 1. You might expect to see more complex management accounting systems, transfer pricing procedures, and some central management functions.

(b) **Crisis of red tape**. The new procedures **inhibit useful action**.

Phase 5

(a) **Growth through collaboration**. The crisis of red tape is resolved by **increased informal collaboration. Control is cultural rather than formal**. People participate in teams.

(b) This growth stage may lead to a '**crisis of psychological saturation**', in which all become exhausted by teamwork. (Greiner did not name this crisis, hence the question mark in the diagram.) Greiner postulates a sixth growth phase involving a dual organisation: a 'habit' structure for daily work routines and a 'reflective structure' for stimulating new perspectives and personal enrichment.

2.6 Greiner's model refers to evolutionary organisational **growth** punctuated by revolutionary **crisis**.

2.7 *Quinn's* concept of **logical incrementalism**, which we encountered in our study of strategy in Chapter 1, is an alternative approach to the nature of organisational growth. Businesses make small adjustments, building consistently on what they have, and adapting to the environment. Change is continuous and gradual. Quinn's model was based, like Greiner's, on a study of real organisations.

Criticisms of organisation life cycle models

Formation

2.8 **Early stages**. Not all organisations are founded by a visionary controlling entrepreneur, selling a product or service.

(a) A new organisation can be formed from the **merger of two existing ones**.

(b) Two or more companies might **collaborate on a joint venture**. The Airbus project, for example, did not start as a small business, but as a result of co-operation between governments and existing companies.

(c) New organisations are created by existing ones and have a substantial complement of staff.

Too many issues

2.9 **The models combine too many issues**: organisation structure, organisation culture, product/market scope, leadership, management style and reward systems. A business can grow quickly in some aspects but not in others. The UK **niche retailers** of the 1980s expanded in terms of the number of sites, locations, employees, and profits growth, but the **product/market scope was very restricted**.

Growth is not the same as effectiveness

2.10 Many organisations can be effective without growth. In fact, growth is **not** the normal state of affairs for many organisations. For example, a doctor's practice can be effective without treating ever-increasing numbers of patients, and an orchestra reaches a maximum size when it needs no more players.

2.11 It is possible to combine a bureaucratic obsession with procedures and efficiency with a strong sense of purpose. Hospitals depend on the devotion and professionalism of staff - but clinical procedures have to be adhered to.

No timescale

2.12 **It gives no idea of the timescale involved.**

(a) For example, the early stages may be very rapid, or may take several years. The longer it takes, the easier, it might be for the organisation to adjust, and no crises may punctuate the process.

(b) Growth models imply a **linear development** over time, whereas the organisation might enjoy different rates of growth at different times of the life cycle, or even decline.

(c) It is not always easy to assess the phase of the life cycle any organisation is actually going through.

Ignores environment and competition

2.13 **The models do not clearly indicate the relationship with the environment.** Organisational growth partly depends on environmental factors.

2.14 The growth of the business can be curtailed by the **growth of competition**. In other words, a business can be hemmed in, but still survive and even prosper.

Case example

Some years ago, an American firm saw a sudden surge in demand for Cabbage Patch dolls, which were relatively unsophisticated toys. The manufacturer expanded operations rapidly, but by the next year, demand had faded significantly.

Question 1

Heifetz and Kyung are partners in a business that makes violins and other stringed musical instruments. They are based in a small workshop in Stoke Newington, north London. They are both experts at their craft. They believe that their future is rosy: Kyung, in particular, realises that as western classical music becomes popular in China, Japan and other Asian countries, demand for instruments will pick up.

Although there is enough demand in the UK to keep them going, both want to expand the business. Kyung asks her brother, who lives in Hong Kong, to help them market their products to Asian orchestras and violinists. Kyung's brother has sent them a number of official forms relating to customs, import and export, and some ideas as to agents. With global trade liberalisation, they assume that exporting will be easy. Heifetz and Kyung hire and train three more skilled instrument-makers.

Required

What issues relating to Greiner's life cycle model are raised by this scenario?

Answer

(a) Although the firm is small, it will very soon need specialist assistance. Despite trade liberalisation, exporting inevitably involves red tape: time must be spent dealing with bureaucracies, filling in VAT forms, and managing relationships with distributors. In addition, somebody has to look after the firm's accounts.

(b) The business shows characteristics of a pre-bureaucratic stage, but it needs detailed technical expertise as mentioned in (a) above. Operations will become bureaucratic, simply to deal with the export side of things.

Greiner's model cannot predict how every organisation will grow as each faces its own unique problems. But it does indicate some of the issues that can arise. You should treat it as a broad generalisation that admits of many exceptions, or as a tool to help you think about organisations, rather than a scientific law.

---

3 ISSUES OF SIZE

Large organisations

3.1 A large organisation uses lots of resources and, typically, employs a lot of people. The problems of large organisations stem mainly from the difficulties of getting a lot of people to work well together. How can large numbers of people share the work that has to be done, and how can their work be properly planned, co-ordinated and controlled?

(a) **Organisation structure**

    (i) **Sharing out tasks and responsibilities**. Who does what?

    (ii) How much **specialisation/functionalisation** should there be?

    (ii) **How many levels of management should there be**? There is a tendency for the management hierarchy to develop **too many levels**. The more management levels there are, the greater the problem of communication between top and bottom, and the greater the problems of control and direction by management at the top.

    (iv) **Delegation**. To what extent should authority be delegated? How much centralisation/decentralisation should there be? Can junior/middle managers be trusted to exercise discretion and make decisions? How should managers be trained and developed?

(b) **Planning and control**

    (i) How should the organisation identify its objectives and set targets for achievement?

    (ii) **MIS**. Formal management information systems to enable managers to plan and control properly must be developed.

    (iii) **Accountability**. The problem of making managers accountable, monitoring performance and setting up effective control systems.

    (iv) **Co-ordination**. The difficulties of co-ordinating the efforts of managers: problems of conflict (line versus staff; interdepartmental rivalries etc).

    (v) **Reward**. Difficulties of setting up a system of rewards that is directly linked to performance appraisal and the achievement of objectives.

    (vi) The different parts of the organisation will not complement each other, and might tend to pull the organisation in different directions.

(c) **Adapting to change**

Large organisations might be slow to adapt to change because of a bureaucratic system of operating and decision-making that stifles ideas for innovation.

(d) **Motivation**

(i) People find it hard to identify themselves with the objectives of a large organisation.

(ii) Difficulties for individuals to see how their efforts contribute to achieving the organisation's objectives (due to narrow specialisation of jobs etc).

(iii) Possible problems in getting employees to enjoy working in a large organisation, where a bureaucratic role culture predominates.

(iv) Decision-making might be slow, with managers not allowed the authority and discretion they would like.

3.2 Increasing size in an organisation causes problems of **co-ordination, planning, control** and the achievement of **economies of scale** and **versatility** in the range of products and services offered.

(a) For example, junior managers might find the organisation so large that they have relatively little influence. Decisions which they regard as important must be continually referred up the line to superiors, for inter-departmental consultations.

(b) At the same time, the top management might find the organisation so large and complex to understand, and changes in policy and procedures so difficult and time-consuming to implement, that they also feel unable to give direction to the organisation. The organisation is therefore a monster which operates of its own accord, with neither senior nor junior managers able to manage it effectively.

3.3 In a large organisation, many of the specialised tasks for junior functional managers, and many day-to-day tasks of junior operational management are routine and boring. Even middle management might be frustrated by the restrictions on their authority, the impersonal nature of their organisation, the inability to earn a just reward for their special efforts (owing to the standardisation of pay and promotion procedures) and the lack of information about aspects of the organisation which should influence their work. These problems are likely to result in poor motivation amongst managers and, consequently, poor motivation amongst their junior staff and a reluctance to accept responsibility.

3.4 **Overcoming the problems of large size**

(a) **Decentralisation and delegation of authority**. Decentralisation should encourage decision-making at lower levels of management. Management motivation and efficiency in target-setting, planning and control should improve.

(b) **A pay policy should provide for just rewards,** perhaps including individual or team bonuses, for outstanding efforts and achievements.

(c) The introduction of **comprehensive management and employee information systems** will enable all managers and employees to understand their planned contribution towards achieving organisational objectives and to compare their actual achievements against their targets.

(d) **Better job design to motivate employees.**

(e) **Delayering.** This is the reduction of levels in the management hierarchy.

Case example

ABB (Asea Brown Boveri)

ABB is often cited in surveys as a company managers most admire. It is a large engineering concern, organised into over 1,000 subsidiary companies in which power is devolved to its lowest level. They are co-ordinated on the basis of business areas, covering particular products.

Given its size and worldwide reach, the firm places importance in getting people to work together: teams are dawn from different nationalities. Thus there are a large number of small operating units, given co-ordination at a strategic level.

Small organisations

3.5 Small organisations face a different set of problems which have to be overcome or lived with.

(a) **Over reliance on a few key individuals**

(b) **No economies of scale**. Higher levels of output spreads cost.

(c) **Small market areas or a restricted range of products** mean that any significant change can imperil their existence.

(d) **Low bargaining power**. They may be unable to get the best discounts from suppliers. (This explains the existence of **buying co-operatives** where small firms club together to get better discounts from suppliers.)

(e) **Cannot raise money**. Many small businesses complain they are unable to raise finance and rely heavily on bank loans. (Many proprietors, however, are unwilling to sacrifice control in order to raise bank finance.

(f) **Cannot afford help**. A small business cannot always pay for the professional expertise needed. A typical entrepreneur is better at some things (eg investing) than others (eg marketing).

(g) **Cash flow**. Large firms often fail to pay their small business suppliers on time.

3.6 Some of the problems can be overcome in the following ways.

- Growth
- Buyer co-operatives
- Specialist services, such as factoring
- Key person insurance

4 CONTRACTION AND DECLINE

4.1 Decline has three causes.

(a) **Environmental entropy**. What should a company do to be successful in a declining industry, if it cannot realistically withdraw? The organisation's environment may no longer be sufficient to support it. For example, the decline in the UK housing market has put many estate agents out of business.

(b) **Vulnerability**. The organisation may for some reason fail to prosper in its environment. They may not pursue the right strategy or choose the right business. They may not be large or strong enough to cope with sudden shifts in demand.

(c) **Organisational atrophy**. The organisation may be too bureaucratic. Its managers may be complacent and unable to adapt.

Declining industries: environmental entropy

4.2 There are two types of decline, as identified by *Kathryn Harrigan*.

(a) **Product revitalisation** occurs when the decline is temporary, for example, when there is a genuine recession in consumer demand.

(b) **Endgame**. A firm (and the industry) is confronted with substantially lower demand permanently.

4.3 Many industries undertook product revitalisation during the recession which started in the late 1980s. Accountancy firms, for instance, tried to expand into general business consulting while maintaining their traditional audit and tax work. The British coal industry has been in a condition of end game since the end of the last national coal strike in 1985.

4.4 Harrigan researched a number of firms in declining industries and arrived at some interesting conclusions.

(a) In endgame conditions, firms which had not competed with each other were drawn into price wars. This knee-jerk response should encourage managers to consider their competitive behaviour before the endgame.

(b) Because the characteristics of declining industries differ (eg some have high exit barriers, some are concentrated, others are fragmented), different strategies are appropriate.

(c) The expectations of competitors about future demand, and the expectations of their customers about future supplies, can have a powerful influence on the nature of the competitive environment.

(d) Forecasting techniques can help firms identify the type of competitor that will leave the industry and the types most likely to remain.

(e) If the industry is falling to a **substitute product**, then firms should **innovate** to capture the new technology.

(f) If products become commodity-like (ie differentiation is not all that significant) then all but the lowest cost competitor will lose market share. In these conditions a cost leadership strategy is appropriate. On the other hand, it might be a good idea to **differentiate** a product, if this is feasible, to build the security of a niche.

(g) Unless a company has the lowest costs, a strong distribution system relative to competitors, or a loyal niche of customers, it might be worth selling the business to a competitor who can make better use of it.

(h) Finally, a firm which is part of a conglomerate might be retained because of strategic relationships with other areas of the conglomerate.

Vulnerability

4.5 An organisation which is **vulnerable** may not be able to withstand a shock or massive change in its environmental domain. Vulnerability can be measured in many ways.

(a) **A sudden change in general environmental factors**. Commercial property companies are vulnerable to changes in interest rates.

(b) **New competitors**. A firm might need certain economies of scale to compete successfully. A firm may not have the resources to build capacity to that extent.

(c) A firm may be vulnerable to **sudden changes in technology**.

4.6   In assessing vulnerability, you can use all the factors identified in Chapter 6.

Declining companies: organisational atrophy

Symptoms

4.7   Companies go bankrupt. Their assets are sold. Their former employees find work elsewhere if they are fortunate, or join the dole queues for life if they are not. Stuart Slatter, from an analysis of UK companies during the severe recession of the early 1980s, identifies **ten symptoms of corporate decline.**

- **Declining profitability.**
- **Decreasing sales volume** (ie sales revenue adjusted for inflation).
- An **increase in gearing** (debt as a proportion of equity).
- A **decrease in liquidity**, as measured, conventionally, by accounting ratios.
- **Restrictions on the dividend policy.**
- **Financial engineering** (eg changes in accounting policies and periods, delays in publishing accounts, sudden changes in auditors).
- 'Top management fear'.
- **Frequent changes in senior executives.**
- Falling **market share.**
- Evidence of a **lack of planning.**

4.8   **These are all observable externally.** Internally, however, there may be a **severe crisis,** whose severity for the long term depends on the behaviour of managers. Slatter identifies **four stages in the crisis.**

(a)   **Blinded stage** or **crisis denial.** Managers are complacent, ignore warning signs or do not appreciate their significance. This may result from poor control systems and poor environmental monitoring. Managers might rest on their laurels. They might be *blinded* to the situation. Prompt action would reverse the trend.

(b)   **Inaction** or **hidden crisis.** When the signs of crisis appear, managers explain them away, or say that there is nothing they can do. The problem is that if they admit something *is* wrong they will be blamed. If a radical change is required, it might adversely affect their position. This second stage sadly means **inaction.** Again corrective action, more severe, might reverse the trend.

(c)   **Faulty action** or **disintegration.** Managers decide that things are amiss and act to do something about them - too little, usually. Moreover, management becomes more autocratic, reducing alternative sources of information. This faulty action might not be enough.

(d)   **Crisis** and **collapse** (or **dissolution**). Slatter says that, in the end, action is impossible. An expectation of failure increases, the most able managers leave, and there are power struggles for the remaining spoils. Eventually, the receiver is called in.

Possible causes

4.9   **Causes of decline** and the **strategies** to deal with them.

(a)   **Poor management.** This should be dealt with by the introduction of new management and perhaps organisation restructuring (this should only be embarked upon once the new executive knows how the firm *really* works, including its informal organisation).

(b) **Poor financial controls**. This can be dealt with by new management, financial control systems which are tighter and more relevant, and, perhaps, decentralisation and delegation of responsibility to first line management of all aspects except finance.

(c) **High cost structure**. Cost reduction is important in improving margins in the long term. New product-market strategies are adopted for the short term (to boost profitability and cash-flow). Growth-orientated strategies (eg as in Ansoff's matrix) are only suitable once survival is assured. A focus strategy (whether cost-focus or differentiation-focus) is perhaps the most appropriate.

(d) **Poor marketing**. The marketing mix can be redeployed. Slatter believes that the sales force of a crisis-ridden firm is likely to be particularly demotivated.

(e) **Competitive weakness**. This is countered by cost reduction, improved marketing, asset reduction (eg disposing of subsidiaries, selling redundant fixed assets), even acquisition, and of course, a suitable product-market strategy.

(f) **Big projects/acquisitions**. Acquisitions can go bad, or there can be a failure of a major project (eg Rolls Royce aerospace once went into receivership because of the cost of developing a particular engine).

(g) **Financial policy**. Firms might suffer because of high gearing. Arguably many of the firms subject to management buyouts financed by interest-bearing loans are acutely vulnerable. Converting debt to equity and selling assets are ways of dealing with this.

Feedback failure

4.10 The acquisition of feedback information is the final stage of the rational decision-making model. In other words, the final stage of the decision process is the monitoring of whether the results have been achieved.

4.11 Some organisations and individuals persist in activities which are undoubtedly failing. In other words, they **escalate their commitment to a decision**.

Case example

The Vietnam war is a good example of an escalation of commitment to a decision, even though many argued from quite early on that it could never be won. However, more and more troops were committed to the war.

Another example perhaps comes from defence procurement, when large sums of UK public money were spent developing the Nimrod airborne warning system: eventually costs were so over budget that the government decided to axe the project and buy an American system, AWACS.

4.12 Why might managers escalate their commitment to a bad decision?

(a) **Managers block out negative information, when they themselves are responsible**. In other words they refuse to believe the decision was wrong but claim instead, for example, that it was badly implemented, and that an injection of money will put things right. In part this is a **cultural problem**, if it means that past ways of working no longer apply.

(b) **Managers or decision makers do not wish to suffer the humiliation of a climbdown** as it might have a wider effect on their reputation. If compromise is seen as a weakness, moral, political or intellectual, then a manager is unlikely to be prepared to risk the poor 'publicity'. In companies whose corporate cultures do not tolerate failure, it might be better for the manager to soldier on in the hope that the situation will sort itself out;

but when this involves committing more and more resources, such nervous wishful thinking can prove very expensive.

(c) **Consistency is valued.** Studies of leadership situations (see section 6 below) indicate that subordinates prefer managers whose leadership style is consistent. Failing to be consistent smacks of weakness or opportunism, even though such a course may be rational. Consistency in a person is valued as it allows people to predict his or her behaviour .

(d) **Mistakes are viewed as failures to be punished rather than opportunities for organisational and/or personal learning**. We discussed learning in Chapter 17. Innovation inevitably involves experimentation: experiments often fail. A company that is not innovative is unlikely to tolerate failure.

(e) **The outcome of the project is uncertain**. It is easy to criticise with hindsight, and the bad decision may have been the best one taken with the information available at the time.

(f) **A failure to understand the principles of relevant costs for decision-making.** As management accountants, you should already know that sunk costs are excluded from decision-making. Not everybody finds this point easy to grasp. People will spend more, to turn a project round.

Turnround

4.13 Companies which recovered did so largely because of the way in which the recovery strategy was implemented. They used a variety of approaches.

- **Contraction** and cost cutting
- **Reinvestment** in organisational capability and efficiency
- **Rebuilding** with a concentration on innovation

4.14 **Turning a company round requires an able top management, with the right mix of skills and experience, to stand outside of the culture of the organisation.** Substantial changes at the top (eg as at Barings) may be needed, and one of the most important **symbols of a new order** is the change of personnel. The development of an effective top management team requires attention to the points below.

(a) What resources does the team have to work with within the company and what could it obtain from the industry?

(b) What is the *ideal* management team given the nature of the crises facing the organisation. For example a firm with poor financial controls may require a team with a financial or systems bias, whereas a firm whose problem was lacklustre products may need a team with a marketing bias.

(c) Against this ideal team, how does the current team shape up? New expertise may need to be imported, or a plan may be needed to enhance the capability of the existing team.

4.15 In the context of change and the top management team we can identify specific leadership roles. **Charismatic leaders** lead by force of personality, which will only be exercised in difficult situations. **Transformational leaders** not only have charisma, but use it to some purpose.

- To create a new vision for the organisation
- To gain acceptance of the new vision
- To force through and 'refreeze' the change

4.16 Despite some scepticism about the degree to which it is possible for individuals to take on some of the attributes of leadership, increasing attention is being paid to the notion of the **visionary leader,** who is capable of transforming the organisation by taking it on to even greater success or by turning it round from imminent collapse.

4.17 Analysis of books about 'visionary leadership' suggests that much the same general motivational and skills qualities apply. Successful leadership is more likely to occur when the person in charge of an organisational possesses some generic leadership characteristics (ie suitable 'traits') and is then able to customise them (ie operate on a 'contingency' basis) to the particular context where leadership prowess is needed.

Case examples

Marks & Spencer

'The American farmer had little time or opportunity to go shopping. So the farmer received a catalogue and was given the novel guarantee of 'your money back and no questions asked'. Providing the service meant also creating new human skills, for example, by organising suppliers to achieve new standards of efficiency. After Simon Marks came back from America in 1924 he remodelled Marks & Spencer to provide high-quality goods at low prices, together with a 'money back' guarantee.'

Habitat

'The inspiration to change things came from asking myself what I had seen on my travels that worked well. For me the markets of France and the ironmongers' shops of France had all the sorts of qualities I found fascinating and exciting. Bringing these ideas together with the market needs in Britain led me to open the first Habitat shops.' (Terence Conran).

John Adair, The Art of Creative Thinking, 1990

---

5 STRUCTURAL REORGANISATION AND DIVESTMENT

5.1 Factors creating pressure for change in organisations structure

(a) **Changes in the environment of the organisation.** For example, greater competition might create pressures for cost-cutting, and so staff cuts.

(b) **Diversification into new product-market areas.** There is a need for better lateral and vertical integration as an organisation becomes more complex and differentiated. A possible role for special co-ordinators can be found. Another issue which might be addressed is when to switch from a functional to a divisional organisation structure.

(c) **Growth.** Employing more people creates problems of extended management hierarchies and poor communication.

(d) **New technology**

(e) **Changes in the capabilities of personnel employed.** These can include changes in education levels, the distribution of occupational skills, employee attitudes to work etc.

(f) **Crisis and turnround** might require changes in the organisation structure.

(g) The existing organisation might be showing signs of **weakness and strain,** such as management overload, poor integration, co-ordination and decision-making, insufficient innovation and weakening control. These are common management problems, but made worse by deficiencies in the organisation structure.

5.2 Restructuring is not always necessary every time that changes take place in an organisation's circumstances. When a problem arises with an organisational deficiency, management has to analyse and diagnose the fault.

(a) What is the scope of the problem?

(b) What is the source of the problem? (It is relatively easy to spot personal problems, when a manager is not doing his job properly, or there are personal rivalries and conflicts, but it is not so easy to diagnose faults in organisational structure.)

(c) Is the problem temporary or permanent, unique or recurrent?

(d) At what level in the management hierarchy and organisation structure is the problem located? This is the point where restructuring will be needed.

Acquisitions and divestments

5.3 A company which is planning to grow must decide on whether to pursue a policy of organic internal growth or a policy of taking over other established businesses, or a mix of the two.

5.4 **Acquisitions are probably only desirable if organic growth alone cannot achieve the targets for growth that a company has set for itself.**

(a) Acquisitions can be made to enter new product areas, or to expand in existing markets, much more quickly. Organic growth takes time. With acquisitions, entire existing operations are assimilated into the company at one fell swoop.

(b) Acquisitions can be made without cash, if share exchange transactions are acceptable to both the buyers and sellers of any company which is to be taken over.

(c) When an acquisition is made to diversify into new product areas, the company will be buying technical expertise, goodwill and customer contracts etc. which it might take years to develop if it tried to enter the market by growing organically.

5.5 However, **acquisitions do have their problems.**

(a) They might be too expensive: some might be resisted by the directors of the target company. Others might be referred to the government under the terms of anti-monopoly legislation.

(b) Customers of the target company might resent a sudden takeover and consider going to other suppliers for their goods.

(c) In general, the problems of assimilating new products, customers, suppliers, markets, employees and different systems of operating might create 'indigestion' and management overload in the acquiring company.

Case example

An example of growth which had to be pursued through diversification and acquisition is Fujitsu. By acquiring the UK firm ICL, not only did Fujitsu find an entry to the European market, but also acquired ICL's experience in *open systems technologies*.

Non-growth strategies and de-growth strategies

5.6 Most strategies are designed to promote growth, but management should consider what rate of growth they want, whether they want to see any growth at all, or whether there should be

a contraction of the business. It might be difficult for you to envisage a company that is hostile to growth, unless there are family companies where members of the family wish to retain personal control and so do not want to see any expansion which calls for substantial new funding. However, the divestment of non-core businesses perhaps to a management buyout, has been quite common in recent years.

Divestment

5.7 Divestment means getting rid of something. In strategic planning terms, it means selling off a part of a firm's operations, or pulling out of certain product-market areas (ie closing down a product line).

(a) A company might decide to concentrate on its core businesses and sell off fringe activities, or to sell off subsidiaries where performance is poor, or where growth prospects are not good.

(b) Selling off subsidiaries at a profit can be a means of raising finance.

(c) Selling attractive subsidiaries can thwart a takeover bid.

5.8 One term that describes divestment is 'demerger'. This is sometimes referred to as 'unbundling'. Demergers are the opposite of mergers. The main feature of a demerger is that one corporate entity becomes two or more separate entities. The newly-separated businesses might have the same shareholders, but they will usually have different people on their board of directors.

5.9 A demerger might take one of two forms.

(a) **A management buy-out** (see below).

(b) **A major demerger of a group**: a well-known and successful example is the break up of ICI into its pharmaceuticals and chemicals components (Zeneca and ICI) in order to release more value for shareholders. This in part resulted from a takeover bid by Hanson Trust.

Management buyouts

5.10 When a firm decides to divest itself of a part of its operations, it will try to get what it can by selling off the business as a unit, or by selling individual assets. Typically, a better price can be obtained by selling the business as a unit, and there might well be many other firms interested in buying it. In recent years, however, there have been a large number of management buyouts, whereby the subsidiary is sold off to its managers. The managers put in some of their own capital, but obtain the rest from venture capital organisations (eg banks), and hope to make a bigger success of the business than the company who is selling it off. Management buy-outs are often associated with ailing subsidiary companies, where the group's management agree to sell off the subsidiary as an alternative to closing it down. An example is MFI.

Strategic factors in a buyout decision

5.11 A management buyout team must answer three important questions.

(a) Can the buyout team raise the finance to pay for the buyout. Buyouts are well-favoured by venture capital organisations, which regard them as less risky than new start-up businesses, and so access to funds is often not a serious problem.

(b) Can the bought-out operation generate enough profits to pay for the costs of the acquisition - ie interest payments on the borrowed finance? If the buyout price is too high, the answer would be no.

(c) Can the buyout team convince its co-investors that it has the management skills, as well as the enthusiasm, to succeed?

Chapter roundup

- Change occurs in the environment, goods/services, technology, management organisation structure or culture.

- Even if an organisation prefers stability, it still has to innovate and it may be faced by discontinuous environmental change.

- Organisations grow and decline for many reasons. Both processes have effects on organisation structure.

- An organisation often has to adapt to maintain its effectiveness over time, as is shown by the Sigmoid curve.

- Many organisations pursue growth, which can be defined in many ways such as profits, market share etc.

- When the 'business' is growing in sales volume, market presence etc, it is almost inevitable that it will employ more people. These give the organisation the opportunity to broaden the product range and specialise.

- Greiner suggests that organisations grow in phases, in which evolutionary growth is punctuated by revolutionary crises. Growth is driven by creativity, direction, delegation, co-ordination and collaboration. Growth is punctuated by crises of leadership, autonomy, control and red tape respectively.

- Problems with these models are: growth is neither necessary nor inevitable; growth need not be accompanied by crises.

- Large and small organisations have different sets of problems. In large organisations these mainly relate to co-ordinating a diversity of activities. Small organisations, however, fail to benefit from economies of scale, and depend heavily on the individuals in them.

- Corporate decline is caused by poor management, poor financial controls, high cost, poor marketing, a variety of competitive weaknesses, a failure of big projects, and financial policy. Turning the situation or acquisition round can mean addressing these issues independently of preconceptions.

- Acquisitions and divestments are examples of growth and decline. Acquisitions can be problematic if there are cultural differences. Divestments enable a firm to concentrate on its core businesses, or to realise a profit on the original investment in the acquisition.

Quick quiz

1 Give examples of different types of change.

2 How does change differ from transformation?

3 What are the implications of the Sigmoid Curve?

4 List some types of growth.

5 Greiner suggests that organisational growth through direction results in a 'crisis of autonomy'. Why?

6 How do you resolve the crisis of red tape?

7 What is logical incrementalism, when applied to organisation growth?

8 What are the problems of large organisations?

9 List three causes of decline.

10 Describe four stages in corporate collapse.

Answers to quick quiz

1 Change in the environment; in products and services; in technology and working methods; in management and working relationships; in organisation structure and size.

2 Buckley and Perkins defined change as gradual and small and transformation as significantly large.

3 Organisations and individuals should embrace change and not wait until the obsolescence of their current practices leads to crisis.

4 Growth may occur in sales revenue, profitability, volume of goods or services sold, number of outlets, number of employees and other matters.

5 There is a limit to the size of organisation that can be directed in detail from the top. As staff numbers grow, the more able come to resent their lack of responsibility.

6 Increase informal collaboration.

7 A process of small increments and adjustments leading to gradual and continuous change.

8 Structure; planning and control; adapting to change; motivation.

9 Environmental entropy; vulnerability; organisational atrophy.

10 Crisis denial; inaction; faulty action; collapse.

Now try the question below from the Exam Question Bank

Number	Level	Marks	Time
Q16	Exam	18	32 Mins

BPP PUBLISHING

Chapter 17

INTRODUCING CHANGE

Topic List	Syllabus Reference	Ability required
1 Models of change	(v)	Evaluation
2 Resistance to change	(v)	Evaluation
3 Corporate culture and change	(v)	Evaluation

Introduction

Change is a feature of the organisation's environment and requires the organisation to change as well in many different ways.

- Change can cause growth and also organisational decline (environmental entropy, vulnerability, organisational atrophy). Many firms fail to accommodate themselves to the necessity for continuous change. Both growth and decline can require structural change.

- Section 2 explains why people resist change and how such resistance is typically articulated (through words and actions).

- In Section 3, we explore the possibilities of culture change across organisations. You should be able to assess the ingredients for an effective culture transformation programme in an organisation.

Learning outcomes covered in this chapter

- Recommend ways in which planned change can be implemented at the organisational and departmental levels.

- Identify opportunities to improve the management of change and communicate recommendations to appropriate managers.

Syllabus content covered in this chapter

- The stages in the change process

- Approaches to the management of organisational development and major cultural and structural change (eg Kanter, Lewin, Peters)

1   MODELS OF CHANGE

1.1   For an organisation to be innovative, and continually responsive to the need for change, a systematic approach should be established, for planning and implementing changes.

1.2 **A step-by-step model for change**

Step 1. Determine need or desire for change in a particular area.

Step 2. Prepare a tentative plan. Brainstorming sessions are a good idea, since alternatives for change should be considered

Step 3. Analyse probable reactions to the change.

Step 4. Make a final decision from the choice of alternative options. The decision may be taken either by group problem-solving (participative) or by a manager on his own (coercive)

Step 5. Establish a timetable for change.

    (a) 'Coerced' changes can probably be implemented faster, without time for discussions.

    (b) Speed of implementation that is achievable will depend on the likely reactions of the people affected.

    (c) Identify those in favour of the change, and perhaps set up a pilot programme involving them. Talk with the others who resist the change.

Step 6. Communicate the plan for change. This is really a continuous process, beginning at Step 1 and going through to Step 7.

Step 7. Implement the change. Review the change. This requires continuous evaluation and modifications

1.3 **Organisational changes need careful planning**. This is true of all but the smallest changes, and it is especially true of major changes. Major organisational changes should usually originate during the corporate planning process. You will recall the first stages in corporate planning from the earlier chapter on the subject.

(a) To establish the organisation's major objectives

(b) To carry out an analysis of the strengths and weaknesses of the organisation, and of the opportunities and threats in its environment

---

Case example

In the UK public sector since 1980, turbulence has been the norm. The transfer of public corporations to the private sector has required new organisation structures and management styles. The proposals for unitary local authorities to replace the existing two tier structure will be a major discontinuity in the operation of local government.

The change process

1.4 In the words of *John Hunt (Managing People at Work)*: 'Learning also involves re-learning - not merely learning something new but trying to unlearn what is already known.' This is, in a nutshell, the thinking behind *Lewin/Schein's* **three stage approach** to changing human behaviour, which may be depicted as follows.

UNFREEZE existing behaviour	→	Attitudinal/ behavioural change	→	REFREEZE new behaviour

1.5 **Unfreeze** is the most difficult (and in many cases neglected) stage of the process, concerned mainly with **selling** the change, with giving individuals or groups a **motive** for changing their attitudes, values, behaviour, systems or structures. If the need for change is immediate, clear and perceived to be associated with the survival of the individual or group (for example change in reaction to an organisation crisis), the unfreeze stage will be greatly accelerated. Routine changes may be harder to sell than transformational ones, if they are perceived to be unimportant and not survival-based.

1.6 **Culture change** is perhaps hardest of all, especially if it involves basic assumptions. Unfreezing processes require four things.

- A trigger

- Someone to challenge and expose the existing behaviour pattern

- The involvement of outsiders

- Alterations to power structure

1.7 **Change** is the second stage, mainly concerned with identifying what the new, desirable behaviour or norm should be, communicating it and encouraging individuals and groups to 'own' the new attitude or behaviour. This might involve the adoption of a new culture. To be successful, the new ideas must be shown to work. Also, the support of junior managers can be enhanced if their status is improved.

1.8 **Refreeze** is the final stage, implying consolidation or reinforcement of the new behaviour. Positive reinforcement (praise and reward) or negative reinforcement (sanctions applied to those who deviate from the new behaviour) may be used.

Discontinuous change

1.9 *Ansoff* suggests that change can be introduced in a variety of ways, and we will discuss some of these approaches briefly.

Coercive change

1.10 **Coercive change is enforced without participation**. Change of culture and power structures is left to the end of the change process. There are several problems with a coercive approach.

- Underestimation of the forces of resistance
- Failure to muster forces in favour
- Failure to attack root causes of resistance
- Management shift their attention too quickly elsewhere
- Failure to ensure implementation.

This approach is necessary in situations of **crisis** where there simply is no time to consult, or where decisions need to be taken quickly. An example is a sudden environmental shock.

Adaptive change

1.11 **Adaptive change occurs when an organisation's environment changes slowly**, but the incremental process of change results in a **major discontinuity**. Adaptive change mirrors this step-by-step: it is change in little stages, and thus has the advantage of minimising the resistance faced at any one time. An example would be the slow demise of the UK's coal industry, with a long programme of incremental cut-backs punctuated, of course, by strikes.

Crisis management

1.12 Ansoff argues (in *Corporate Strategy*) that 'there is an increasing likelihood that the firm will fail to perceive some rapidly developing and novel discontinuities until they forcefully impact upon the firm. When a change appears to imperil the firm's survival and places the firm under severe time pressures, the firm is confronted with a crisis'.

1.13 Crisis has the effect of inducing panic - which managers must do what they can to minimise - but **it can also promote an immediate willingness to change**: it can be the necessary 'unfreeze' process before an organisational change.

1.14 If there is a crisis on the horizon, there are three options.

(a) Convince the others of the crisis and prepare preventative measures.

(b) Accept that the crisis will happen anyway and prepare to capitalise on it by acting as saviours.

(c) Trigger an early artificial crisis, 'usually by inventing an "external enemy" who threatens survival of the firm. This is an approach which has been used by political leaders throughout history.' Artificial crises reduce resistance, and perhaps build up support for recovery.

Managed resistance

1.15 Most of the time, a half way approach between coercive change and adaptive change is needed. Adaptive change is too slow. Ansoff recommends a 'managed resistance' method for dealing with it.

- Prepare the ground for change.
- Gather support to give momentum to the change.
- Plan the change process.
- Design behavioural features.

1.16 A strategic diagnosis will provide necessary information.

- The nature of the environmental change
- The time the firm has to deal with it
- The changes in management capability required
- The units of the organisation affected.

1.17 A behavioural diagnosis analyses the disturbance caused to the cultures and power structures in each unit. Areas of resistance can be mapped, perhaps using a **force field analysis** (see below)

1.18 After unnecessary resistance has been minimised three further strategies can be suggested.

(a) Resistors, if they cannot be won over, should perhaps be excluded from the change process.

(b) The change should be spread over the longest possible time.

(c) Make individuals responsible for implementation also responsible for decision making.

1.19 *Huczynski and Buchaman* give a summary of Rosabeth Moss Vianter's recipe for introducing change, in their book *Organisational Behaviour*. She advises change agents to define their projects in ways that make them sound:

BPP
PUBLISHING

Triable	The change should appear capable of being subjected to a pilot before going the whole way
Reversible	Convince your audience that what you are proposing can be changed back to the status quo if it falls to pieces – irreversible changes are seen as risky
Divisible	Where the change has a number of separate dimensions, present these as potentially independent aspects of a broader change programme – so when single issues cause problems the whole package doesn't have to fold
Concrete	Make the changes and their outcomes tangible and avoid expressing what will happen in abstract and general terms which do not convey an accurate feel for the proposals.
Familiar	Make proposals in terms that other people in the organisation can recognise, because if what you propose is so far over the horizon people can't recognise it, they'll feel out of their 'comfort zones' and start resisting
Congruent	Proposals for change should where possible be seen to 'fit' with the rest of the organisation and be consistent with existing policy and practice
Sexy	Choose projects that have 'publicity value' – in terms of external or media relations, or in terms of internal politics – what will the local press go for –what will excite the chief executive?

Based on Rosabeth Moss Kanter, The Change Masters: Corporate Entrepreneurs at Work

1.20   In The Change Masters, Kanter distinguished between firms with an **integrative** approach and those with a **segmentalist** approach. The integrative approach is taken by innovative firms that see problems as wholes and produce visionary solutions, developing their abilities in the process. Segmentalist firms stifle entrepreneurial innovation by taking narrow, functionally based views of any problem. The integrative, innovative approach is monitored in a variety of ways.

(a)   Encouragement of a culture of pride in the organisation's achievements

(b)   De-layering the hierarchy

(c)   Improvement of lateral communication and working across functional boundaries

(d)   Wide distribution of information about company plans

(e)   Decentralisation and the empowerment of entrepreneurially inclined people at lower levels in the organisation

2   RESISTANCE TO CHANGE

2.1   Change may affect individuals in several areas.

(a)   There may be **physiological** changes in a person's life, both as the natural product of development, maturation and ageing, and **as the result of external factors**: (a change in the pattern of shift-working, for example, may temporarily throw the individual's eating, waking and sleeping routine out of synchronisation with the body's sense of time).

(b)   **Circumstantial** changes - living in a new house, establishing new relationships, working to new routines - will involve letting go of things, perhaps 'unlearning' old knowledge, and learning new ways of doing things.

2.2 Above all, change affects individuals **psychologically**.

    (a) It may create **feelings of disorientation** before new circumstances have been assimilated: you may have felt this on waking up in an unfamiliar room, or performing a familiar task in an unfamiliar setting at college or at work.

    (b) Uncertainty may lead to insecurity. This is especially acute in changes involving work, where there can be very great pressures for continuity and fast acclimatisation.

    (c) The secure basis of warm, accepting relationships may be up-rooted; the business of forging new relationships can be fraught with personal insecurity, risk of rejection, the feeling of being an outsider.

2.3 Change can affect the individual's **self-concept** quite radically.

    (a) A new **psychological contract** may result from the change, bringing with it new expectations, challenges and pressures, in the face of which the self-image may have to be revised - perhaps, initially, with an uncomfortable experience of dissonance.

    (b) A new set of models may have to be confronted, if the change involves a new role set and new relationships.

    (c) The individual's **uncertainty about being able to cope with new circumstances can shake his or her sense of competence**. Many people feel guilty and inadequate as beginners, even though they know, and are told, that it is perfectly natural and acceptable, that their performance will improve as they get used to it.

    (d) Change can be particularly threatening if it is perceived as an **outside force or agent** against which the individual is powerless. This may be a blow to the concept of self as the controller of its own destiny.

Resistance to change at work

2.4 Resisting change means attempting to preserve the existing state of affairs against pressure to alter it. Despite the possibly traumatic effects of change *per se*, as discussed above, most people do *not* in fact resist it on these grounds alone. **Many people long for change, and have a wealth of ideas about how it should be achieved.**

2.5 Sources of resistance to change itself may include age and inflexibility, strong needs for security and emotional instability. Sources of resistance to particular proposed changes, (eg in location, methods of working, pay structure), may include the following:

    (a) **Attitudes or beliefs**, perhaps arising from cultural, religious or class influences (for example resistance to changes in the law on Sunday trading).

    (b) **Loyalty to a group and its norms**, perhaps with an accompanying rejection of other groups, or outsiders (for example in the case of a relocation so that two departments share office space). Groups tend to close ranks if their independent identity is threatened.

    (c) **Habit, or past norms**. This can be a strong source of clinging to old ways, whether out of security needs, respect for tradition, or the belief that 'you can't teach an old dog new tricks' (for example resistance to the introduction of new technology).

    (d) **Politics** - in the sense of resisting changes that might weaken the power base of the individual or group or strengthen a rival's position. Changes involving increased delegation may be strongly resisted by senior management, for example. In the same way the introduction of automation, or new methods, may be seen by the workforce as an attempt to devalue their skills and experience in the job market: they will be superfluous, or will be 'starting at the bottom again', and will have lost their position of strength as suppliers of labour in demand.

(e) The **way** in which any change is put forward and implemented.

2.6 **Reactions to proposed change**.

(a) **Acceptance** (whether enthusiastic espousal, co-operation, grudging co-operation or resignation)

(b) **Indifference** (usually where the change does not directly affect the individual: apathy, lack of interest, inaction)

(c) **Passive resistance** (refusal to learn, working to rule)

(d) **Active resistance** (deliberate 'spoiling', go-slows, deliberate errors, sabotage, absenteeism or strikes)

2.7 *John Hunt* highlights a number of responses that may not **look** like resistance on the face of things, but are **behaviours aimed at reinforcing the status quo**. There are a number of responses that the manager should learn to recognise.

(a) Pleas of ignorance: ('I need more information').

(b) Delayed judgement: ('let's wait and see ...'), perhaps stalling for time with comparisons ('there are other ways ...').

(c) Defensive stances: ('This isn't going to work', 'It'd be too expensive', 'It's the wrong time to ...').

(d) The display of various personal insecurities: ('I won't be able to cope', 'I won't see my team anymore', 'We won't have control over our planning any more', 'Why can't we just go on as we are?'); fear, anxiety, resentment at the manner of change, frustration at perceived losses.

(e) Withdrawal, or disowning of the change: ('Oh well. On their heads be it', 'I'm not interested in flexitime anyway').

Question 1

It is interesting to set side by side the comments of Sainsbury's director of personnel and a senior official of the shop worker's union Usdaw, as reported in *Personal Management Plus* in February 1992. See if you can tell which is which!

(a) 'I have taken a close personal interest, and so have my colleagues, to ensure that in every branch the people who are working are those who volunteered. Not working on Sunday is not going to affect promotion prospects, it is not going to affect people's pay, and it is not going to affect our attitude to them.

'There are some who say "I will not work on Sunday because I feel it's not right to do so". There are others, and this includes managers, who say: "I am not going to work on Sunday because I want to play football" and we say: "That's a nuisance, isn't it and we find a way round it".'

(b) 'Connor maintains some retailers have ways of making their staff work Sundays without resorting to blackmail. "Very clever retail employers work through the ranks. They take the weakest, the people who have less than two years' experience and who have no rights for unfair dismissal, then they pick the starry-eyed people who think they are going to be managing director, then they pick the people who work low hours and need a few bob. Then they come to the resolute minority and say: "You are out of step".'

Overcoming resistance to change

Force field analysis

2.8 It is also necessary to assess the impact of change on the political system of the organisation.

2.9 *Kurt Lewin* developed a simple technique of visualising the change process called **force field analysis**. This can be used to identify ways of dealing with an unsatisfactory situation. It is based on the idea that in any group or organisational situation there is an **interplay of restraining and driving forces that keeps things in equilibrium**. Force field analysis maps the forces that are pushing toward the preferred state and the restraining forces, which are pushing back to the current state. They can then be presented in a chart. The example below describes a public sector organisation whose management are introducing a performance review system.

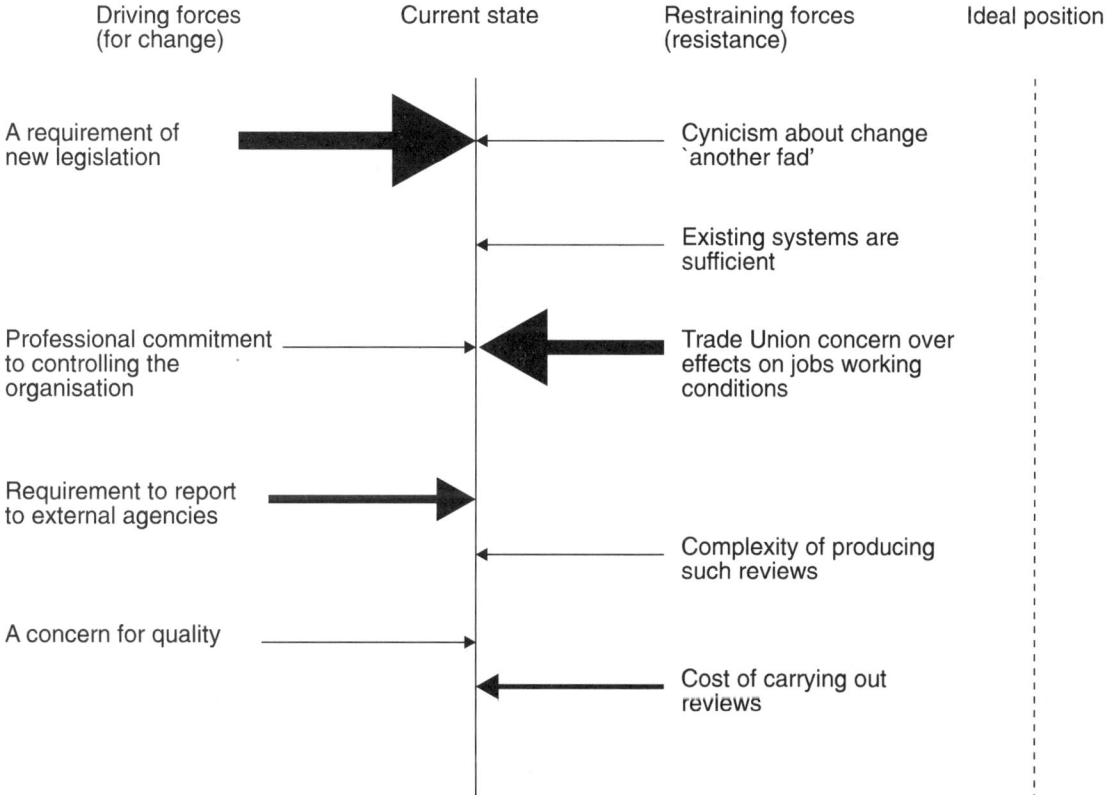

2.10 Let us imagine a group of workers who are producing at 70% of the efficiency that might be expected on purely technical grounds. This being so, their output can be visualised as a **balance** between two opposing sets of forces, ie **driving forces** which are propelling their output upwards and **restraining forces** which are preventing it from going beyond the 70% level.

2.11 Note that these driving forces and restraining forces represent **perceptions** entertained by the workers themselves. They are not merely a list of impersonal advantages and disadvantages because, as is often the case with complex scenarios, an advantage for one person turns out to be a disadvantage from someone else's point of view. If the workers in question were to increase their output, that may prove beneficial for the organisation's management team, but the workers themselves would feel their job security to be threatened.

BPP
PUBLISHING

Question 2

Before going on, can you think of some *restraining forces* which, in the eyes of the workers concerned, deter them from producing more than 70% of what is technically feasible? Equally, can you think of some *driving forces* - again, in the eyes of the workers involved - which ensure that output remains at the 70% level without falling to, say, 60%?

Remember that your driving and restraining forces have to be the kinds of arguments which would be meaningful for the workers themselves, so you have to try to put yourself in their place and visualise how kinds you would feel: in other words, you must *empathise* with the kinds of feelings, attitudes, beliefs, emotions and goals likely to be uppermost in their minds.

2.12 **Restraining forces**

(a) Dislike of the work itself

(b) Fear that if they produce more, the organisation will then be unable to sustain sales at the higher level of output, so redundancies will ensue.

(c) Fear that once higher output norms have been established, the organisation will expect such norms to be sustained permanently.

(d) Dislike of the supervisor, the management and even the organisation as a whole, thereby making the workers unco-operative and resentful.

2.13 **Driving forces**

(a) Fear of dismissal if output falls below a reasonably well-defined rate acceptable to or tolerated by the management.

(b) Financial incentives, without which output would be significantly lower than 70%.

(c) Fear of losing special privileges, such as concessionary prices for the organisation's products or services.

(d) Response to pressure from the management - and thus a desire to reduce that pressure to acceptable proportions.

2.14 Once the equilibrium has been established, the organisation may be perfectly content, provided that a 70% level of performance is viewed as reasonable. Alternatively, management may believe that the disruption 'costs' arising from any disturbance to be status quo may outweigh the potential 'benefits' involved.

2.15 On the other hand, if management wants to increase output levels to, say, 80%, then logically this can only be done in **either** of the following ways.

(a) **Overcoming resistance** through strengthening the driving forces, ie increasing management pressure, enhancing fears of dismissal and so forth

(b) **Reducing resistance** by weakening the forces that currently hold down output, for example through job redesign, adoption of a more people-centred management style

2.16 **Overcoming resistance tends to be the more popular strategy**. Overall, the approach appears to succeed because management works very hard, applies pressure and knocks a few heads together (eliminating some, if necessary), but it does create resisting forces which are costly to organisational flexibility and efficiency in the long run, as well as damaging people at all levels.

2.17 *Chris Argyris*, commenting on 32 major changes in large organisations, says that not one was fully completed and integrated even three years after the change had been announced. 'That

is, after three years there were still many people fighting, ignoring, questioning, resisting, blaming the re-organisation without feeling a strong obligation personally to correct the situation.'

2.18 The essential characteristic of **overcoming resistance** as a strategy for change is that **increasing any of the upward 'push' factors** will prompt an **equal and opposite reaction** on the other side of the equilibrium: management gets what it ostensibly wants - an increase in production - but at the cost of more tension, conflict, suspicion and hostility. With **reducing resistance**, on the other hand, the same objective is accomplished as output rises, but the resultant balance of forces operates at a significantly lower level of tension.

Question 3

Consider a major change in your organisation in the past three years. Draw up a force field analysis indicating who proposed change and the main sources of resistance to it. Was the change successfully implemented?

Introducing the change

2.19 There are three important factors for managers to consider when dealing with resistance to change.

- The **pace** of change
- The **manner** of change
- The **scope** of change

2.20 Changes ought generally to be introduced slowly. Apart from 'people problems', there may be a long planning and administrative process and/or financial risks to be considered, for example in a re-location of offices or a factory: a range of alternatives will have to be considered, and information gathered. Change is, however, above all a 'political' process: relationships are changed, and must be reformed, old ways have to be unlearned and new ways learned.

Pace

2.21 The more gradual the change, the more time is available for questions to be asked, reassurances to be given and retraining (where necessary) embarked upon. People can get used to the idea of new methods - can get acclimatised at each stage, with a consequent confidence in the likely success of the change programme, and in the individual's own ability to cope.

(a) Presenting the individuals concerned with a *fait accompli* may short-circuit resistance at the planning and immediate implementation stages. But it may cause a withdrawal reaction (akin to 'shock'), if the change is radical and perceived as threatening, and this is likely to surface later, as the change is consolidated - probably strengthened by resentment.

(b) **Timing** will also be crucial: those responsible for change should be sensitive to incidents and attitudes that might indicate that 'now is not the time'.

Manner

2.22 The manner in which a change is put across is very important: the climate must be prepared, the need made clear, fears soothed, and if possible the individuals concerned positively motivated to embrace the changes as their own.

(a) **Resistance should be welcomed and confronted,** not swept under the carpet. Talking thorough areas of conflict may lead to useful insights and the adapting of the programme of change to advantage. Repressing resistance will only send it underground, into the realm of rumour and covert hostility.

(b) **There should be free circulation of information** about the reasons for the change, its expected results and likely consequences. That information should appear sensible, clear, consistent and realistic: there is no point issuing information which will be seen as a blatant misrepresentation of the situation.

(c) **The change must be sold to the people concerned**: people must be convinced that their attitudes and behaviours need changing. Objections must be overcome, but it is also possible to get people behind the change in a positive way. If those involved understand that there is a real problem, which poses a threat to the organisation and themselves, and that the solution is a sensible one and will solve that problem, there will be a firm rational basis, for implementing change. The people should also be reassured that they have the learning capacity, the ability and the resources to implement the plan. It may even be possible to get them really excited about it by emphasising the challenge and opportunity by injecting an element of competition or simply offering rewards and incentives.

(d) **Individuals must be helped to learn,** that is, to change their attitudes and behaviours. Few individuals will really be able to see the big picture in a proposed programmed of change. In order to put across the overall objective, the organisation should use **visual aids** to help conceptualise. Learning programmes for any new skills or systems necessary will have to be designed according to the abilities of the individuals concerned.

(e) The effects of **insecurity,** perceived **helplessness,** and therefore **resentment,** may be lessened if the people can be **involved** in the planning and implementation of the change, that is, if it is not perceived to have been imposed from above.

Scope

2.23 **The scope of change should be carefully reviewed.** Total transformation will create greater insecurity - but also greater excitement, if the organisation has the kind of innovative culture that can stand it - than moderate innovation. There may be hidden changes to take into account: a change in technology may necessitate changes in work methods, which may in turn result in the breaking up of work groups. Management should be aware of how many various aspects of their employees' lives they are proposing to alter - and therefore on how many fronts they are likely to encounter resistance.

Question 4

Watch out for examples of organisations undergoing change in the press and see how it is being handled. A particularly good source should be articles about how companies are responding to the new opportunities of the single European market, but technological change, takeovers, new conditions of work and relocations are amongst the many other examples you may see reported.

Also, note carefully how your own organisation handles changes, or mishandles them. Are you, or any of your colleagues, inclined to resist change?

3   CORPORATE CULTURE AND CHANGE

Cultural change

3.1   'Changing a culture to increase a corporation's effectiveness is a hazardous undertaking,' says *Hampden-Turner*. He recommends a number of steps that senior managers, perhaps with the advice of management consultants, should take.

3.2   Senior managers, if they wish to change a culture, have to know about it in detail. Hampden-Turner suggests **six modes of intervention**: these produce a knowledge about how the culture works.

(a)   **Find the dangers ('locate the black sheep').** The best way to find out about how a culture works is to **violate** it, by doing something culturally shocking. If you break the unwritten rule, then the force of the culture will be mobilised against you. Change managers need to find out about previous cultural rebels, so they can plan their attacks more circumspectly. In short, cultural **taboos** are elicited.

(b)   **Bring conflicts into the open.** Interviewing and observation are the principal tools of cultural investigation. Interviews identify what people **believe as individuals**, as opposed to what they **affirm as employees**. The interviewer should uncover dilemmas (eg safety *versus* performance).

(c)   **Play out corporate dramas.** The manager or consultant then discusses the culture with its members. 'A repressive culture may simply deny that remarks qualifying or criticising it were ever made.' ... 'A narrow or low context culture may agree that such remarks were made, but treat them as the utterances of private persons, irrelevant to the common task.'

(d)   **Reinterpret the corporate myths.** Corporate stories passed round to recruits indicates something about competing value systems. Sometimes these corporate myths have to change. Hampden-Turner cites the experiences of *Volvo* in France. The French sales force considered the cars they were selling to be boring: after a long trip to Sweden, when they were shown around the factories, they changed their views.

(e)   **Look at symbols, images, rituals.** Rituals are used to celebrate achievement, or to mark changes (eg in a merger): 'changing a corporate culture can mean that new symbols, rituals and approaches are devised.'

(f)   **Create a new learning system.** Cultures filter and exclude information. They need to be modified to accept new types of data.

3.3   Any programme of cultural change involves three steps.

- Identifying and exposing the **hidden assumptions** of the new culture
- Trying to identify the **conflicts** hidden in the culture
- Identifying cultural **mechanisms for change**

3.4   Culture is part of a process of organisation restructuring. The commitment of senior management is important if it is not to be viewed cynically.

Unhealthy cultures

3.5   *Edwin Baker*, in 1981, observed twelve corporations which developed **unhealthy corporate cultures**. He found a common pattern.

(a)   The organisation **flourished initially** under its founder who created, usually without conscious effort, a cohesive group of employees who shared his beliefs and values.

(b)   On the founder's retirement the organisation continued to flourish but many employees became **rigid and insular** in their thinking and behaviour.

(c) Concern for **survival** faded and, as a result, so did values regarding speed, flexibility, innovation and concern for the customer.

(d) Increased growth led to **formalisation** and the development of rules and procedures. Divisions occurred between employees and management because of specialisation. Communication and willingness to accept responsibility decreased.

(e) Employees identified with their departments, not with the organisation as a whole.

(f) Corrective action needed to challenge problems of mature products and markets met inertia. It was thwarted by the rigid culture.

3.6 In one case the rigidified culture led directly to bankruptcy. Baker warned that: 'changing the distinctive culture of a large, old organisation is enormously difficult and may take years'. There are clear parallels here both with Greiner's **life cycle model** and Harrison's description of **role culture.**

Culture gaps

3.7 *Ralph H Kilmann* suggests the following steps for closing 'culture gaps'.

- Find out about what **norms of behaviour** are currently present.
- Decide the ways in which norms need to be changed.
- Establish new norms.
- Identify **culture gaps between the norms**.
- Close culture gaps.

3.8 The sorts of **norm** which Kilmann is talking about relate to **attitudes** toward performance/excellence, teamwork, communication, leadership, profitability, staff relations, customer relations, honesty and security, training and innovation. **Positive norms** of behaviour are those where individuals identify their own goals with those of the organisation. **Negative norms** are represented by insularity, slowness, complacency and hostility. The difficult task, obviously, is to establish new and positive norms of behaviour. A consistent approach is needed and certain features are essential.

(a) Top management commitment.

(b) Modelling behaviour - management should be seen to be acting on the new norms themselves, not merely mouthing empty words about change.

(c) Support for positive behaviour and confrontation of negative behaviour.

(d) Consistency between the evaluation and reward system and positive behaviour (linking pay to acting on positive norms).

(e) Communication of desired norms.

(f) Recruitment and selection of the 'right' people.

(g) Induction programmes for new employees on the desired norms of behaviour.

(h) Training and skills development.

Most research has shown that, in a large organisation, shifting the value system or culture can take between three and eight years to bring about.

3.9 Why might it take so long? One of the disadvantages of strong cultures is that, as we have seen, they **discourage the questioning of their basic assumptions**.

3.10 Furthermore, culture is reflected in an organisation's **recruitment policies**. People are recruited who conform to the corporate culture, who 'fit in', irrespective of their technical or other qualifications.

3.11 In some cases, recruitment is also a means of perpetuating the old order, a sort of cultural nepotism where people promote others with similar values to themselves. In other cases, recruitment is a means of developing a new corporate culture from scratch.

Case example

On 3rd July 1993, British Airways opened a new aircraft maintenance hanger in Bristol, on the principles of Japanese-style management (as reported by the *Financial Times*). BMAC was careful in who it chose to work at the plant. It was wary of mechanics accustomed to sloppy work in local car repair garages and wanted people who already had a flexible approach to their work. Half the 340 staff recruited so far have never worked on aircraft and only 31 came from elsewhere in BA.

The management ideas include flexible working, identical uniforms for workers and a single canteen.

3.12 Culture can also have a significant impact on the effectiveness of mergers and takeovers.

Case example

UK high street banks acquired broking and jobbing firms in the City of London, as well as 'merchant banks'. There were newspaper reports of conflicts in culture arising from the merger of the different cultures.

Chapter roundup

- Change occurs in the environment, goods/services, technology, management organisation structure or culture.

- Change involves structural and behavioural factors. Resistance to change results from individual uncertainties and distrust of management. Some of this may arise from poor information. Some resistance may result from uncertainty about the nature of the change itself, or from poor information.

- Corporate culture is often the hardest matter to change, because it is often unwritten, and resistance can be powerful. Change agents need to expose the hidden assumptions of the corporate culture and offer alternatives.

- There are a variety of models of the change process. Force field analysis identifies where the likely problems might be found and where effort can be expended.

Quick quiz

1   Describe a change model.

2   What is meant by 'refreezing'?

3   What are the problems with coercive change?

4   What causes resistance to change?

5   What is force field analysis?

6   What are the stages of an organisation development programme?

Answers to quick quiz

1   Determine the need or desire for change. Prepare a tentative plan. Analyse probable reactions. Choose from available options. Establish a timetable. Communicate the plan. Implement. Review.

2   The final stage of the Lewin/Schein three-stage approach in which the desired new behaviour is consolidated.

3   Underestimating resistance; not coercing hard enough or long enough; failure to ensure implementation.

4   Attitudes, beliefs, loyalties, habits and norms, politics.

5   Lewin's analysis of the driving and restraining forces which underlie any group or organisational equilibrium.

6   Management awareness of need; disclosure of objectives; data gathering and diagnosis; consensus on strategy; implementation and monitoring.

Now try the question below from the Exam Question Bank

Number	Level	Marks	Time
Q17	Exam	18	32 Mins

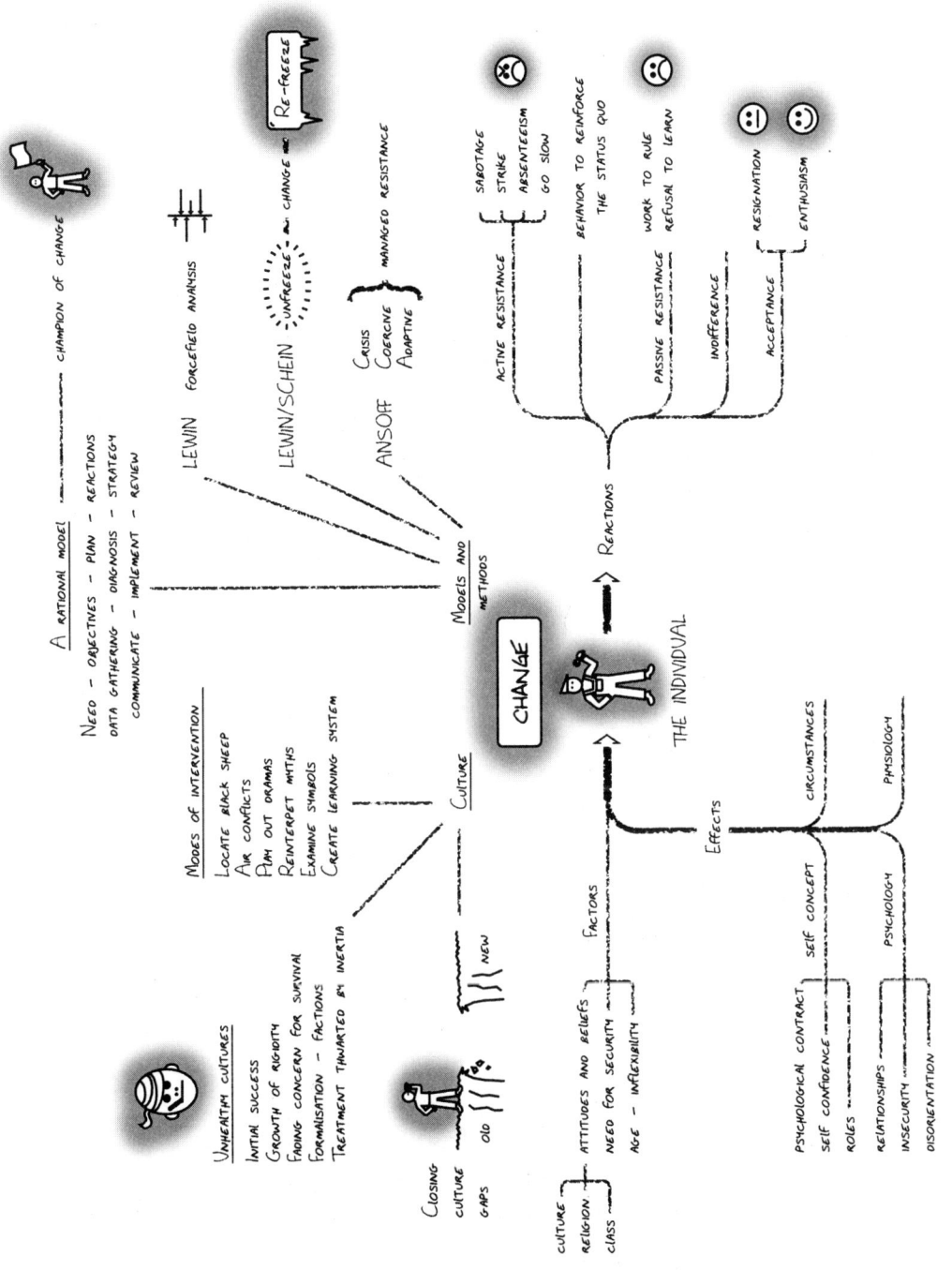

Exam question bank

1 STRATEGIC MANAGEMENT   *36 mins*

The process of strategic management is sometimes defined as comprising strategic analysis, strategic choice and strategic implementation.

(a) Briefly describe each of these three stages, and comment on their interrelationship.   **16 Marks**
(b) Briefly describe an alternative model of strategic management.   **4 Marks**

Total marks = 20

2 MISSION STATEMENT   *36 mins*

The managing director of TDM plc has recently returned from a conference entitled 'Strategic planning beyond the '90s'. Whilst at the conference, she attended a session on Corporate Mission Statements. She found the session very interesting but it was rather short. She now has some questions for the accountant.

'What does corporate mission mean? I don't see how it fits in with our strategic planning processes.'

'Where does our mission come from and what areas of corporate life should it cover?'

'Even if we were to develop one of these mission statements, what benefits would the company get from it?'

You are required to prepare a memorandum which answers the managing director's questions.

20 Marks

3 ENCOURAGING INNOVATION IN A LARGE ORGANISATION   *36 mins*

How can senior managers set out to encourage innovation and entrepreneurial attitudes in their own organisation?   **20 Marks**

4 CORPORATE CULTURE   *36 mins*

Handy defines 'culture' as 'the way we do things around here'. What precisely does this mean? How does a corporate culture come into existence? What are the benefits and disadvantages of a strong corporate culture (like that commonly attributed to organisations like IBM)?   **20 Marks**

5 SOCIAL RESPONSIBILITY   *36 mins*

Social responsibility may be defined as the obligations which an organisation has towards society and the broad environment in which the organisation operates. Management therefore, should concern itself with the way in which the organisation interacts with its environment. Explain how and to what extent should management recognise social responsibility extending beyond the boundaries of the organisation.   **20 Marks**

6 CONTINGENCY THEORY   *36 mins*

'The contingency approach to organisational design evolved as a direct reaction against the 'one-best-way' panaceas of classical theory and the human relations school'. Outline the major features of the contingency approach and show how it can be distinguished from the other two theories mentioned in the quotation.   **20 Marks**

7 ORGANISATION PRINCIPLES   *36 mins*

Illustrate with examples the management principles associated with:

(a) line organisation; and
(b) matrix organisation.

What are their relative merits?   **20 Marks**

8 THE MARKETING CONCEPT

36 mins

What is the 'marketing concept'? Comment on its relationship to other business orientations. **20 Marks**

9 RUS PLC

20 mins

RUS plc operates a chain of hotels. Its strategy has been to provide medium-priced accommodation for business people during the week and for families at weekends. The market has become increasingly competitive and RUS plc has decided to change its strategy. In future, it will provide 'a high-quality service for the discerning guest'.

(a) Summarise the financial and organisational implications of RUS plc's new strategy. **5 Marks**

(b) Discuss the contribution that RUS plc's management accountant could make to the new strategy.

6 Marks
Total marks = 11

10 JOB DESCRIPTIONS

32 mins

(a) Discuss the following issues related to job descriptions.

(i)	Their purposes	**5 marks**
(ii)	Their benefits	**5 marks**
(iii)	Their dangers	**5 marks**

(b) What would be your policy regarding the use and design of job descriptions? **3 marks**
Total marks = 18

11 CARROT AND STICK

36 mins

In *Turning People On: The Motivation Challenge*, Andrew Sargent states that: 'Gone the days when managers could resort to the 'carrot and stick' approach to motivate the workforce.' What do you think Sargent means by this remark, and how far do you agree with Sargent's sentiments? **20 Marks**

12 TRAINING

36 mins

Pavlov Products Limited specialises in veterinary pharmaceuticals and nutrition. It employs scientists and assistants in its laboratories, and production workers in the factory. It also has a sales and marketing function and a finance function.

(a) How should companies like Pavlov Products Ltd identify the training and developmental needs of management, professionals and staff? **8 marks**

(b) How should companies like Pavlov Products Ltd implement development and training programmes? **12 marks**
Total marks = 20

13 PERFORMANCE APPRAISAL SYSTEMS

36 mins

(a) What are the features of an effective performance appraisal system? **10 Marks**
(b) What are the advantages and disadvantages of performance appraisal systems?

10 Marks
Total marks = 20

14 LEADERSHIP STYLE

36 mins

It has been observed that different styles of leadership are required at different stages of an organisation's development

(a) Define 'leadership style' and illustrate your answer with reference to any one well-known classification of leadership styles. **8 Marks**

(b) Explain why the style of leadership may need to change as an organisation passes through the various stages of birth, growth, maturity and decline. **12 Marks**
Total Marks = 20

15   CONSTRUCTIVE CONFLICT   *32 mins*

What are the symptoms of conflict in an organisation? How can a manager convert conflict into constructive competition?   **18 Marks**

16   ORGANISATION LIFE CYCLE   *32 mins*

(a)   Describe the stages of an organisation's life cycle, according to Greiner's model. How useful do you think such models are?   **12 Marks**

(b)   What changes do you think will occur in the role of the management accountant in each phase of the life cycle?   **6 Marks**

Total marks = 18

17   BRINGING ABOUT CHANGE   *32 mins*

(a)   Why is it sometimes difficult to bring about change in organisations?   **9 Marks**

(b)   What are the key processes that help to bring about the successful implementation of change in organisations?   **9 Marks**

Total marks = 18

Exam answer bank

1 STRATEGIC MANAGEMENT

(a) It is important to note that strategic management goes beyond strategic planning - it is a distinct mode of management which proceeds from analysis to implementation and shares the same functions - planning, organising, directing and controlling - as operations management.

Strategic analysis

The first step in the process involves analysis of the situation in which the organisation finds itself. This means identifying the conditions prevailing in both the internal and external environment and the effects of these conditions on the organisation. The following matters will need to be addressed.

(i) *SWOT analysis* (internal strengths and weaknesses, external opportunities and threats). This might include some of the following.

(ii) *Competition analysis*. The organisation must analyse who its competitors are, how and why they are competing, and whether and how competition will increase. The nature of the industry's competitive forces should be addressed.

(iii) *Customer analysis*. In many markets the needs/demands of customers are becoming increasingly sophisticated and complex.

(iv) *Cultural analysis*. The culture or 'feel' of an organisation is seen as being of critical strategic importance. An organisation which has an enterprising, innovative and unique culture will be attractive to investors, customers and employees. Culture must therefore be analysed to see what kind of message it is giving out about the organisation.

(v) *Social analysis*. This can be seen as part of customer analysis since it attempts to identify how the complexity of modern society impacts on the organisation and its customers. It will take into account demographic and economic changes, changes in attitudes in society (such as towards environmental issues) and changes in political attitudes (for example, the favourable light in which the Government views initiative).

Strategic choice

Having analysed where the organisation is, the next step for the strategic manager is to decide where it wants to go. This process of strategic selection involves the following further steps.

(i) Define the company's mission or overall objective: this is often a financial aim - such as to increase the earnings per share ratio - but can sometimes be expressed in rather less precise terms, such as 'to achieve excellence, add value and improve the quality of life'.

(ii) Derive the company's objectives from the mission: having a set of objectives enables management:

(1) to organise and explain the purpose and direction of the business in a small number of general statements about goals

(2) to test the validity of these goals as a means of achieving the organisation's purpose

(3) to predict behaviour

(4) to appraise the validity of decisions about strategies and budgets (by assessing whether these are sufficient to achieve the stated objectives)

(5) to assess and control actual performance.

Objectives should enhance the medium and the long-term future of the company, and may be set for particular functional areas such as marketing, finance and profitability, production, sales, industrial relations, productivity and new development.

(iii) Develop strategies by which these objectives may be met. These can take the form of plans of increasing detail which indicate how the particular objective, say of increasing market share, can be fulfilled by marketing, advertising and sales strategies.

When formulating mission, objectives, strategies and plans the organisation will have to have regard to:

(i) the results of the strategic analysis indicating the current position of the organisation

(ii) the availability of funds and resources in order to carry out the strategies adopted

(iii)   the state of the external environment which will impose pressures on the organisation's achievement of its aims

(iv)   the effect of its strategic selection on the structure of the organisation.

Strategic implementation

Having formulated strategies and plans it only remains to implement them. This will almost certainly involve changes to the way things are done if the process of strategic management has been followed through from first principles. Areas in which the implementation of strategies is likely to cause change are:

(i)   the organisation's structure (such as new subsidiaries, new reporting lines, redefined responsibilities)

(ii)   the organisation's culture (there may have to be a move from bureaucracy towards a task culture if it has been identified that the organisation is in an unstable environment)

(iii)   the quality of all outputs - this may well have to improve

(iv)   attitudes towards innovation, entrepreneurship and individualism

(v)   the degree of control exercised over subordinates, given new emphasis on innovation

(vi)   personnel - the organisation needs to acquire the services of the right personnel to put strategies into practice.

(b)   The process outlined above is usually called the *rational model*. In the real world, people are not entirely logical nor do they have all the information they might like. Lindblom suggests that most strategy making actually proceeds in small incremental steps and in a rather disjointed manner. He used the term *disjointed incrementalism*.

The process involves small scale extensions of past policies. The developments are selected from a limited range of possibilities and may involve a political bargaining process of *partisan mutual adjustment*. An important aspect of the process is that it is largely reactive; unforeseen events provoke a response.

Critics called this model *muddling through*. Quinn suggested that an incremental approach could be satisfactory if managers set a broad direction for developments. This would be *logical incrementalism*. Managers would consciously proceed in small steps whose results could be tested for suitability.

2   **MISSION STATEMENT**

To: Managing Director
From: Anne Accountant
Date: 29 February 200X
Subject: Mission Statements

Contents: Introduction
           Mission statement and strategic planning
           Originating a mission statement
           The scope of mission statements
           The benefits of mission statements

Introduction

A *mission* can be defined as a business's basic function in society. It is often visionary, open-ended and has no time limit for achievement. It is possible however to reach a more expanded definition of mission to include four elements.

(a)   *Purpose*. Why does the company exist, or why do its managers and employees feel it exists?

(i)   To create wealth for shareholders, who take priority over all other stakeholders.

(ii)   To satisfy the needs of all stakeholders (including employees, society at large, for example).

(iii)   To reach some higher goal and objective ('the advancement of society' and so forth).

(b)   *Strategy*. This provides the commercial logic for the company, and so defines:

(i)   the business the company is in

(ii)   the competence and competitive advantages by which it hopes to prosper.

(c)   *Policies and standards of behaviour.* Policies and strategy need to be converted into everyday performance. For example, a service industry that wished to be the best in its market must aim for standards of service, in all its operations, which are at least as good as those found in its competitors. In service businesses, this includes simple matters such as politeness to customers, speed at which phone calls are answered, and so forth.

(d)   *Values.* These relate to the organisation's culture, and are the basic, perhaps unstated beliefs of the people who work in the organisation. For example, a firm's moral principle might mean not taking on an assignment if it believes the client will not benefit, even though this means lost revenue. An example of this can be found in the standards of professional ethics required of accountants.

A *mission statement* is a document embodying some of the matters noted above. A mission statement might be a short sentence, or a whole page. It is intentionally unquantified and vague, and is sometimes seen as a statement of the guiding priorities that govern a firm's behaviour. Mission statements are rarely changed, as otherwise they have less force, and become mere slogans.

(a)   *Purpose*

(i)   The firm's purpose might be described in terms of more than just self interest. A pharmaceutical company might define its corporate mission as 'the well-being of humanity'.

(ii)   The firm's responsibility to its stakeholders.

(b)   *Strategy*

(i)   The statement should identify the type of business the firm is engaged in.

(ii)   The statement should perhaps identify the strategy for competitive advantage the firm intends to pursue.

(c)   *Values*

(i)   The statement should identify values that link with the firm's purpose.
(ii)   The values should reinforce the corporate strategy.

(d)   *Behaviour standards*

(i)   Defined standards of behaviour can serve as benchmarks of performance.
(ii)   Individual employees should be able to apply these standards to their own behaviour.

(e)   *Character*

(i)   The statement should reflect the organisation's actual behaviour and culture, or at least its aspirations for improved behaviour and culture.

(ii)   The statement should be easy to read.

Objectives, on the other hand, are the embodiment of a mission statement in a commercial context. They specify the meaning of a mission in a particular period, market, or situation.

Mission statements and strategic planning

The relationship between mission statements and strategic planning is an ambiguous one. In some cases, the mission statement is prepared after the strategic plan is drawn up as a sort of summary of it. However this would only be done if there was a major change in the company's direction.

Whilst the mission inspires corporate objectives, the strategy is a means for fleshing them out. The strategy also provides directions for specific context. The mission statement cannot institute particular strategies but it can indicate priorities. Say an investment company prided itself on investing funds in companies which it regarded as behaving ethically, and its mission statement contains a clause which says that the company is 'to invest clients' funds in companies whose products promote health'. It would be unlikely to invest in tobacco firms, but no indication is given as to which shares to buy, on which stock exchanges, when to sell, what returns to expect, and so forth.

Originating a mission statement

A mission statement originates at the highest levels of the organisation. It is possible that, given a mission statement is meant to inspire as well as direct, a process of consultation with employees should take place to determine what the mission statement should be, or to assess what would be laughed out of courts. A company which declared its commitment to customer service in a mission

statement, but whose practices for years had been quite the opposite, would have problems in persuading employees to take it seriously. The fact that the employees were consulted about the current ethos in a formal procedure would make the mission statement more effective. The mission statement would be introduced as part of an attempt to change the culture of the organisation.

The scope of mission statements

All areas of corporate life can be covered by a mission statement. This is because it is broadly based, and as a statement of an organisation's values and objectives, it should affect everyone in the organisation. That means its scope is wide-ranging. If it did not affect everybody in each department, from managing director to clerk, then its power would be lessened, and its purpose poorly satisfied.

For example, if a company's mission highlights the provision of *good quality* products and services, then this does not only include the way in which products are made and services delivered, but the way in which commercial relationships are conducted. Given that a successful business requires, in the long term, good commercial relationships, 'quality' applies to these as well.

The benefits of mission statements

The benefits of mission statement are that they:

(a)   describe what the company is about

(b)   provide a guiding philosophy where there are doubts about the direction a company should take, or a decision an individual manager or employee should make

(c)   display the area in which the company is operating

(d)   enable the communication of a common culture throughout the whole organisation

(e)   stimulate debate as to how the mission can be implemented.

3   **ENCOURAGING INNOVATION IN A LARGE ORGANISATION**

An essential job of the senior manager is to establish the organisational climate that encourages and nurtures creativity and innovation. Cultural expectations regarding the way things are done must be built up so that they become deeply ingrained and wide ranging in the organisation.

Innovation is the process of creating and applying something new, such as new methods, products or services, so that the organisation benefits from bringing them into use. The benefit will be to satisfy wants and thus earn profits.

Innovation and entrepreneurial attitudes are best nurtured in a climate that permits and actively encourages new ideas and new ways of doing things. Managers must teach members how to perceive, think and feel in relation to problems and how to cope with external adaptation and internal integration. Conflict must be contained and channelled constructively to find new and better ways of achieving results. This process helps managers anticipate change and plan for it.

To create the climate that will encourage and reward innovation, managers must do the following things.

(a)   Set clear objectives and spell out the freedom to achieve them. Guiding beliefs will focus strategy and give creativity purpose and direction. Managers must be dynamic but also tolerant - they must encourage commitment.

(b)   Offer recognition and reward for creative behaviour and for tasks well done. For creative individuals the scope to think creatively and to achieve results may, to some extent, be its own reward.

(c)   Encourage new ideas and be willing to listen to subordinates' suggestions. Managers must make it clear that they welcome ideas for improving things and making changes. Employees must be allowed to participate with their managers in making decisions to change things that will affect them.

(d)   Permit more interaction between employees within their own work group and between work groups. The creation of a more permissive climate encourages ideas and information to flow and new perspectives on problems and opportunities to be developed. The use of 'quality circles' can improve participation, communication, productivity and efficiency as well as create a sense of teamwork.

(e) Accept and allow for failure. Some ideas may prove impractical and lead to lost time and resources. This must not be allowed to stifle creativity.

To be entrepreneurial is to take risks and show initiative in an attempt to make profits. Managers must encourage certain attitudes and build up certain abilities. The main drive that motivates the entrepreneurial person is a high need for achievement. The manager must therefore promote and encourage the following attitudes and motivations.

(a) The desire for responsibility and accountability for results.

(b) The willingness to take moderate risks in an attempt to achieve high performance.

(c) Self confidence and the willingness to make judgements.

(d) Future orientation to search for and anticipate future opportunities and plan for their successful exploitation.

(e) The willingness to organise work and obtain resources to achieve goals. Entrepreneurs want to get the job done efficiently.

Senior managers must provide a supportive environment and encourage all managers to search for business opportunities.

4   CORPORATE CULTURE

Defining culture

Handy's definition neatly sums up the meaning of culture, which is the complex body of shared values and beliefs of an organisation.

Schein has defined culture in a more detailed way as 'the pattern of basic assumptions that a given group has invented, discovered or developed, in learning to cope with its problems of external adaptation and internal integration, and that have worked well enough to be considered valid and therefore, to be taught to new members as the correct way to perceive, think and feel in relation to these problems.'

IBM has been cited in the question as a company with a strong culture. Other examples of 'the way we do things around here' can be found at Procter and Gamble and at Hewlett Packard. At Procter and Gamble all parts of the organisation's activities focus on product quality. At Hewlett Packard all employees are encouraged to be innovative and the culture is one which encourages individuals to experiment.

How a corporate culture comes into existence

Corporate culture develops along with the organisation as it grows. The development of a particular culture may be deliberate, perhaps through the issuing of policy documents and by selecting and retaining only certain types of employee. Alternatively, the culture may develop more naturally as a result of the leadership style of the organisation's senior managers.

It has been suggested that an organisation's culture develops from three main sources: the organisation's origins, its technology and the dramatic events in its history.

To demonstrate the effect of an organisation's *origins* on the development of culture we can cite the two founders of Philips, who had distinct personal work preferences. One founder preferred technical work, the other concentrated on sales and commercial work.

An organisation's *technology* can give clues to the development of the underlying culture. For example an engineering culture will be very different from mass production culture.

Dramatic events include events such as a recession, a major new product development or a significant lay-off of staff, which could change or mould an organisation's set of shared values or beliefs.

The benefits of a strong corporate culture

A strong corporate culture exists where there is a very clear set of values and beliefs in the organisation. There are a number of benefits in this and Peters and Waterman, in their book *In search of excellence* found that 'dominance and coherence of culture' was an essential feature of 'excellent' companies. The benefits can be listed as follows.

(a) Motivation and satisfaction of employees may be improved by encouraging commitment to the organisation's values and objectives, fostering satisfying team relationships and using 'guiding values' instead of rules and controls.

(b) The organisation will present a positive image in its environment. The cultural attributes of an organisation will affect its appeal to potential customers and suppliers, employees, potential shareholders and so on.

(c) An organisation's culture may encourage adaptability, by supporting innovation, risk-taking, willingness to embrace new methods and so on.

(d) A background of unchanging values (or values which change more slowly, over a longer time-scale, as a result of mere superficial changes) can act as a platform for change, and for the acceptance of change by individuals who may desire some familiarity and security to be retained.

The disadvantage of a strong corporate culture

(a) Culture may be an obstacle to change because by its nature it is a force for continuity and cohesion. If culture itself is continually adapting, there will be none of the sense of security and order and coherent self-image that Peters and Waterman observe in successful business cultures.

(b) Culture establishes patterns of thought and behaviour as a basis for future action. In other words, it establishes *attitudes*. Attitudes are notoriously hard to change - harder than behaviour.

(c) Culture tends to be a force for cohesion and may cause a tendency for 'groupthink' or a cosy complacency, a consensus which is resistant to outsider input and information which contradicts or threatens the group. This sense of infallibility and blindness to dangers in the present course can obviously be detrimental to an organisation's prospects of survival in a changing environment.

5 SOCIAL RESPONSIBILITY

Social responsibility is a hard term to define, but many would say it means acting with regard to social welfare. *No* organisation would ever admit to being socially *irresponsible* and many organisations claim to act responsibly on social issues.

For an organisation to act with social responsibility, it should align its goals with those of the wider society of which it is a part. Whether a society as such has easily defined goals is hard to assess: the purpose and direction of society, not to mention the means by which those goals are achieved, are generally political decisions rather than commercial ones. Is the wider society limited to the national economy or the world as a whole? The consequences of a global corporation acting with social responsibility in one society may cause it to act *without* social responsibility in another. Moreover, a business almost certainly has its own objectives, which, in the long term, it claims will enhance social welfare, if only that the creation of wealth as a result of business activities is felt to be of benefit to society as a whole.

The managers of organisations, however, which seek to be socially responsible rarely start off with a theoretical notion of social responsibility which they then seek to implement. Rather, organisations which act responsibly do so in *response* to pressures from their various *stakeholders*. Some of these pressures are outlined below.

Employees

Employees are *internal* stakeholders. Their relationship with the organisation is twofold. Firstly, it is their labour which keeps the organisation in operational existence. Secondly, as citizens they are members of the wider society in which the organisation exists.

Employees value the certainty and regularity of wages, in other words that the employing organisation will honour the contract of employment. To act with social responsibility also implies a concern and respect for safety in the workplace, whether this relates to equipment, building, or hours worked. (It is believed that repetitive strain injury arises from too much uninterrupted time at the word processor.)

The organisation's social responsibility includes adaptation to other pressures on employee's lifestyles. Workplace crèches, for example, are of great assistance to working women, but employers are unlikely to introduce them without any consequent commercial benefit. If, for example, the cost of labour turnover is higher than the cost of running workplace crèches and if labour turnover is reduced significantly by a workplace crèche, then the crèche can be justified (in financial terms).

Management has a certain amount of discretion, but this is circumscribed by law. Health and safety for example is the subject of regulation, as it was felt that commercial imperatives would not justify the expense, and that employers are not necessarily altruistic. Other benefits are won as the result of the relationship between management and organised labour.

The exercise of social responsibility towards the workforce is constrained by the law, by organised labour, and in some instances by the recognition that social responsibility can be of benefit in encouraging employee loyalty and skill.

Customers

Customers are stakeholders in that they pay for the organisation's output of goods and services. Here the situation is more complex. In some consumer goods sectors, public attitudes - with some direction from government and lobby groups - have made the environmental impact of an organisation's activities open to public comment. This has led suppliers to reduce CFCs in aerosol cans, and to introduce ranges of goods which are supposed to be friendly to the environment.

Finally, it sometimes happen when a firm bids for a contract with a local authority, for example, that *contract compliance*, by which the contract is only awarded to a firm which operates an equal opportunities policy, will be required of any successful bidder.

Suppliers

In multinational corporations, the exercise of social responsibility is distributed over several countries, but again, management will only let it override commercial objectives if it either is part of the inbuilt culture of the firm, or if the voice of public opinion in the market is strong. An example is the use of rainforest hardwoods: some consumer organisations are suggesting boycotting these products.

A supplier may also make restrictions on the end-use of products a condition of sale. For example, a supplier of high-technology items may require that these are not re-exported to the enemies of the nation where the supplier is based.

Professional bodies

Control is exercised over certain members of management by their membership of professional bodies, which have standards of ethics and conduct.

Elected authorities

Society's elected political representatives are external stakeholders and can affect management in a number of ways, by legislation as has already been mentioned, by influencing the climate of public opinion, or by trying to persuade commercial organisations to follow a particular line or policy. An example is business sponsorship of the arts in the UK. (The tenor of government policy has been to reduce government funding and to encourage commercial organisations to avail themselves of the marketing opportunities thereby provided.)

Shareholders

Shareholders are connected stakeholders. The main interest of shareholders is profit, and they might have objections to money being spent on projects which are socially responsible but which reduce the return on the investment. As many shareholders are large institutions like pension funds, then *their* duties can be adversely affected by the use of organisational resources on activities which do not make a profit.

It is possible that some shareholders, and other commentators, would assert that the creation of wealth is the only desirable social objective of a business and anything which intervenes in this objective is damaging in the long run.

Management issues

Social responsibility has costs and benefits for an organisation, and management have to weigh up the conflicting demands of different stakeholders. There is also the problem of managing social responsibility policies and activities so that the most effective use is made of the resources allocated for the purpose. This means:

(a)   monitoring the expectations people have of the organisation, as an enterprise which trumpets its environmental friendliness will be expected to live up to its claims in all areas

(b)   achieving the maximum good publicity from the project

(c)   selecting an appropriate choice of socially responsible activities which can be divided between:

(i)   ensuring that the firm's core activities are conducted in a socially responsible way

(ii)   subsidising, supporting or sponsoring those activities which are for public welfare (eg charitable donations, Prince's Trust) etc

(d)   clearly distinguishing between what are the minimum acceptable standards in a particular situation, and what are additional to them.

6   CONTINGENCY THEORY

Following the emergence of the open systems approach (or 'analogy') and its recognition of environmental influences on the organisation, an essentially pragmatic view was developed which argued that *no* single theory can guarantee the organisation's effectiveness. Essentially, 'it all depends'.

This *contingency approach* aims to suggest the most appropriate organisational design and management style *in a given set of circumstances*. It rejects the universal 'one-best-way' approach, in favour of analysis of the internal factors and external environment of each organisation, and the design of organisation and management as a 'best fit' between the tasks, people and environment in the particular situation. As Buchanan and Huczynski put it: 'With the coming of contingency theory, organisational design ceased to be 'off-the-shelf', but became tailored to the particular specific needs of an organisation.'

The contingency approach grew from the results of a number of research studies which showed the importance of different factors on the structure and performance of an organisation, and indicated that there is in fact no inevitable correlation between the structures and cultures prescribed by previous theories and organisational effectiveness. Joan Woodward, for example, demonstrated that 'different technologies imposed different kinds of demands on individuals and organisations and that these demands have to be met through an appropriate form of organisation'. Lawrence and Lorsch, Burns and Stalker found that different types of *environment*, with a different pace of *change* and degree of uncertainty, suited different organisation structures and cultures: Burns and Stalker's 'mechanistic' and 'organismic' systems, for example. Fiedler, Handy and others suggest that group effectiveness is contingent upon a number of variables, not only the leader and the group but the 'situation', the task and environment of the group.

According to Tom Lupton: 'It is of great practical significance whether one kind of managerial "style" or procedure for arriving at decisions, or one kind of organisational structure, is suitable for all organisations, or whether the managers in each organisation have to find the expedient that will best meet the particular circumstances of size, technology, competitive situation and so on.'

This absence of 'prescription' is the main factor that sets contingency theory apart from classical and human relations 'theories', which attempted to formulate a set of principles which, if applied, would lead to the efficient and effective functioning of an organisation.

The other main difference is in 'orientation'. Classical theory was essentially an *organisational* theory, while human relations was a *management* theory. Each concentrated on a particular aspect of the work situation, seen as most important at the time: in a sense, human relations emerged as a 'corrective' approach, from a critical perception of classical theory - in the same way that contingency theory evolved from a critical perspective on both.

The classical approach to management was primarily concerned with the structure and activities of the *formal* organisation. Effective organisation was seen to be mainly dependent on factors such as the division of work, the establishment of a rational hierarchy of authority, span of control and unity of command.

The practical application of Taylor's 'scientific management' approach was the use of work study techniques to break work down into its smallest and simplest component parts, and the selection and training of workers to perform a single task in the most efficient way.

The classical school contributed techniques for studying the nature of work and solving problems of how it could be organised more efficiently.

Human relations thinking was founded by Elton Mayo, whose response to classical ideas was that: 'We have failed to train students in the study of social situations; we have thought that first-class technical training was sufficient in a modern and mechanical age. As a consequence, we are technically competent as no other age in history has been; and we combine this with utter social incompetence.'

Mayo was responsible for the major early social research project known as the Hawthorne Studies, from which emerged the approach emphasising the importance of human attitudes, values and relationships for the effectiveness of organisations. It concentrated mainly on relationships and the concept of social man, with an emphasis on how employees' social or 'belonging' needs could be satisfied at work. This was called the 'Human relations' movement.

These ideas were followed up by various social psychologists - eg Maslow, McGregor, Herzberg and Likert - but with a change of emphasis. People were still considered to be the crucial factor in determining organisational effectiveness, but were recognised to have more than merely physical and social needs. Attention shifted towards 'higher' psychological needs for growth and self-fulfilment. This was labelled the *neo-Human Relations School*.

Contingency theory was founded on research evidence showing that the principles advanced by the two previous schools did not necessarily correlate with organisational effectiveness. The need for organisation structures to be *adaptive* (Lawrence and Lorsch, Burns and Stalker) rather than universal, on classical principles, became clear. Mayo's human relations ideas failed to make an impact at the Hawthorne plant once applied. Contingency thinkers moved away from particular aspects and into consideration of the 'whole' organisational system and its environment.

Another difference between the schools was the viewpoint of those behind them. The classical theorists were mainly early practising managers - such as Henri Fayol and F W Taylor. They analysed their own experience in management to produce a set of what they saw as 'principles' applicable in a wide variety of situations. The human relations approach, however, was pioneered mainly by social scientists - rather than practising managers - and was based on research into human behaviour, with the intention of describing and thereafter predicting behaviour in organisations. Contingency Theory, as befits its flexible nature, has been championed by a wide variety of researchers, writers and managers in a number of disciplines.

7   ORGANISATION PRINCIPLES

(a)   *Line organisation* refers to a way of deploying authority in an organisation. It is based on the principle of the scalar chain which links superiors and subordinates. Authority, commands etc flow *down* the scalar chain from superior to subordinate. Accountability flows upwards, so that subordinates are responsible to superiors. The scalar chain is the term used to describe the organisation's management hierarchy, that is the chain of superiors from the lowest to the highest rank.

A line organisation will be divided into departments, each headed by an executive responsible to the highest authority and deriving power and authority from it. Departmental heads will, in turn, delegate to sub-department heads and so on down the scalar chain. The department divisions may be based on, for instance, function, geography, task or political affiliation or a mixture of these bases. Formal communication is up and down the lines of authority. If, however, communication between different branches of the chain is necessary, horizontal communication saves time and is likely to be more accurate, as long as superiors know that such communication is taking place.

An organisation has many such chains of authority and command, but all of them originate at the topmost management authority which in a company is the board of directors. Managers at different levels in the hierarchy are all links in a chain of command.

There might be a tendency for chains of command within a single organisation to get longer as the organisation grows older; the length of the chain of command is a function of:

(i)   the size of the organisation
(ii)   the type and complexity of the products it makes or services it provides
(iii)   the diversity of its products and services
(iv)   its geographical spread
(v)   the number and complexity of controls required
(vi)   the type of people it employs.

No rules have been (or can be) laid down for how chains of command should be structured, but a general observation is that chains of command should be kept as short as possible, consistent with sound management.

The *span of control* or span of management refers to the number of subordinates working for the superior official. In other words, if a manager has five subordinates, the span of control is five. Various writers of the classical school, such as Fayol, Graicunas and Urwick, argued that the

managerial span of control should be limited to between three and six. Their arguments were based on the twin beliefs that:

(i)   there should be tight managerial control from the top of the organisation; and that

(ii)   there are physical and mental limitations to a manager's ability to control people and activities.

To ensure effective control, the number of subordinates and tasks over which a manager has supervisory responsibilities should therefore be restricted to what is physically and mentally possible. A narrow span of control offers:

(i)   tight control and close supervision (better co-ordination of subordinates' activities)
(ii)   time to think and plan; managers are not burdened with too many day to day problems
(iii)   reduced delegation; a manager can do more of his work himself
(iv)   better communication with subordinates, who are sufficiently few to allow this to occur.

The army is a classic example of a line organisation. Different ranks have defined authority and power. Another example of line organisation is a traditionally structured finance department in a commercial company. The junior cashier reports to the cashier supervisor who reports to the treasury accountant who reports to the chief accountant who reports to the divisional financial controller who reports to the finance director who reports to the chief executive. Each of these people, apart from the junior cashier, is likely to have more than one subordinate (eg the chief accountant will have not only the treasury accountant but also a financial accountant and a management accountant as subordinates).

(b)   *Matrix organisation*

The concept of *matrix organisation* has emerged, dividing authority between functional managers and product or project managers or co-ordinators. This is a way to give a formal status in a line organisation departmented by function to necessary groupings of people in different functions. Communication and co-ordination are, in a way, both horizontal and vertical.

Matrix management first developed in the 1950s in the USA in the aerospace industry. Lockheed-California, the aircraft manufacturers, were organised in a functional hierarchy. Customers were unable to find a manager in Lockheed to whom they could take their problems and queries about their particular orders, and Lockheed found it necessary to employ 'project expediters' as customer liaison officials. From this developed 'project co-ordinators', responsible for co-ordinating line managers into solving a customer's problems. Up to this point, these new officials had no functional responsibilities. With increasingly heavy customer demand, Lockheed eventually created 'programme managers', with full authority for project budgets and programme design and scheduling. This dual authority structure may be shown diagrammatically as a management *grid*.

Matrix organisation is also used in multinationals. For example a person might report to:

(i)   a functional boss
(ii)   a regional or country boss.

Matrix management thus challenges classical ideas about organisation in two ways:

(i)   it rejects the idea of one person, one boss
(ii)   it subverts the bureaucratic ethic of authority based on status in the formal hierarchy.

The *advantages* of a matrix structure are said to be the following.

(i)   *Greater flexibility*

      (1)   *People.* Employees develop an attitude geared to accepting change, and departmental monopolies are broken down.

      (2)   *Tasks and structure.* The matrix structure may be short-term (as with project teams) or readily amended.

(ii)   *Re-orientation.* A functional department will often be production-orientated: product management will create a market orientation.

(iii)   A structure for allocating responsibility to managers for end-results.

(iv)   Inter-disciplinary co-operation and a mixing of skills and expertise.

(v)   Arguably, motivation of employees by providing them with greater participation in planning and control decisions.

The disadvantages of matrix organisation are said to be as follows.

(i)   Dual authority threatens a conflict between functional managers and product/project managers.

(ii)   One individual with two or more bosses is more likely to suffer stress at work.

(iii)   Matrix management can be more costly - product management posts are added, meetings have to be held, and so on.

(iv)   It may be difficult for the management of an organisation to accept a matrix structure and the culture of participation, shared authority and ambiguity that it fosters.

8   THE MARKETING CONCEPT

The marketing concept has been defined as a 'management orientation or outlook, that accepts that the key task of the organisation is to determine the needs, wants and values of a target market and to adapt the organisation to delivering the desired satisfaction more effectively and efficiently than its competitors'.

In other words, customer needs and the market environment are considered of paramount importance. Since technology, markets, the economy, social attitudes, fashions, the law and so on are all constantly changing, customer needs are likely to change too. The marketing concept is that changing needs and attitudes must be identified, and products or services adapted and developed to satisfy them. Only in this way can a supplier hope to operate successfully and profitably (if the supplier of the goods or service is a profit-making organisation).

Some firms may be *product oriented* and others *sales oriented*, although a firm should be *marketing oriented* to be successful in the longer term.

(a)   A product oriented firm is one which believes that if it can make a good quality product at a reasonable price, then customers will inevitably buy it with a minimum of marketing effort by the firm. The firm will probably concentrate on product developments and improvements, and production efficiencies to cut costs. If there is a lack of competition in the market, or a shortage of goods to meet a basic demand, then product orientation should be successful. However, if there is competition and over-supply of a product, demand must be stimulated, and a product-oriented firm will resort to the 'hard-sell' or 'product push' to 'convince' the customer of what he wants.

(b)   A sales oriented firm is one which believes that in order to achieve cost efficiencies through large volumes of output, it must invest heavily in sales promotion. This attitude implies a belief that potential customers are by nature sales-resistant and have to be persuaded to buy (or buy more), so that the task of the firm is to develop a strong sales department, with well-trained salesmen. The popular image of a used car salesman or a door-to-door salesman would suggest that sales orientation is unlikely to achieve any long-term satisfaction of customer needs.

The marketing concept should be applied by management because it is the most practical philosophy for achieving any organisation's objective. A profit-making company's objective might be to achieve a growth in profits, earnings per share or return on shareholder funds. By applying the marketing concept to product design the company might hope to make more attractive products, hence to achieve sustained sales growth and so make higher profits.

Another implication of the marketing concept is that an organisation's management should continually be asking 'what business are we in?' This is a question which is fundamental to strategic planning too, and the importance of developing a market orientation to strategic planning is implicit in the marketing concept.

(a)   With the product concept and selling concept, an organisation produces a good or service, and then expects to sell it. The nature of the organisation's business is determined by what it has chosen to produce, and there will be a reluctance to change over to producing something different.

(b)   With the marketing concept, an organisation commits itself to supplying what customers need. As those needs change, so too must the goods or services which are produced.

If the marketing concept is to be applied successfully, it must be shared by all managers and supervisors in an organisation. 'Marketing is a force which should pervade the entire firm. It must enter into the thinking and behaviour of all decision-makers regardless of their level within the organisation and their functional area' (Boyd and Massy). 'Marketing' in its broader sense covers not just selling, advertising, sales promotion and pricing, but also product design and quality, after sales service, distribution, reliability of delivery dates and in many cases (such as the retailing industry) purchasing supplies. This is because the customers' needs relate to these items as well as more obvious 'marketing' factors such as sales price and how products are promoted.

Another way of expressing the important point made above is: 'most firms have a marketing or sales department, but the marketing concept should be shared by managers in every department'.

It could also be suggested that marketing should aim to maximise customer satisfaction, but within the constraints that all firms have a responsibility to society as a whole and to the environment. Not only is there the idea that 'high gross national product also means high gross national pollution' but also there is a need to make efficient use of the world's scarce and dwindling natural resources.

(a) Some products which consume energy (motor cars, houses) should perhaps make more efficient use of the energy they consume.

(b) It may be possible to extend the useful life of certain products.

(c) Other products might be built smaller, so that they make use of fewer materials (products made using microtechnology).

9 **RUS PLC**

(a) *Financial and organisational implications*

RUS is chasing a different market, targeting high spending customers whose requirements will be different. Investment in buildings and fixtures includes:

(i) decoration
(ii) changes to room sizes (eg conversion of pairs of single rooms into suites)
(iii) more luxurious furnishings
(iv) perhaps expanded restaurant and kitchen facilities
(v) swimming pool, gymnasium etc
(vi) more opulent spaces
(vii) enhancing the hotel's grounds and gardens
(viii) carparking facilities.

Other expenditure will arise from:

(i) more staff, to provide the service required
(ii) more training
(iii) the greater variety of food offered to guests (hence kitchen costs will rise)
(iv) advertising to reach the target segment.

There will be few customers but they will be paying more.

Organisationally, the increased numbers in staff must be given more training, and existing staff will have to learn to cater differently for the new customers. Furthermore, there is unlikely to be the same deployment of staff as before, catering for family and business customers at different times. More effort will need to be spent on management and marketing. Quality circles could be introduced.

(b) The management accountant's contribution to the new strategy is as follows.

(i) To provide cost and revenue information in the initial research and planning phase, and to forecast future income and expenditure.

(ii) To cost any improvements to buildings and furnishings.

(iii) To suggest an appropriate pricing policy.

(iv) To raise external finance (eg from the bank) if substantial capital investment is needed and borrowing is necessary.

(v) To draw up tactical plans and budgets for the changeover.

(vi) To set up and operate new management accounting systems to monitor and control the hotel's performance.

(vii) To suggest appropriate non-financial performance measures, in particular with relation to quality of service.

(viii) To consider if the hotel's new clients will need services such as travellers cheques encashment etc, if they are from overseas.

(ix) To provide regular and suitable management information.

10 JOB DESCRIPTIONS

Tutorial note. Don't lose marks by ignoring the last part of the question, in which your own opinion is sought.

Examiner's comment. Good answers showed 'the dangers of job descriptions against a broad-brush discussion of bureaucratic/mechanistic and organic systems...No marks were awarded for candidates who presented a suggested job description framework, since the question was about policy rather than about detail'. Some candidates wrote about person specifications etc, evidently confusing them with job descriptions.

(a) (i) A *job description* is a written statement of the important responsibilities of a job, and their organisational and operational interrelationships. Although they vary from firm to firm, a typical job description might contain the job title, a list of duties, reporting relationships, and hours of work.

In recruitment, a job description can the used to determine identify the skills needed from the new recruit. This is especially true if a pre-existing position is to be filled, rather than one created from scratch. (A person specification can be developed from a job description.)

A job description makes clear what a person is expected to do, and thus makes it easier for the organisation to function.

Job descriptions can be used for job evaluation purposes, as they focus the attention on the job, in comparison with other jobs.

(ii) *Benefits of job descriptions*

Job descriptions are an essential way in which the organisation allocates labour and carries out its activities. If work processes are standardised, as in a bureaucracy, then the job description will function as a part of the socio-technical system of the organisation. A job description, by defining the relationships of the position to other positions, is a part of organisation structure.

One of the economic benefits of organisations is that they permit division of labour and specialisation. Job descriptions can enforce these features by writing them into the work that people do.

Some people value certainty and security, and a job description, by precisely delineating what a person must do, can provide such psychological assurance.

They can be used in the appraisal, discipline or grievance process, so that the employee is appraised as to what he or she is expected to do. They can be appealed to in case of dispute.

They can pinpoint weaknesses in the organisation structure, if there are disputes as to authority.

(iii) *Dangers of job descriptions*

These days people are supposed to be more flexible, and people might end up taking on functions in addition to those in their job description. It thus becomes a waste of time, perhaps even discouraging teamworking.

We have suggested that job descriptions are suitable for bureaucracy, in which individual positions are outlined. Bureaucracies encourage commitment to the job as such rather than to the firm or its wider mission; this is because the job has been defined from the outset.

By contrast, an organic organisation requires a continual redefinition of the task in the light of the organisation's wider mission. Job descriptions focus on the detail of the job not on the wider mission of the firm.

Job descriptions assume that the job designer knows best in advance how a job should be done and, as such, they might be relics of scientific management. It is possible that, if adhered to rigidly, they can inhibit individual and organisational learning, by artificially prescribing the relationships between positions and inhibiting creative team work. Moreover, many job descriptions do not employ the wider systems thinking perspective which might be considered necessary for organisational learning.

They may be inappropriate for some jobs, especially those which cannot be broken down into a sequence of repetitive routine tasks. For certain jobs, such as customer care, the job description may not outline those items which make a particular difference.

(b) *Policy regarding the use of job descriptions*

> *Tutorial note.* Here is one set of suggestions, but you could quite easily have come up with something quite different.

    (i)   Job descriptions should be brief, should focus on *what* the employee is expected to achieve, as opposed to *how* this is done, except where there are vital reasons to specify procedures.

    (ii)   Job descriptions should contain a paragraph about the context of the job.

    (iii)   A job description should identify the skills and competences a person is expected to bring to the job.

    (iv)   It should support the mission of the organisation so that where appropriate the employee cannot easily evade responsibilities at the margins of what he normally does.

    (v)   Job descriptions should be given to the holder of each part and to their supervisors. They should form that basis of any scheme of appraisal.

    (vi)   Job descriptions should be kept up to date by the holders and their supervisors, mediated by the HR department, to prevent gaps or overlaps developing.

11   CARROT AND STICK

The 'carrot and stick' approach to motivation uses both rewards and punishments to motivate behaviour in employees which displays adherence to organisational norms and the pursuit of organisational as opposed to purely personal objectives.

Rewards, or positive motivators, in the carrot and stick approach, include extrinsic rewards, such as more pay, bonuses and so forth, and intrinsic rewards (such as a sense of recognition or of being liked). Punishments include dismissal, demotion and reprimand.

An implication of the carrot and stick model could be that it assumes that all human beings have the same attitude to work and motivation. Underlying this model is a behaviourist 'common sense' which would suggest that good behaviour can be conditioned by rewards and punishments of a fairly simple kind. Good behaviour, as it is conditioned, can thus be replicated in any number of individuals.

Sargent's statement implies that this model of motivation, where manipulative managers can dangle rewards and threaten punishments as a means to generate higher levels of performance, is out of date and no longer appropriate, and moreover, is no longer used.

In its place, some writers argue that management now have a more sophisticated repertoire of motivational techniques at their disposal. Some of them involve far reaching cultural changes, but there is a recognition that, as human beings are complex, so too are their expectations of, and behaviour in, the workplace.

Some more complex theories of motivation, such as Maslow's hierarchy of needs, Herzberg's two factor theory, Expectancy theory and Handy's motivational calculus, have been around for some time. Moreover, personnel departments or interviewers generally take into account factors of individual personality (eg is the interviewee by nature industrious?) when interviewing. In practice, therefore, the carrot and stick approach, which suggests that all people can be motivated in the same way, has never been taken to its logical conclusion and applied universally or completely.

The argument that the carrot and stick approach is a thing of the past is developed from a number of trends in management that have been apparent over the past few years.

An important motivating factor, as it were, for businesses has been the establishment of Japanese factories in the UK, and the success of Japanese industry as a whole in the decades since World War II. Companies afraid of this competitive threat have looked to see how their own performance can be

improved. It has been common to attribute part of the success of Japanese companies to the management culture, and employee motivation is part of this. In particular:

(a) employees' skills are necessary in suggesting improvements to the company's performance, so that more is required of them than simple adherence to present rules: instead their creativity is valued

(b) it is believed that communication between management and workforce is much better

(c) it is realised that employee participation in decision making can improve productivity in some cases, and so this would lead to an emphasis on group harmony.

A second factor has been the growth in the service sector, where 'people' issues are often more important than technical ones in providing services and generating repeat business.

Another factor perhaps is the increasing amount of technology that is used, which means that valuable expertise possessed by both management and staff. This is helpful if the workforce can share the greater commitment to organisational objectives as management.

Broadly speaking then, Sargent is proposing that management is (or if not, should be) much more sophisticated in its approach to motivation. Ways should be found to involve the employees far more than before in decision making, so that adversarial attitudes between managers and staff can be abandoned. Motivation is a matter of hearts and minds, as well as wallets and pockets.

It is likely that Sargent's statement is an over generalisation for a number of reasons.

(a) In some sectors, 'carrots' certainly have been a motivating factor in recent years. An example is given by the financial services sector, where teams of brokers, for example, depart to different employers offering more money. Government policy in the 1980s (tax cuts to provide incentives) evidenced a belief in economic incentives. Whether that belief is justified is another question.

(b) The stick is still used in disciplinary matters (eg adherence to rules).

(c) Organised labour is less powerful than before. Management has tried to channel workers solidarity to the benefit of the company. New forms of participation and 'empowerment' (to use the American term) go hand in hand with a decline in workers' power in other areas. There is perhaps less need to use the carrot and stick than before.

(d) The biggest stick of all is, arguably, redundancy, although management can shift the blame for wielding it on to general economic conditions, or on to Japanese competition. The contraction in manufacturing jobs has led to a more compliant workforce. To put it another way, the need for work and security is a powerful motivating factor in some regions, and so the workforce is willing to adopt whatever new techniques are felt necessary.

(e) Skills shortages and demographic trends. In certain high tech industries there are skill shortages. Management therefore tries to keep those workers whose skills it most values, and to employ their services productively. If this means satisfying an employee's higher needs (on Maslow's hierarchy) then so be it.

(f) The increase in part time employment has also increased manager's power to use the stick to enforce labour discipline, as the threat of unemployment is quite severe.

To conclude, then, a decline in the institutional power of organised labour power gave management power to reorganise working practices. This has coincided with Japanese competition, whose success has been in part attributed to employee involvement and harmony.

The carrot and stick approach is not excluded by these developments, as it may be the approach which most effectively motivates certain individuals or groups, or is most appropriate to certain work situations.

12   TRAINING

Training is the 'systematic development of the attitudes, knowledge and skill patterns required by an individual in order to perform adequately a given task or job'.

(a) **Identifying training and developmental needs**

There are two interlocking sets of needs: the **needs of the organisation**, and the **needs/capacities of the member of staff** or manager.

Strategic impact. Many organisations are realising that training cannot be narrowly technical, but must be part of a wider strategy to promote organisational and individual learning.

Training needs resulting from change

(i) A new computer system will require skills training in that system.

(ii) A change in corporate culture (eg customer care programmes, enhancing customer service) will require different attitudes and capabilities from different members of staff.

(iii) Technical training will be necessary for some positions (eg senior accountancy positions might require the CIMA qualification).

Training in conditions of stability

(i) **Operational departments**, perhaps with the help of strategic planners, can suggest to the training department areas of work where they think that training might be beneficial.

(ii) The **personnel or training department** itself may **require** levels of training for new staff and to upgrade or maintain current skills.

(iii) Training needs will be identified by considering the gap between:

    (1) Job requirements
    (2) The ability of the job holder

In Pavlov Products there are a variety of training needs.

(i) Managers will have to deploy different management and leadership styles for the production workers and the research scientists, as the jobs of these two groups are different.

(ii) Researchers might need training in management skills, although they themselves would be expected to keep abreast of technical developments in their fields and would use training sessions to communicate any new insights.

(iii) Staff might contribute to the training of their colleagues (on the job training) and need to be advised of new techniques: modern approaches to factory organisation would suggest that the involvement of staff in setting standards and in studying work leads to enhanced efficiency. Training will thus be part of sharing good news. ·

(b) **Implementing a training programme**

Training objectives

Training objectives are tangible, observable targets which trainees should be capable of doing at the end of the course.

Training methods

(i) Residential courses.
(ii) Day courses or lectures.
(iii) Programmed learning, perhaps with computer assistance. This is interactive.

Costs and benefits

The training course should only go ahead if the likely benefits are expected to exceed the costs of designing and then running the course. The problem here is not so much in estimating costs, but in estimating the potential benefits.

(i) Costs will be the costs of the training establishment, training materials, the salaries of the staff attending training courses, their travelling expenses, the salaries of training staff etc.

(ii) Benefits might be measured in terms of:

    (1) Quicker working and therefore reductions in overtime or staff numbers
    (2) Greater accuracy of work
    (3) More extensive skills.

The benefits are more easily stated in general terms than quantified in money terms.

When the training course has been designed, it may be decided to have a pilot test of the course. The purpose of the test would be to find out whether the training scheme appears to achieve what

it has set out to do, or whether some revisions are necessary. After the pilot test, the scheme can be implemented in full.

Review and evaluation

(i) **Ask the trainees** whether they thought the training programme was relevant to their work, and whether they found it useful.

(ii) **Measure what the trainees have learned** on the course, perhaps by means of a 'test' at the end of the course.

(iii) **Study the subsequent behaviour of the trainees** in their jobs to measure how the training scheme has altered the way they do their work. This is possible where the purpose of the course was to learn a particular skill.

(iv) Find out whether the training has affected the work or behaviour of **other employees not on the course** - eg seeing whether there has been a general change in attitudes arising from a new course in, say, computer terminal work. This form of monitoring would probably be reserved for senior managers in the training department.

(v) See whether the training (all training schemes collectively) has contributed to the **overall objectives** of the organisation. This too is a form of monitoring reserved for senior managers and would perhaps be discussed at board level in the organisation.

13 PERFORMANCE APPRAISAL SYSTEMS

(a) Most large firms have a regular system of appraising staff. The objectives of staff appraisal systems are to help in developing staff members to their full potential and to enable the organisation to allocate their human resources in the most efficient way possible. To achieve these objectives an effective appraisal system is likely to incorporate certain key characteristics.

(i) Reports on employees should be made out in writing and at fixed intervals. Staff appraisal is a sensitive operation and a written record of the assessment may remove any doubts or uncertainties which arise at a later date. The report is part of a record, the personnel record, which charts an employee's progress within the organisation. The intervals at which the appraisal should be carried out depend on the nature of the employee's work. For specialist staff who move from one long-term assignment to another, appraisal may be appropriate after each assignment is completed. For staff engaged in more routine work, an interval of six months or a year may be suitable.

(ii) Written reports should be objective. An employee's superior may be inclined to assess harshly to excuse his own poor performance; alternatively, an easy-going relationship during day-to-day work may make a superior feel reluctant to be critical, especially if his subordinate's promotion prospects may be harmed. One way of improving objectivity is to make the assessment form very detailed: the more specific the assessor is required to be, the less margin there is for subjective responses.

(iii) Appraisal should be consistent throughout the organisation. This can cause problems in organisations which, like banks, have many semi-autonomous branches. Again, the use of detailed assessment forms (standard throughout the organisation) will help, but the assessment form is only the beginning of the appraisal process and care must be taken to ensure consistency in the later stages too.

(iv) Assessments should be discussed with the person assessed. If employees do not know what is being written about them they will not be able to improve in areas where shortcomings have been noted. This could cause particular frustration if the assessment system is used as part of a process of selecting staff for promotion.

(v) Persons conducting the appraisal interviews should be trained and experienced in the necessary techniques.

(vi) The employee should be encouraged to contribute to the appraisal process. Ideally, he should have sight of the written assessment in time to consider his response before being called to interview. During the interview the emphasis ought not to be on problems and obstacles, but on opportunities. The interviewee should be encouraged to talk about his career plans, his knowledge and skills and how they could be put to better use, and to make suggestions for improving the way his work is carried out.

(vii)   There should be adequate follow-up after the interview has taken place. If the system is to be effective, staff must have confidence in it. This will only happen if results are seen to follow from the assessments.

(b)   *Advantages of appraisal systems*

(i)   They enable the organisation to gather information about the skills and potential of employees and to identify training needs.

(ii)   They provide a system on which salary reviews and promotions can be based.

(iii)   They help to develop the employee's potential by directing his attention to particular strengths and weaknesses.

(iv)   They allow the employee and his assessor to discuss and agree on personal objectives.

(v)   They may contribute to staff motivation.

Disadvantages of appraisal systems

(i)   The subjective element in such systems cannot be entirely eliminated.

(ii)   They depend for their success on a mutual confidence between the assessor and the employee assessed. In practice, it is difficult to achieve that confidence.

(iii)   It is difficult to go beyond appraisal of past performance, which may be an inadequate guide to future performance in a different job. If an appraisal scheme is used as a guide to promotion potential this is a serious disadvantage.

(iv)   They often do not lead to improvements in performance. Criticism of areas where performance has been weak can lead to a defensive response and future performance may actually deteriorate.

(v)   There are many posts, particularly in technical roles, where further promotion is impossible, performance is standardised at a high level and experience is infinitely valuable. To the incumbents of such posts a formal appraisal system may seem like a waste of time.

14   LEADERSHIP STYLE

(a)   **Leadership is the art of managing people's performance to achieve goals.** Leadership behaviour can be analysed according to the leader's general approach to his or her subordinates. This general approach is called leadership style and is usually considered to lie somewhere on a **spectrum ranging from autocratic through consultative and democratic to laissez-faire.**

Ashridge Management College studies in the UK distinguished **four main styles.**

The tells style. The manager makes all the decisions and requires unquestioning **obedience.** This is very efficient in fast but routine work as decisions are made quickly. However, it does not allow for routine feedback from subordinates or permit the use of initiative so it is much less effective under fluid and changing conditions.

The sells style. The manager still makes all the decisions but puts effort into **motivating subordinates** by explaining the reasoning behind decisions. This is still a largely one way process, but can obtain greater commitment and flexibility of action as staff understand the overall situation and intention.

The consults style. The manager takes account of **staff input into decisions** but has the final word. This style makes use of staff knowledge, skill and experience and can improve commitment. However, the search for compromise can inhibit vigorous action.

The joins style. Decisions are made entirely democratically. High levels of motivation can ensue, but the leader's authority may be undermined and the decision making process can be very slow.

The studies found that subordinates generally preferred the consults style but usually felt that their managers used the tells or sells styles. Also subordinates disliked working for managers **who did not have a consistent style.**

(b)   When a business is being set up from scratch, it will live almost from hand to mouth, making mistakes, exploiting opportunities and solving problems as they arise. There will usually only be a small group involved. Whether they are partners or a single principal and a few employees, the ethos is likely to be one of vision, creativity, flexibility, and community spirit. Effective leadership is

therefore likely to be rather **democratic,** to encourage commitment and make maximum use of the available talent, when possible. However, founders with clear ideas of where they are going may be quite **autocratic,** and **crises are best managed firmly.**

A company which grows successfully will eventually find its progress limited by the **finite abilities of the founders.** They will discover that they cannot do everything and the **skills of professional specialists** like accountants, sales people and production engineers must be obtained if the concern is not to stagnate. Top management will now be at one remove from their staff, operations will be more complex and **a participative style will be more difficult to use.** For many companies this is a time of crisis as the founders lose their way.

If successful growth continues, overall management of the company can develop in different ways. **A simple, stable environment** may allow continuing firm direction from the top. However, a **complex or rapidly changing environment** may require extensive delegation of authority: a laissez-faire style of top management, in other words. On the other hand, severe external threats may still require a firm hand at the top.

A company can **decline** for a variety of reasons, including **management failure.** When decline is identified and acknowledged, hard decisions have to be taken, often redundancy and other severe effects on employees. This requires very competent leadership which can combine firmness of purpose in implementing difficult programmes with a maximum of consultation, communication and sympathy with the victims. The balance is very difficult to strike.

15   CONSTRUCTIVE CONFLICT

Conflict can be defined as a failure to reach common agreement; it can also be an indicator of poor quality relationships within an enterprise. The existence of conflict is often reflected in the struggle for power within organisations.

The tendency for conflict to occur gave rise to the industrial relations function of personnel management. Industrial relations personnel have specific responsibility for effective negotiation so that conflict can be resolved and utilised as a mechanism for building understanding and common purpose within organisations such that industrial harmony is created.

Conflict becomes a problem to an organisation when it upsets the atmosphere of the working environment such that a disruptive, unco-operative or negative culture begins to develop. The main symptom of conflict is the expression by employees of a dissatisfaction with the current situation in the work environment.

People (either as individuals or a working groups) may develop entrenched viewpoints - they refuse to budge from their strongly held views. They may develop erratic behaviour patterns - directing their pent-up emotions against people or objects. This can be evidenced in a range of behaviour from actually damaging industrial equipment to a tendency to short temper and resentment towards management.

A more common symptom of conflict is negativity - the propensity to look at everything that goes wrong in the firm, or at every initiative management attempt, in a negative manner. A spirit of non-co-operation may emerge where there is underlying conflict. Workers may, short of taking industrial action, insist on working to rule - only performing the essentials of their contracts of employment and refusing to co-operate in any other activities.

There are also other, less overt symptoms of conflict to consider.

People may fantasise - feeling hopeless to change the day-to-day situation, they switch off from work and daydream to escape the reality of the conflict-culture of the organisation. Such people are usually apathetic to both their jobs and to relationships at work. Poor quality work is a consequence of such behaviour.

People may exhibit regressive tendencies - individuals return to an earlier and less mature personality in order to cope with the frustrations brought on by the conflicts - some individuals may start to behave like children.

Some people may repress their feelings, anxiety levels will grow to the extent that they some eventually suffer from cumulative stress trauma - thought by some behavioural scientists to be the industrial disease of the 1990s. They will often, under such conditions be off sick from work for long periods of time. High sickness statistics can therefore by symptomatic of an organisation in conflict.

BPP PUBLISHING

Handy summarises the symptoms of conflict as:

(a)   poor communications, in all directions

(b)   interpersonal friction

(c)   inter-group rivalry and jealousy

(d)   low morale and frustration

(e)   proliferation of rules, norms and myths; especially widespread use of arbitration, appeals to higher authority, and inflexible attitudes towards change.

Conflict can be positive especially where managers use it to develop competitiveness within the organisation. Conflict is an essential part of change and creativity, especially when considered with regard to the management and development of teams.

To maximise individual, or team potential, management must first eliminate insecurity - development of a detailed and mutually acceptable grievance procedure will ensure that employees feel that any conflict arising from working conditions or unfair treatment will be dealt with fairly - this done, the manager will be free to focus on personality conflicts between employees and between work groups.

By creating a positive, open culture and through the development of carefully selected work teams a management can use conflict to increase productivity and enhance performance. The members of a well-structured working group will display loyalty to each other and a high level of work commitment to the team. Groups of well-briefed and well-led teams competing against one another against planned targets can do much to harness natural conflicts and to develop the potential of the organisation as a whole.

A manager will need to consider the application of motivational incentives, and performance rewards in order to maximise the effectiveness of competition. A manager could consider multi-skilling, the creation of quality circles, job enrichment and delegate responsibilities as agents to improve the performance potential of work teams whilst staff noticeboards, in-house newspapers and periodic team appraisals and team prizes would demonstrate to all involved the rewards of team competition.

Competition can:

(a)   set standards, by establishing best performance through comparison
(b)   motivate individuals to better efforts
(c)   identify the best performers.

In order to be fruitful, competition must be *open*, rather than *closed*; or, rather, must be *perceived* by the participants to be open rather than closed. Closed competition is a zero-sum game, where one party's gain will be another party's loss. One party can only do well at the expense of another, in competition for resources and recognition. Open competition exists where all participants can increase their gains, for instance, by productivity bargaining.

If competition is perceived to be open, the rules are seen to be fair, and the determinants of success are in the competitor's control, competition can be extremely fruitful. The observations of Peters and Waterman on the motivation effect of comparative performance information supports this view. If these preconditions are not met, competition may again degenerate into conflict.

16   **ORGANISATION LIFE CYCLE**

(a)   *Greiner's model*

The *organisation life cycle model* was suggested by Greiner. It assumes that, as an organisation ages, it grows in *size*, measured perhaps by the number of employees and diversity of activities. This growth is characterised by a number of discrete phases. Each phase is characterised by:

(i)   a distinctive factor that directs the organisation's growth;
(ii)   a crisis, through which the organisation must pass before achieving the next phase.

(1)   *Phase 1.* The organisation is small, and is managed in personal and informal ways. The founders of the business are actively involved in operations. Apple Computers, for example, started up in a garage. However, sooner or later there comes a need for distinct management skills, relating less to products and marketing issues and more to co-ordination of the organisation's activities. This is a *crisis of leadership*.

(2)   *Phase 2.* Clear direction is provided by professionalising the management. At the same time, there are more employees. This initial enthusiasm might be tempered by loss of autonomy and the growth of hierarchy. The problem arises in that of delegation. The top finds it harder and harder to keep in detailed control as there are too many activities and it is easy lose a sense of the wider picture. Employees resent the lack of initiative and their performance falters. There is a *crisis of autonomy.*

(3)   *Phase 3.* The response to the problems of Phase 2 is delegation. This has the advantage of decentralising decision-making and giving confidence to junior managers. However, this in itself leads to additional problems of co-ordination and control. Over-delegation can result in different departments acting sub-optimally. There is a *crisis of control.*

(4)   *Phase 4.* The addition of internal systems, procedures and so forth to ensure co-ordination of activities, optimal use of resources etc. This increased complexity results in a *crisis of red tape.*

(5)   *Phase 5.* The crisis of red tape is resolved by increased informal collaboration. Control is cultural rather than formal. People participate in teams. Greiner thinks that this growth stage may lead to a crisis of psychological saturation, in which all become exhausted by teamwork. He postulates a sixth growth phase involving a dual organisation: a 'habit' structure for daily work routines and a 'reflective structure' for stimulating new perspectives and personal enrichment.

Greiner's model describes organisational growth as inevitably punctuated by crisis. A different approach adopted by Quinn was *logical incrementalism.* This means that businesses make small adjustments, building consistently on what they have, and adapting to the environment. Change is continuous and gradual. This alternative model was based, like Greiner's, on a study of real organisations.

Another criticism is based on the fact that not all organisations are founded by a visionary controlling entrepreneur, selling a product or service.

(i)   A new organisation can be formed from the merger of two existing ones.

(ii)   Two or more companies might collaborate *jointly* on a joint venture. The Airbus project, for example, did not start as a small business, but as a result of co-operation between governments and existing companies.

(iii) New organisations are created by existing ones and have a substantial complement of staff.

The model perhaps combines too many issues: organisation structure, organisation culture, product/market scope, leadership and management style.

It is possible to combine an obsession with procedures and efficiency (bureaucracy) with a strong sense of mission. Hospitals depend on the devotion and professionalism of staff - but clinical procedures *have* to be adhered to.

The growth of the business can be curtailed by the growth of competition. In other words, a business can be hemmed in, but still survive.

(b)   *The management accountant's role in each phase*

Management accounting deals with management information and control.

In *Phase 1*, it is unlikely that there would be a distinct management accounting function at all. This is because the organisation is small, and will not be able to afford an elaborate finance department. It is possible that bookkeeping will be contracted out to a firm of accountants. Or perhaps a small team of technical staff, reporting to the accountant, who may have a seat on the Board as a finance director, will do all the accounting jobs, including tax returns, company accounts, monthly management accounts etc.

In *Phase 2*, the management as a whole becomes professionalised, and you would expect to see the finance function growing in importance. If no qualified accountant has been employed until now, one will be found. The accountant will have to exercise staff authority over other professional managers. Increased attention will be paid to supplying detailed management information to the senior management.

In *Phase 3*, extensive delegation would suggest a need for systems of performance evaluation, profit centre analysis etc. Specific management accounting skills come into their own in this stage.

Phase 4, which is ended by a crisis of red tape, might be characterised by an efflorescence of accounting controls, exercised by functional authority.

Phase 5 should engender a more sober look at the nature and purpose of accounting controls. Informal collaboration can be supported by information systems which contain modelling facilities, executive information systems should be able to drill down into basic data.

17   BRINGING ABOUT CHANGE

(a)   *Reasons for difficulties in bringing about change*

(i)   Change may be expensive, particularly if major innovations in working procedures are planned. There may be a tendency to assume that the present methods are working satisfactorily and that any marginal improvement will not be worth the cost.

(ii)   Change involves planning in advance, consultation and negotiation. Managers who are thinking of introducing change may be daunted by the administrative hurdles to be overcome.

(iii)   Policies and procedures become fixed and inflexible. It can be difficult for people who have become accustomed to them to understand that alternative methods are possible to achieve the same aims.

(iv)   Employees often resist change which:

(1)   alters the pay or status of an individual relative to that of other individuals
(2)   lessens the value of their experience
(3)   causes disruption to their social life (eg shift-working or relocation)
(4)   is associated with job insecurity (eg technological innovation).

(b)   *Key processes in successful implementation of change*

(i)   Planning. This should begin with a definition of the objectives to be achieved by the proposed change. In environments where change takes place at a rapid pace this may be more of an ideal than a target achievable in practice, but in principle all change should be planned. Where major changes are proposed, this is obviously all the more important and a significant amount of time may need to be devoted to planning.

(ii)   Consultation. Interested parties should be invited to express their views on the need for the proposed change and on the methods for implementing it. It is possible that quite different means may be proposed at this stage for achieving the defined objectives. At the least, the process of consultation should help to minimise opposition to change: people will be unable to complain that the change has been forced on them if they have been given the opportunity to suggest alternative approaches.

(iii)   Communication. This is important before, during and after the change. Before the change takes place, all employees affected by it should be notified of its aims and its intended effects. Efforts should be made to minimise resistance; this may involve explaining that the change will not lead to redundancies, that adequate training will be given to all staff in any new procedures and that benefits for employees are expected to arise from the change. As the change is introduced steps should be taken to communicate progress so that employees are not left in the dark. Any transitional procedures should be clearly explained; for example, if a computerised system is being introduced a form of parallel running may be needed. In that case staff would need to know that for a time they are expected to process data through two systems in parallel.

(iv)   Monitoring and review. At all stages the progress of the change should be monitored and employee reactions recorded. Comparison with the original plan will show where implementation of the plan is being carried out successfully and where improvements are needed. Finally, review of the whole process after it is complete will indicate where follow-up action is required to tidy up loose ends. It will also provide benefits when future changes are planned because lessons will have been learnt.

Index

Note: **Key Terms** and their references are given in **bold**.

BPP PUBLISHING

See overleaf for information on other
BPP products and how to order

CIMA Order

To BPP Publishing Ltd, Aldine Place, London W12 8AW
Tel: 020 8740 2211. Fax: 020 8740 1184
www.bpp.com Email publishing@bpp.com
Order online www.bpp.com

Mr/Mrs/Ms (Full name)

Daytime delivery address

Postcode

Email

Date of exam (month/year)

Daytime Tel

	Texts 7/01 £20.95	Kits 1/01 £10.95	Passcards 1/01 £5.95	Tapes 9/00 £12.95	Videos 7/00 £25.95	i-Pass 8/01 / 1/02	i-Learn 1/02 £19.95	MCQ cards 7/01 £5.95
FOUNDATION								
1 Financial Accounting Fundamentals	£20.95	£10.95	£5.95	£12.95	£25.95	£24.95		£5.95
2 Management Accounting Fundamentals	£20.95	£10.95	£5.95	£12.95	£25.95	£24.95		£5.95
3A Economics for Business	£20.95	£10.95	£5.95	£12.95	£25.95	£24.95		£5.95
3B Business Law	£20.95	£10.95	£5.95	£12.95	£25.95	£24.95		£5.95
3C Business Mathematics	£20.95	£10.95	£5.95	£12.95	£25.95	£24.95		£5.95
INTERMEDIATE								
4 Finance	£20.95	£10.95	£5.95	£12.95	£25.95	£29.95	£19.95	£5.95
5 Business Tax (FA 2001)	£20.95 (9/01)	£10.95	£5.95	£12.95	£25.95	£29.95	£19.95	£5.95
6 Financial Accounting	£20.95	£10.95	£5.95	£12.95	£25.95	£29.95	£19.95	
6I Financial Accounting International	£20.95	£10.95						
7 Financial Reporting	£20.95	£10.95	£5.95	£12.95	£25.95	£29.95	£19.95	
7I Financial Reporting International	£20.95	£10.95						
8 Management Accounting - Performance Management	£20.95	£10.95	£5.95	£12.95	£25.95	£29.95	£19.95	£5.95
9 Management Accounting - Decision Making	£20.95	£10.95	£5.95	£12.95	£25.95	£29.95	£19.95	£5.95
10 Systems and Project Management	£20.95	£10.95	£5.95	£12.95	£25.95	£29.95	£19.95	
11 Organisational Management	£20.95	£10.95	£5.95	£12.95	£25.95	£29.95	£19.95	
FINAL								
12 Management Accounting - Business Strategy	£20.95	£10.95	£5.95	£12.95	£25.95			
13 Management Accounting - Financial Strategy	£20.95	£10.95	£5.95	£12.95	£25.95			
14 Management Accounting - Information Strategy	£20.95	£10.95	£5.95	£12.95	£25.95			
15 Case Study				£12.95	£25.95			
(1) Workbook	£20.95							
(2) Toolkit for 11/01 exam: available 9/01	£19.95							
(3) Toolkit for 5/02 exam: available 3/02	£19.95							

Total [ ]

POSTAGE & PACKING

Study Texts

	First	Each extra	
UK	£3.00	£2.00	
Europe***	£5.00	£4.00	£
Rest of world	£20.00	£10.00	£
			£

Kits/Passcards/Success Tapes

	First	Each extra	
UK	£2.00	£1.00	
Europe***	£2.50	£1.00	£
Rest of world	£15.00	£8.00	£
			£

Breakthrough Videos

	First	Each extra	
UK	£2.00	£2.00	
Europe***	£2.00	£2.00	£
Rest of world	£20.00	£10.00	£
MCQ cards	£1.00	£1.00	£

Grand Total (Cheques to *BPP Publishing*) I enclose a cheque for (incl. Postage) £ [ ]

Or charge to Access/Visa/Switch

Card Number [ ][ ][ ][ ][ ][ ][ ][ ][ ][ ][ ][ ][ ][ ][ ][ ]

Expiry date [ ]   Start Date [ ]

Issue Number (Switch Only) [ ]

Signature